THIS
LITTLE LIGHT
OF MINE

THIS
LITTLE LIGHT
OF MINE

THE LIFE OF
FANNIE LOU HAMER

Kay Mills

A DUTTON BOOK

973.049
HAMER
MIL

DUTTON
Published by the Penguin Group
Penguin Books USA Inc., 375 Hudson Street,
New York, New York 10014, U.S.A.
Penguin Books Ltd, 27 Wrights Lane,
London W8 5TZ, England
Penguin Books Australia Ltd, Ringwood,
Victoria, Australia
Penguin Books Canada Ltd, 10 Alcorn Avenue,
Toronto, Ontario, Canada M4V 3B2
Penguin Books (N.Z.) Ltd, 182–190 Wairau Road,
Auckland 10, New Zealand

Penguin Books Ltd, Registered Offices:
Harmondsworth, Middlesex, England

First published by Dutton, an imprint of New American Library,
a division of Penguin Books USA Inc.
Distributed in Canada by McClelland & Stewart Inc.

First Printing, January, 1993
1 3 5 7 9 10 8 6 4 2

Excerpts from Sally Belfrage, *Freedom Summer* (Charlottesville, Va.: University Press of
Virginia, 1990), reprinted with permission of the publisher.

Songs from "Fannie Lou Hamer: Songs My Mother Taught Me," produced by Bernice
Johnson Reagon and printed with permission of folklorist Worth Long.

Excerpts from *Malcolm X Speaks*, edited by George Breitman, copyright 1965, 1989 by Betty
Shabazz and Pathfinder Press, reprinted with permission of Pathfinder Press, New York.

REGISTERED TRADEMARK—MARCA REGISTRADA

LIBRARY OF CONGRESS CATALOGING-IN-PUBLICATION DATA
Mills, Kay.
This little light of mine: the life of Fannie Lou Hamer/Kay Mills.
p. cm.
Includes bibliographical references and index.
ISBN 0–525–93501–0
1. Hamer, Fannie Lou. 2. Civil rights workers—United States—Biography.
3. Afro-Americans—United States—Biography. 4. Civil rights movements—United
States—History—20th century. 5. Afro-Americans—Civil rights. 6. Mississippi—Race
relations. 7. Afro-Americans—Civil rights—Mississippi. I. Title.
E185.97.H35M55 1993
973'.049607302
[B]   92–19713
                                                        CIP

Printed in the United States of America
Set in Quorum Book and Plantin Light
Designed by Julian Hamer

Contents

The path of the just is as the shining light,
that shineth more and more unto the perfect day.

—PROVERBS 4:18

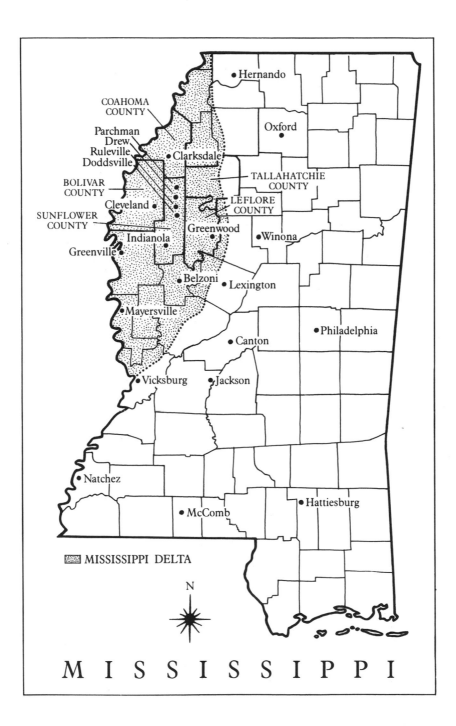

COAHOMA
COUNTY

Parchman
Drew
Ruleville
Doddsville

• Hernando

• Oxford

• Clarksdale

TALLAHATCHIE
COUNTY

BOLIVAR
COUNTY

LEFLORE
COUNTY

Cleveland •

SUNFLOWER
COUNTY

Greenwood

• Winona

Indianola •

Greenville •

• Belzoni

• Lexington

• Philadelphia

•Mayersville

• Canton

• Vicksburg

• Jackson

• Natchez

• Hattiesburg

• McComb

▦ MISSISSIPPI DELTA

N

M I S S I S S I P P I

"My Mind, It Was Stayed on Freedom"

FANNIE LOU HAMER was poor and unlettered. She walked with a limp. A short, stocky black woman, for much of her life she worked weighing the cotton picked on a white man's plantation in the heart of the Mississippi Delta. She lived in a small frame house that had no hot water and no working indoor toilet—while her boss's dog had its own bathroom inside the main house. She had an earthy sense of humor, an ability to quote vast passages from the Bible, and the respect of those who knew her. They counted on her to straighten out disputes and intercede in the white community when necessary and knew that she and her husband, Pap, would take in children other families could not raise. She knew there was much wrong with America, but until the civil rights movement came to her town, she could do little about those wrongs.

The summer that the movement reached Fannie Lou Hamer's hometown of Ruleville—1962—she was forty-four years old, and she could not vote. She wanted that right, and in her struggle to achieve it she became a symbolic figure who inspired countless other Americans, those who met her and many who never did. Like many Delta blacks, she lived for a time a life of resignation, making the best of what she had and trying to enjoy her family and her friends. But she was ready when a movement came to Mississippi that could match her mountainous talents.

Mississippi and other southern states had effectively taken the vote from their black citizens by requiring them to pass a test to register, one they almost always failed because it was administered by people who did not want them to pass. A black person too well educated to be denied the right to register was often forced to choose between voting only for white candidates or not voting at all.

The intimidation was usually economic. The few good jobs that black people could get in rural Mississippi were as teachers in the all-black school system. A white board of education and a white superintendent controlled all teaching jobs. Most black people picked cotton or cleaned and cooked for white people. They may have rebelled in their own private ways—spitting in the soup is a favorite tale—but most dared not speak out. The only people with any measure of independence were black preachers and funeral directors; many of them squandered even that minimal independence by currying favor with whites.

Those who found neither outright exploitation nor indirect subservience palatable left Mississippi for East St. Louis, the South Side of Chicago, Gary, or Detroit. Those who demanded fair treatment at home often were forced to head north as well or risk joining the ranks of the lynched. The trees and bayous of the Delta are often the only features on the flat landscape; they also served as the tools of repression when blacks were hanged or dumped off a bridge, never to be seen alive again. Fannie Lou Hamer knew all these landmarks only too well. The cruelty of the Delta was only part of white supremacist violence that marked Mississippi as the most repressive state of the South.

By almost any measure, black Mississippians had little share in the American Dream of opportunity as they entered the 1960s. The focus of early organizing drives in the Delta was the right to vote— but few could worry about voting when there were almost no jobs left picking cotton and no proper schooling to qualify a black person for whatever jobs did exist. Few could worry about voting when children went hungry and rain poured through holes in the roof, or when children died in fires caused by primitive stoves in unheated shacks. Or when people went to the hospital only to die. Or when the white world was deliberately leaving blacks further behind, and when its rear guard of white sheriffs turned their dogs on those trying to assert their rights, and men riding at night fired shotguns at them or tried to burn down their barns. A few black southerners like Medgar Evers had braved the night, too, signing people up for the National Association for the Advancement of Colored People, trying to get people to vote, resisting this violent system even before Dr. Martin Luther King, Jr., burst into the headlines with his leadership of the Montgomery, Alabama, bus boycott.

There were thus a handful of people, but only that, ready to hear the message of the young civil rights workers when they arrived in Ruleville in August 1962. The workers called their gatherings "mass meetings" for psychological reasons, but sometimes the mass was fairly small. They met at a church because that was the only place a gathering of black people wouldn't arouse whites' suspicions. In between the singing, they would preach. Their message was one of hope and faith—hope that people would hear their words about the value of voting, faith that they would be sufficiently brave to make the word deed. Then they asked who would go with them to try to register. Fannie Lou Hamer put up her hand. That night she changed her own destiny and that of a great many others, black and white. She would lose her job, be jailed and beaten, for her beliefs. She symbolized one aspect of what the movement hoped to accomplish: to embolden local people to resist a harsh and violent system.

From this humblest of beginnings, Mrs. Hamer would go on to challenge the president of the United States, the national Democratic Party, members of Congress, and the American people about fulfilling the promises of democracy. She recognized the shortcomings in the nation's electoral and educational systems. She opposed the war in Vietnam from the beginning, and she was thrilled by seeing Africans govern themselves. She organized programs to feed poor people, tend to their ills, house them, clothe them, train them for jobs. She ran for office. She recognized the need for women of all races to work together for political and social goals. She encouraged young people to set and achieve their own goals.

She was not some ethereal being who lived unscathed amid poverty. Her health and formal education were severely stunted by her surroundings; her penetrating analysis of society was at times dismissed by those who picked apart her unlettered grammar or could hear only her Delta dialect. She was thoroughly human: she snored, she cracked earthy jokes, she mimicked bigoted people. She understood the fears held by violent whites— suffered as a result of them—but she did not hate them for she was a true Christian. She often was undiplomatic: she could flay a public official or those less resolute than she on a moment's notice. She was not perfect, but she was, to many who worked with her under the most life-threatening conditions, the most inspirational person they ever knew. They drew from her and Mississippians like her a self-confidence that helped them later in facing their own difficulties, achieving their own successes.

She died poor because she gave away much of what she earned or raised. She thought she was dying forgotten because few people visited her during the debilitating illnesses of her last years, and because many turned away from her when she no longer had money or energy to give to their needs. Yet more people who had been active in the movement, famous and unknown, turned out for her funeral than she ever realized honored and revered her.

I met Fannie Lou Hamer only once, in 1973. A decade earlier, I had seen her dramatic nationally televised testimony at the 1964 Democratic National Convention, when black Mississippians were challenging the seating of their state's all-white delegation. Had I not met her that once, I would not have believed the stories of her influence. It will be said, because I am white, that I cannot fully understand the life of a black Mississippi sharecropper. That is correct. I can only try as best I can to re-create it through words. This criticism is one that would have saddened Fannie Lou Hamer deeply, for it indicates that we still see ourselves divided and thus limited by race, not enriched by it.

In 1973 I was a reporter based in Washington, and I was preparing a series of articles on the civil rights movement, using as a peg the artificial device journalists so often use: an anniversary. In this case, it was the tenth anniversary of the 1963 March on Washington. What, I wanted to know, had happened since then? Were conditions better? And what had happened to some of the people who had fought for change? I selected a northern city, Chicago, where I had attended graduate school and had held my first full-time job, as one locale for my reporting.

I also chose a southern state, Mississippi. This bastion of segregation had had the furthest to go; its racial violence had been the most widespread. It had claimed the lives of three young civil rights workers, James Chaney and Andrew Goodman and Michael Schwerner. And Emmett Till and Medgar Evers and how many more? And it had Fannie Lou Hamer. I had seen her on television, read about her bravery, and always wanted to meet her. Now I had my chance.

I drove up to the yellow brick house in Ruleville's black quarter, and she escorted me inside. It was summer, and Mississippi was living up to its steamy reputation. Even steel magnolias would wilt under that sky, in that humidity. I didn't know it then, but Mrs. Hamer had been in ill health, had barely made it through the Democratic National Convention the year before. She was deeply discouraged. She took me to see Freedom Farm, the cooperative that she had been trying to develop. It was failing. She talked to me about Mississippi politics. In their ongoing resistance to the Voting Rights Act of 1965 and all of that law's implications for sharing power, the Mississippi legislature and many of the state's counties were making people reregister to vote in the early 1970s. As a result of the state's willful footdragging, many blacks who had risked their jobs and even their lives to register felt the vote was no longer worth the effort. There were few black officeholders—none wielding real power in Sunflower County, where Mrs. Hamer lived, and few in many of the Delta towns. Had signing up to vote helped them get better jobs? Why bother? Mrs. Hamer had every reason to be depressed. But she would keep talking about the need for change until the day she died four years later.

I was mesmerized as she talked, as I had been when watching the Atlantic City convention. There, she had glared at the TV camera and rejected the compromise President Lyndon Johnson wanted the upstart black Mississippians to accept: two token seats instead of full representation as the official delegation on the floor of the convention. "We didn't come all this way for no two seats 'cause all of us is tired," she roared. I had never heard a black woman speak in such commanding fashion. Or perhaps had, as a child in a southern setting; those were personal commands. This was the voice of deeply felt convictions in an amoral political arena.

That day in the Delta, I naively asked Fannie Lou Hamer how life was different in 1973 from 1963. That was, after all, the focus of my series. Her answer could have been the material that fills this book. But she simply looked at me directly, with those deep brown eyes, and as if teaching a slow child—kind, too tolerant, perhaps—she replied: "If you had turned up the road to my house in 1963, you might have been stopped before you got here, probably arrested. That's how tense it was." Everybody in town would have known a white lady was there, she said, and would have been driving by to check it out. She paused, not needing to add what the drive-bys would have done then. Come to think of it, she added, they probably all know you're here today—they're just not driving by.

I did not realize then that she had, in just a few sentences, analyzed a major change in Mississippi. The naked, brutal repression was gone. Economic conditions for many black people were no better, but the fear of talking freely to anyone, the fear of having a white person visit your house, was gone for many people. Not for everybody. Many people, black and white, are still bound by chains dating back to the days of slavery. But now a black child born in Mississippi is not automatically forced to choose between leaving or becoming a second-class citizen. Too many still are unable to achieve, but there is more hope today. Black people now vote, they serve as mayors and legislators and health officials, they work as independent-minded teachers or bank clerks or restaurant managers. That is part of Fannie Lou Hamer's legacy; this is her story.

CHAPTER 1

"This Little Light of Mine"

TIME WAS WHEN the flat and endless horizon of the Mississippi Delta was broken only by rows of slow-moving people turning the earth with mules in the early spring, chopping cotton through the staggering summer heat, and stooping to pick that cotton from September through November. It was weary work that bent the back, calloused the hands, cut the fingers, and numbed the soul. It also had no reward in this world because the white landowner got what profit there was. The black people trudging through the fields could only sing out to God to carry them along until they could rest on some distant shore.

It was a world of harsh contradictions: there was absolutely nothing romantic about the life, but at the same time there were moments of sublime beauty as a flock of birds flew over a field in a perfect V formation at sunset or a child smiled as a fish caught the hook in the quiet down by the river. It was, at least, a life out of doors, not confined to concrete and crowds. It was a world many black people refused to leave even as their brothers and sisters filled the trains north.

Today cultivators and giant mechanical pickers cross the fields. They have driven the black workers off the land, into small, fading towns or out of the state entirely. Tufts of cotton that float wispily off trucks headed for the gins still cling to the shoulder of the road and the landscape looks much the same. But now the people are gone.

Fannie Lou Hamer was born into that old Mississippi but died in the new. She began life humbly and ended it the same, like countless other poor Mississippians. But some alchemy of inborn intelligence, deep spirituality, strong parents, love of country, and a sharecropper's gutty instincts for survival made her different. Make no mistake about it: "There were many strong leaders in Mississippi," says Rims Barber, who worked with them all in the Mississippi movement, "but she was a cut above."[1]

Jim and Ella Townsend had twenty children, fourteen boys and six girls. Fannie Lou was the youngest, born October 6, 1917, in Montgomery County, Mississippi.[2] Her birth helped her family survive one more winter. In those days, plantation owners often paid $50 to a woman who produced a future field hand; that money enabled the Townsends to buy necessities after the crops were in and their normal income was gone.[3] Two years after their last child's birth, the Townsends left the hill country in the center of Mississippi and moved to the Delta flatlands to E. W. Brandon's plantation in Sunflower County. They were part of a massive shift among black people after World War I, as thousands migrated north in search of jobs and others replaced them in the Delta.

As the 1920s began, Sunflower County was a typical Delta county: owned by whites, worked by blacks. There were few places of entertainment, and those few were for whites only. Blacks had to use their own cafés and transportation, or do without. Gas stations, as they were established, either had "white" and "colored" rest rooms or none at all for black people. The water fountains in public buildings were labeled "White" and "Colored." Hotels for black travelers in Mississippi were so rare that they were remarked upon. Black people were expected to go to the back door—never the front—of a white person's home.

The towns and fields in which everyone, black and white, lived and worked were linked by dirt roads, which turned to mud in the spring rains and torrential August thunderstorms. On the horizon beyond the field hands at work, only a few oak, pecan, red gum, and cypress trees, usually along riverbanks or bayous, broke the table-top landscape. All the rest had been cleared for King Cotton. Sunflower County, in the state's northwest quarter one hundred miles north of the state capital, twenty-five miles from the Mississippi River to the west, had—and has—few attractions for outsiders. Its largest town was, and still is, Indianola (1990 population: 11,500). The local rivers provide both food and recreation, and as Fannie Lou and her brothers and sisters were growing up, the family could go fishing in the Quiver River or a bit farther away in the Sunflower or Big Eddy. The catch included mud catfish and crappie. Flooding remained a springtime danger, tornadoes a summer threat.

The hard life started young. "I never will forget, one day—I was six years old and I was playing beside the road and this plantation owner drove up to me and stopped and asked me, could I pick cotton?" Mrs. Hamer told an audience years later. "I told him I didn't know and he said, 'Yes, you can. I will give you things that you want from the commissary store,' and he named things off like Crackerjacks and sardines," a Daddy Wide Legs gingerbread cookie, and other treats for which the child would never have money herself.

"So I picked the 30 pounds of cotton that week, but I found out what actually happened was he was trapping me into beginning the work I was to keep doing, and I never did get out of his debt again." It was clear Fannie Lou knew how to work. The next week she had to pick 60 pounds. "By the time I was 13, I was picking two and three hundred pounds."[4]

The large Townsend family picked tremendous amounts, 55 to 60 bales of cotton, 500 to 600 pounds to the bale. But at the end of each year, when the accounts were totaled, sharecroppers in Mississippi often owed landowners money rather than earning any. If they cleared any money, it was never enough to get ahead; they had to borrow over the winter. Each spring the landowner advanced the seed for the crop. He gave sharecroppers a "furnish," money to pay for food and clothes and other supplies until the crop was laid by. Sharecroppers often had no choice but to use the plantation commissary, the rural equivalent of the company store, where the plantation owner, not the law of supply and demand, set the prices.

Most sharecroppers lacked the education to keep records of what they had borrowed and what they were owed after giving the landowner half the crop. But one year L. C. Dorsey, a friend of Mrs. Hamer's who also grew up on a Delta plantation, kept records for her own family. Although she was only a schoolchild, she felt her father was being cheated, a fate shared by many Delta sharecroppers. Her careful accounts showed, at year's end, that her father should get $4,000—or at least $1,000 even after subtracting "plantation expenses," the catch-all "when there was nothing else they could legitimately add to your debt." Came settling day, her father had to accept $200. "People were locked into this system," Dorsey said, "and the fear and lack of control made them take that. There was no protest. There was no saying, I'm not going to take that. There was nobody else you could appeal to. *Nobody else.*"[5]

One year Jim Townsend did manage to make some money. "He said, 'You know, we ought to buy some mules and wagons, because if I can rent some land, I can make a better living for my children,' " Mrs. Hamer said.[6] People who worked the land viewed renting as better than sharecropping because the black farmer could keep more of his crop for himself. But blacks renting also posed a threat to whites, who wanted to preserve their work force.

"They didn't have machines like they have now," Mrs. Hamer recalled decades later. "They had mules. So my father bought three precious mules. I'll never forget their names because we *loved* them because they was ours. He bought three mules: Ella, Bird, and Henry. Ella was a white mule and Bird was kinda tan and Henry was jet black, but they were beautiful to us." He also bought two cows, one of which was named Della. He bought a wagon, some plow tools, and cultivators. "We were doing pretty well. He even started to fix the house up real nice and had bought a car." One night while the Townsends were away from home,

> this white man went to our lot and went to the trough where the mules had to eat and stirred up a gallon of Paris Green [poison] into the mules' food. It killed everything we had. When we got there, one mule was already dead. The other two mules and the cow had their stomachs all swelled up. It was too late to save them. That poisoning knocked us right back down flat. We never did get back up again. That white man did it just because we were getting somewhere. White people never like to see Negroes get a little success.

Ella Townsend protected her children fiercely, even taking on the boss man on one occasion when he slapped her youngest boy. She worked hard, too, as Ben Sklar, proprietor of a cavernous dry goods store on Ruleville's shopping street for more than five decades, recalled. "She'd go out there with two or three of her youngest children and they'd gather a bale of cotton" after the regular picking had been done. "In those days that was worth about $100. They were hardworking people. They were not moochers."[7]

When a plantation owner would tell the Townsends that they could gather cotton scraps left in his fields, Mrs. Hamer reminisced, "we would walk for miles and miles and miles in the run of a week. We wouldn't have on shoes or anything . . . the ground would be froze real hard. We would walk from field to field until we had scrapped a bale of cotton. Then [my mother would] take that bale of cotton and sell it, and that would give us some of the food that we would need. Then she would go from house to house and she would help kill hogs. They would give her the intestines and sometimes the feet and the head and things like that and that would help to keep us going. So many times for dinner we would have greens with no seasoning and flour gravy."[8]

The diet was poor, and the medical care just as bad. Fannie Lou Hamer limped badly throughout her life, either from polio or from a childhood accident—a fact never clearly established. She thought she had had polio, but in later years her husband learned that one of her brothers dropped her while tending her when she was a baby; her leg was never set properly, thus the limp.

Like the poverty, the toil was endless. Fannie Lou dragged her cotton sack behind her as she worked with her family in the fields. People wanted a better life, and her mother would express that longing in song:

> I'm going to land on the shore.
> I'm going to land on the shore.
> I'm going to land on the shore,
> Where I'll rest for evermore.
>
> The preacher in the pulpit,
> With the Bible in his hand—
> He preaching to the sinners
> But they just won't understand.
>
> I'm going to land on the shore.
> I'm going to land on the shore.
> I'm going to land on the shore,
> Where I'll rest for evermore.
>
> I would not be a white man,
> White as the dripping of snow.
> They ain't got God in their heart.
> To hell they sho' must go.[9]

It was a life, then, not only of constant toil but also of little gain. White people had solid homes, perhaps not the antebellum mansions of Natchez, but comfortable houses with separate rooms for eating and cooking and talking and sleeping. The Townsends lived in a wood plank shack with no electricity, running water, or indoor plumbing. Whites ate meat and vegetables. The Townsends often had only bread and onions. The whites wore shoes; Ella Townsend would tie her children's feet in sacks so they wouldn't freeze, but their feet still got so cold and dry that their skin sometimes cracked open. The whites had heat; the blacks didn't. Often young Fannie Lou would stand where the cows she was rounding up had been resting so she could get her feet warm.[10] The whites did no work that Fannie Lou could see; her parents, her brothers and sisters, her black neighbors did it all. "Being a very small child I thought it was because of our color that made something wrong. I remember telling my mother one day. I said, 'Mother, how come we are not white? Because white people have clothes, they can have food to eat, and we work all the time, and we don't have anything.'

"She said, 'I don't ever want to hear you say that again, honey.' She said, 'Don't you say that, because you're black!' She said, 'You respect yourself as a little child, a little black child. And as you grow older, respect yourself as a black woman. Then one day, other people will respect you.' "[11]

The child grew up amid poverty and also violence. Black people took what they were handed at settling time, or in the courts, or in the streets of the small towns, whether they liked it or not. In the decade before Fannie Lou was born, white Mississippians lynched an estimated eighty-three black men, two white men, and one black woman. "The year Fannie Lou Townsend reached her third birthday [1920], 13 lynchings took place in Mississippi." Only Georgia, with fourteen, had more.[12]

But some rebelled. When Fannie Lou was eight years old, a man working on a plantation near Drew, the next town north of Ruleville, could stand no more. The plantation owner often wouldn't pay Joe Pullum for his farm labor, but he did give him $150 to pick up some farm workers from the hill country. Instead of fetching the workers, Pullum used the money to fix up his house; he figured the $150 was owed him. The white man went to Pullum's house with a gun and asked him what he'd done with the money. "The white man got mad and shot Mr. Pullum in the arm," Mrs. Hamer recalled.

> Mr. Pullum ducked in the house and got his Winchester and killed that white man dead. Well, the white man that was sitting out in the buggy saw this and he lit out for town, which was Drew. The Negro knew what this meant. As soon as that man got to town, he'd be coming back with a lynch mob and they would hang him. So he got all the ammunition he had and went on out to Powers Bayou and hid in the hollow of a tree.
>
> The lynch mob came. I ain't ever heard of no one white man going to get a Negro. They're the most cowardly people I ever heard of. The mob came to get Mr. Pullum, but he was waiting for them and every time a white man would peep out, he busted him. Before they finally got him, he'd killed 13 and wounded 26. . . . The way they finally got him was to pour gasoline on the water of the bayou and set it afire. When it burned up to the hollowed-out stump, he crawled out. When they found him, he was unconscious and was lying with his head on his gun. They dragged him by his heels on the

back of a car and paraded about with that man for all the Negroes to see. They cut his ear off and for the longest time it was kept in a jar of alcohol in a showcase in a store window at Drew.[13]

Pullum had taken his toll, though. "It was a while in Mississippi before the whites tried something like that again."

White supremacy ruled the courts as well. One of the most celebrated crimes of the century occurred when the hideously beaten, bloated body of Emmett Till, a Chicago teenager visiting relatives, was found floating in the Tallahatchie River in nearby Leflore County in 1955. He had supposedly flirted with a white woman. The two white men who admitted abducting Till were acquitted of his murder. A month later, Clinton Melton, a black man working at a gas station, was slain by a white customer in nearby Glendora. That man was also acquitted.[14]

Black children like the Townsend family and their neighbors could not aspire to much schooling, especially the boys, who had to help break the land in the spring. School for black children in the Mississippi Delta started in December, once the cotton was in, and ran through March. Often children didn't have warm clothes or shoes, so they couldn't attend classes. School would let out until the cotton was planted and the initial weeding done. Then followed two summer months of school, with children sitting in stifling class-rooms in Mississippi's humid heat. Often no schools existed for black children, and classes were conducted in tenant farmers' cab-ins, stores, churches, or other private buildings. Mississippi spent less on black children's education than any other state. It spent less on its black students than on whites, paid black teachers less than white teachers, and invested less in buildings for black students. As late as 1950, Sunflower County's Board of Education reported that there were no four-year black high schools, that there were no publicly owned black school buildings, and that "the colored schools . . . as they now exist, are in deplorable condition."[15]

Even so, school was an early light in Fannie Lou Townsend's life. She won spelling bees and recited poetry, and she sang up a storm.[16] She left school after the sixth grade to help support her family, but she always wanted to read and know what was going on in the world. "After I stopped going to school, whenever I was in the [plantation owner's] house and I'd have to sit with a sick person or something, I'd stretch out and read." Years later, she recalled jumping off moving trucks full of workers "to retrieve newspapers and pieces of magazines caught in the cotton along dirt roads between fields and of picking through the trash behind the big house just to have something—anything—in print to read."[17]

The quality of education in Mississippi always distressed Mrs. Hamer, especially the way black children were portrayed in the few books those children had to read. "When I was in public school," she said once, "the state of Mississippi was responsible for doing a very sad thing. When I was in school—it must have been in a child's third reader—I read about a little child and this little child was black and his name was Epamonandus. First place, it was stupid to put a word that big in a book for a kid. Second place, it was a disgrace the way they had this little child and the things that he was doing." The child was portrayed as stupid, as were his mother and his grandmother.[18]

As she became a civil rights activist, Mrs. Hamer was forever angry that better educated black people would not get involved. Once she scolded educators for what they had failed to teach black students: "Why at that time didn't some of you tell us about our heritage? Why didn't you tell us about some of our history? Why didn't you tell us that it was a black man, Dr. Drew, that learned to give blood transfusions and had to die in a hall in South Carolina when he couldn't get blood for hisself? I didn't know until I was 50 years old that the first man to die in [the American] Revolution was a black man [Crispus Attucks]. . . . You going to have to teach what is necessary to teach."[19]

After she left school, Fannie Lou worked long days with her family. At night they would roast peanuts. They made up their own entertainment. Fannie Lou's father would tell jokes, or she would sing. The family slept on cotton sacks filled with dry grass or corn shucks. Her father died in 1939. She watched as her mother went blind from an accident. "My mother was clearing up a new ground trying to help to feed us for $1.25 a day. She was using an axe, just like a man, and something flew up and hit her in the eye." Eventually she lost her sight because she could not get to a proper specialist.

> I began to get sicker and sicker of the system there. I used to see my mother wear clothes that would have so many patches on them, they had been done over and over and over again. She would do that but she would try to keep us decent. She would be ragged and I always said if I lived to get grown and had a chance, I was going to try to get something for my mother and I was going to do something for the black man of the South if it would cost my life; I was determined to see that things were changed.[20]

As her brothers and sisters left home to seek a better life "up South" in cities like Chicago, Fannie Lou, the youngest, stayed to care for her parents. "My mother got down sick in '53 and she lived with me, an invalid, until she passed away in 1961. And during the time she was staying with me sometime I would be worked so hard I couldn't sleep at night."[21]

In 1944, Fannie Lou Townsend married Perry Hamer, a tall, strong sharecropper who had gone down to the Delta from Kilmichael in Montgomery County thirteen years earlier to "scout about." He was thirty-two when they were married, and she was five years younger. In the winter, "Pap," as he was known, would shoot rabbits and squirrels so they would have meat. For recreation, the Hamers liked to go fishing for catfish or perch, using earthworms for bait. Mrs. Hamer cooked and canned, always teaching the children she raised to store food so they would not have to do without. People who went to the house to talk politics in later years—and there were swarms—would find themselves handed a bowl of peas to shell, and Mrs. Hamer insisted on feeding them with whatever food she had on hand.

The Hamers lived on the Marlow plantation outside Ruleville in a small home. Mrs. Hamer considered the house "pretty decent." It had running water—although no hot water—and a bathtub. There was an indoor toilet, but it didn't work. "When we asked the man to fix it, he said we didn't need it. We had to use the outside toilet. That didn't bother me too much," she said, "till one day when I was cleaning the boss's house. I had cleaned one bathroom and was working on another when his daughter came up to me and said, 'You don't have to clean this one too good, Fannie Lou. It's just Old Honey's.' Old Honey was the dog. I just couldn't get over that dog having a bathroom when [the owner] wouldn't even have the toilet fixed for us. But then, Negroes in Mississippi are treated *worse* than dogs."[22]

The plantation owners had been in Sunflower County several generations by then, and W. D. Marlow, Jr., had been county sheriff. The Marlow place is east of Ruleville, reached on a road that winds off the highway and along the Quiver River. In the days when the Hamers lived there, W. Dave Marlow IV said, there were seven or eight families on the place. One of his childhood memories is hearing the Hamers down by the river. She could really sing, he recalled, and Pap would whistle.[23] The women on the plantation, black and white, did canning and cooking together. Mrs. Hamer often washed clothes and cleaned for Marlow's grandmother—and during World War II she sent cookies to his father, who was in the service in the Philippines and then a military policeman in occupied Japan. It was that man, W. D. Marlow III, who was running the farm when the young Student Non-Violent Coordinating Committee (SNCC) members started visiting the workers in his fields.

For black people, life was much the same from plantation to plantation. Mae Bertha Carter, a friend of Mrs. Hamer's, worked on a plantation outside Merigold, not far from Ruleville. Sometimes they chopped cotton together, and Mrs. Carter remembered the routine well. Those days you went from "can to can't," from daylight to dark.

Cotton was planted in April, since "May cotton didn't do so good." So from May on, "you get up before sunrise and go in the kitchen and get some breakfast. You fixes what you had, and about sunup we were in the fields, choppin' cotton," recalled Mrs. Carter. Chopping cotton meant first thinning the tiny plants as they started coming up, leaving about a hoe's width between them. The next time through the fields, the worker would pull the weeds around the plants. People would do a field once, row by row, then start through again. The landowners wanted the field clean every time. Hoeing at least meant a person could stand up and not stoop in the fields, but it also meant working on June and July days when the temperature was 100 and the humidity not far behind.

Between the last hoeing and the first picking toward the end of August, there was a short respite, then people picked cotton until the end of November. To get a bale of cotton, which is about 500 pounds, sometimes people had to pick 1,500 pounds, because cotton contains seeds that are removed in the ginning process, reducing the weight. "When you start picking the cotton," Mrs. Carter said, "that's when the sun beats on your back and you've got to get out there and pick. You can't go out there and stand up; you've got to pick because them scales gonna tell when night come how much cotton you picked. . . . You've gotta get that cotton out before the weather comes." So people got up before daylight and went out to pick in the dew. "You be wet. Your clothes were wet. And you're picking cotton at sundown. We picked from Monday morning until Saturday night because we were picking so that the kids would go to school."

Mrs. Carter often found that the cotton resisted her attempts at picking, and she would have cuts across her knuckles from the plants. Wearing gloves did little good; the gloves got in the way of getting your hand well into the bud. "If you get a good season and it rain a lot, it'll come out good. But when the sun is out a lot, it won't come out good." When the picking was easiest, people hated to go home. At the height of the season, they often did not stop to eat. They would put some sweet potatoes on the stove in the morning, and then about noontime the kids would bring the sweet potatoes to the field. And we'd sit on our sacks. Sometimes we didn't sit on the sacks. Sometimes we'd be eating that sweet potato and picking that cotton. And then we had a big jug of water down in the fields because if you go [away to get water], you'd lose a lot of time picking cotton.

You'd get up in the morning—and I did this a lot of times—get up early in the morning, about four o'clock and put the clothes on the line and then go to the fields. I washed many a night after I'd been picking cotton. My husband, he worked so hard, so he always made it convenient for us. He'd go down in the truck patch and he'd bring the sweet potatoes home or bring the peas or the beans home, and we'd sit up and shell the peas and beans at night and then put 'em on. You had to plan it. If you don't, that cotton'll be out there until Christmas.[24]

Late in the day people would still be in the fields, picking. There might be many of them, but they were "lonesome in the field." The work was so hard and the future held so little hope. At that time of day, Mrs. Hamer would hear her mother's voice, dragging out a song as she'd haul her cotton sack up a long, long row.

Oh, Lord, you know just how I feel.
Oh, Lord, you know just how I feel.
Oh, Lord, you know just how I feel.
Oh, Lord, you know just how I feel.

Oh, Lord, they say you'd answer prayer.
Oh, Lord, they say you'd answer prayer.
Oh, Lord, they say you'd answer prayer.
Oh, Lord, say you would answer prayer.

Oh, Lord, I'm comin' to you again.
Oh, Lord, I'm comin' to you again.
Oh, Lord, I'm comin' to you again.
Oh, Lord, comin' to you again.

As she sang others in the field would join in:

Oh, Lord, we sure do need you now.
Oh, Lord, we sure do need you now.
Oh, Lord, we sure do need you now.
Oh, Lord, sure do need you now.[25]

Mrs. Hamer often said that she was so tired when she went home that she wasn't sure where she got the strength to cook what little food they had. She and Pap made it through some rough winters, she confessed, because he had a little juke joint—a place where people could drink and dance—and they made liquor.

This, then, was the environment that produced Fannie Lou Hamer. Others grew up in the same circumstances, amid the same poverty, the same violence. What set her apart?

She herself pointed to her mother as one of the strongest influences on her life. "My mother was a great woman. She went through a lot of suffering to bring the twenty of us up, but she still taught us to be decent and to respect ourselves, and that is one of the things that has kept me going."[26]

Her faith also contributed to Fannie Lou Hamer's strength. She joined the Strangers Home Baptist Church at age twelve and was baptized in the Quiver River. Many of her religious principles she learned at home, from her mother. One of the most important lessons she was taught was that hating made one as weak as those filled with hatred. She would hold to her mother's teaching, as an astonished Andrew Young discovered when he went to get her out of jail in Winona, Mississippi, in 1963. Young, then the trusted aide of Dr. Martin Luther King, Jr., shared his mentor's commitment to nonviolence as a tactic to shame white society into recognizing black grievances. He had met Mrs. Hamer while he was running a citizenship education project; she was arrested while returning from one of those training sessions. "She was instinctively an extremely nonviolent person who really was so polite and was so generous to her jailers, for instance—the people who had been beating her," Young said, "that we could not conceive of the way they were chatting—that these were the same people who had been beating her for a week. But that was very deliberate on her part."[27]

What her mother had taught her, she passed on to her friends and neighbors. The first time Unita Blackwell, later a dear friend and civil rights ally, met Mrs. Hamer, she heard the story about the brutal treatment she had received. "She could just keep you spellbound. I was so angry that day, listening to all of her stuff and she said, 'Baby, you have to love 'em.' I said, 'This woman is crazy.' She explained it to me that we have to love them and they are sick. That was a continuous thing—she kept that going that they were sick and America was sick and it needed a doctor and we was the hope of America."[28]

Mrs. Hamer knew the Bible well and regularly attended small black churches near her home. The church in Mississippi was one of the most segregated institutions in the state, and it still is. Christianity should be "being concerned about your fellow man, not building a million-dollar church while people are starving right around the corner," Mrs. Hamer said. "Christ was a revolutionary person, out there where it was happening. That's what God is all about, and that's where I get my strength."[29] She quoted the Bible more naturally than most ordained ministers could. "You know the Scriptures says, 'Be not deceived, for God is not mocked; whatsoever a man sow, that shall he also reap.' And one day, I don't know how [white people are] going to get it, but they're going to get some of it back," she said of the whites opposing civil rights workers. "They are scared to death and are more afraid now than we are."[30]

"A radical in the deepest sense of the word," she sought to "understand, expose and destroy the root causes of oppression," said the Reverend Edwin King, a United Methodist minister who worked closely with Mrs. Hamer. "She questioned many things about the misuse of power in this land—things many of us are still afraid to understand. But hatred of her enemies, hatred of whites or any person, she resisted. 'I feel sorry for anybody that could let hate wrap them up,' " she used to say. " 'Ain't no such thing as I can hate anybody and hope to see God's face.' "[31]

"She was deeply religious," recalled John Lewis, the indomitable civil rights leader who first met Mrs. Hamer after he became chairman of the SNCC in 1963. "She really believed in some power or some source much greater [than she]. . . . 'Whether I want to do it or not, I got to,' " she would say. " 'This is my calling. This is my mission.' "[32]

And she loved her country. "She had this knowledge of the Constitution, what this country was supposed to be," Lewis added. "She would talk about it. 'Live up to the creed. Live up to the Declaration of Independence, to the Bill of Rights.' I think she really believed in America and she wanted to make it real."[33]

She was a friend, a person respected in her own black community and able to deal with the white. In the midst of rough times, she always had a moment to hear a neighbor's problem. She was sometimes the despair of her husband, who said that from the moment she got up in the morning until the moment she went to bed, she had people in the house, seeking help. If anything was wrong, she'd go speak up, said Cora Harvey, who lived on the same plantation.[34] White and black sought her help.

"One time she came in to buy a dress," storekeeper Ben Sklar remembered. "I said to her, 'Fannie Lou, when you get through shopping, come to the back of the store. I have a favor I want you to do for me.' " Sklar, who trusted Mrs. Hamer even though he disagreed with her "philosophy of the NAACP," had taken a check from someone and it had come back from the bank. "I said, 'Fannie

Lou, you know who this is. I need you to help me get my $225.' She said she'd call me in thirty minutes. Within the thirty minutes, she called me and said, 'You can cash that check now. It'll go through this time.' "[35]

And she could sing. Countless times, music helped her overcome her own fears and calm those of others. Her own talent fit perfectly the roots and needs of the civil rights movement. Born as it was out of the southern black church, the movement was especially rich in its songs and its singers. It poured forth with music, breathed it, depended on it to conquer fear and inspire action. People sang what they lived; the songs of endurance for Ella Townsend's generation became songs of deliverance for her daughter's.

Her mother had sung children's songs to her when she was little. Her church taught her its hymns and its spirituals. Her life often gave her nothing but time in which to sing them—time in the fields, time at the ironing board, time fishing along the rivers and bayous. And later, time on marches, even time in jail. Her allies in the civil rights movement taught her their songs, and she became the unofficial song leader almost wherever she went. At training sessions, her robust voice and emphatic presence carried people with her in song, bringing together those who had been strangers, making them comfortable enough to talk easily.

How do you describe a voice? What was the quality that carried people along? It was an untutored voice, although Mrs. Hamer had been singing in church and performing for her family since she was a child. It was not even a bell-like voice, because it had a touch of huskiness, especially after an hour of reaching into the spirit and pouring out songs. It could be contralto, said her old friend, the entertainer Harry Belafonte, who often sang with her, but it could also be almost bass. Pausing a long time before he answered the question about Mrs. Hamer's voice, Belafonte finally replied: "I can't describe her voice—as a voice. I have got to always talk about Fannie Lou Hamer singing and the *power* of her voice because there was a mission behind it and in it. I can describe Marilyn Horne, and I can describe Leontyne Price. [The] closest might be Mahalia Jackson, because certainly when Mahalia sang, there was a mission in her song, especially when she sang anywhere in the movement."[36]

Folk singer Pete Seeger was often in the South during movement days and appeared in New York with Mrs. Hamer as well. He described her voice by using the word *African* because of that ancient tradition from which she came. But you couldn't describe it, he said: "You have to hear it. It's like Louis Armstrong when he was asked, 'What is jazz?' He said if you have to ask, you'll never know." One thing her voice was *not* was high; big, yes—high, no. "When she sang 'This Little Light of Mine' in the key of C," Seeger explained, "most men and sopranos would put it in the key of G, five notes higher. She couldn't get it much lower down without being in a tenor's range."[37]

If Mrs. Hamer had a theme song, it was "This Little Light of Mine." One of the last times Seeger saw her, at an anti-war rally in Madison Square Garden in New York, he sang it for her. He recalled that usually one person would start a song, "and others gradually join in, adding harmony. The melody is never twice the same, as inspiration hits different people, who lead off with different verses. It became common to start with the name of the city or state one was singing in at the time, and then broaden the geographic area," so people would be singing about letting their little light shine all over Georgia or Mississippi, or all over the South, or all over the world.

Seeger, who taught many people all over the world the songs of the movement and brought the songs of the world back to the United States, emphasized that he learned much from Mrs. Hamer and others like her. "I felt that although I could pick a guitar and get a crowd singing, up here"—and he tapped his head—"there was an awful lot that I had to learn about music from people like her. So, if she was [at an event], I would be following her lead. Get her tempo. Get her syncopations."

It is one thing, Harry Belafonte said, to sing to amuse someone or yourself. "It's another thing to sing where there is a passion behind what you do, because the singing in and of itself is created for the purpose of touching something and someone. And Fannie Lou sang that way. I don't think there was ever a wasted hum when she sang." Belafonte, still helping to raise money for causes decades after he first met Mrs. Hamer, said that sometimes he sings at benefits and wishes that he could just be finished with the performance. But Mrs. Hamer, he said, always sang with a mission. "When she sang, it transcended all other considerations at the moment. And when she evoked singing at times, I always felt that she felt it was needed in order to break a mood or something that was happening at the moment. That song from the heart would bring another dimension when everybody got back at the end of the song to the business."

She sang songs of humor as well. She loved children, and sometimes when she had a child sitting on her lap, she would break into some folk song, like "Little boy, little boy, yes, ma'am, how many toes you got?" Every song had a purpose, Belafonte recalled. For him, in every one of her songs, he could hear "the struggle of all black America. . . . I thought that when she sang, there was indeed a voice raised that was without compromise the voice of all of us."[38]

Mrs. Hamer herself recognized the power of song. "Singing," she told an SNCC worker in Ruleville,

> is one of the main things that can keep us going. When you're in a brick cell, locked up, and haven't done anything to anybody but still you're locked up there and sometimes words just begin to come to you and you begin to sing. Like one of my favorite songs, "This Little Light of Mine, I'm Going to Let It Shine." This same song goes back to the fifth chapter of Matthew, which is the Beatitudes of the Bible, when he says a city that sets on a hill cannot be hid. Let your light so shine that men would see your good works and glorify the father which is in heaven. I think singing is very important. It brings out the soul.[39]

There was one more crucial element that molded a poor share-cropper into a leader: it was anger, touched with sorrow, about her lack of control over her own life. Without her knowledge or permission, Fannie Lou Hamer was sterilized in 1961.

She was in her early forties—past most women's childbearing years, and indeed two pregnancies had ended in stillbirths. The Hamers had talked about having children of their own and were raising two girls, one of whom had been taken in when she was born because her mother was unmarried. The other had been badly burned when a tub of water spilled on her and her large, impoverished family had been unable to care for her. "We had a little money so we took care of her and raised her. She was sickly, too, when I got her, suffered from malnutrition," Mrs. Hamer said.[40] She felt she could easily have cared for more.

But, wrote Perry Deane Young in the *Washington Post,* "Fannie Lou Hamer went into the hospital to have a small uterine tumor—'a knot on my stomach,' she called it—removed. She was recuperating from the operation when she heard what they were saying in the big house at the plantation. Vera Alice Marlow—cousin of the doctor and wife of the plantation owner—told her cook and the cook told Mrs. Hamer's cousin who told her: Fannie Lou had been given a hysterectomy."[41]

Little did she know at the time that sterilizations of poor black women would become a national issue in the next decade. In just one of many instances, twelve- and fourteen-year-old sisters, Minnie and Mary Alice Relf, were sterilized at an Alabama family planning clinic. Their mother, who couldn't read, signed a form that she did not understand; she thought her daughters would merely receive anti-fertility shots. Their lawsuit brought to national attention a situation of which poor, rural black women were long aware. Mrs. Hamer had been telling anyone who would listen about such cases for years. "If he was going to give that sort of operation, then he should have told me. I would have loved to have children. I went to the doctor who did that to me and I asked him, Why? Why had he done that to me? He didn't have to say nothing—and he didn't." There was no way she could consider suing. "At that time? Me? Getting a white lawyer to go against a white doctor?" she told Young. "I would have been taking my hands and screwing tacks in my own casket."

A year later, then, when the civil rights workers came to Ruleville, Mrs. Hamer was ready. She drew her strength from many sources: surviving the poverty and violence of the sharecroppers' life, always wanting to help others, singing the songs of the black church and the black field hands, learning about her country and believing in its promises despite her personal experiences. Her greatest power, however, was spiritual, a trait shared by many of her background. "It's the coming up against elements, both natural and human, in this period of their lives," that tested them and gave them strength, said Bob Moses, a dominant force in the Mississippi civil rights movement. "Those who survived both in an inner sense and an outer sense had learned how to reach down to some deep consciousness, a deeper place in themselves in order to survive."[42]

CHAPTER 2

"I Been 'Buked and I Been Scorned"

MARY TUCKER was in her late sixties when the Freedom Riders came to Sunflower County. Some of the early civil rights workers who went to Mississippi had actually ridden the buses that had crossed the South, testing segregation, facing angry mobs who beat them and burned their buses. Others had sat in at segregated lunch counters, seeking service. Others joined up specifically to help with voter registration in Mississippi. Local people called them all Freedom Riders, no matter their movement history or organization. When were the Freedom Riders coming? Would they come to this little town?

"There wasn't but a few of us would accept them because people were scared," Mrs. Tucker said, recalling those days in 1962. "I kept some of them and Joe McDonald kept some and we had a small church. . . . They'd go in and hold a service, and so I began to listen at the service to find out what it was" that brought them to the community. These young people were walking the unpaved streets of the black quarter in town and talking to people sitting on their front porches, or visiting the plantation cabins in the country. They held meetings when they could find a church or a hall. They were asking people to register to vote.

As Mary Tucker listened, she thought about Fannie Lou Hamer, who as a child used to go with her to church and Sunday school and follow her home. Coming from a large family, Fannie Lou loved the attention she got from Mrs. Tucker, who had only one child living.

I said, "Lord, I believe I'll go out in the country and get Fannie Lou. I want her to come in here and hear this because I believe it would mean something to her." So I did. And I said, "Fannie Lou, I want you to come to my home." She said, "What for, Tuck?" I said, "I want you to come to a meeting. We're having a civil rights meeting. . . . We're learning how to register and vote so you can be a citizen." She said, "Tuck, they taught us that mess in school and that's turned me off like that."

"I felt real bad but I wouldn't let on," Mrs. Tucker said. "I said, 'Well, you come on.' . . .

"I began to grieve about it. The next day evening she came out here. She said, 'Tuck, I come to beg your pardon. I never sassed you before in my life and it hurt me so bad when I thought about what I had said to you. I come to beg your pardon.' "[1]

Fannie Lou Hamer went to the meeting that Monday night at 7:30 at Williams Chapel Church. First, James Bevel, a young minister with Dr. Martin Luther King, Jr.'s, Southern Christian Leadership Conference, preached. His theme was from Matthew, chapter 16, verse 3, "discerning the signs of the times." He tied his text to voter registration. Then a leader of the Student Non-Violent Coordinating Committee, James Forman, spoke. "He told us . . . we could vote out people and they talked about, you know, hateful policemen and how they had been elected and if we had a chance to vote, you know, that we wouldn't allow these people to be in office because we could vote them out," Mrs. Hamer said. "It made so much sense to me because right then, you see, the man that was our night policeman here in Ruleville was a brother to J. W. Milam, which was one of the guys helped to lynch this kid Emmett Till. . . . Then they asked who would go down there Friday and try to become a registered voter. I was one of the persons that held up my hand."[2]

In so doing, she was defying decades of restrictive laws. When the Democratic Party, the party of the slaveholders and the Confederates, had regained control of the state after Reconstruction, its members wrote blacks' right to vote out of existence. Resistance bred only retaliation, and the pattern persisted well into the middle of the twentieth century. Resistance was especially difficult and dangerous in Mississippi, where there were fewer large cities than in other southern states and less tradition of a black middle class, with its education and some economic independence. Black people in the Delta were particularly dependent on white goodwill, and if they showed the least sign of questioning that outwardly benign authority, they would come up against skull-busting local police. A chief architect of white resistance, Senator James O. Eastland, lived in Sunflower County, and the influential segregation-forever Citizens Council had been organized there as well.

That August night in 1962, the civil rights movement was gathering momentum for its most massive confrontation with white power structures across the South. Scattered black individuals had resisted harsh laws and economic conditions for generations. The histories are now being written that trace the earliest ripples of this resistance in the decades preceding the 1950s.[3]

The oldest, and most moderate, of the civil rights groups was the National Association for the Advancement of Colored People (NAACP), whose lawyers prodded the cause through the courts. The NAACP battled discriminatory election laws and overturned the doctrine that "separate but equal" school systems were fair to black children, thus triggering massive white resistance across the South. In Mississippi, many of the adults who formed the backbone of the movement in its early days were NAACP members, but they were often isolated and had reason to be scared. As soon as NAACP representative Medgar Evers and his allies might line up parents to protest school desegregation, white pressure would force those parents into silence.

As the lawyers filed their briefs and argued their cases, black communities around the South were starting to defy unfair laws and officially condoned lawlessness. In June 1953 black citizens had started boycotting the segregated bus system in Baton Rouge, Louisiana. They refused to ride the buses in Tallahassee, Florida. And they walked and carpooled to work for over a year, from December 1955 well into December 1956, rather than ride the Montgomery, Alabama, buses, whose drivers made them sit in the rear and give up their seats to white passengers. With the *Brown v. Board of Education* decision of the U.S. Supreme Court, the Montgomery bus boycott helped mark the beginning of the modern civil rights movement.

Triggered by Rosa Parks's refusal to give up her seat on a city bus and galvanized by leaflets prepared by Jo Ann Robinson of Alabama State College and others in the Women's Political Council, the boycott launched a young minister named Martin Luther King, Jr., into international prominence. Absolutely committed to nonviolence but seeking change at a faster pace than the courts allowed, King seized the high ground with his sermons and leadership. He soon helped found the Southern Christian Leadership Conference (SCLC), placing black clergymen at the head of this new phase of the struggle.

Students would be the next to enlist. A handful of young black students braved mobs of angry whites as they entered Central High School in Little Rock, Arkansas, in 1957. Then college students took up the cause, sitting down to request service at a lunch counter in Greensboro, North Carolina, on February 1, 1960. As sit-ins spread across the South, SCLC staff member Ella Baker convinced her organization to help coordinate the protests by bringing young people together at a meeting held Easter weekend of 1960 at Shaw University in Raleigh, North Carolina. SCLC wanted the students to become a youth auxiliary, but the students, encouraged by Baker, resisted and formed their own organization, the Student Non-Violent Coordinating Committee, known as "Snick" for its abbreviation, SNCC. Baker saw a critical need for a group that could reach out to grass-roots people and help them set their own agenda, and she felt SNCC would be better able to do that than the SCLC and its hierarchically oriented ministers.

In May 1961, an integrated group, including John Lewis, boarded a bus in Washington, D.C., for the first Freedom Ride— with whites in the back of the bus, blacks in the front. They intended to try to use segregated lunch counters and rest rooms at bus stations across the South to show that blacks were denied the equal access to interstate travel to which federal law entitled them. Whites stoned one bus in Anniston, Alabama, and burned it six miles outside the city. A mob assaulted other riders in Birmingham. City police arrested the riders and dumped them beside the highway just across the Tennessee state line. In Montgomery, there was another brutal attack, and in Jackson the Freedom Riders were arrested and sent to maximum security at the Mississippi State Penitentiary at Parchman in Sunflower County. In Albany, Georgia, hundreds of black demonstrators campaigned against discrimination in public facilities and faced arrest in 1961 and 1962.

Despite this surge of activity across the South, Mississippi remained among the most intractable states. Its resistance was total. When Governor Ross Barnett cried, "Never!" in the face of federal court orders to admit a black man, James Meredith, to the University of Mississippi, President John F. Kennedy sent in hundreds of federal marshals. A campus riot ensued in September 1962 and two people were killed. There was not even that protection, ineffective as it proved, for those seeking change in the small towns of the Delta.

But quiet organizing was occurring. Medgar Evers, hired as a field director for the NAACP late in 1954, helped gather evidence after Emmett Till was killed and encouraged black customers to boycott merchants who perpetuated segregation. Profoundly concerned that blacks could not achieve their economic goals until they gained political freedom, Evers was working with John Doar and his staff from the Justice Department's civil rights division. Amzie Moore, an NAACP member in Cleveland, Mississippi, was also signing up members in the Delta.

Evers and Moore had both served with U.S. military forces during World War II, Evers on Omaha Beach and Moore with the Air Force in Burma. When they returned to Mississippi, they bristled at being denied the freedoms for which they thought they had been fighting. When Medgar Evers and his brother, Charles, tried to vote, for example, an armed mob stopped them. "We fought during the war for America, Mississippi included," Charles Evers said. "Now, after the Germans and the Japanese hadn't killed us, it looked as though white Mississippians would."[4]

John Doar remembered going to Medgar Evers's house for breakfast as he sought to document how Mississippi prevented black people from registering or voting. "I had all these county maps. We laid them out and he would tell us which counties were most likely [targets] and where people lived. We would go to see them without asking anybody directions and ask who else might have tried to register and then we'd get the FBI" to do longer interviews.[5] First, the Justice Department filed suit in Clarke, Forrest, Walthall, Tallahatchie, Jefferson Davis, and Panola counties to force local clerks to register blacks. In August 1962 Doar's department brought a massive suit, U.S. v. Mississippi, against the entire state's discriminatory election procedures.[6] Medgar Evers's involvement, and his outspokenness in trying to force the city of Jackson to hire more blacks, made him a key target of segregationists' hatred in the Mississippi of the early 1960s. He had to train his wife and children to sit away from windows and hit the floor whenever they heard sharp noises.

The United States might oppose Mississippi in court, but it had virtually no enforcement power in the streets. Civil rights workers faced local police with billy clubs, as well as thuggish night riders firing into homes and setting fire to churches and halls where meetings had been held. Under pressure to shed its passive role, the Federal Bureau of Investigation insisted that it was an investigative arm of the federal government, not a police agency. Even as an investigative unit, its men often asked only the questions they were told to ask. What, the rights workers asked, could force the federal government to protect people trying to exercise rights that those living in other parts of the country took for granted?

Waiting for the federal government to take case-by-case,

county-by-county action meant waiting for relief that might not come for years. The civil rights workers in Mississippi wanted to send more and more black people to the courthouse to claim their rights of citizenship, to build a moral force behind their claims. This portion of the Mississippi story started in large part when Amzie Moore met Bob Moses. Moore worked for the Post Office, and he traveled the Delta with a barbershop quartet, which was sometimes a cover for his NAACP work. Moses, an extremely soft-spoken young man with a master's degree from Harvard who had been teaching mathematics at Horace Mann, a private school in New York City, went south in the summer of 1960 for volunteer work at SCLC headquarters. Bored there, he traveled the Deep South at his own expense at the urging of Jane Stembridge, who was running the SNCC office. He met Moore and, as they talked, a plan emerged to achieve what both men wanted: political activity among black Mississippians directed at the problems they themselves decided should be resolved.[7]

Because there were not for the moment the meeting places nor the equipment available in Moore's hometown of Cleveland, Mississippi, Moses switched his focus to McComb when another activist, C. C. Bryant, invited him to southern Mississippi in 1961. Moses and a small band of young people canvassed the black community to try to sign up voters and were arrested on various charges, such as interfering with the police or disturbing the peace. That August, Moses was beaten in Liberty, Mississippi, by the sheriff's cousin, who was quickly acquitted. The next month, Herbert Lee, a local black man who had been working with Moses, was killed by a member of the state House of Representatives, who was also cleared. The young people convinced only a few people to register, and they received little or no help from the federal government. Although deeply frustrated, they were building a cadre of workers who would soon fan out over the state.

The next year Moses and the other young people who had joined forces with the Student Non-Violent Coordinating Committee arrived in the Delta. SNCC set up its main office in the black community in Greenwood, a cotton center in Leflore County on the southeast corner of the Delta. Charles McLaurin from Jackson, then twenty years old, became the field secretary most consistently identified with the efforts in nearby Sunflower County. Only a handful of black people were registered to vote in that county, and it was hard to find even that handful on election day. Fear that they would lose their jobs or even their lives kept people off the voting rolls and away from the polls. Fear made them look over the shoulder of the student talking to them and out at the white person cruising by in a pickup truck, shotgun racked in the rear window. Even by the spring of 1965, after 2½ years' work, there were only 155 black people registered in Sunflower County out of 13,524 of voting age, or 1.1 percent of the population. More than 7,000 whites were on the voting rolls, 80 percent of those eligible.[8]

The Justice Department had moved two years earlier in Forrest County in southern Mississippi. Why did the department, confronted with these statistics, not move until 1963 to sue the Sunflower County clerk for obstructing black voter registration? Years later, John Doar said Sunflower had not been "one of the counties Medgar Evers identified as a place we could go and find people who would talk to us."[9] Doar also acknowledged that the earliest suits did not include Sunflower "probably because it was Senator Eastland's county." James O. Eastland, who chaired the Senate Judiciary Committee, lived in Sunflower County in the town of Doddsville. A major landholder, he had an office in the bank building in Ruleville.

"If we had gone out of our way to seek out Sunflower County, the suspicion would have been aroused that we were just seeking publicity," Doar said. "It would have made it harder to clear cases through the Justice Department. It would have made it harder to deal with Eastland because he was chairman of the Judiciary Committee. We didn't make a deliberate effort to avoid Sunflower County, but we didn't go about our job with the feeling that we needed to start in Sunflower County."

There was a reason few in Sunflower County would talk to the federal government. The county had a reputation as one of the worst counties for blacks in the state—so bad that Marian Wright Edelman, working then as a young civil rights attorney and traveling all over Mississippi, always made sure she was out of Sunflower by dusk.[10] Civil rights workers said Sunflower's reputation for violence stemmed in part from a 1904 lynching in Doddsville that set the tone for decades.

Eastland's family played a key role in that incident. The way contemporary newspapers recounted the story (it was covered as far away as New York), James Eastland, uncle of the senator who became his namesake, had an argument with a black servant, Luther Holbert. "James Eastland was one of two brothers who owned a plantation of 2,300 acres near Doddsville. . . . The brothers were well fixed financially and were successful and highly respected planters," according to the *Greenwood Enterprise*.[11]

James Eastland was but 21 years of age, and was murdered Wednesday morning [February 3, 1904] at 9 o'clock, when he went

to Holbert's cabin, about two miles from his home. He had in company with him a negro named Albert Carr, who was also killed by
Holbert at the same time. The object of the visit was to warn Holbert
from molesting another negro who works for the Eastlands. The
woman with whom Holbert was living had brought on the trouble
between the two negroes. As young Eastland and the negro Carr
entered the cabin, they were shot down, Carr falling first on the
veranda and Eastland being found on the bed in the room with a
bullet hole in his forehead. Two shots from his revolver had been
fired.[12]

A posse went after Holbert, who had fled to the bayous with his
wife. Another black person was killed when the mob showed up at
Eastland's plantation. Then two innocent black people, one of
whom bore a resemblance to Holbert, were killed by the mob near
Belzoni in Yazoo County. "They were working in a field when
armed men approached, and, fearing that harm might come to
them, broke to run, when they were fired upon and killed."[13] The
hunt "engaged two hundred men and two packs of bloodhounds in
a four days' chase across four counties," said the *New York Daily
Tribune,* adding that the search stirred the section of Mississippi
"almost to frenzy."

Two young men, V. H. Lavender and E. L. O'Neal, captured
Holbert and split the reward of $1,200 from W. C. Eastland (Sena-
tor Eastland's father) when they turned their captive over to him.
Two brothers of the slain Eastland had "led the posse, forgetting
rest and sleep—all else save the spirit of the lamented dead which
cried for vengeance." Both were present when Holbert and his wife
were burned that Sunday afternoon.[14]

The Holberts, caught after running for miles on foot through
canebrakes and swamps, were tied to stakes in the presence of a
thousand people, although, as the *Tribune* reported, "there is nothing in the story to indicate that Holbert's wife had any part in the
crime."[15] As the funeral pyres were being prepared, the *Vicksburg
Evening Post* account added,

the blacks were forced to hold out their hands while one finger at a
time was chopped off. The fingers were distributed as souvenirs.
The ears of the murderers were cut off. Holbert was beaten severely,
his skull was fractured, and one of his eyes, knocked out with a stick,
hung by a shred from the socket. . . . The most excruciating form of
punishment consisted in the use of a large corkscrew in the hands of
some of the mob. This instrument was bored into the flesh of the
man and woman, in the arms, legs and body, and then pulled out,

the spirals tearing out big pieces of raw, quivering flesh every time it was withdrawn.[16]

At least a thousand people were reported to have watched as, "more dead than alive," Holbert and his wife were "led to their horrible doom," headlined the *Greenwood Commonwealth*.[17] "Several citizens who realized the enormity of the offense which was about to be committed mounted a stump and tried to dissuade the mob from its purpose," but they were drowned out by cries of "Burn them! Burn them!" Holbert escaped the flames several times, but finally writhed and died. A reporter noted: "It was a scene such as a man wants to witness only once in a lifetime."

Doddsville, where this incident occurred and where James Oliver Eastland, the future senator, was born November 28, 1904, sits almost squarely in the middle of long, narrow Sunflower County. It is five miles from Ruleville. Although the lynching occurred more than a decade before Mrs. Hamer was born, it was the kind of gory story firmly imprinted in local folklore. Civil rights workers heard the story from local people in 1964 without learning for sure until years later whether it was true.

Another celebrated lynching occurred in the county in 1929 after a black prisoner killed a guard while escaping from the penitentiary at Parchman, about fifteen miles north of Ruleville. He was chained to a log and burned slowly. "Now and then," according to the account in the *Memphis Press-Scimitar*, "someone would step forward and throw a little gasoline on the blaze. The whole burning took a little more than an hour. The Negro was alive and screaming 40 minutes of that time."[18] Fear was not, therefore, an inexplicable emotion in Sunflower County.

Down through the years, Mississippi politicians campaigned on the strength of their efforts to fight any breakdown of racial segregation, any weakening of the "southern way of life." They had to be racist demagogues to be elected, many would argue today; it was beyond the realm of comprehension that any successful politician would speak of bringing black and white together in any but a patronizing fashion. That kind of leadership was politically suicidal. No one led the charge harder than Senator Eastland.

One could not have invented two more disparate characters than Fannie Lou Hamer and James Oliver Eastland. They lived no more than a dozen miles apart, yet they lived in worlds that never touched except in the most menial ways until the civil rights movement occurred. One worked the land; the other owned vast tracts of land. One craved schooling yet attended only through the sixth grade; the other was educated at universities and law schools across the South. One lived in a three-room house with no indoor plumbing; the other had a home in Washington and a spacious house on his plantation outside Doddsville. One could not vote until she was in her midforties; the other was elected to the state House of Representatives when he was twenty-four years old. One sued to try to break down school segregation in Sunflower County; the other vilified the Supreme Court for handing down the school desegregation decision. One urged her neighbors, black and white, to vote, to work within the democratic system, to give it meaning in order to try to change their lives; the other argued that Mississippians did not have to obey the Supreme Court.

In a speech in Senatobia, in August 1955, for example, Eastland told his audience, "You are not required to obey any court which passes out such a ruling. In fact, you are obligated to defy it!"[19] In December, he spoke to the convention of Citizens Councils, which had been set up expressly to oppose school desegregation. He told the audience, which included Mississippi's governor, a congressman, and forty state legislators: "The Supreme Court of the United States, in the false name of law and justice, has perpetrated a monstrous crime. It presents a clear threat and present danger to the very foundation of our republican form of government. The anti-segregation decisions were dishonest decisions. They were dictated by political pressure groups bent upon the destruction of the American system of government, and the mongrelization of the white race."[20]

Eastland also fought against repeal of the poll tax, against anti-lynching laws, and consistently referred to blacks as "an inferior race." Named to fill a U.S. Senate vacancy in 1941, Eastland was elected to a term in 1942. He remained a staunch opponent of communism, socialism, and liberalism until he left the Senate in 1978. He rose to be chairman of the Senate Judiciary Committee, where he boasted about bottling up civil rights bills and where he helped set the course for the federal judiciary for many years. During the Kennedy administration, Eastland traded his approval of the NAACP attorney Thurgood Marshall's nomination to be a federal appellate judge in return for appointment of W. Harold Cox, a college friend and son of a Sunflower County sheriff, to the U.S. District Court. "Robert Kennedy is said to have discovered [the reason for delay in confirming Marshall] one day when, meeting Eastland in the corridor, he was accosted with this quasi-threat: "Tell your brother that if he gives me Harold Cox, I will give him the nigger!" reported Robert Sherrill.[21] Cox got the judgeship.

Eastland's rage and highhanded tactics focused on whites as well as blacks. Facing a tough reelection challenge in Mississippi in 1954, Eastland thundered that communists were behind the school desegregation cases working their way through the courts. As chairman of a Senate internal affairs subcommittee, he investigated alleged communist influence in labor unions, schools, the arts, and newspapers—institutions that might undermine his view of the proper order of life. He convinced many a Mississippian that the Red Menace, not legitimate black grievances, was behind concern over civil rights. But Alabama papers were outraged when Eastland went after Virginia Durr of Montgomery, a crusader against discriminatory poll taxes and the sister-in-law of Supreme Court Justice Hugo Black, and her husband Clifford, who had been an attorney in the Roosevelt administration. The *Montgomery Advertiser* branded the attack as "the type of character lynching which Southern Senators should deeply resent."[22]

But Eastland was not curbed; instead, he won reelection and continued to do so in 1960, 1966, and 1972. In 1966, he boasted in a speech that he was "another Southern reactionary" and that the people of his state "approved that kind of reactionary."[23] He voted against anti-poverty programs and helped seriously cripple the initial Head Start program developed in Mississippi. He voted against the Civil Rights Act of 1964 and against the Voting Rights Act of 1965.

Eastland's example set the tone in his home county. He may, as reported, have given homes to people who worked on his plantation and were in danger of losing jobs to mechanization, but his paternalism did not translate into political accommodation. Sunflower County was a harsh environment for civil rights workers, harsher still for the people who lived there and flirted with freedom. In mid-August 1962, for example, Ruleville Mayor Charles Dorrough, Sr., warned a black city employee that he was not going to allow civil rights to be forced on the town. Anyone attending a voter registration school, he said, "would be given a one-way ticket out of town, and if that would not do it, they would use whatever they had available."[24] Later that same month police in Indianola, the county seat, arrested six SNCC workers, including Robert Moses and Charles McLaurin, on a charge of distributing literature without a permit. They had been taking leaflets door-to-door announcing a mass meeting in the black community.[25]

Moses was by then a key SNCC organizer conducting voter registration work under the umbrella of a civil rights coalition called the Council of Federated Organizations, or COFO. COFO brought together the Congress of Racial Equality (CORE), which had been active in the Freedom Rides, SCLC, a somewhat reluctant NAACP, and SNCC. It was an uneasy coalition that would last through the summer of 1964. COFO's work was financed in part by the Voter Education Project in Atlanta, a foundation-backed effort that was supported by the Kennedy administration in hopes of channeling the young workers away from the direct action that had led to so many clashes in McComb and elsewhere. Although many of the SNCC workers—Moses, Hollis Watkins, and Curtis Hayes among them—were veterans of the jails and streets of tough southwestern Mississippi, they still scarcely knew what to expect in the Delta, beyond certain repression.

Charles McLaurin, a handsome young man who often wore black sunglasses against the Mississippi glare, had recently arrived in Ruleville from Jackson. He filed regular reports to SNCC or Voter Education Project headquarters in Atlanta, often describing the smallest details with the sharp eye of a newcomer to the region; his writing revealed a realist with occasional touches of an almost poetic sensibility. Soon after he arrived, he described the plantations on which "the Negroes live in little huts made of old boards nailed to a frame sometimes held up by legs. In the huts there is one, two or three rooms . . . and the only light is from an open fireplace in the middle of the room. This fireplace serves many as a means of keeping warm for reading and writing, cooking the meals and just whatever the family wants to do."[26]

By the time he arrived in Ruleville, "the Negroes had already made some attempts to register and the whites was upset." In mid-August, McLaurin went into the community with a group of about fifteen local boys and girls, going

> from door to door, telling people of their right to vote and how with the vote they could get better schools, jobs, paved streets and all these things citizens should have. The people most of them owned little homes right in the town. Some had to depend on credit and small loans from white people to keep up the payments on the homes, and [for] this reason many of them said they could not get down to register to vote. Some said they would go later.

McLaurin knew that the people were frightened, and he refused to give up, canvassing day after day. He knew he had to let people get to know him and to think about his message. Soon he ran afoul of the mayor, who told him that he and the other workers weren't needed there, "that they had schools to teach the Negroes all they needed to know." But McLaurin's strategy was to teach adults who could not go to school and didn't know their rights. That was precisely what the local authorities, who soon arrested McLaurin, did not want them to learn.

Arresting civil rights workers was always aimed as much at scaring the local community as at intimidating the workers, so once McLaurin was released, he and his group

> went walking through the Negro community so they could see us and know we were out of jail. We felt that by us walking around the community it would cause people to stop us to ask questions about what had happened. This would give us a chance to bring out things that we might not bring out otherwise; we wanted the community to start asking questions and to be informed about what happened. This we felt was one of the first steps to becoming a good citizen.

When mass meetings began that August at Williams Chapel Church, "the police would come by with a big police dog in the car and stop people on their way to the meetings and tell them to go home. Some did and others did not."[27]

McLaurin himself drew his courage from the people he accompanied to register at the courthouse in Indianola. He was afraid, he said, not so much of dying as of the powers of the sheriff and the courts. People would not have been as afraid of the night riders who shot into their homes, McLaurin wrote, had it not been that sheriffs sided with those night riders and policemen arrested the blacks who had been shot by the mob, charging *them* with breach of the peace.[28]

By mid-August 1962—less than two weeks before Mrs. Hamer would make the trip herself—McLaurin had found only three elderly women who were willing to go to Indianola to try to register. "This was the day I learned that the numbers were not important. I learned that a faithful few was better than an uncertain ten." They rode through Doddsville. That was the place, as McLaurin wrote in his report to SNCC headquarters, "where many years ago the burning of Negroes was a Sunday spectacle where whites young and old delighted at this evil which killed the spirit of the old Negroes and set the stage of the place-fixing of young ones not yet born."[29] The old ladies "would point toward the West and say Eastland owns this town as far as the eye can see." As they rode, McLaurin tried to imagine whether there would be mobs outside the courthouse as there had been when people had tried to register in other Mississippi towns.[30] McLaurin's knees were quivering and his brow was sweating, his stomach sinking, as they drove up to the old brick courthouse in the county seat. "I was filled with fear but this I must do; do this or continue to die."

The women took charge then. "They got out of the car and went up the walk to the courthouse as if this was the long walk that [led] to the Golden Gate of Heaven, their heads held high. I watched from a short distance behind them; the pride with which they walked. The strong convictions that they held as they walked up the steps into the building."[31] Their resolve could not, however, unlock the door to the circuit clerk's office. The women were told the office was closed. They went home, proud but unregistered. They tried again the next day. McLaurin was told the clerk would be gone for a month.

On August 31, Mrs. Hamer and seventeen others—more than the workers had expected—turned out to go to Indianola. With the help of Amzie Moore, who lived nearby, they rented a bus. Mrs. Hamer went prepared for the worst. "I don't know why, but I just had a feeling 'cause the morning I left home to go down to register, I carried some extra shoes and a bag because I said, 'If I'm arrested or anything, I'll have some extra shoes to put on.' "[32]

"When we reached Indianola," Charles McLaurin said, "the bus pulled up in front of the courthouse and the people got out and kind of just milled around a little bit because it was a place that a lot of blacks had some hesitancy to go because it first of all represented the seat of power, the jail, and all of the things that blacks wanted to stay away from."[33] There was a brief stalemate. "Then this one little stocky lady just stepped off the bus and went right on up to the courthouse and into the circuit clerk's office. I didn't know this was Fannie Lou Hamer."[34]

Mrs. Hamer was almost forty-five years old when she went this first time to try to register. "When we got down there," she said, "it was so many people down there, you know, white people, and some of them looked like the Beverly Hillbillies . . . but they wasn't kidding down there; they had on, you know, cowboy hats and they had guns; they had dogs."

Circuit Clerk Cecil Campbell was hostile when Mrs. Hamer told him the group had come to register. All but two of them would have to leave, he said, so Mrs. Hamer and Ernest Davis stayed and took the literacy test. "It was rough," Mrs. Hamer said. A prospective voter had to fill out a long questionnaire with personal information, written just so, with every *t* crossed and *i* dotted. She had to tell where she worked, and she knew why. "Well, see, when you put by whom are you employed, you fired by the time you get back home.'' Applicants had to give their place of citizenship and answer whether they had been convicted of bribery, theft, arson, embezzlement, forgery, or bigamy.

Finally, the registrar would bring out a big black book and give the potential registrant a section of the state constitution to interpret. Registrars thus could easily pass those they wanted to pass and fail any others. Whites passed; blacks rarely did. In Mrs. Hamer's case, Campbell pointed to the sixteenth section of the Mississippi Constitution. It was a section, she said, "dealing with facto laws and I knowed as much about a facto law as a horse knows about Christmas Day."[35] She flunked the test.

Later in the day, the group headed back to Ruleville. Soon a police car pulled the bus over and arrested the driver. The charge: his bus was too yellow. It looked too much like a school bus, the police said. The driver was taken back to Indianola. "While the driver was away, the people on the bus became restless and afraid," McLaurin recalled.

> They didn't know what was going on. They began to talk about their fear, to worry. Such things as, "I sure hope we don't get put in jail." "I gotta go home. My family will be coming in from the field." Or, "I gotta cook dinner." In the midst of all this grumbling about the problems, a voice, a song, a church song, just kind of smoothly came out of the group. "Down by the Riverside." Or "Ain't Gonna Let Nobody Turn Me Around." "This Little Light of Mine."

That voice was Fannie Lou Hamer's. Her singing calmed many of the riders on the bus. It carried over the nervous chatter, and it soothed even as it inspired. The other riders could get their minds off what faced them at home by joining in and humming. The young civil rights workers drew strength from these poor people of the Delta, and they from the workers, as the bus rolled down the highway. It was the first time that Fannie Lou Hamer drew upon this well of talent in public service. Combined with her fiery stump-speaking style and her personal courage, the power of her voice would remain stamped in the mind of many a Mississippian, many an American, in the coming years. "So Fannie Lou Hamer was on that bus," McLaurin said, "and, as a result of her songs, came forward."[36]

But the day was not over. The bus driver was handed a stiff fine. Nobody had much money, but among them his passengers scraped up $30 and that was acceptable. When the bus returned to Ruleville, Mrs. Hamer went back to the Marlow plantation where she had worked for eighteen years.

Her husband, Pap Hamer, remembered the day well. "That day at twelve o'clock, me and my little girls, we went to the house for lunch. OK. Here come Mr. Marlow across there. He asked me where was Fannie?" The conversation went on:

"I don't know. She gone to town there somewhere."

"No, she ain't gone to town. She gone down to Indianola to redish," *redish* being Mississippi vernacular for registering. "We ain't gonna have that now."

"What's that going to do?" Mr. Hamer remembered asking.

"Oh, it's going to happen. It ain't going to do nothin' but stir up a lot of stuff. It's going to happen, but we ain't ready for it now."

Mr. Hamer thought about what his boss had said. "I thought, 'Hell, there must be something to it or why would he want to raise hell about it?' I thought about it all that evening. Well, they made it home late that evening and he had told me to tell her when she come to go back down there and get her name off that book if she wanted to stay out there." When Mrs. Hamer returned, her husband was putting the cotton trailers away, so the Hamers' daughters, Dorothy and Vergie, told her what the boss had said.

"It was night when I got to the house," Mr. Hamer said, "and so I asked her, 'Did the children tell you what Mr. Dee [Marlow] said?' She said, 'Yeah.'

"I said, 'Well, what you going to do?' She said, 'I didn't go down there to register for Mr. Marlow. I went down to register for myself.'

"I said, 'OK, then.' A few minutes after I got through talking to her, here he come. He wanted to know, asked me did I tell her?" Mr. Hamer replied: "I sure did."

"What she say?"

"She in there. She'll tell you herself." He called his wife to the door.

The boss said, "Fannie, you've been down there to Indianola to register today, didn't you?"

"Yessir, Mr. Marlow, I sure did."

"Well, if you want to stay here and everything go like it always is, you better go back down there and get your name off that book."

"Mr. Dee, I didn't go down there to register for you," Mrs. Hamer repeated. "I went down to register for myself." It was a line she would come to repeat again and again around the country. It was a line that took unshakable courage to speak, black woman to white boss in Sunflower County, Mississippi, in 1962.

The boss left, and the Hamers talked some more. She said she wasn't going to take her name off the registration forms, Mr. Hamer recalled. "And I said, 'Well, you know you can't stay out here. I said, 'Now you and the kids pack your clothes and I'll take you all out to town.' ''[37]

The next morning the boss told Mr. Hamer to tell his wife to come back home, that things would be like they always were. He relayed that message to his wife. She replied: "That's what I'm trying to get out of now. Things be like they always was. I want some change." She did not accept his offer. Years later, Marlow's son, Dave, said that his father hadn't meant to throw her off his place; he was, however, clearly irked at the number of people who had been coming to the fields to get people to register and told Mrs. Hamer that she should keep her distance from them.

When she reached Ruleville that night, Mrs. Hamer went to the voter registration meeting. She said she had been thrown off the plantation and had no place to go. "I thought I'd come out here and tell you all." Her friend Mary Tucker was there and spoke up: "Don't say you ain't got nowhere to stay as long as I got a shelter— if I ain't got but one plank, you stick your head under there, too.' And she said, 'Thank you, Tuck.' And Joe McDonald said, 'If you ain't got room, I got room.' And we just put our arms around her."[38]

When Mrs. Hamer told what had happened, the young SNCC workers could not find words to describe how they felt about the sacrifice that she had just made. So two of them, Dorie Ladner and Colia Liddell, started singing. "It was all we could do under the circumstances," said Ladner, who had been in a caravan of civil rights workers' cars accompanying the bus to Indianola that day. "She was older than we were—she was in her forties and we were in our twenties and she followed us. We had the audacity to do that. We didn't know what it meant to be afraid or have responsibilities to pay the mortgage or feed our children. But Mrs. Hamer went a step further than I did because I didn't have those responsibilities and she left her husband, she left that little house in which they were living." Ladner said she still thinks about how brave it was for a woman from a plantation to go down that long winding road to leave her home, knowing a sheriff could bring her back, knowing that she could be shot at any moment.[39]

Mrs. Hamer stayed with friends—the few brave enough to house her—for several days. Then Mr. Hamer became afraid that some white person might try to kill her. He took her to relatives who lived in the country in Tallahatchie County. "She didn't stay gone long before she come back," Mrs. Tucker recalled, "and when she come back, she said, 'Well, killing or no killing, I'm going to stick with civil rights.' ''[40]

While Mrs. Hamer was away from Ruleville, there were repri-

sals. On just one day—September 3, 1962—these incidents occurred, all connected to the vote drive: a black city worker in Ruleville was fired, two black dry cleaning establishments were shut
down, Williams Chapel Baptist Church was told it was losing its tax
exemption and free water, and a plantation bus driver was told that
henceforth he would need a hard-to-obtain commercial license to
ferry workers to the field. The fired city worker's wife had been
going to the voter registration classes. The dry cleaners were owned
by blacks. The suddenly uninsured church was a meeting place for
voter registration workers. And the mother of the harassed bus
driver had registered to vote. That man, Fred Hicks, was told by the
bus owner: "We gonna see how tight we can make it—gonna make
it just as tight as we can. Gonna be rougher and rougher than you
think it is."

That same day, Bob Moses and Amzie Moore were walking
down a street when a white man in a pickup truck pulled up along-
side them. Were they the folks who were getting people to register?
They replied that, yes, they were. Could they come to his plantation
to register people? Yes, they answered, they could come. If that was
so, then "I've got a shotgun waiting for you, double barrel," the
man said and roared away.[41]

The civil rights workers knew that they, as outsiders, could not
combat this climate of intimidation alone. They needed to develop
local leaders, people who came from the same backgrounds as those
they were seeking to lead to the polls, people who understood the
fears and could help overcome them. Since its founding, the Student Non-Violent Coordinating Committee had operated on the
principle that the people should make their own decisions. Without
a mass base, there would be no local organization remaining once
the students left. Change had to flow from the people's concerns,
whether those concerns centered on education or better roads or
food for hungry children. And leadership had to rise from those
people as well or they would only be substituting one master for
another. In Sunflower County, Bob Moses soon realized that Mrs.
Hamer was exactly the kind of natural community leader that
SNCC sought.

For more than a decade, she had gone to the Mound Bayou
Day celebrations in the all-black community in neighboring Bolivar
County, celebrations organized by a doctor named T. R. M. How-
ard. Howard was an outspoken black man who stood up for him-
self, and many people thus were fearful to be seen with him. Not
Charles Evers. He had not yet succeeded his brother, Medgar, as
NAACP leader, had not yet become one of the state's leading black

politicians, but he knew that the freedoms the group discussed would be considered incendiary by their white neighbors in the Delta. "I think back in those days there were only six or seven of us, say, who wanted to be free and were willing to pay the price." There were Medgar Evers, who had lived in Mound Bayou and sold insurance there; Amzie Moore; Aaron Henry, a druggist and NAACP activist from nearby Clarksdale; a few other men; and Fannie Lou Hamer. At Mound Bayou Days, Evers added, "We'd all be there, and a few others, meet there. They had to be the strongest niggers in the state because there wasn't anybody else going to come. So we kind of got to be a family like."[42]

Fannie Lou Hamer was a person in search of a freedom movement. "She told me that she had always wanted to get involved with something to help her people but she just didn't know exactly how or what to do," Charles McLaurin recalled. "She had read about the Freedom Rides into Jackson and around the country, about the various student sit-ins around the country, and she was really waiting for an opportunity."[43]

SNCC provided it. "If SNCC hadn't of come into Mississippi, there never would have been a Fannie Lou Hamer," she told a student later. "They treated me like a human being, whether the kids was white or black. I was respected with the kids, and they never told nobody what to say, nobody. Everything you heard us screaming and saying . . . nobody tell us to say that. This is what's been there all the time, and we had a chance to get it off our chests, and nobody else had ever give us that chance. . . . They brought every hope into the state of Mississippi."

Fannie Lou Hamer had a presence. She was smart. And as a poor black southern sharecropper, she represented the soul of the people whom the movement wanted to represent. As disfranchised people were starting to assert themselves, she stepped forward, voicing her own concerns and those of her neighbors. She had a personal story, which would only grow more compelling the more she endured. And she had a voice with which to tell it. Virtually everyone whose path crossed hers remembered first and foremost her singing and her speaking.

Bob Moses had heard the voice; intuitively, he knew what might lie behind it. So that fall of 1962, he asked McLaurin to locate the lady who had been evicted from the plantation and had sung all the church songs on the bus. McLaurin was to go to Tallahatchie County where Mrs. Hamer was staying and ask her to go with him to Nashville for a SNCC rally. Moses wanted her to tell reporters her story about registering and losing her job.

McLaurin didn't know the Delta well then, but he found that most people knew of Mrs. Hamer. Gradually, he got directions from black people driving tractors in the fields or walking along the streets.

> Finally, though a few miles out of the way, I was told that I would find a little cabin at the top of a hill in Cascilla, just off the road . . . and that the house would have two sides with a corridor running right down the middle. After driving in the pouring rain for hours, I finally located the little house on the side of the hill right by the road with smoke coming out of the chimney and the two sides as I was told and the corridor right down the middle.
>
> I knocked on the first door to the left and someone said come in. I walked into the building. There was a woman with her back to the door putting wood in this little pot-bellied stove. It was red hot. I never will forget it because it was raining and it was a little bit cool. And I said, "I'm looking for Fannie Lou Hamer." And she turned around and said, "I'm Fannie Lou Hamer."

McLaurin told her that Moses had asked her to go to Tougaloo College in Jackson and from there to Nashville for a meeting. "And she said, 'I'll be ready in a minute.' In other words, nobody had contacted her really that I know of. She had not been told that somebody was going to pick her up. But yet she just got right up, got her stuff together and we got in the car and left for Tougaloo."[44]

McLaurin stood with Mrs. Hamer for many years. He was like a son to her, she said once. The young man was learning every day the lesson that the elderly ladies had taught him at the Indianola courthouse weeks earlier. Those women, he said, had been victimized by white faces all their lives and suddenly walked up to one of them and said they wanted their rights. "This did something to me," he wrote. "It told me something. It was like a voice speaking to me, as I stood there alone, in a strange place and an unknown land. This voice told me that although these old ladies knew the risk involved in their being there, they were still willing to try. It said you are the light, let it shine and the people will know you, and they will follow you, if you show the way, they will go, with or without you."[45]

CHAPTER 3

"I Want My Freedom Now"

ONCE FANNIE LOU HAMER tried to register to vote, there was no turning back to life on the plantation. Her course, and that of her husband, was irrevocably altered. Other dramatic days lay ahead for her, but in that fall of 1962 and spring of 1963 there were only painstaking organizing and educating, filled with setbacks to match each small step forward.

In Nashville, she was the center of attention. She personified many of the reasons the students with whom she was meeting had become involved in civil rights: the dream that, with a modicum of help and more than a bit of heroism, ordinary people could transform their lives. Organized for two years then as the Student Non-Violent Coordinating Committee, these young people had been at work in several states, trying to build confidence among the local people. They learned again and again, as if the lesson needed repetition, each individual's stories of economic dependence or violent intimidation. If people went to a civil rights meeting, much less opened their homes to rights workers, the next thing they knew the boss would be saying, "Don't do that." Courthouse doors slammed in the faces of those few who did gather their courage to try to register to vote.

Workers in rural Georgia had some success—a few hundred blacks had been registered; Mississippi was barely awakening to the movement.[1] That a sharecropper evicted from her home for trying to register had not only refused to retract her application but would also come to tell these SNCC members her story, and possibly work with them, represented only a small step—but one that provided incentive to keep going.

Charles McLaurin was getting to know Mrs. Hamer better.

"On the way to Tougaloo we talked about many things which we would later work on as organizers," he recalled. "Mrs. Hamer was about forty-four years of age, and I was twenty-one, but there was no barrier between us." Once they got to Tougaloo, they joined other SNCC workers and carefully planned their route to Nashville. Around midnight three cars left, carrying Mrs. Hamer and a handful of the earliest SNCC fieldworkers—Lafayette Surney, Curtis Hayes, Hollis Watkins, Charles Cobb, McLaurin, and six others. It was in Nashville, McLaurin said, "that the SNCC family learned of Mrs. Hamer's ability to move people with her speeches and her way of expressing reassurance in her songs."[2]

Fannie Lou Hamer the speaker cajoled audiences, scolded them for not daring to take action, then embraced them by sharing her own hopes and fears with them. She inspired the students in Nashville by telling her own story. She quoted the Bible. In her speeches, she poked fun at cowardly men who, if they weren't under the bed, were under the porch. She mimicked people others would dare not mimic, like Dr. Martin Luther King, Jr. She criticized presidents, and she shamed people who had suffered less than she had into daring to do as much as she and others were doing. She berated educated people who were not doing what she was trying to do with less schooling. She urged her neighbors not to hate whites but to help them—sometimes suggesting that they help them out of office. Later, she would urge her northern friends to contribute money or time to that effort.

She rarely spoke from a prepared text. One time she tried it in a radio appearance, recalled her friend and fellow civil rights worker Victoria Gray, and it didn't work. They were appearing together in Clarksdale, and they both had scripts. Mrs. Gray read hers well, but Mrs. Hamer had trouble. After it was over, Mrs. Hamer said, "Gray, I messed that up."

"You don't need a script," Mrs. Gray recalled replying. "Whenever you get a script, just go through it and see what they want you do say and then put it aside. And she said, 'Do you think that's so?' And I said, 'I know it's so. I've seen you before. And you don't need a script.'"[3]

The Nashville conference, then, launched Mrs. Hamer as a movement speaker. After the meeting, she did not return home for several months. She and the SNCC Freedom Singers toured the country, raising money for the organization's work throughout the South. Mrs. Hamer was making the shift from private outrage to public person. The transition was gradual that first year until more and more of the movement leaders—and their lawyers—saw her ability to sweep all into her orbit and electrify audiences with her story. Her world would expand well beyond the confines of Ruleville; her travels made some of her neighbors jealous and at times annoyed her husband, who thought she gave too much of herself, getting little in return. She in turn worried about Pap and the girls, who by then had moved into town, until she reached home safely again. She thrived on the attention and would miss it when it disappeared.

In many communities, women stepped into movement leadership because in the South at that time it was simply too dangerous for a black man to stand up to the system. He would lose his job, possibly his life. The fact that the Student Non-Violent Coordinating Committee and not Martin Luther King's Southern Christian Leadership Conference was the most visible presence in Mississippi enhanced women's roles as well. Ministers—men—dominated SCLC while SNCC and its political offshoots in Mississippi relied on grass-roots people. Where there were grass roots, there were women.

The movement worked through churches, even when some local ministers feared to become involved. Who did the church work? "Who's the people that really keeps things going on? . . . It's women," said Unita Blackwell, one of the early leaders in the rural town of Mayersville near the Mississippi River.

> The women is the ones that supports the deacon board. They holler the amen. The women is the ones that support the preacher. . . . Without women in these churches and whatever in the United States, you wouldn't have many people there. . . . So in the black community the movement, quite naturally I suppose, emerged out of all the women that carried out these roles. We didn't know we was leaders. You knew you did things, but you never saw it as a high political leadership role.[4]

Some have argued that black women were able to play such an active role in areas where leadership was foreclosed for men because the black women were invisible to white eyes. Charles Evers speculated that whites, accustomed to having black women working in their homes, were not as threatened by them as by black men. "Maybe there was a tendency there because of the motherhood that black women had shown to all whites—every white had more'n likely come in touch sometime with a black woman—she'd cooked for them, she made the beds, she washed the dirty clothes, she'd nurse 'em, she'd babysit while mom and dad went out and had a good time. Somehow they came into that very personal, intimate relationship with black women." Civil rights leaders in Mississippi relied heavily on Mrs. Hamer, Evers added, because they had found that, in general, the black woman was the only person who was nearly free. "She could get into more doors, and could say things that we couldn't say and still stay alive, so we pushed Fannie and she did that."[5]

Yet Charles Payne of Northwestern University found that some of the most violent reprisals were against women. "Women who were even rumored to be part of the movement lost their jobs. Every adult woman I interviewed got fired, except for those who quit because they expected to get fired. Women were regularly clubbed at demonstrations or beaten in jail. The homes of women activists were regularly shot into. Any women in the Delta who contemplated joining the early movement had to be aware of all this."[6]

In the fall of 1962, then, Fannie Lou Hamer was one of the few converts to the movement in Sunflower County. Most people remained too fearful, too dependent on whites to challenge their power. Even though Amzie Moore had introduced the civil rights workers to the few people interested in voter registration, they had made limited headway. Charles McLaurin and others talked to fifty or sixty black people and found that their so-called leaders—teachers and preachers—were "the most hated people in the community."[7] Instead of being leaders, they often proved the most timid; they felt they had the most to lose. They had made their uneasy peace with the system, and any dealings with these student upstarts could only challenge their tenuous gains. The SNCC workers faced their task of building leaders. "We began to talk with the old ladies and men," McLaurin reported to the Voter Education Project in Atlanta. If young people saw their elders taking part, they, too, might try to register.

In August, McLaurin and company had persuaded five people to go to Indianola, then nine, then the eighteen who included Mrs. Hamer. In September there were more mass meetings; six more people tried to register. "The people was having a good time singing Freedom songs," McLaurin reported. Little children could be heard singing, "Ain't Going to Let Nobody Turn Me Around" and "We Shall Overcome." Everybody, he said with his understated eloquence, "was talking about Freedom."[8] There seemed to be progress.

Then on the night of September 10—the same day the U.S. Supreme Court said the University of Mississippi had to admit

James Meredith—shots were fired into the homes of the McDonalds, the Tuckers, and the Sisson family, all of whom had either housed rights workers or been active in the registration drive. The shots into the Tuckers' house hit just above where Fannie Lou Hamer's head would have been resting had she still been there.

Herman Sisson had planned to take his granddaughter and a friend to college in Jackson the next day. After dinner, Sisson was reading the newspaper, and Marylene Burkes, twenty, and nineteen-year-old Vivian Hillet were sitting on the couch, talking. "Bam, Bam, and then after a few minutes another shot, Bam," Sisson said.[9] Hattie Sisson shouted for help, and her husband and their neighbors got the girls, who had been hit by the shots, into the car. At the hospital, Sisson saw the mayor of Ruleville, who approached him and said, " 'You done that yourself, trying to lay it on somebody else. You done that yourself, get out of here, go on out of here.' "

Mrs. Sisson, who was at home, said the mayor stopped by there as well. " 'I was looking for this to happen,' " she quoted him. " 'I was looking for this to happen. Lot more should have gotten this.' " He said it was like Carl Braden, the journalist allied with the civil rights cause, whose house in Kentucky was burned after the Bradens rented it to a black family. "He pulled a stunt, burned down his house to get publicity," the mayor insisted as he left.[10] In fact, a neighbor saw the car from which the shots were fired. He said the driver, who had his arm out the window, was a white man.[11]

Rebecca McDonald had been reading the Bible and decided to take a bath before she went to bed. A gunshot broke a window. The McDonalds turned the light out, and Joe McDonald got his single-barrel twelve-gauge shotgun. Later that evening the local police, including the brother of J. W. Milam, acquitted in the Emmett Till killing, arrived to check what had happened. One officer said the mayor had ordered him to take McDonald's shotgun if he had one. He asked whether there were another gun, then started searching the house, overturning the studio couch. McDonald asked whether he had a search warrant, and the man replied that he knew nothing about that, adding: "Joe, we gonna get to the bottom of this thing and find out what we can do about it. You been listening to some strange folks anyhow, to cause this trouble to happen."[12]

SNCC worker Charles Cobb, meanwhile, had telephoned Bob Moses in Jackson, then had gone to the North Sunflower County Hospital to check on the condition of the two girls, one of whom had been shot in the leg and the other in the head and shoulder. While he was there, Mayor Dorrough came in and grabbed the address book in which he was taking notes. He arrested Cobb and told the police officer who took him to jail, "He looks like the type of person who would do this." The next morning, Cobb explained to Dorrough that he had been taking notes because he felt the shootings were connected with the voter registration project. "The mayor agreed in a way," Cobb said. "He said, 'I think you all shot at those houses; you were disappointed at the lack of violence here; and you need the publicity to get money from the North.'"[13] The FBI investigated but, like the local officials, proved most interested in asking whether the civil rights workers were asking for money or had fired the shots themselves. "The FBI did more to frighten [our] people than to help them," Charles McLaurin reported.[14]

Activity in the black community halted abruptly after the shooting. SNCC workers could not attract anyone to meetings or be invited inside their homes. People were afraid to be seen with SNCC workers or have letters sent by them to their homes. They told McLaurin "that if we had not come to Ruleville all this wouldn't have happened. So most everybody in the community was down on us, and we had to do something to get them on our side."

The setbacks dictated a new approach. The civil rights workers realized that they needed to win back people's confidence, and, as they did in other communities across the South where people lost jobs and homes because they dared try to vote, they switched to helping provide the basic necessities of life. The young workers, many of whom had dropped out of school or put off college to join the movement, were in it for the long haul; one SNCC worker stayed in Ruleville at all times so the people would see that the young people had no intention of getting them into trouble and then leaving.

The workers went from house to house asking about everyday problems. They took people into town to shop. They helped pick cotton. They cut wood. September and October were spent trying to recreate that feeling of "togetherness and friendship" before resuming any overt new civil rights activity.[15]

Nevertheless, the intimidation continued. "We were able to keep a place to stay because of Mr. Joe and his wife," McLaurin reported. "Many times the Mayor told Mr. Joe to get us out of his house or he would have real trouble, but Mr. Joe stood his ground." Joe McDonald finally lost his job hauling laborers; even then, he would not put the workers out.

November witnessed little improvement. The Delta had had a dry year so the heavy machines had been able to pick most of the cotton, leaving little to be picked by hand. "Mrs. Willie Mae Robinson, who sharecrops on a plantation near Ruleville, picked twenty bales of cotton this season," the SNCC workers reported, "yet she only cleared three dollars for the entire year."[16] Other sharecroppers said they had had Social Security taxes deducted even though they had no Social Security numbers. "Mrs. Irene Johnson of Ruleville, who is active in the voter registration drive there, reports that even her ten-year-old son has had Social Security taken from him."[17]

The bosses were angry because of the registration drive, and "the bank would not loan money to people that had tried to register or if anyone in their family had attempted."[18] To survive through the winter months in which there was no employment, seasonal workers traditionally relied on surplus food such as meal, rice, flour, and dry milk, available through a federal commodities distribution program. Mississippi started tightening the screws. In the past, all a person had to do to get the commodities was sign up. By late 1962, however, an applicant had to have the registration form countersigned by his boss or by "a responsible person," which usually meant a white person. Because of the voter registration drive, "the 'responsible people' were not particularly inclined to favors for the Negro," the SNCC workers wrote.[19]

Farm workers hesitated to go to Ruleville city hall to sign up for the commodities because that meant going to the same building where the police station was located, "and they fear the police most of all."[20] Those who did go were directed instead to Indianola, and many did not have cars to make the trip. But even if they went to the county seat, they had to stand in the cold while only two or three people were allowed inside to tell "the history of their lives." If a white person took "his Negroes" down, McLaurin said, he could take them inside; others would have to stand out in the cold in a line all day.[21]

The SNCC workers quickly saw the connection. "Commodities are the only way many Negroes make it from cotton season to cotton season," they reported. "If this is taken from them, they have nothing at all; and the success of our voter registration program depends on the protection we can offer the individual while he is waiting for his one small vote to become a part of a strong Negro vote. It doesn't take much to tide over the rural Mississippi Negro, but the commodities are vital."[22] Diane Nash Bevel, one of the SNCC workers, contacted the Agriculture Department in Washington. Agriculture secretary Orville Freeman's intervention changed the attitude at the local welfare office, where the staff became somewhat more helpful in signing people up for the commodities. As a result, more people in the black community started talking to McLaurin. "So you see we are not only voter registration workers but lawyers, welfare workers, preachers and anything the people need."[23]

By late 1962, forty-one people had gone from Ruleville to the courthouse in Indianola to try to register. Four of the nine who had gone in August had finally been registered. Rebecca McDonald, told she hadn't passed, was so provoked that she went down again by herself and took the test. "Mrs. McDonald is one of the hard fighting old ladies who have stuck it out and truly do believe," McLaurin noted.[24] With these small gains, "the community . . . is beginning to perk up a little," SNCC workers could report. "The people are asking questions about voting and other things citizens should know. They continually ask about the FBI and what is going to happen about the shooting in Ruleville."

And Fannie Lou Hamer was back. On November 22, 1962, she spoke at a meeting of twenty to thirty people at a home in Ruleville. She told them how she had lost her job but said that it was important that every person in Ruleville try to register.[25] Early in December, the Hamers moved into a rickety frame house that friends made available in town on Lafayette Street just east of the main U.S. highway that runs through Ruleville. Mr. Hamer had finished working out the cotton season. Then he, too, was evicted. Neither of the Hamers could find regular work; they existed on the ten-dollar weekly stipend that SNCC started paying Mrs. Hamer that December. McLaurin noted Mrs. Hamer's return in his report to Atlanta: "This is good, because she is as you know the lady that was put off the Marlow plantation for going down to register. She is a very good singer and can do most anything." She knew all the people on her plantation, he added, "and they all respect her and we feel that she will play a big part in getting people from the plantation to register."[26]

On December 4 Mrs. Hamer returned to Indianola to take the voter-registration test again. This time she was asked to interpret a section of the Mississippi Constitution concerning the state House of Representatives. Since her last attempt to register, she had studied the state constitution with the help of some of the SNCC workers. "So that time I gave a reasonable enough interpretation."[27] She told the registrar he had better let her sign up because she was going to keep coming back until he did.

In December, Mrs. Hamer circulated a petition to help get food commodities for poor families. She was letting civil rights workers use her home for meetings, and "through her, we have been able to get people from some of the plantations to meet with us and two have gone to register," they reported. Marlow, the Hamers' boss, who had evicted the couple, kept telling Perry Hamer that his wife could come back to the plantation if she would withdraw her voter application. She wouldn't.[28]

Early in the new year, 1963, she went to Indianola to find out whether she had passed the voting test. "Mrs. Hamer returned with joy in her eyes." She had passed. The next day, Fannie Lou Hamer, Irene Johnson, Hattie Sisson, and Ruby Davis went to Ruleville city hall and signed their names on the books there so they could vote in city as well as county elections.[29] That August Mrs. Hamer would try to vote in the primary election, only to be told that she couldn't because she had not been paying poll tax for two years. She hadn't paid poll taxes because she hadn't been registered, of course.

As the winter of 1962 wore on into 1963, people in Ruleville needed warm clothes as well as food. Winters had always been hard financially for blacks in the Mississippi Delta, but farm mechanization and the farmers' antagonism toward the voting drive turned fortune even colder that year. Various civil rights organizations collected clothing in the North, and in February one hundred people crowded the McDonalds' home for food and clothes. About twenty said they would go to Indianola to register.

That winter, the Hamers were repeatedly harassed by local authorities because they were active in the voter-registration program. At one point, they received a $9,000 water bill, which Mrs. Hamer protested.[30] How, she asked, could she owe so much when her house had no running water?

It was at about this point that Charles McLaurin was able to make a startling report to Rebecca McDonald, who had tried to register five times already. Because of a mixup in voter records, or deliberate misinformation from county authorities, it turned out that she was already a registered voter, and had been for ten years. "Man, you should have seen her face when I told her this news," McLaurin reported.[31]

Voter-registration efforts were still piecemeal. To combat their lack of success, civil rights workers were training local people to teach their neighbors how to read, how to take the voter-registration test, and what citizenship meant. The Southern Christian Leadership Conference provided much of this training. In March Mrs. Hamer took one of the SCLC courses. And in April she went to Dorchester, Georgia, for more citizenship teacher training.[32]

The Dorchester program was one of the incubators of the civil rights movement, unknown to most Americans but crucial in the early 1960s because of its role in helping mold existing, but raw, talent into trained workers. The SCLC had taken over this training from Highlander Folk School in the Tennessee mountains. Myles Horton, then a young Tennessee disciple of the social gospel, started Highlander Folk School in 1932 to help poor mountain people help themselves, operating on the principle that the concerns of the people themselves would guide the program. By the 1940s and 1950s, more black people—those who were economically independent of whites—started attending sessions at Highlander. Interests at the school, often labeled communist by its detractors, evolved toward civil rights. Highlander staff and visitors developed methods to teach adults how to read and how to sign up to vote. Septima Clark, a former Charleston, South Carolina, teacher who consistently ran afoul of education authorities because of her insistence on equal pay with whites, was a prime mover in this effort; so were Esau Jenkins, of Johns Island, off the South Carolina coast, and Bernice Robinson, a hairdresser from the area.[33]

While she was still SCLC executive director, Ella Baker had urged her boss, Dr. Martin Luther King, Jr., and the rest of the organization's leadership to stress this kind of education. She saw the wisdom in developing grass-roots leaders. Finally, her message sank in. King asked Myles Horton to help develop such a program for SCLC; Horton in turn suggested that SCLC take over the Highlander program. The training had outgrown Highlander's capacity—and the school itself was constantly harassed by the Tennessee authorities. They ultimately forced its closure. Andrew Young, a Congregational church minister then employed by the National Council of Churches in New York, went to Georgia to direct the SCLC program. Dorothy Cotton was assistant director and education consultant.

"When we were helping them learn to read and write better, we would use the Constitution as the content material or newspapers or other things that were relevant," Cotton said. The instructors would ask the people why they wanted to learn to read. One would want to write to her son; another wanted to be sure he wasn't being cheated. Some wanted to vote. Then they would learn what they needed to accomplish those goals. "We were also trying to teach [these prospective teachers] what makes for an interesting class," Cotton recalled. "I would ask a group what was habeas corpus, hoping no one would know, then I'd tell them. Then I'd ask them to define citizenship. We'd thrash it over. Some people thought it meant having moral character and so on. But then at the end I'd ask them again what was habeas corpus and they couldn't remember because I'd told them. But because we'd talked about citizenship, they knew that. We were teaching what to teach *and* how to teach."[34]

For the training, people from around the South would travel to a turn-of-the-century schoolhouse south of Savannah that the Congregational church had given the people of the area as a community center. It accommodated fifty-five or sixty people.[35] The Reverend James Bevel, who had preached the night Mrs. Hamer decided to try to register to vote, scoured Mississippi for people to be trained at Dorchester; in April a group including Fannie Lou Hamer made the trip with Bevel's wife, Diane.[36]

"We rode on a bus from Cleveland, Mississippi, to Dorchester, Georgia," recalled Leslie McLemore, then a Rust College student. "After dinner every night we would sing. That was the first time I heard 'The Drinking Gourd,' " a song used on the antislavery Underground Railroad that then became a civil rights movement standard. "Andy Young taught that to us. Mrs. Hamer was clearly the song leader in that group. It's probably where she learned many of the freedom songs. She already knew all the spirituals line and verse."[37]

The training was important to her, and she was important to other trainees. "Mrs. Hamer immediately took over a leadership role," Andrew Young recalled, because in the opening session people would talk about their experiences. "She was always very open" in talking about what had happened to her. And "any time there was a slow period in the discussion, she would just start up one of those good ol' hymns and so there was no question about her leadership ability."[38]

Dorothy Cotton agreed. "She became the dynamic personality in the Mississippi group. We would ask them to describe the work they were doing in their hometowns, and she would shine her light in these workshops. This was a folk workshop so even if we were talking about the Constitution, we started our sessions singing, and she was a powerhouse. I would stress her determination no matter what she was talking about, and people caught this spirit.

"Our purpose was to see how people could unbrainwash themselves—and that's a direct quote from one of the people in one of my sessions." The people needed to develop the self-confidence, quashed at home, that they could conduct business for themselves. "We taught them how to make long distance phone calls. A lot of people didn't know how to do that. We taught them how to use bank drafts. These were people who, when they got any money, they put it under the mattress. We needed to teach them to use banks. We introduced them to political officials. We wanted to demystify the political process and build a base from which folks could operate."[39]

In May 1963, Mrs. Hamer was selected to receive more training at a similar two-week program in which Bernice Robinson taught in Charleston, South Carolina. The training programs brought scholars like Vincent Harding and John Henrik Clark into contact with grass-roots people like Fannie Lou Hamer who would be on the front lines of the movement. Folksinger Guy Carawan, generally credited with helping transform "We Shall Overcome" from a little known song into the anthem of the civil rights movement, attended with his wife and their baby and taught the group more songs.[40]

Attending the Charleston training sessions with Mrs. Hamer was June Johnson, a teenager from Greenwood, Mississippi, who became involved in the movement even though her mother forbade her to distribute voter-registration leaflets or do any canvassing. Bell Johnson, a tall woman who worked as a cook and raised twelve children, was a strict disciplinarian, but her daughter was just as strong-minded. June would sneak out to distribute leaflets, her mother would punish her, and she would sneak out again. Mrs. Johnson eventually took part in the movement herself, but that spring she gave her permission for June to go to Charleston reluctantly and only after she learned that Annell Ponder, a college graduate working for SCLC in Greenwood, would be in charge.

Black parents, knowing the risks of crossing whites, remembering Emmet Till's fate, were often horrified at what their children were doing. It was the mothers and fathers who would lose what little security they had, even as their children faced losing their lives. June herself wasn't sure whether she was initially more interested in the issue or simply "wanted to be around new guys" in town.

Johnson had first heard Mrs. Hamer speak at the Friendship Baptist Church just down the street from her home in Greenwood. Passing by, she heard through the open window "this lady who had such an eloquent voice." Johnson walked up the steps and peeked in the doorway. "I was really impressed with her and the things that she was saying. She had a very unique way of dealing with the Bible. She was a very Christian religious woman, and she knew the Bible well."[41]

June left Greenwood with Annell Ponder and Mrs. Hamer on a Sunday morning. "We tried to integrate the bus terminal here in

Greenwood while we were waiting for that bus," Johnson said, "but we didn't have enough time, so we said we would deal with that when we got back."[42]

Once the group reached Charleston, Mrs. Hamer visited the Old Slave Mart. Standing there, she could imagine how black families had been ripped apart a century earlier, how possibly her own ancestors had passed through that port. She saw the ads for slaves for sale; one of them read, "Crippled but a good breeder." She saw the stump from which slaves were sold, from which children were torn from their mothers' arms. "They keeps it nice and shellacked," she recalled.[43] That visit had a profound impact and helped her understand some of the songs and stories of her grandmother, who had been a slave. "She used to tell us how she was first a Gober and then a Bramlett," Mrs. Hamer said. "I didn't know what to make of it when I was a child, but since I've grown, I realized that it was the name that the white people gave her. So I never will know what my name really was, because the white people took it from my grandmother."[44]

The trip to the slave mart deepened Mrs. Hamer's resolve to help collect the debt that she felt America owed black people. For her efforts, she would soon be repaid in violence at the hands of Mississippians who regarded her as little better than her enslaved ancestors.

CHAPTER 4

"It Isn't Nice to Go to Jail"

THE SOUTH THROUGH which the Mississippians traveled home had exploded that spring. Dr. Martin Luther King, Jr., and the Reverend Fred Shuttlesworth led adults and children into the streets of Birmingham seeking an end to that city's harsh segregation, and Chief Eugene "Bull" Connor's police turned their dogs on the demonstrators. Water from high-pressure fire hoses slammed into the black demonstrators, and the photos flashed around the world. The NAACP's Medgar Evers tried to get the city of Jackson to hire black police officers, led a boycott against local merchants who supported segregation, and was granted television time never before given a black leader in Mississippi to respond to one especially harsh message from the city's mayor. Early in June, Roy Wilkins, the cautious NAACP leader who sought to distance his organization from King's incendiary tactics, had been arrested with Evers on a picket line in Jackson, and four days later John Doar of the Justice Department helped the first black student enroll at the University of Mississippi Law School. Governor George Wallace was threatening to bar two black students from attending the University of Alabama. These events placed the Kennedy administration under intense pressure to drop its bystander role in civil rights.[1]

Fannie Lou Hamer, June Johnson, and the other Mississippians thus headed home with both apprehension and new zeal for their mission, trained now in new techniques to achieve their goals. A few minor skirmishes quickly reminded them of the segregated society they were up against, but the main event awaited them in the Winona jail.

With their renewed confidence, the travelers sat down at the whites-only lunch counter in the bus station during a layover in Columbus, Mississippi. Several police officers stared at them and made remarks, but they were served.[2] Then, as they boarded the bus for Winona, the last major stop before their destination of Greenwood, the bus driver placed a little white girl at the front of the line ahead of Mrs. Hamer and June Johnson and the rest, telling his black passengers that "niggers were not to be in front of the line." Mrs. Hamer objected strongly and asked the driver for his name and number.

She was still talking about the incident as the bus left, Johnson said. "She talked about the Bible. She talked about how we had been treated. And she was going to do something about it. I think this infuriated the man."[3] The group sang freedom songs as the bus moved through Mississippi. At every brief stop along the way—in a little town between Mayhew and Starkville, in Eupora, in Stewart, and in Kilmichael—the driver made a telephone call. Judging from the number of law officers on hand when the bus rolled into Winona, county seat for Montgomery County, Johnson decided the driver had been calling ahead about his passengers.

What followed in the next few days drew little attention at the time but would go down in civil rights movement history. The events at the Winona jail became the core of Mrs. Hamer's powerful story about the forces unleashed upon her when she tried to become a first-class citizen. On a larger scale, the Winona incident and its aftermath showed that even though the federal government might be moved toward some action in behalf of its black citizens, there was only so much it could do faced with a recalcitrant state and local law officers bent on repression. National power did not travel well.

The bus carrying the travelers home from Charleston arrived in Winona about 11:15 on June 9, 1963, a Sunday morning. Some of the passengers got off to use the rest rooms; others wanted something to eat. Annell Ponder, the SCLC staff member traveling with the group, described what happened next:

> Three or four of us got off the bus and went in the café to be served, and we sat down at the lunch counter and when we sat down there were two waitresses back of the counter and one of them just balled up her dishcloth . . . and threw it against the wall behind us. She said, "I can't take no more," and so right after she said that, the chief of police and highway patrolman came from the rear area of the café and came around and tapped us on the shoulder with the billy clubs. Said, "Y'all get out—get out."[4]

When he tapped her, Ponder stood up and said, "You know it's against the law to put us out of here, don't you?"

The patrolman replied, "Ain't no damn law, you just get out of here!"

The group stood outside, joined by Euvester Simpson, who had tried to use the rest room. One of the policemen had told her to go to the one that was for "colored." Ponder decided to write down the license plate number of the patrol car and while she was doing that, the patrolman and the chief of police came out of the restaurant. "The chief of police said, 'You're all under arrest. You're under arrest. Get in that car there.' They had us get into the patrolman's car. As we were getting in the car, Mrs. Hamer got off the bus and asked us if we wanted them to go on down to Greenwood. So I said yes, and then the police chief hollered out, 'Get that one there; get that one there—bring her on down in the other car.'" Mrs. Hamer said later that as she was getting into the car, one of the law officers kicked her and cursed.

The caravan traveled the few blocks to the Montgomery County Jail, a small one-story brick building located in a residential neighborhood within walking distance of downtown stores and offices. The prisoners went in to the booking room, where they milled around for several minutes. It was not clear what the charges against them were. Soon the only man in the group, James West, was put in a cell with several other male prisoners; Mrs. Hamer and Euvester Simpson were taken to a small cell, and Annell Ponder and Rosemary Freeman were put next door.

Traveler and law officer alike basically agreed on what had happened at the bus station. There was, however, some dispute over why the officers were there. They said the café owner asked them to come in and that several white patrons had complained about the travelers' behavior. The café owner testified later in federal court that she had not called them in, nor had any patrons complained.[5] The stories diverged dramatically, however, about events that occurred once the prisoners entered the jail.

After the other women were placed in cells, June Johnson remained in the booking room. The police asked the teenager what she thought they should do. She replied that she thought they were supposed to protect people. Then the police hit her, she said. Later, when the men were tried on brutality charges, the law officers said fifteen-year-old June started the trouble by refusing to go to a cell and sitting down on the floor in the booking room. Any bruises she had, they contended, were received when they had to drag her across the floor.[6] She said she was hit without provocation and knocked down, adding that when she wanted to take a shower to clean up, the law officers, who controlled the water temperature from outside the area, tried to scald her.

Then the officers brought Annell Ponder into the booking room and put Johnson in the cell in her place. Ponder said that June's face was bleeding and she was crying when she passed her. There was blood on the floor where she had been. The officers started hitting Ponder, accusing the workers of being "down there stirring up shit and the more we stir the more it stank." They were accused of planning a demonstration. The police kept after her to say, "Yes, sir." Ponder replied to one of the men that she didn't know him well enough to say that.

He was amazed that a black woman displayed such boldness, "and then after that they kept trying to get me to say, yes, sir, and I wouldn't and they kept hitting me from one to the other, and around, and this went on for about 10 minutes, talking and beating," Ponder said. "I'd say there were at least three of them . . . kind of gave us the runover with blackjacks, a belt, fists, open palm and at one point the highway patrolman hit me in the stomach. . . . They really wanted to make me say yes, sir, and that's one thing I wouldn't say."[7] The police said later that Ponder had also refused to go into a cell and sat down on the booking room floor.

"By this time it was Sunday afternoon. They brought us something to eat. A man kept saying, 'You, black, African-looking son of a bitch.' This is what they kept calling me. One man kept insisting that I call him mister. So I asked him at one point why it was so important, and then he'd just get angry again and start hitting me again." She was placed in a cell by herself and not beaten again, although she was continually insulted.

The jailers took James West into a cell known as "the bullpen." Roosevelt Knox, a twenty-three-year-old farm worker who was in jail for forging a check, said later in court that the highway patrolman hit West; then a deputy told the other inmates that he wanted them to whip West with a blackjack. After they beat West, the police chief and sheriff gave them each a drink of corn whiskey. "After we had drinken the whiskey," Knox said, "Mr. Tommy Herrod brought a lady back there to us, and then he told us he want us to whip this lady."[8]

One of the law officers had gone into Mrs. Hamer's cell and asked her where she was from. "I told him Ruleville, Mississippi, and he said, 'I'm going to check.' " He also asked her whether the group had been trying to hold a demonstration at the bus station. He cut her off before she could answer and went to check her story. "So, I know by me being one of the persons that works with this voter registration, when he checked, well, that was really going to put me on the spot for sure. So, when he walked back in, he says, 'Yes, you live in Ruleville,' and says, 'You the big—' and

I have never heard that many names called a human in my life."[9]

A Mississippi highway patrolman asked Mrs. Hamer where she had been and why she had been in Charleston, South Carolina, according to an FBI report on the incident. "She told him she had gone to a citizenship training school, and he contradicted her, saying, 'You went to march' and 'You went to see Martin Luther King' and 'We are not going to have it.' "[10]

One of the officers called her "Fatso," and they took her to the bullpen. The highway patrolman gave one of the inmates a blackjack, and Mrs. Hamer remembered that he said, " 'I want you to make that bitch wish she was dead.' " He also threatened the black inmates that if they didn't use the blackjack on her, "You know what I'll use on you."[11]

The inmate told her to lie down on the bed. "You mean you would do this to your own race?" she asked him.

"You heard what I said," the highway patrolman ordered.

"So, then I had to get over there on the bed flat on my stomach, and that man beat me—that man beat me until he give out." After the prisoners beat her, she nearly passed out as she got off the cot. But the officer said, " 'Hell, you can walk.' It was all kinds of language he used." For weeks afterward, she could not sleep on her back.

The women in the other section of the jail had heard the screaming. Soon Mrs. Hamer was taken back to her cell. Euvester Simpson was brought into the room where Mrs. Hamer had been beaten and made to lie down on the cot. "The man literally had his hand drawn back to beat me when somebody came in and said, 'Stop!' " she recalled. "I had to believe the phone calls had started to come in."

No one else was beaten. Euvester Simpson stayed up that entire night, pressing a cold, wet towel to Mrs. Hamer's forehead. She had a headache, her blood pressure was high, and she was running a temperature. Where she had been beaten, her body was bruised and swelling. "The only way we could manage to get through that ordeal was to sing any song that came to mind," Simpson said.[12]

"We were not allowed medical treatment, phone calls," said June Johnson.

> The food was terrible, so we all ended up going on a strike. We would sing. We would sing a lot of the songs, and [Mrs. Hamer's] particular song that she would sing while in jail was "When Paul and Silas Were Bound in Jail." She still had a good spirit in spite of her

[ordeal] but she really suffered in that jail from that beating. I mean, her body was so black and her skin felt like—I don't know if you ever felt a snake skin but it would be rough, it was like raw cowhide.[13]

Mrs. Hamer could hear some of the men in the booking room plotting to kill them. "They said, 'We could put them son of bitches in Big Black, and nobody would never find them.' See, so many been put in Big Black River, and that's what they wanted to [do to] us. But it was one guy there, and I thank God that he was there, and he just rebelled against them killing us."[14]

By the following night, the workers were sure that someone at the SNCC office in Greenwood knew what was happening. They hadn't checked in as they were always supposed to do; others who had been on the bus and had not been arrested would have arrived in Greenwood to report what had happened.

They were right. Hollis Watkins, one of the young SNCC workers, started calling police stations and sheriffs' offices in all the little towns throughout the area, bluffing that he knew the missing workers were there and that police intended to kill them. "Understanding and knowing the mentality of the local officials," Watkins said, "if they felt that nobody was watching them or nobody knew about what they were doing, they would get away with it, being isolated. So one of the most important things we wanted was to let them know that they're not isolated, other people know about them, know what they're doing. I placed the call and told them we knew they had 'em and we knew they were intending to kill 'em."[15] To strengthen his bluff, he added that the FBI also knew about the planned killings.[16]

The workers were also calling reporters they knew. Some were not far away—just over the Mississippi line in Tuscaloosa, Alabama. As Pat Watters and Reese Cleghorn later reported:

One reason the national press didn't converge on Winona was that the arrests occurred on the eve of Governor Wallace's stand in the door at the desegregation of the University of Alabama. Most of the reporters who were then the nation's main contact with what happened in Southern civil rights struggles were in a motel room in Tuscaloosa when the first word of Winona came in. "We ought to be there instead of here," one of them said. But they weren't.[17]

Only scattered wire service stories, largely based on material called in by Julian Bond from the SNCC office in Atlanta, appeared in a few newspapers. The release of the workers, with no mention of beatings, marked the first time Mrs. Hamer's name appeared in the *Delta Democrat-Times,* the only newspaper in the area that reported with any regularity and even-handedness on the civil rights movement under both its Pulitzer Prize–winning editor Hodding Carter and later his son, Hodding Carter III. Her name was, however, misspelled as Jamer. The *New York Times* carried two brief stories about the arrests on inside pages.[18] There was no on-the-scene reporting, and the lack of national attention to incidents such as the Winona jail beatings and other violence against blacks would later prompt Mississippi movement leaders to intensify their campaign by bringing white students into the state. As they suspected, the reporting climate changed once those students were present.

As Mrs. Hamer and her companions sat in their cells, Wiley Branton, head of the Voter Education Project, had been calling the jail, trying to arrange bail. None of the jailers told the civil rights workers about his calls. They were taken to court early in the morning on Monday, June 11, thinking someone would be there to represent them. No one appeared. "They didn't have anything like a trial—they just asked us questions, and nobody recorded anything," Ponder said. "That trial was nothing but a farce and we just said as little as was necessary." No charges were recorded against June Johnson because she was only fifteen; the rest were fined $65 each for disorderly conduct and $35 each for resisting arrest.[19]

Meantime, in Greenwood, Lawrence Guyot, a SNCC staff member who had frequently worked with Mrs. Hamer in Sunflower County, became concerned when the group did not return as scheduled. "I had encouraged people to go to Dorchester," and the other SCLC training sessions, Guyot said.[20] "And I knew they were missing. So we were calling around. I remember calling that jail and saying, 'Do you have these individuals?'

" 'No, we don't have them. We've got some niggers over here.' "

Receiving no straight answers on the phone, Guyot and Milton Hancock made the short drive from Greenwood to Winona. Guyot was standing on the sidewalk outside the jail, talking to a policeman, when the officer hit him for no apparent reason. Right then, "I knew we were going to jail so I didn't hit them back." Some of the highway patrolmen remembered Guyot from demonstrations in Greenwood. One said, "Oh, you're the nigger who wasn't afraid of the dogs"—referring to the police dogs that had been used to subdue civil rights protesters.

"The sheriff told Guyot and myself to get our black ass out of town," Milton Hancock recalled. The patrolman asked them whether they were NAACP members and they said no. "Then he asked Guyot was he in 'that shit in Greenwood?' Guyot said no. Then he asked Guyot will it hurt your mouth to say yes, sir, or no, sir? Guyot replied, 'No, it won't.' "[21]

"They charged me with disturbing the peace and resisting arrest," Guyot said. "When we got inside and they started beating me, it was very methodical. I knew—they threatened to burn my genitals—I knew that I had to stay conscious, otherwise I was dead."[22]

Guyot's jailers took him outside, where some two hundred whites were milling around, and showed him to the crowd so they would be sure to recognize him in the future. He was taken back inside and told to sign a paper that he had driven to Winona, was drunk, and fell when he got out of the car. "I refused to sign it. I had never driven a car in my life." In fact, he had refused to learn to drive for just that reason: Guyot wanted to be sure that if he were ever arrested on charges related to driving a car, people would know the charges were false.

The jailers also tried to trap Guyot. "They put me over in a section by myself. . . . They left the cell door open. I called out so the other prisoners could hear me. I said, 'Look, the cell door's open. Somebody come lock it.' " And they left a knife outside his cell door. "I made sure it got out of my cell so it didn't have my fingerprints on it. I think what they were trying to do was get me to walk out of my cell so they could shoot me. 'Cause they said to me a couple of times, 'Well, Guyot, you're causing so much trouble, I tell you what we're going to do. We're going to let you out tonight at twelve o'clock and you can walk to Greenwood.' " Soon, Guyot said, the jail was getting calls from New York, New Jersey, Washington—people alerted through the SNCC network. "That saved my life."

"Guyot looked like he was in a bad shape," Mrs. Hamer recalled later. She said that was the first time she had seen him not smiling.[23]

With Guyot gone from the Greenwood office, the responsibility of trying to free the workers fell next to a newly arrived student from Yale Law School who was on her summer vacation. Eleanor Holmes Norton had met Bob Moses on one of his forays north and had promised him she would go to Greenwood that summer. He had told her there were few black lawyers in Mississippi, and few lawyers who would handle civil rights cases.[24]

NAACP leader Medgar Evers had tried to convince Norton to work in Jackson, but she kept her pledge to go to Greenwood, where she found that Moses was returning from a trip north and Guyot had been jailed in Winona. She was thus the oldest person at the SNCC office. Norton called the Greenwood police chief, summoned her most authoritative voice, and told him she was a law student and she planned to go to Winona herself.

" 'The only thing I'm asking you is one thing—to call before I go,' " she told the chief. " 'Let 'em know I'm coming. . . . I know exactly what my rights are, and I'm only coming over to see if I can get them out of jail.' I don't know what he said on the phone. I went over there and I was let into the jail. And I think all that's due to the police chief."[25]

But the young law student had no bail money. She had to leave empty-handed. In the meantime, a group from the SNCC office tried to see the prisoners. Before they could get in, one policeman questioned them sharply, young Ida Holland reported to SNCC headquarters.[26] "You did not come over here to start any damn trouble, did you?" one officer asked.

"I said, 'Trouble? I don't understand what you mean.' He replied, 'The same damn thing the others did.' I told him, 'No, sir, not yet.' "

When the visitors got to jail, Ida Holland first saw Annell Ponder. Her face "was swollen and she had a black eye. She could barely talk, but she looked at me and whispered, 'Freedom.'

"We saw the others: June Johnson had been beaten, her face was swollen. Mrs. Fannie Hamer was beaten also. The two other girls looked to be in good condition." Holland, who became a university English professor and playwright, asked the jailer whether she could give the prisoners some books. He said, "Don't bring any of that NAACP shit." As they left the jail, she reported, a plainclothesman said, 'You are all welcome to Winona anytime you want to come, but don't start any of that same shit.' "

Holland's group visited the jail twice on June 10. The prisoners were not released until June 12, when Andy Young, James Bevel, and Dorothy Cotton arrived. They had been in Birmingham at a meeting when they heard that the rights workers had been jailed and that several were beaten because they wouldn't say "sir." "It wasn't that they were being impolite," Young recalled. "Annell Ponder is one of the sweetest persons you'd ever want to meet, but she was just very strong and very stubborn."[27]

Young speculated that several things saved him and his companions from jail. One:

Bevel and I were both southerners who were very comfortable with Southern mores. I mean, Bevel stayed in Mississippi at least 10 years and never went to jail. . . . I never went to jail unless I wanted to go to jail. Part of it was just not being afraid of white southerners and being willing to talk to them and go out of your way to put them at ease. So that going in to town we made it a point to stop by the grocery store and a gas station. . . . You wanted to have a full tank of gas leaving. But you also wanted people to see you and you want them to talk to you. Soon as you walked into a town, into a grocery store, they called the sheriff and let him know you were there.[28]

The law officers thus were not only warned of their imminent arrival but also given a chance to size them up as both self-confident and nonviolent.

The second saving point, said Young, was that Wiley Branton of the Voter Education Project made a key phone call. Young, Bevel, and Cotton had just arrived at the jail when the phone rang. "I don't think they really knew who Wiley was—whether he was a Justice Department person or what but anyway they were very, very nice to us."

Locked in her cell, Mrs. Hamer had been wondering how Christian people could do to her what her jailers had done. She talked with the jailer's wife, who said she tried to live a Christian life. "And I told her I would like for her to read two scriptures in the Bible, and I told her to read the 26th chapter of Proverbs and the 26th verse," Mrs. Hamer said. "She taken it down on a paper and then I told her to read the 17th chapter of Acts, the 26th verse, and she's taken that down, but she never did come back after then. I don't know what happened."[29]

She might have read the verses. The twenty-sixth chapter of Proverbs warns about the folly that befalls fools, sluggards, and busybodies, as well as those who hate. Verse 26 reads, "Whose hatred is covered by deceit, his wickedness shall be showed before the whole congregation." Verse 27 adds, "Whoso diggeth a pit shall fall therein: and he that rolleth a stone, it will return upon him." The reading from Acts that Mrs. Hamer had recommended to the jailer's wife was one she quoted often, that God "hath made of one blood all nations of men for to dwell on the face of the earth." She had raised no hand to hit back at her jailers. "I hit them with the truth, and it hurts them."[30]

Dorothy Cotton was astonished at Mrs. Hamer's charity. "When we got there, I remember the jailer standing around saying pleasantries to me. Then Mrs. Hamer and Annell came out of the cell and Mrs. Hamer pointed to him as the same one that had beaten her. I felt intense anger—I could have done real harm to him, and he had been standing there talking friendly to me."[31] Mrs. Hamer, however, simply commented on the weather.

At 4:00 P.M. June 12 Andrew Young posted the workers' bond. When they left the jail, they learned that Medgar Evers had been killed in front of his home in Jackson the previous evening after returning from a meeting. "I don't think that they intended for us to leave that jail," Guyot said. "I think as cruel as it may sound, the timing of the Medgar Evers assassination put a lot of pressure on them to let us out of there."[32]

Enter the FBI. SNCC's Willie Peacock had contacted the Justice Department from Greenwood to report the jailing. In Atlanta, Julian Bond had advised the local FBI office of the arrests as well. Director J. Edgar Hoover sent urgent teletypes to the Memphis FBI office on Monday, June 10, advising that three of the people held in the Winona jail might have been beaten, and if the victims charged that law enforcement officers were involved, the agent should immediately investigate.[33]

Early the next day, Agent Clifton O. Halter from Memphis interviewed some of the victims at the jail; names of those interviewed—and anything they said—has since been deleted from a June 12 report to Washington. Mrs. Hamer told the agents she would make no statement until she was released from jail. The civil rights workers said later they hadn't been sure the agents really were from the FBI. After the shootings in Ruleville the previous September, with no culprits found, Mrs. Hamer didn't trust the FBI not to tell her jailers what she said.[34]

FBI agents interviewed the local law officers, as directed. However, FBI files are so thoroughly censored, even in the 1990s, that it is impossible to determine the value or timeliness of any information the agents obtained. For example, one memo to Washington from the Memphis FBI office deletes the name of someone from "MSHP," presumably John Basinger of the Mississippi State Highway Patrol, whom the FBI attempted to interview on June 11. He refused to be interviewed except in the presence of (deleted) and the Mississippi attorney general. Another attempted interview was, presumably, unsuccessful. "(Deleted) advised that he did not desire to furnish any information pertaining to this matter and declined to be interviewed."[35]

The FBI files do show that Attorney General Robert Kennedy was paying attention to the arrests. For example, he called C. A. Evans at the FBI early the Monday evening after the workers were jailed "and advised that he was particularly interested in this case, which involves police brutality."[36]

After the group was released, FBI agents talked to Mrs. Hamer briefly in Greenwood and noted that "her left forearm and the palms of her hands were bruised. No other bruises were visible. Mrs. Hamer advised that her buttocks and back area were bruised and she was complaining about her back and buttocks injuries. She advised that she intended to go to Dr. W. T. Garner that afternoon and advised she had no objection to Dr. Garner releasing the results of her examination to the FBI."[37] Other agents interviewed Mrs. Hamer in Atlanta on June 13 after she and Annell Ponder arrived to confer with officials of the Southern Christian Leadership Conference.

FBI agents showed Mrs. Hamer photographs of law officers who might have been involved in the Winona incident, and she identified several of them. But she complained repeatedly over the quality of the bureau's investigation. "When the FBI finally came to take pictures," Mrs. Hamer complained, "they had me hold my hands up; they took pictures of the front, but didn't take any of my back where I was beaten."[38] A year later, she testified about the jailing at a hearing in Washington. After that hearing, agents visited her at her home in Ruleville. "During this interview she was extremely hostile in her manner, showed little respect for the FBI, and stated the FBI 'is a rotten bunch,'" the agents reported. "She advised she has no trust for the FBI and stated that numerous instances of violations of Negro Civil Rights have been furnished to the FBI and nothing ever became of these complaints. The FBI's jurisdiction in Civil Rights matters was explained to Mrs. Hamer. Her opinion of the FBI could not be changed."[39]

The FBI had an inadequate and neglected staff in Mississippi, and some of those agents worked more closely with local police than with those challenging police authority. Much of the nation was no more advanced than the bureau in its thinking on civil rights. Nonetheless, the FBI's performance in this period was considered "far from adequate" by John Doar, who worked on many of the earliest suits involving voter intimidation in the South. The bureau's lackluster performance stemmed in part from the "very real difficulties it faced operating in the complex legal network of the caste system," said Doar and an associate in a 1971 assessment. "These states were largely still a part of the American frontier, riddled with bewildering rural patterns of secrecy and silence, almost designed to make the work of any investigative agency difficult, if not impossible."[40]

Civil rights workers not only distrusted the FBI but also eyed the Justice Department warily. Annell Ponder and Fannie Lou

Hamer went first to Atlanta after their release from the Winona jail, and Martin Luther King, Jr., sent them to Washington. They had no reason to be optimistic that they could press the federal government into action. Although the Kennedy administration had brought down the wrath of white Mississippi by helping James Meredith enroll as the first black student at the University of Mississippi in 1962, the president had proved lukewarm about pushing civil rights legislation before Congress. In addition, the Justice Department, headed by the president's brother Robert, had repeatedly declined requests from Bob Moses to protect civil rights workers, insisting that that was not the government's role.[41]

But the Kennedys' attitude was changing. On June 11, while Mrs. Hamer was still in jail, the president had spoken on national television about fulfilling America's promise to all its citizens. The demonstrations in Birmingham and other parts of the South "have so increased the cries for equality that no city or state or legislative body can prudently choose to ignore" this moral crisis, Kennedy said.[42] Within hours after Kennedy had spoken, Medgar Evers lay dead in his own driveway, the victim of a sniper.

In response to the Winona beatings, the Justice Department filed both civil and criminal charges. It was one of the earliest cases in which the federal government filed charges against southern law officers for their treatment of black Americans. "There wasn't any doubt that they had been pretty badly beaten up," said H. M. Ray, then U.S. attorney in Oxford who was in Washington for a meeting at the time.[43]

On June 17, the Justice Department filed a civil complaint in the federal court in Oxford to try to stop any additional prosecution against the six originally arrested in Winona.[44] Attorney General Robert F. Kennedy made this announcement: "The prosecution of the six constitutes an unlawful and unconstitutional interference with Interstate Commerce Commission regulations forbidding racial discrimination." Named as defendants were the city of Winona, Mayor Martin C. Billingsley, Police Chief Thomas Herrod, and Montgomery County Sheriff Earle W. Patridge. Kennedy called the arrests of the civil rights workers "baseless" because blacks had a right to use the station facilities and they had "left and were standing peaceably outside the terminal" when Herrod arrested them.

On September 9, the Justice Department filed criminal charges as well. It charged the sheriff, police chief, a highway patrolman, and two other men of beating and kicking the prisoners, thus violating their constitutional rights. Attorney General Kennedy said the defendants had conspired to punish six of the prisoners and to force five of them to sign statements against their will. The men were charged under Section 242 of Title 18 of the United States Code, which makes deprivation of rights by law enforcement officers a federal offense.[45]

Neither *U.S. v. City of Winona*, the civil suit, nor its criminal counterpart, *U.S. v. Patridge, Herrod, Surrell, Basinger and Perkins*, is a well-known case. But they did put on the public record more of the details of what went on during those four days in Winona. They also show how difficult it was to gain convictions when a case involved the word of black against white in a courtroom in Mississippi in 1963.

In the civil case, the government charged that the defendants violated Interstate Commerce Commission (ICC) rules barring race discrimination in transportation between states and at stations that served interstate passengers. The Justice Department pointed out that Winona officials clearly knew the law because Assistant Attorney General Burke Marshall had written to Mayor Billingsley in January 1962 about the city's policy of segregation at the bus terminal. Marshall said that this policy and the arrest of two black youths in November 1961 at the terminal restaurant violated ICC rules. A few weeks later the mayor assured a Justice Department attorney that the city would not interfere with implementation of the ICC rules.[46] The federal government asked that the city of Winona stop any prosecutions of the civil rights workers. The federal government never got the desired injunction against segregation at the bus terminal, but neither were the civil rights workers taken to court again, except as witnesses in the criminal suit against the law officers. In May 1964, the civil case was dismissed with Justice Department concurrence.

The law officers pleaded not guilty to the criminal charges on November 11, 1963. The case was set for trial December 2 in the federal courthouse in Oxford only a few blocks from the University of Mississippi campus, scene of the confrontation—and two deaths—over James Meredith's enrollment a year earlier. Many black people felt Oxford was still a hostile place. So the civil rights workers stayed with families in Holly Springs, some twenty-five miles to the north. There was even a black café in Oxford that refused to serve the group. "We could not go in there," June Johnson recalled. "We could not go into the Holiday Inn. We were told to stay in the Justice Department office and they would go and get our food."[47]

Civil rights workers mistrusted many southern judges, even

those in federal courts. Men like W. Harold Cox of Mississippi and E. Gordon West of Louisiana simply failed to apply the law fairly. Cox, for example, was Senator James O. Eastland's law school roommate and had compared blacks to "chimpanzees" who "ought to be in the movies rather than being registered to vote." West once refused to order a voting registrar to reopen his office after it had been closed for six months.[48] Claude F. Clayton, who sat in Oxford, seemed cut of somewhat different cloth. Named to the federal bench by President Dwight D. Eisenhower, Clayton was a general in the Mississippi National Guard and carried himself ramrod straight. He was, as H. M. Ray recalled, "an outstanding jurist . . . very strict. . . . He didn't let in any improper evidence." Nor did he ever show any sign of bias.[49] He was also very smart and careful in how the record was constructed in cases he heard, John Doar recalled. "If he could do something to preserve the caste, he would," Doar said.[50] Some of the civil rights workers also felt that Clayton conveyed to the jury a sense that the plaintiffs were "only" Negroes and thus not to be taken as seriously as white law officers.

Perceptions of the fairness of the trial varied. "They picked an all-white jury to try the policemen, and there were lots of white students from Ole Miss in the courtroom with Confederate flags," June Johnson recalled. "We wondered why we'd come there; there was no justice."[51]

As the trial began, the American press was preoccupied with the aftermath of the Kennedy assassination. The transcript of the trial, and not the media, provided the only record of the proceedings. There was no wide broadcasting of the testimony of the black people involved, no coverage or interviews on the courthouse steps about the law officers' side of the incident. How might history have been different, what different restraints might have been placed on those who arrested Chaney, Goodman, and Schwerner the following summer had the details of the Oxford trial been more fully known?

Annell Ponder, thirty at the time and the well-spoken holder of a bachelor's degree in elementary education and a master's degree in social work, was the first witness. Prosecuting attorneys St. John Barrett, John Rosenberg, and H. M. Ray made the small but critical point of showing respect by always using courtesy titles for their witnesses: Miss Ponder, Mrs. Hamer, Mr. West. The defense, following the southern custom that black people so resented, would address "Annell" and "James" as they moved through their questioning.

Annell Ponder told of the incident at the bus station and the jail, adding that after one officer struck her in the face, he asked why she had been writing down his car's license number.

> I told him that in our work if we run into any problems we have to write as accurate a report as possible, and we were doing that in order to make a report that would be truthful. So he said, "What kind of report?"
>
> And I told him we usually make reports like that if we have trouble and we send them to the federal government. Well, then he wanted to know who the federal government was. He said, "Who? You mean Bobby Kennedy?"
>
> And I said, "No. The federal government."

Testimony concluded on the first day of the trial with the chief defense attorney, Mississippi's assistant attorney general, Will S. Wells, asking Ponder about the trip to Atlanta after her release. SCLC had paid the travel expenses. "That's Dr. Martin Luther King's outfit; is that right?"

"It's the organization he heads."

The following morning the government called Fannie Lou Hamer, and Wells's cross-examination zeroed in on the same topic.

"Do you mind telling us who paid your fare to go to Washington?"

The SCLC, Mrs. Hamer replied.

"And that's headed by Dr. Martin Luther King, isn't it?" Wells asked.

"Yes."

"Did you and Annell discuss this matter with Dr. King or any other representative of the SCLC before you went to Washington?"

"Yes. We talked with Dr. King. We talked with—"

"In other words, you reported to Dr. King in Atlanta about what had happened, is that right?"

And so, Wells went on, "the Southern Christian Leadership Conference paid your way for you and Annell Ponder to fly to Washington, and you went straight to the Justice Department when you got there, didn't you?"

"No, I didn't go straight to the Justice Department. I went to a hotel."

"Well, then you did go to the Justice Department?"

"Yes."

"And conferred with Mr. St. John Barrett, the gentleman who is sitting there, didn't you?"

"Yes."

After speaking at length about her beating, Mrs. Hamer also testified that she had written a statement dictated by Basinger, who made her say that she had not been mistreated and that she had been fed well in jail. Her only means of resistance was to write the statement poorly.

Asked why she wrote the statement, Mrs. Hamer replied: "He had his gun, and I know what I had gone through that Sunday, and I didn't have no other choice. But I ask him one time—I say, 'Do you mean I been treated good and can't sit down?' "

After Mrs. Hamer testified, Barrett set about trying to verify the injuries the women had reported. He entered into evidence pictures taken by FBI photographers in Washington, then called Dr. Garner. She had examined Annell Ponder and Fannie Lou Hamer immediately after their release from jail. She said that Ponder's left eye was bloodshot, her right thigh was bruised and swollen, and her upper back had welts on it. As for Mrs. Hamer, Dr. Garner testified: "Both of the buttocks were blue and black all over, and this extended all the way down to both knees and the dorsal aspect. Both buttocks and these areas involved were indurated [hardened] and inflamed, and there were harder places right at the creases of both buttocks. She had a bluish discoloration of the left arm and her hands were tender to touch."

Barrett asked the doctor what she thought had caused the bruises on Mrs. Hamer's buttocks and thighs.

"Well, I would say they are due to trauma."

"Due to some sort of one or more blows?" the attorney asked.

"Yes, sir."

"Is that correct? Did you observe any abrasions on the skin?"

"No, sir, I did not."

"In your opinion, could the condition that you observed on Mrs. Hamer have been caused by her being dragged across the floor?" Barrett went on.

"No, sir," Dr. Garner replied. "I have never seen anything like this. I would say not."

"Could it have been caused by falling down or suddenly sitting down?"

"No, sir."

Barrett was raising a vital question. The law officers repeatedly testified that the women who were beaten had all sat down on the floor of the booking room and refused to move. Was the women's version of their beating possibly false? Absolutely not, said H. M. Ray, who was on the prosecution legal team. Ray saw the women in the days immediately after the Winona incident. "There was never any doubt in my mind how it happened." The women "really had been badly beaten." Their injuries could not have resulted from being dragged across the floor.[52]

The law officers stuck to their story. Questioning Thomas Herrod, who had been Winona's elected police chief for three years, Wells asked what happened at the jail. June Johnson sat down on the floor, Herrod said, adding: "We tried to get her up. She wouldn't get up. So then we just had to drag her around."

"Did she resist in any way?"

"Yes. She kicked and fought, but we got her around."

No one struck or kicked Johnson, Herrod said, adding that Annell Ponder also "fought, kicked and hollered." No one hit her, either, Herrod said. Then they brought Mrs. Hamer from her cell. She, too, "sat down in the floor and said she wasn't going, and started hollering, kicking and carrying on."

"Fannie Hamer, I believe is the rather large—"

"Right."

"—woman."

"Yes, sir," said Herrod, indicating that it took three of them to drag her back into her cell.

"Now, while she was in there, was she hit or struck by anybody?" Wells asked.

"No, sir."

Herrod also denied that either West or Mrs. Hamer had been turned over to other prisoners in the jail to be beaten.

Basinger was the next defense witness. A highway patrolman for five years, he lived in Winona. He recalled that Mrs. Hamer, when questioned by the police chief, refused to give her date of birth.

"Sometimes that's a woman's privilege after she reaches a certain age, I believe," Wells commented. "Then what happened?" he asked Basinger.

"Well, she—she went through the same procedure, just like if—just like they'd been coached to do stuff like this; just sat down in the floor and started hollering like they were being beaten, stuff like that, and they went through the same procedure, the other two."

"Were you and the chief able to get her back by yourself or did you have to have help?"

"Well, she—she put up a good fight," Basinger said. "We'd catch ahold of her; she'd snatch loose and she would turn over in the floor; and finally we got—the chief got ahold of one arm and I got ahold of the other one and Mr. Perkins assisted us in putting her into the jail."

The stories remained at direct odds as each of the civil rights workers and law officers testified. The officers' attorneys concentrated intensively on events at the bus station and spoke repeatedly of the group's connection with civil rights organizations based outside the state.

Then Judge Clayton instructed the jury about the law. He read Section 42 of Title 18, U.S. Code, which prohibited anyone from depriving another person "of any rights, privileges, or immunities secured or protected by the Constitution or laws of the United States"—other than clearly prescribed punishments—because of his race or color. Clayton explained that the law had been passed to carry out the provisions of the Fourteenth Amendment. Law officers could not summarily punish people in their custody, Clayton said, adding that the prosecution had to prove its case; the defense did not have to produce any evidence. He also explained the concept of "reasonable doubt."

After the noon recess, the lawyers for each side presented closing arguments, Barrett first. He narrated what had happened at the bus station, stressing that the group that was arrested was

> taken in two separate cars to the jail. They don't resist—don't resist. They get out of the cars, without resistance. They go into the jail, without resistance. They assemble in the booking room of the jail where at least there was some questioning and maybe some taking of personal possessions; but, in any event, no resistance. With the exception of June Johnson, they're distributed among various cells. No resistance. No resistance.

Barrett also attacked the credibility of the defense witnesses and defended the testimony of his own witness, Sol Poe. Now he's "up there in the state penitentiary in Parchman. He's in the custody of the state of Mississippi. He's a Negro. He was a prisoner in that jail, and he came down and told you people: 'It's the truth. It's the truth. These defendants made me beat that woman. They made me beat James West, and they gave me whiskey' to warm up to the work a bit when he wasn't having too much stomach for it. Why, do you think he's lying? Do you think he could lie?"

When one of the defense attorneys, Chatwin Jackson, delivered his summation representing Sheriff Patridge, his principal point was that if anyone had conspired, it was the civil rights workers, not the law officers. "Annell Ponder tells you that she is a full-time employee of what one witness referred to as SINK [*sic*], I believe, and that's the Student Non-Violent Coordinating Committee, headed, as she said, by the Dr. Martin Luther King," said Jackson. Ponder recruited five children

and they were children, too, from 15 years up; they ought to have been in school over there instead of running all around the southern part of the nation, but she recruited them—and she took them—and where did she take them—all expenses paid by SINK?

She took them to an island off the coast of South Carolina, I believe, or maybe North Carolina, took them to an island, to a school, to teach them in the precepts of the organization which she represents, and this school was sponsored by SINK, but it was actually put on by the infamous Highlander Folk School of Knoxville, Tennessee. . . .

Returning to Mississippi, the group used rest rooms and a lunch counter "customarily used by white people," Jackson said. Law officers, seeing that white people were angry, took the workers to jail. "Do you think that their interest is primarily the seeing of justice done in this particular case or . . . could the overall purpose of these so-called victims be to so conduct themselves as to cause the very thing that we have here now and thereby intimidate the officers of the state of Mississippi?"

Wells, the principal defense attorney and assistant state attorney general, continued in the same vein: "Now what have we got, gentlemen? We've got a group of professional agitators that have been picked up here by the Southern Christian Leadership Conference, headed by Martin Luther King, who, in my opinion, is the most vicious demagogue that's come out of the South in my life."

"Wait a minute," interrupted Judge Clayton. "We're not trying Dr. Martin Luther King."

"I beg the court's pardon."

"No characterization of him is in the record," Judge Clayton admonished. "The jury will disregard counsel's remark about a person with whom we are not concerned in the trial of this case."

"I apologize, if the court please," Wells said. "I got carried away with myself."

The civil rights workers, Wells resumed, had been taught

how to go about creating incidents. Some of you people have seen on television some of these sit-in demonstrations and when they can get a television audience, they sit down in the middle of the street and the officers have to pick them up and carry them in the paddy wagon. I know some of you have seen it. But when they didn't have a television audience at the bus terminal in Winona on this Sunday, they waited until they got down in the jail and did it. Now, you've got these kind of people on the one hand and you've got elected, trusted officials on the other hand. Which group would you rather believe?

Finally H. M. Ray, the U.S. attorney, closed for the prosecution. He cautioned the jurors "that the real evidence in this case is down there at the jail, gentlemen. It doesn't matter if these victims were all communists. It doesn't matter what they were doing."

Trial by a jury—not summary punishment outside the law—was a precious right, Ray said, using as an example events in Dallas, Texas, only a few days earlier. President Kennedy had been assassinated, yet even a man who had "done a dastardly act," as had accused assassin Lee Harvey Oswald, deserved trial by jury under the American system, Ray added. Instead, he had been punished—killed—outside the law. "I'm sure you, as fellow Mississippians and fellow Americans, do not believe that a citizen, whether he's a police officer or anyone else, has the right to punish [someone who has been arrested] until he has been punished by the court, if the court in its wisdom sees fit to punish him."

Thank God, Ray went on, "that we live in a country where we have a right to trial by jury. Do we want to do away with this right of trial by jury, gentlemen? Are we worried about these foreign ideologies that are creeping in? The surest way in the world to do away with it, gentlemen, is this: if you do believe the evidence beyond a reasonable doubt and go out and acquit these defendants, gentlemen, you're making a bad thing worse."

The trial was not a case against the state of Mississippi, Ray counseled, but rather against a group of individuals. He scored the defense for talking about Highlander School, the rest room, the lunch counter. "I think you recognize that that's exactly a tactic of counsel in trying to get your mind off the facts in this case. There was very little discussion of the facts in this case."

Of the prisoners who had testified about beating Mrs. Hamer and West, Ray said that it would be nice, "if we had gentlemen of your caliber down there to testify, but gentlemen, gentlemen of your caliber do not frequent the jails, are not imprisoned—you have to necessarily rely on those who are available. . . ."

He concluded:

I ask you to do this: whether you're citizens of Tippah County, Calhoun County or whatever county you may be from, I ask of you, if you believe the evidence beyond a reasonable doubt, that you show the other people in this state and in this nation that you are not different from anyone else and that you can, as a matter of fact, find and decide a case on its individual facts. Let us go forth, gentlemen, to do our duty in the land that we love, and let us have faith that right makes right, and to that end let us try to do our duty.

Judge Clayton sent the jury out at 4:29 P.M. to consider its verdict. At 5:45 P.M., slightly over an hour later, the jury returned.

"You may be seated. Have you agreed on your verdicts?"

"Yes, sir," replied the foreman.

"Will you pass those to the clerk, please?"

The clerk read the verdict. "United States of America against Earle Wayne Patridge, Thomas J. Herrod, Jr., William Surrell, John L. Basinger and Charles Thomas Perkins. We, the jury, find the defendants not guilty."[53]

CHAPTER 5

"Keep Your Eyes on the Prize, Hold On"

FANNIE LOU HAMER came out of jail and away from the Oxford trial more determined to become a first-class citizen, and her story spread. "I came in after her and I began to hear things about this woman in Sunflower County, this Fannie Lou Hamer," said Annie Devine of Canton, who would work with Mrs. Hamer in the coming months. "Myself with others realized that there is a woman that can do all these things. And when she got herself beat in Winona, that was a greater woman."[1] She would sing "Nobody's Going to Turn Me Around" better than anybody else, Mrs. Devine said. She had proved nobody was going to turn her around. "Why not follow somebody like that? Why not just reach out with one hand and say, just take me along?"

Mrs. Hamer did not jump from the jailhouse to center stage in Atlantic City—the public appearance that would rivet her message onto the consciousness of many Americans—without months of continued SNCC organizing and the attendant frustrations. She would run for Congress, she would participate in a new political party, she would work with the young people who volunteered to come into the state. She did it all to show black people not as brave as she that they could get involved, that they could make a difference in ending the violence that intimidated them. "We been waitin' all our lives," she told a visiting journalist, "and still gettin' killed, still gettin' hung, still gettin' beat to death. Now we're tired waitin'."[2]

It was a season of despair. Too little money was coming in for voter-registration work, and too many sharecroppers were out of work. SNCC had been organizing in Mississippi for two years, yet had little to show for its efforts in terms of either increased numbers of registered voters or great awareness of black Mississippians' plight spreading beyond the borders of the state. The civil rights workers knew that they needed help but argued into the long winter nights about how best to secure that help. People who had been bound together in struggle became snappish under the strain. Mrs. Hamer, still recovering from her beating, could not heal the frustrations of these young people who meant so much to her, listen as she would to their complaints.

The Voter Education Project (VEP) pulled much of its financial support out of Mississippi in November 1963, citing poor results. It felt the same amount of money, used elsewhere, could help sign up more voters. Director Wiley Branton said that the Justice Department had so far failed to win any favorable court action in its suits filed in Mississippi, and that VEP was "very concerned about the failure of the federal government to protect the people who have sought to register and vote or who are working actively in getting others to register."[3]

This left little money to pay the civil rights workers' subsistence allowance or to buy gas for the cars to take people to the registrars' offices. And there still was not enough clothing for people who had lost their jobs because they tried to register. Mrs. Hamer sent an appeal to SNCC for help that fall. Perhaps, she wrote, some people don't know how it is living in the country rather than in a heavily populated area. "There is so much territory to cover if one wants to get to all of the people and not some of them." Some of the targeted people lived eight and ten miles apart; workers could not walk these distances in a short time. "When we've reached these people and persuaded them to go to the courthouse and register, then we need cars to carry them there. The courthouse is twenty-six miles from where I live and farther away from the people who live ten and twenty miles away from my home."

Why did this still matter to her? "My family and I have suffered greatly since I started working with the movement," Mrs. Hamer wrote. "Although we've suffered greatly, I feel that we have not suffered in vain. I am determined to become a first-class citizen. Some people will say that we are satisfied with the way in which we are living, but I am not. I've never been satisfied because we've always worked hard for little or nothing. So if registering to vote means becoming a first-class citizen and changing the structure of our State's Government, I am determined to get every Negro in the State of Mississippi registered. By doing this, we can get the things we've always been denied the rights to. I can say this, we need a change in Mississippi; I'm sick of being hungry, naked, and looking at my children and so many other children crying for bread."[4]

Jane Stembridge, the white SNCC staff member who had

encouraged Bob Moses to start his travels through the South, now worked in Greenwood and reported back to Mary King in the Atlanta office:

> Mary, it's one of those honest autumn days when the only right thing to do is walk, for a long way, for a long time. The wind is warm, but it's strong across the land and down these little streets, that bound our lives and our days right now.
>
> The report from the field is one of sadness, one about human beings destroying one another, loneliness. With all the forces of human fear and hatred against us, we must somehow draw together around the fire, around the table. But, instead, we are destroying each other. Is that also a result of the system? Is that the atonement? Some of us have finished a good hot dinner; others didn't eat because they were angry with those who did eat for various and separate reasons. . . . On days like this, one gets most angry at the South for all the loneliness it has produced, all the lack of direction, the stored up tears.[5]

Even petty frustrations caused serious problems. One worker couldn't get to a hearing on a traffic citation because his car's manifold was broken. Another was in Itta Bena and had no transportation to Greenwood to pick up leaflets for a mass meeting. Another was struggling with lack of money for a program in Winona. The group was reorganizing the library and preparing for a clothes distribution. Art classes were about to begin. But for the moment, Jane Stembridge wrote, "There is nothing to tell—no facts, no figures. Just faces, angry words and people wandering around . . . stopping to shout, and the constant wind."

Stembridge found herself wondering "if the sum total of field reports, clothes distribution, mass meetings and voting will make us love [each] other more or if anything will or if it matters. If we were in Ruleville, we should have pecans and coffee with Mrs. Hamer and a few songs for freedom . . . but we are in Greenwood, 960 on your dial, and fighting each other and meanwhile missing the point."

Something dramatic had to be done. The old Mississippi seemed to be winning. Any whites who abhorred the violence still hesitated to speak out. The civil rights workers conducted a mock election that fall with two candidates clearly identified with civil rights: black druggist and NAACP activist Aaron Henry of Clarksdale for governor and white chaplain Ed King from Tougaloo College for lieutenant governor. Henry had been selected as head of the Council of Federated Organizations, which was coordinating the voting drive, and wanted to show that black people would vote if only they could register. The COFO organizers set up their own polling places, spread the word about the candidates and their platform, and—at the same time white Mississippi was about to vote for governor and lieutenant governor—cast their ballots at the beauty parlors and the churches that dared to participate. Black and white alike were allowed to vote in this mock election, although the most effort was concentrated on turning out the black vote to prove the point. Eighty thousand people, most of them unregistered, cast "freedom votes."

The freedom-ballot candidates had a clear platform of proposed changes in Mississippi's justice, economic, and education systems.[6] Foremost was a call for "security in the belief that the laws will be fairly enforced and security of personal safety," guarantees considered essential for "freedom of mind and action." Henry and King's platform called upon the state to stop supporting the actions of extreme racists with money channeled to them through what was supposed to be an investigative agency, the State Sovereignty Commission. The platform also urged ending segregation in all state facilities, appointing more blacks to local police forces, making intimidation of voters a crime, passing fair employment laws, establishing a low-interest loan program for owners of small farms, completely integrating the public schools, and spending more money on education. These recommendations were considered radical in many quarters in the Mississippi of 1963.

Amid the frustrations, the freedom vote campaign "was definitely a step forward for the movement. It allowed us for the first time to organize on a statewide basis," SNCC staff member Ivanhoe Donaldson wrote in a memo.[7] With Yale and Stanford students who had been recruited to go to Mississippi to help,

We were able to penetrate communities and make valuable contacts where we have never been able to operate before. Not only was the mock election able to produce 80,000 plus votes (enough to have made Rubel Phillips governor instead of Paul Johnson [had blacks been able to vote in the official election]), but we laid the foundation to establish a really statewide voter registration campaign, and to raise serious legal questions about the seating of Jimmy Whitten, Congressman from the heavy Negro populated 2nd District (Delta) when he comes up for re-election this spring. It showed the Negro population that politics is not just "white folks'" business, but that Negroes are also capable of holding political offices.

Donaldson concluded: "The mock election also points up that whites can work in Mississippi (at least white males). A lot of leg work which we didn't have the manpower to accomplish" was done by the Yale and Stanford students, including canvassing in some of the hard core areas: Sunflower and Leflore counties. "The final point is that if we are to take advantage of the foundation this election has allowed us to lay around the state, we've got to set up voter registration programs immediately in all these areas. In this way, SNCC can make an example of Mississippi to the nation, pointing out that this intolerable system is to exist no longer."

Recruited through Allard Lowenstein, later a prominent anti-war activist and congressman from New York, the Stanford and Yale students worked in Mississippi for only a few weeks. Should COFO bring more students back for the summer for a massive registration campaign across Mississippi? SNCC workers, who had borne the brunt of the Mississippi fieldwork, debated the question in lengthy staff meetings. One side felt that until whites were involved as workers—and even as victims of the violence that the voter-registration drives were generating—whites in power would ignore Mississippi. The other side argued that rural blacks were just starting to believe that they themselves could change their lives; to bring in whites now would negate whatever tentative gains they were making.

For her part, Mrs. Hamer didn't care whether the young people were black or white. The people of Ruleville and Mississippi needed help; they should take anyone they could get. "If we're trying to break down this barrier of segregation, we can't segregate ourselves," she declared at one SNCC meeting in Greenville in November 1963.[8]

"I was one of the ones that was adamantly opposed," SNCC worker Hollis Watkins said, citing long-range implications. With an established group that was used to running its own affairs, a highly competent outsider might take over management for a short time and the experienced group could still function when the outsider left, he said.[9] "But if you come into a situation where you have new leadership developing that is not sound, that is not solid, who had to be nurtured, then when you give them that break from that, then you start back at zero" when the outsiders leave. That would be even tougher, Watkins reasoned. And "in most cases, that's what happened."

SNCC was debating a question that still troubles many thoughtful Americans: how does an organization, or a nation, move beyond race while still recognizing the role it plays? This particular SNCCathon started at seven at night, ended around midnight. "Everyone was very tired," Howard Zinn wrote.

The meeting was called to a close. Everyone stood up, and locked hands, every single person there in the circle, and sang, "We Shall Overcome," stanza after stanza. I had heard the song sung many times at various meetings with deep passion, but never quite like this. I felt that people were gripping each other's hands tighter than usual. When they came to the stanzas "We shall brothers be" and "Black and white together," the voices somehow grew louder, more intense. People looked at one another. A few broke hands and applauded. The song came to an end, and the people at the meeting, talking in low voices, moved out together into the darkness.[10]

In the end, the decision was made to try to recruit one thousand students from campuses outside the state. COFO started sending out the word, arranging to screen potential summer workers, alerting the government and the press about the summer plans, paving the way with a campaign to reach the public with more information about conditions within Mississippi. For its part, SNCC also held a public session in Washington both to help its own members learn more about government and to show the government the problems of Mississippi. Mrs. Hamer, still recovering from her beating and about to testify at the Oxford trial, went to Washington for the sessions, which would represent an important stage in her emergence as a national figure.

Some three hundred SNCC workers attended the Thanksgiving weekend leadership conference despite the assassination days earlier of President John F. Kennedy. Kennedy had finally been moving toward some understanding of black southerners' grievances, and rights workers feared that Kennedy's death and the ascension of Texan Lyndon Johnson to the presidency might retard what little progress had been made. Johnson would surprise them. He felt enormous pressure to create national stature for himself, to try to outdo the Kennedys, and he chose the arena of civil rights and later poverty to display his legendary legislative arm-wrestling skills. Fannie Lou Hamer would be one of those outsiders who kept up constant pressure on this consummate insider to try to accomplish the goal of equality at the polling place, on the job, and at the schoolhouse.

"We would be derelict in our duty to our people and to President Johnson if we had a moratorium" on civil rights activity, SNCC executive secretary James Forman said as the Howard sessions opened. Author James Baldwin, delivering the keynote speech, agreed.[11] Then Bob Moses spoke, giving a clue about the summer to come, one that failed to register on much of the press present. He talked about voter-registration work in Mississippi, saying that no significant changes would occur until a confrontation between federal and state authorities occurred. SNCC's job was to "bring about just such a confrontation . . . to change the power structure," Moses said.[12] Bayard Rustin, the longtime black organizer who had just directed the massive March on Washington, said, "SNCC must help Mr. Johnson—but to help Mr. Johnson means to create an atmosphere in which he is pushed even further."[13]

The meat of the conference, however, were presentations by representatives of government agencies or private organizations about manpower training, migrant health care, rural development, education, and civil rights. "It was a very massive, probably over-produced conference," recalled organizer Mike Thelwell. It got to be pretty heavy going. People's spirits were sagging. One of the Mississippi staff members stood up and suggested that Mrs. Hamer come forward to speak.

"That was the first time I set eyes on her," said Thelwell, now a professor at the University of Massachusetts.[14]

> Now, you know all the people on the local level in the movement were special to us. We called them Mr. and Mrs.—Mr. Steptoe, Mr. Turnbow, Mrs. Hamer—so she looked like another local person to me. Then she started to talk. The room had been full of random conversation. Slowly it came to attention. She talked about what had happened in Winona. Now, there were not just Southern people there. There was SNCC staff from all over. We had college students who had come down from New York and other places. So it was the first time they heard her, too. There were tears in lots of people's eyes. And then she starting singin' "This Little Light of Mine."

> This little light of mine,
> I'm gonna let it shine,
> Oh, this little light of mine,
> I'm gonna let it shine.
> This little light of mine,
> I'm gonna let it shine,
> Let it shine, let it shine, let it shine.

> All over Mississippi,
> I'm gonna let it shine,
> All over Mississippi,
> I'm gonna let it shine,
> All over Mississippi,
> I'm gonna let it shine,
> Let it shine, let it shine, let it shine.

That, Thelwell believed, "was her national debut as a public presence and articulator of the spirit of the movement."

Mrs. Hamer coupled her own story with a shrewd analysis of economic and political power in the United States, of steps blacks and poor whites needed to take to obtain equal benefits in America. Her unlettered voice gave her words a power that no amount of grammatical correctness could have infused.

Eleanor Holmes Norton, who remembers hearing virtually all of the civil rights orators, maintained that Fannie Lou Hamer may have had no equal, save only Dr. King. Mrs. Hamer was not, she said, the kind "to reel off a bunch of one-liners, not to put together a bunch of catchy phrases—although she could do that." What captured Norton's respect

> was the capacity to put together a mosaic of coherent thought about freedom and justice, so that when it was all through, you knew what you had heard because it held together with wonderful cohesion. . . . She also, let us not forget, would break out into song at the end of her things, and I'm telling you, you've never heard a room flying [like one] that Fannie Lou Hamer set afire. Her speeches had themes. They had lessons. They had principles. And then when you had heard all that said with such extraordinary brilliance—like WOW, that's what it is. She has put her finger on something truly important that all of us had felt but she had said. You heard that all the time. What really gets you is that person somehow concretizes an idea that you had never quite been able to fully form. And she did that in this extraordinary ringing style and then ended up singing "This Little Light of Mine." You never needed to hear anybody else speak again.

Nobody sang "This Little Light of Mine" as Fannie Lou Hamer sang it. "I'm convinced she chose that song for a reason," Norton said, "that she knew that summarized her life. All she was was a little light, and she fastened upon the notion that every little light could make a difference. The reason that she fastened upon it, I think, is that she saw walking off that plantation had made a difference. That one little act had made a difference."[15]

Because of her ability to capture the essence of the struggle in Mississippi in compelling language that all could understand, Mrs. Hamer soon expanded the scope of her travels, which until then had been fairly limited. Now, sharecropper would meet archbishop. SNCC knew that only a federal presence in Mississippi would reduce the possibility of violence as the registration campaign escalated. Its leaders felt that an appeal to Attorney General Robert

Kennedy might get the administration to act, and that Mrs. Hamer, symbolizing the grass-roots nature of the movement, might make the most effective appeal. Trying what the workers thought was the best path to the attorney general, they decided that Mrs. Hamer should go to Boston to see Cardinal Cushing, who was close to the Kennedy family. Dorothy Zellner, who was working with Friends of SNCC in Boston, would go with her to the cardinal's residence.

"One of our big problems was about what to wear," Zellner recalled. "There was a lot of joking and laughing about that. The next thing was what to call the cardinal. We were guessing. She didn't know whether to say 'your honor' or 'sir.' So we asked someone, who said you have to call him 'Your Eminence.' " Mrs. Hamer

> was from the Delta, and she spoke like a person from the Delta. She said, "Dottie, I laugh even when I think about it. If I'm not careful, this is gonna come out 'your enema.' " We decided the easiest way was to call him "sir" to avoid any embarrassment.
>
> Then the next question was whether she should kiss his ring. Mrs. Hamer was a Protestant so that wasn't appropriate. We decided she shouldn't kiss his ring. Then there was the question [of what would happen] when we actually got to start our meeting. You were supposed to genuflect. Mrs. Hamer said, "If I get down on my knees, I'm never going to get up. You could rip your dress or run your stockings."
>
> Finally, we did get to the cardinal's residence. I remember it as extremely lavish. My recollection is that we never had a sit-down meeting; we encountered him in the hall. We told him we had come to talk to him about help for Mississippi. We asked him to talk to the president. And he said, "My president is dead." And he walked away. . . . We had worked ourselves into quite a state, and it was anti-climactic at the end.[16]

Let down by the failure of her mission, Mrs. Hamer returned to Mississippi. It was winter. People were cold, and needier than usual in a Mississippi winter because they were still losing their jobs because of either farm mechanization or retaliation against the voter-registration efforts. Her work, and that of others in the movement, was complicated by the seeds of distrust sown by the State Sovereignty Commission, which spied on her as she worked on a clothing drive in Ruleville in February 1964.

The commission was established by legislation in 1956 to protect Mississippi's "sovereign rights" after the U.S. Supreme Court ruled in the *Brown* decisions that school segregation was unconstitutional. "If you say you're for state's rights, that means you're for segregation," said longtime commission director Erle Johnston.[17] "That meant state control of schools." Johnston said he had been "a practical segregationist," knowing that changes were coming and trying to work around them. The commission's primary job had become surveillance of the civil rights movement to preserve white sovereignty. "First, it was political, the fear that if blacks got enough votes, they could become the power structure. Second was the fear that integration might lead to intermarriage and, as they used to say, mongrelization of the races."

"The whole state wanted the movement watched," Johnston insisted. "The Sovereignty Commission was just the instrument."[18] White Mississippians felt threatened by the civil rights movement because equality with blacks would mean equality with people they thought, generally speaking, were capable of no more than field work or household drudgery. That is all black people had been allowed to do; thus, that must be all they were capable of doing. Otherwise moral people somehow separated themselves from their morality, from their own religious principles, and opposed civil rights activity.

So white Mississippi did not object as, over its seventeen-year existence, the commission investigated hundreds of people for alleged civil rights leanings and "subversive" activities. But it did more than investigate. It planted stories with friendly newspaper reporters or publishers—including one in 1964 to publicize claims that the Reverend Martin Luther King, Jr., was linked to the Communist Party. It played a role in the dismissal of the president of Tougaloo College, a school then considered too chummy with the civil rights movement. In the mid-1960s, it helped Senator John Stennis with his investigation aimed at discrediting the Child Development Group of Mississippi, which started the Head Start program in the state and which white Mississippi politicians saw as a threat to their control of federal money that flowed into the state.[19] And it helped screen jury members for the trials of Byron de la Beckwith, charged with the 1963 sniper slaying of NAACP leader Medgar Evers. Decades later, when this jury tampering was revealed in commission papers, Beckwith was reindicted.

Johnston, commission director from 1963 to 1968, insisted that the commission "never harassed anybody." It would report to the government if a voting rights march was going to be held "just so they would have some officers on hand." It was, by his account, an investigative agency, and he disputed attempts to paint it as "a big super-spy organization." All he was trying to do was "keep law and order and prevent violence."[20] Commission opponents have argued that it repeatedly provided groups like the white segregationist Citizens Councils with information and money that helped foster violence against rights workers.

The commission spied at every level of the movement.[21] Sovereignty Commission investigator Tom Scarbrough went to Ruleville in February 1964 at the request of Mayor Charles Dorrough. The mayor was concerned about a shipment of 30,000 pounds of clothing that had arrived from Friends of SNCC in Boston and Cambridge, Massachusetts, that Mrs. Hamer was distributing.[22] Dorrough had asked commission director Johnston to find out from the state attorney general's office what legal action might be taken against "these known local agitators"—including Mrs. Hamer— "who were distributing this food and clothing to recipients provided they would go to the courthouse to try to register to vote."

The attorney general's office said no laws were being violated unless the truck containing the shipment was blocking traffic. Scarbrough advised Dorrough, however, that some of those receiving the relief might "be driving up to the distributing point in fine automobiles and it was highly likely that many of the local Negroes would not get the benefit of any of the products, and it is possible they might be irritated by not being able to get the relief. I advised him to get in touch with his local paper to see if they could not get a pretty good story which could expose the group who were distributing this food."

The investigator talked to a woman who said Mrs. Hamer refused to give her any food or clothing unless she tried to register. "She said she did not feel she was qualified to try even to register as she would not know whom she was voting for and what their duties were." Scarbrough talked to a local planter who said "he had on his place some, what he considered, trustworthy colored people." He had told them to go down to Fannie Lou Hamer's place to ask for some of the clothing and food. They got the same message: not until you try to register. The clothing was yet another weapon in Mrs. Hamer's organizing arsenal.

"I next talked with Mr. C. C. Campbell, circuit clerk of Indianola, Mississippi, to determine how successful this food and clothing bribe had been in getting Negroes" to try to register. Campbell replied that applications had increased considerably since the food had arrived, but "they were the caliber of Negroes who were totally unqualified to pass any kind of mental test."

Scarbrough thought there might be some connection between the clothing shipment and the presence in Mississippi the previous fall of students from Yale University who worked on the mock election (he evidently thought Yale was in Cambridge, where the shipment had originated). "It might be interesting to know who are the forces there who were behind the movement in Cambridge and what organizations they are affiliated with."

In another effort to upset the program, Mayor Dorrough had announced on the radio that everyone should go to Mrs. Hamer's for clothing and food. Hundreds of people showed up, and members of Ruleville's Citizenship Club—people who had already tried to register—talked to them about voting. More than four hundred people went to the courthouse to try to sign up.[23] Later, when more clothing arrived, the mayor told people again to go get the clothing and if they weren't given it, just to take it. "I went and talked to the mayor," Mrs. Hamer told a reporter. "I told him not to boss us around. 'We don't try to boss you around,' I told him."[24]

The harassment, official and not, was building because movement strategy was paying off on some fronts. After a Tougaloo student and a British student from Yale were arrested for trying to attend a whites-only concert in Jackson, John Lewis of SNCC asked VIPs to send their regrets to Mississippi to protest discrimination, and they did. People ranging from baseball great Stan Musial to classical pianist Gary Grafman cancelled appearances in Mississippi in those early months of 1964. British author Stephen Spender and several other writers cancelled appearances at a literary festival in Columbus, Mississippi. James Webb, who ran America's space program, cancelled a speech to what would have been a whites-only dinner in Jackson. The U.S. Department of Commerce and the Small Business Administration withdrew their sponsorship of a foreign trade seminar at the University of Southern Mississippi, segregated at the time. *Bonanza* star Dan Blocker withdrew from an appearance at the Jackson coliseum, saying that he "would find an appearance of any sort before a segregated house completely incompatible with my moral concepts—indeed repugnant."[25]

The courts were also ordering registrars to allow blacks to sign up to vote. In January 1964, the U.S. Supreme Court affirmed a federal appeals court decision that Forrest County registrar Theron Lynd had to give equal treatment to black and white voter applicants. During a time when no blacks had been registered, Lynd had signed up nearly two thousand white voters without requiring them to fill out forms or interpret the state constitution. Not long after the decision, SNCC held a Freedom Day demonstration in the southern county's major city, Hattiesburg, as blacks lined up to try to register. Lynd still would let only two people into his office at a time, forcing the rest to stand outside in the rain. SNCC leaders had gathered from around the state—Lawrence Guyot, who was directing operations in the city; Bob Moses, jailed that day for standing on a sidewalk and failing to move on when ordered; and Fannie Lou Hamer along with Aaron Henry, John Lewis, and Ella Baker. On the picket line, author and activist Howard Zinn wrote that Mrs. Hamer was "moving along with her characteristic limp" outside the courthouse, "holding a sign, her face wet with rain and turned upwards, crying out her song against the sky: 'Which Side Are You On?' "[26]

With encouragement from her SNCC allies, Mrs. Hamer had decided to take her protests even more directly into the political arena. She would run for Congress against Jamie Whitten, a major power in the House of Representatives who had held his office since 1941. The candidacy was doomed from the start, if the objective was winning the congressional seat. But throughout the 1960s, Mississippi civil rights workers frequently entered political contests they knew they would lose in order to demonstrate that there was no great mystery to becoming involved. Potential voters could at last see themselves and their issues reflected in real political candidates and political debates.

Mrs. Hamer kicked off her campaign for Congress on March 20 in Ruleville and campaigned the next day in Minter City, Philipp, Sunnyside, Money, Wakeland, Schlater, and finally Greenwood. She told the audiences in Ruleville and Greenwood that she intended to campaign despite the atmosphere of intimidation and the obstacles to success.[27] "She feels that as an American she has the right to conduct a campaign for Congress the way candidates all over the country do," her supporters wrote in a press statement. Acknowledging the uphill nature of her race, her press statement said that "even though Negroes are a clear majority of the folks old enough to vote, it is very hard for the majority of people who have lived there all their lives to elect a person to office. No Negro in the Delta has held a municipal, county or state office in this century, except in the all-Negro community of Mound Bayou."

Mrs. Hamer was not given to overstatement; that there was an atmosphere of intimidation was made clear by events in the church-burning summer to come. Not only had she lost her job and been jailed and beaten for her voter-registration efforts, she had had telephone threats against her life and had heard that a black man had been hired to kill her. She thought she had seen him case the neighborhood several times.[28] One of the SNCC workers said she would be campaigning in "the roughest territory in the world outside of South Africa." It was fantastic, he said, "to be planning a campaign where a primary consideration is whether the candidate will get killed."[29] Later she would receive hate mail—including a heart with a dagger through it—from out of state after her testimony at the 1964 Democratic National Convention. She had a matter-of-fact response to the threats, saying that she was never sure when she left home whether she'd get back. "Sometimes it seems like to tell the truth today is to run the risk of being killed. But if I fall, I'll fall five-feet four-inches forward in the fight for freedom."[30]

Mrs. Hamer specifically wanted to target Jamie Whitten. "In late 1961," she said, "the United States government wanted to start a program of training tractor drivers so they could command good wages from the planters" and could get jobs in the midst of the mechanization of cotton farming. The Delta Council, the organization of area planters, had received the Labor Department's approval for the program, which would have helped them prevent damage to expensive machinery and would have provided them with workers trained at government expense.[31]

"About 2,400 of the workers to be trained would have been Negroes and the other 600 would have been whites," Mrs. Hamer said.

> The classes would have been integrated. Negro and white workers would have had the chance to get to know and understand each other. When Jamie Whitten heard about the program, he said, "I hope this does not mean that this is the entering wedge into Labor Department supervision of wage rates and hours in agriculture, which would upset the local economy." What he meant was that he was afraid there'd be more money for the workers and less for the planters— that's what he calls "upsetting the local economy."[32]

After a meeting with Delta planters in Cleveland, Mississippi, on January 8, 1962, Whitten killed the training program in Congress, Mrs. Hamer said. Race had overshadowed even the benefits the farmers had anticipated. They were worried about federal control, she added. "It's funny they don't worry about 'federal control' when it comes time to get their subsidy money every year from the United States government."

Mrs. Hamer also criticized Whitten for supporting higher beef prices at the expense of consumers and opposing federal aid to education. "Even the white children are getting the short end of the stick," Mrs. Hamer said, although "Jamie Whitten has got the whites thinking they're doing real well because more money is spent on their children than on Negroes."[33]

The night that Mrs. Hamer had opened her campaign, SNCC fieldworkers Mendy Samstein and George Green went to Ruleville with hundreds of leaflets for her to use. They arrived soon after midnight and were driving through the black community when Ruleville police stopped them. Samstein, white, was questioned about what he was doing "with that nigger." When Green did not respond to one officer's question, the man took out his gun and shoved it into his stomach. The police arrested the pair and took them to the jail.[34] One officer said, " 'I still don't know what you people do,' " Samstein reported. "When I said we were concerned with Negro participation in politics, he replied that 'we don't have any nigger politics in Ruleville.' " Ultimately, Mayor Dorrough charged Samstein and Green with violating the curfew and going through a stop sign. Samstein replied that the Supreme Court had ruled that curfew laws for adults were unconstitutional. " 'That law has not reached here yet,' " Dorrough responded. The men paid their fines and were released.

Although Mrs. Hamer's campaign stressed the conditions of black people in Mississippi, she also wanted to appeal to white voters. She and John Lewis had argued with Lawrence Guyot during the 1963 mock election that ballot boxes should be taken into white neighborhoods around the state as well as black communities, but they lost that round.[35] Mrs. Hamer said that all Mississippians suffered in their present circumstances and that their elected officials really didn't represent the people. She pledged that if elected, she would work to develop all parts of the state and help all people, regardless of race or personal circumstances.[36] She remained an integrationist throughout her life, a source of knowledge for poor whites in her community as well as poor blacks.

Music played a role in her political campaign, as it did in virtually all her appearances. It was common to adapt a song to the needs of the moment, and Mrs. Hamer used the tune of "Oh, Mary," for one such adaptation. As Bob Cohen, director of a tour of musicians called the Mississippi Caravan of Music recalled,[37] the resulting campaign song went like this:

> If you miss me in the Missus kitchen,
> And you can't find me nowhere,
> Come on over to Washington
> I'll be Congresswoman there.

Another:

If you miss me in the Freedom fight
And you can't find me nowhere,
Come on over to the graveyard
I'll be buried over there.

Just before the campaign ended, Jerry DeMuth, a freelance writer working for *The Nation,* visited Mrs. Hamer in her small frame house. He described the large pecan tree in the front yard, the butter bean and okra plants in gardens on either side of the house, and the challenger who had come forward to oppose Jamie Whitten. "Her deep powerful voice shakes the air as she sits on the porch or inside, talking to friends, relatives and neighbors who drop by on the one day each week when she is not out campaigning," DeMuth wrote.[38] "Whatever she is talking about soon becomes an impassioned plea for a change in the system that exploits the Delta Negroes.

" 'All my life I've been sick and tired,' she shakes her head. 'Now I'm sick and tired of being sick and tired.' "

Mrs. Hamer told DeMuth one way her civil rights activity had affected her family. Not only had she and her husband both lost their jobs, her daughter Dorothy had trouble finding employment. Several months earlier she had been looking for work and her prospective employer said, " 'You certainly talk like Fannie Lou.' When the girl replied, 'She raised me,' she was denied the job. 'She has a job now,' " Mrs. Hamer told DeMuth, but " 'they don't know she's my child.' "

Talking about the Winona jail incident, Mrs. Hamer added: "We're tired of all this beatin', we're tired of takin' this. It's been a hundred years and we're still being beaten and shot at, crosses are still being burned, because we want to vote. But I'm goin' to stay in Mississippi, and if they shoot me down, I'll be buried here."

Mrs. Hamer campaigned throughout the Second District, although she had to miss a week of campaign time because of bad health. She would be plagued the rest of her life with problems stemming from her beating, such as a blood clot that affected the sight in one eye and kidney problems, as well as from hypertension, diabetes, and a heart disorder. Nonetheless, she carried on until the June 2 primary. She and the other three black candidates running under the banner of the new Freedom Democratic Party—Victoria Gray for U.S. Senate, James M. Houston for Congress from the Third District, and the Reverend John E. Cameron for Congress in the Fifth District—were defeated.

Why, asked *Washington Post* columnist Sue Cronk, did the two women, Mrs. Hamer and Mrs. Gray, bother to wage what would clearly be losing campaigns? After all, Cronk pointed out, "neither Victoria Gray nor Fannie Lou Hamer has a chance of winning. Of the 553,000 registered voters in Mississippi at the close of 1963, only 28,000 were Negroes, despite the fact that 422,256 Negroes are eligible."[39]

"We feel the time is ripe to begin to let people know that we're serious about this whole thing of becoming first-class citizens," Mrs. Gray responded. "It's not just a sudden burst of energy; we're not going to grow tired and give up. We think our candidacies will have a terrific psychological impact on both races." Victoria Gray, younger than Mrs. Hamer by a decade, had sold cosmetics and household goods in the Hattiesburg area before she became active in the movement. She had tried five times to register before the Forrest County registrar decided she had passed the literacy test—after the Justice Department filed suit against him.

The unremarkable primary voting marked the end of one campaign and the beginning of another, far from unremarkable, that would change the state forever: Freedom Summer. Movement workers in Mississippi, goading President Johnson toward turning his well-honed skills to work on a civil rights bill, had decided after more late-night discussions to bring out-of-state students into Mississippi to help register voters. They knew that until white students were at risk, no one of influence in America would focus on the violence blacks faced whenever they tried to assert their rights. White students were stirring out of their lethargy of the 1950s, and one thousand ultimately came, including many who went on to hold political office themselves, sit as judges, edit newspapers, and inspire other social protest movements.

Not only did these volunteers need orientation, the nation did as well. Reporters were briefed, members of Congress informed. To try to alert the nation to the denial of rights the young people would seek to correct, the organizers of Freedom Summer held a hearing in Washington on June 8, 1964, a few days after Mrs. Hamer and Mrs. Gray had lost their bids for Congress. Unsuccessful in an attempt to have Congress conduct the hearing, the civil rights organizers instead set up a panel that included the former president of Sarah Lawrence College, several authors, a New York judge, and child psychiatrist Robert Coles. The testimony at the hearing led Representative William F. Ryan of New York and some of his congressional colleagues to ask the Justice Department to send federal marshals to protect the summer volunteers. The request went unheeded.

First came Lawrence Guyot, jailed and beaten with Mrs. Hamer in Winona. Asked specifically whether there had been any changes by the mere fact of a federal trial of a sheriff and police chief in that case, he told the panel, "In Mississippi, as long as you have Federal district judges who are appointed by senatorial courtesy, a white man doesn't have to worry about the Federal Government. The Federal Government in Mississippi is the white man."[40]

Soon Mrs. Hamer testified, telling about losing her job and being beaten and jailed for trying to become a first-class citizen. She told about harassment she faced routinely, efforts clearly designed to intimidate her day by day to drop her political activity. "We have a curfew only for Negroes," she said. "It was a little before Christmas. My husband got up at five o'clock to go to the washroom. As he walked out, we heard a knock at the door and he opened the door. He said, 'Come in.' Two policeman walked in—and asked him, what was he doing up at this time of night?

"Not only have I been harassed by the police," Mrs. Hamer said, "I had a call from the telephone operator after I qualified to run as congresswoman. She told me, 'Fannie Lou, honey, you are having a lot of different callers on your telephone. I want to know do you have any outsiders in your house? You called somebody today in Texas. Who was you calling, and where are you going? You had a mighty big bill.' I said the bill was paid. 'Well, I wouldn't let no outsiders come into my house,' the operator added.

"I said, 'What do you mean, outsiders?'

" 'Well, we are going to check on this, and we just don't want no people from outside your house coming in and making outside calls.' "

There would be a hot summer in Mississippi, Mrs. Hamer added, "and I don't mean the weather." People were getting prepared. "They have been riding with the guns. But Ruleville is a very small town. There are about 2,000 people in there. . . . And the mayor, he would ride around and tell folk don't let the outside people come into their homes, because after they stay awhile, they would just beat them up. But they say, 'Don't say nothing to old Fannie Lou Hamer about it.' "

Mrs. Hamer was followed by Elizabeth Allen of Liberty, whose husband, Louis Allen, had witnessed the murder by a state legislator of Herbert Lee, a black man who had been active in voter registration with Bob Moses in southwestern Mississippi. Trying to stay alive, Allen, also black, had testified to one set of facts about the case in court, yet had told the FBI the truth. That word got out, and he was killed the day before he planned to leave the state.

Hartman Turnbow, a movement stalwart from Tchula in

Holmes County, testified about his house's being firebombed and shot into at 3:00 A.M. about two weeks after he had tried to register to vote. Charging out of the house, "I saw two white men and one of them no sooner he saw me he shot at me. . . . I had my .22 already in position and I just commenced shooting at him right fast." Meantime, someone was shooting into the front of the house. The men fled, "then myself and wife and daughter went to pumping water and we put the fire out. And that is what I got for going to register."

"Was anyone arrested. . . ?" Turnbow was asked.

"I was," Turnbow said.

Sheriff Andrew Smith had come to investigate. Turnbow knew the sheriff well. One of their last encounters had been at the courthouse, when the sheriff stood looking at a group of local black people who wanted to register. One hand on a blackjack, the other on a pistol, Smith had asked, " 'All right now, who will be first?'

"And the 14 of us got scared, looked one at the other one," Turnbow testified. "So . . . I just stepped out of the 14. I said, 'I will be first, Mr. Smith.' " After the firebombing, the sheriff told Turnbow he thought he could have set the fire. "Do you think I would set my house on fire and don't have no insurance on it?" Turnbow asked. "I had borrowed money from the FHA to make a crop year and the tractor is hard to crank, and it is sitting beside the house, and there was my pickup sitting there, and there is no insurance on anything and even myself, 'and then you think I would set my house on fire to burn up everything?' "

This was Mississippi on the eve of Freedom Summer. In Ruleville, in Holmes County, in Jackson, white Mississippi was talking about the "invasion" about to descend upon the state, throwing up the spectre of black and white young people fornicating in public places, hippies who never bathed, communists under every bed. The local press headlined the impending arrival of outside agitators. The state legislature passed laws restricting rights to assemble and speak. The state and communities expanded their police forces, and the city of Jackson bought a crowd control vehicle that so closely resembled a tank that it soon was called "Thompson's tank," after Mayor Allen Thompson.

The anticipation was felt in homes as well as in the streets. Many a Mississippi white remembered a father who thought he got along well with black people who fulminated at the evening news on television as it showed demonstrations, sometimes in their very own hometowns. Mothers exhibited tensions never seen before. Many a black child remembered the confusion, fear among some, a sense of exhilaration and deliverance among others, as they watched the news on television or saw demonstrations on their own streets and at their local courthouses. Lines were being drawn.

The students were coming. First they had their orientation at Oxford, Ohio. Bob Moses, James Forman, Hollis Watkins, Fannie Lou Hamer, and other Mississippi veterans were there. "You are not going to Mississippi to try to be heroes," Moses told the young volunteers at one training session. "You are heroes enough just going into the state. This is not a Freedom Ride. The point is to stay out of jail if you possibly can, and don't put yourself in any unnecessarily dangerous situation. You have a job to do. If each of you can leave behind you three people who are stronger than before, this will be almost 3,000 more people we will have to work with next year. This is your job."[41]

The orientation taught the volunteers how to withstand blows from billy clubs and kicks to the groin, how to defend themselves and not strike back. The young volunteers also encountered the first tensions between them and the more veteran workers, many of whom remained unconvinced about the wisdom of bringing in inexperienced whites. At one point, feelings boiled over when the group saw a film involving a white registrar of voters, a "parody of 'massive resistance.'" The volunteers found the man comical. He *was* ludicrous, but the young blacks, who had been working under intense pressure in Mississippi, saw nothing funny in the filmed image. They had already seen him in the flesh, and they knew of his bigotry.[42]

Fannie Lou Hamer went to Oxford to help with the orientation. Help? She dominated it, in the view of historian James Silver, who called her the "indomitable, untutored philosopher from Jim Eastland's county."[43] First, she helped break the ice as the volunteers arrived on campus. She sang out:

> If you miss me from the back of the bus,
> You can't find me nowhere,
> Come on up to the front of the bus
> I'll be riding up there. . . .

"Her voice gave everything she had," Sally Belfrage wrote in her chronicle of that summer,

> and her circle soon incorporated the others, expanding first in size
> and in volume and then something else—it gained passion. Few of
> them could know who she was, and in her plump, perspiring face

many could probably see something of the woman who cleaned their mother's floors at home. But here was clearly someone with force enough for all of them, who knew the meaning of "Oh, Freedom" and "We Shall Not Be Moved" in her flesh and spirit as they never would. They lost their shyness and began to sing the choruses with abandon, though their voices all together dimmed beside hers.[44]

She sang, and she tutored. She represented the grass roots, telling the volunteers things they needed to know about the people with whom they were about to work and live. Above all, "Our religion is very important to us—you'll have to understand that." If they did, she indicated, they would also understand that they were the answer to the faith of the people of Sunflower County.

Hatred should have no place in their thoughts, she told them, just as hatred had no place in hers. Hatred of black for white solved nothing, she said, adding, "The white man is the scaredest person on earth. Out in daylight he don't do nothin'. But at night he'll toss a bomb or pay someone to kill. The white man's afraid he'll be treated like he's been treating the Negroes, but I couldn't carry that much hate. It wouldn't solve any problems for me to hate whites because they hate me. Oh, there's so much hate! Only God has kept the Negro sane."[45]

"Help us communicate with white people," Mrs. Hamer said during one session held in paralyzing heat. "Regardless of what they act like, there's some good there. How can we say we love God, and hate our brothers and sisters? We got to reach them; if only the people coming down can help us reach them."

As the meeting ended with many questions about the students' own fears still hanging unanswered—they could be answered only when the students reached Mississippi—Mrs. Hamer led the singing with "Go Tell It on the Mountain." The students sang and clapped and Mrs. Hamer improvised. "Who's that yonder dressed in red?/Let my people go./Look like the children Bob Moses led."[46] And so the students went to Mississippi.

Some had not even left the orientation site when they learned that one among their number, Andrew Goodman of New York, was missing along with James Chaney, a local black man who had been recruited by CORE's Mickey Schwerner. The trio had gone into the country in Neshoba County to check on a church burning. They were arrested, then released, and never seen again. They had not checked in with their contact, and they were presumed dead. Their disappearance, and the massive manhunt that followed, confirmed both the worse fears of violence predicted for the summer and the belief of veteran rights workers that it would take white deaths to spur national outrage. The burned hulk of the car in which Chaney, Goodman, and Schwerner had been riding was found, yet a swamp-searching, river-dragging operation failed to locate their bodies. Only after a paid informant spoke up did authorities find the young men buried in an earthen dam on a farm southwest of Philadelphia, Mississippi, just days before the Democratic convention in August.[47]

Against this backdrop of violence, and anticipation of more violence that was almost as paralyzing, thirty volunteers came to work in Ruleville.[48] It was a mecca of civil rights work because of the presence of Rebecca and Joe McDonald, Mary Tucker, Ruby Davis, Irene Johnson, and Fannie Lou Hamer, among others.

That spring one of the volunteers, Len Edwards, then a law student at the University of Chicago and now a judge in San Jose, California, had received a long letter from Mrs. Hamer after he had volunteered to go to Mississippi. She obviously had taken some time and care to write it, and it "was warning about the Mississippi Highway Patrol, telling me how dangerous it was to come down."[49] It was the first clue that Edwards, son of California Congressman Don Edwards, had about the "shockingly different mood and atmosphere I would find in Mississippi." Edwards was impressed that Mrs. Hamer, with whom he would live for part of that summer, had taken the time to write. The letter came straight from her heart, he said. "She didn't mess around. There was no politeness." Edwards called Mrs. Hamer "the most inspirational person I've ever met . . . the purest of heart."

Mrs. Hamer was on the road when the volunteers arrived, but "from the moment she arrived from Oxford, mothering her brood of teachers for the Freedom School, black and white Ruleville knew that Fannie Lou was back. Her compact, heavy body was immediately recognized, and her booming voice, scolding, singing, or laughing, was freedom itself," wrote Tracy Sugarman, an artist and volunteer that summer.[50] Sugarman made many sketches of the people with whom he worked, and he said that Mrs. Hamer was in only two because she was always in motion: she had a "kinetic quality" that never allowed her the repose necessary for a sketch.

People always knew when she was back in town, when she was at a mass meeting, Sugarman said, because the decibels, already rising, rose a bit more when she sang. Her voice "bellowed out and you knew that they were hearing it across the highway. The Klan guys used to hang out at the gas station. [People] said you could hear her all over Sunflower County when she sang."[51]

Each time she would return from her many travels that summer, the house soon filled up with people. Whenever she had time, she would sit in her yard with some of the students. "She would describe how people wanted to compromise" with the system at every turn, to take just a small change instead of insisting on full rights, Len Edwards recalled. She would not do that. "The right answer was clear to her. She would make fun of them. . . . We were laughing and crying at the same time." Edwards was surprised at how open Mrs. Hamer was with these young people she had not known before that summer. "It was as if we all knew the right answer—and she included us in that group—and we had to get people to do it. She understood those who wanted to compromise, but she wouldn't do it herself."

Mrs. Hamer smoothed the way for the white volunteers on occasion. "She and I went to a number of churches together," Edwards recalled.

> When she walked in with white civil rights volunteers, that said something. She'd get rolling and she'd compliment us for putting off important things and coming to Mississippi to do this. It showed blacks and whites worked together. She'd say, "The rest of you out there, are you ready to move?" We never talked black and white with her; what's right versus what's wrong was the issue for her. She knew I knew what had to be done. That was a great compliment to me. She knew that I loved her.

At these meetings, Mrs. Hamer would galvanize people when she started to sing. "She always started with 'This Little Light of Mine' and sang one or two other songs. Her talk was also singing— she was telling people, whatever her audience, whether civil rights workers or local people, what they had to do." She always knew who her audience was. "I never had the feeling she was on automatic pilot," saying the same thing over and over in canned phrases as some politicians do. "Her energy level was such that everything she said was fresh."[52]

Clothing was still arriving from the North, and Mrs. Hamer continued to insist that people had to try to register before she would give them dresses or shirts or trousers. Mrs. Hamer would round up the people for volunteers to take to the courthouse. Edwards drove a Corvair, and four giant women would pile into the little car, and they'd tear down to Indianola. "The women were scared to death but they were motivated by Mrs. Hamer. They wanted the clothing. They didn't get registered but by going down, they were making a political statement." It was, for most of them, the first overtly political step they had ever taken.

Local harassment started almost immediately. On June 24, white youths drove through the black community where the volunteers were staying and threw bottles at cars and houses, breaking several windows.[53] The next night someone threw a firebomb at Williams Chapel Church just around the corner from the Hamers' home. At 2:30 A.M. Pap Hamer heard the bottle crash, saw the flames, and called the fire department.[54] The church, which SNCC and COFO had used for meetings, escaped extensive damage because eight gasoline-filled plastic bags spread out around the small building failed to ignite. Another night there was a phone call that Mrs. Hamer would be shot that night. "We got her over to someone else's house," Edwards recalled, "and we got shotguns and waited for the cars to drive by. They never did. We weren't necessarily going to shoot but wanted to be ready."[55]

Generally, the white volunteers lived peacefully in the black community, but local whites drove by the community center—the focus of the civil rights activity—almost daily to yell insults or throw trash. "I have had white ladies on two separate occasions tell me I was a Communist nigger lover, then give me an obscene hand gesture," Edwards said in a report he filed that summer with SNCC.[56]

Ruleville, white and black, was not used to seeing white and black young people walking together, working together, much less holding hands or riding motorcycles together. The reaction of white Ruleville worried Mrs. Hamer, Tracy Sugarman said, recalling that Mrs. Hamer was like a mother hen or a sorority mother.

> She used to get furious . . . when the black and white kids would go hand in hand into town. . . . She was afraid for them, and she was afraid it was going to ignite violence and she was perceptive enough to pass that on. She did, and everybody cooled it. The kids felt they were back on campus sometimes. Being nurtured in the black community, they had a feeling of being safe, but of course they weren't safe. And she knew that, and she knew it was a matter like that [—he snapped his fingers—] because any trigger could have set it off. [Whites] would come through the quarter with no license plates at all hours of the night. It was a dangerous situation. So they listened to Mrs. Hamer.[57]

White students were also getting black high school students involved. They worked in voter registration and started agitating for change at the all-black high school. Edwards and an attorney volunteer tried to talk with the Ruleville Central High School principal about the questions the students had raised, but a policeman arrived and told them they had to clear any appointments at the school with the superintendent. The principal was black; the superintendent was white.[58]

While the white volunteers settled in with comparatively few problems, blacks in the community fared less well. "Almost all the Negroes who are known to support the civil rights movement in Ruleville have lost their jobs," Edwards reported. There were frequent threats of physical harm, probably more than the white volunteers knew about because many of the local people simply told no one about them. That August, however, Mrs. Hamer reported seeing one of the men who had her beaten in the Winona jail the previous summer. That evening she received a phone call from someone who said, "We know where you are now, Fannie Lou, so don't try to get away. You're going to end up in the Mississippi River tonight." Nothing happened.

Newspapers made up stories about "all-night biracial orgies in the community center," Edwards reported. "Several papers have commented on the Communist activities that are going on in Ruleville. . . . Mayor Charles Dorrough was heard to say on his morning radio show, 'Watch out for those Communist agitators around here.' " So intense was feeling against the voter-registration workers that the Ku Klux Klan burned a large cross on the mayor's front lawn, presumably because the movement had gained a foothold in Ruleville despite his hostility.[59]

Pap Hamer had let the civil rights workers set up headquarters in the Hamers' parlor. Phones rang, typewriters clattered, people ate at odd hours, reporters dropped by, students sprawled in the shade under the pecan tree. Mr. Hamer's privacy was destroyed. His life had changed the instant his wife tried to register; she was frequently away in the years afterward and he groused, but, as she always said, he was there backing her up. "He accepted the changes with the quiet, appraising calm that he wore like a protective garment," Sugarman wrote. He knew how to hide his anger; he no longer had work to provide for his family. " 'I drink,' he told me one day. He said it simply, without apology," Sugarman added. " 'When I work, I don't drink. But when I'm not working, I like to drink.' "

One day, Mayor Dorrough drove by the Hamers' home, took a look around, and asked Pap Hamer how he felt, having white men sleeping in his house. Mr. Hamer stood silently for a minute. Then he replied: "I feel like a man . . . because they treat me like a man."[60]

In many Sunflower County communities, local police regularly followed voter-registration workers who were out canvassing. It was hard enough to get wary people to talk when no one really wanted the workers to be there, when no one would shake hands, talk, or even look directly at them. "Don't you want to register?" Edwards would ask. "The answer often was 'No,' the speaker's eyes shifting to the yard," wrote a visiting *Saturday Evening Post* reporter who accompanied Edwards on his rounds. "And even when it was 'Yes,' the conversation usually went no further. 'Don't you want a better life for your children?' Len finally began to ask in desperation. 'No, suh,' came the answer, the eyes flicking at the white police car as it moved past. 'No, suh.' "[61]

In Drew, five miles north of Mrs. Hamer's hometown, twenty-five civil rights volunteers and local residents were arrested in connection with a voter-registration drive July 15. City attorney Pascol Townsend called in all the parents of the young people who had been picked up and reportedly called Representative Don Edwards, who had visited his son that summer, "Castro's secretary" and blasted all the COFO workers as communists. Townsend asked all of the people there to have nothing to do with the civil rights workers.[62]

Some of the antagonism Mrs. Hamer faced came from the black quarter as well. "There was envy for a lot of reasons," Tracy Sugarman recalled,

> quite aside from the notoriety, because here was a woman with a reputation, and there would be journalists coming in and people asking questions about Fannie Lou Hamer and stuff. She was the conduit through whom clothes and a lot of support was coming down, and she rode herd on that and she got the best out of it for the movement. . . . People were envious of the fact that she was comfortable with these outsiders because they weren't. . . . Here were rural people, black people—suddenly this whole thing was in their midst . . . and she was the reason for it. If she hadn't been there, they would have been a lot safer, they felt. . . . She shamed a lot of people into being Christian.[63]

Fannie Lou Hamer and her allies were tired of waiting for help with voter registration. They were ready to step onto the national stage to challenge President Lyndon Johnson and the Democratic Party to back them in this dangerous, deadly work. After the frustrations of the previous winter, after the meddling of the State

Sovereignty Commission, after all the deaths, the black Mississippians had landed squarely in the headlines as their churches were burned and their summer visitors threatened. They weren't talking abstract concepts of freedom now or shadowboxing with democracy. They were forming their own Mississippi Freedom Democratic Party to get ready for the next, critical round.

CHAPTER 6

"Everybody Knows about Mississippi, God Damn"

THE MISSISSIPPI FREEDOM DEMOCRATIC PARTY (MFDP) began life as an organizing tool. People living amid violence and discrimination needed a way to overcome their justifiable fears in order to take action. MFDP provided them with a vehicle through which they could learn about the political system and see how its decisions affected them, even if they lived in the poorest, most remote hamlets. The party gave them a voice, a way to take collective action so they weren't challenging the system all by themselves. The Freedom Democrats had an immediate goal—unseating the all-white Mississippi delegation of the regular Democratic Party at the 1964 convention. But they felt the means to that end was also important: that is, the participation of black people of all backgrounds.

Challenging the regular Democrats in Mississippi was but one part of the Freedom Summer activity. But it was this challenge that aggressively took the action to the politicians. It forced political leaders from around the country to judge the issues this predominantly black group was raising and to take a stand. It offered a vehicle for people from around the country, not just those who had volunteered to work in Mississippi, to express to their own states' delegates in Atlantic City their views on civil rights in Mississippi. And it would write Fannie Lou Hamer into American political history.

Mrs. Hamer remained at the core of MFDP from the day it was founded, through the long weeks of organizing in Mississippi, and when the challengers took center stage along the Boardwalk and in the convention hall. The movement had created the space—a media role—for someone who would embody its goals,

Bob Moses said later, and she was ready to walk right into that space.[1] Many others faced just as much danger, had suffered just as much hardship. She was the one who could tell their story and sing their song, and reporters quickly recognized her symbolism.

The Mississippi Freedom Democratic Party was officially established at a meeting of several hundred people in Jackson on April 26, 1964. Moses had already consulted Washington attorney and Democratic Party insider Joseph Rauh about whether challenging the regular state party had a prayer of succeeding. Rauh thought it could, because the Democrats and Republicans might be courting voters favoring stronger civil rights laws.[2]

The MFDP founders had decided they needed their own party because Mississippi's Democratic Party was preventing blacks from voting. The "regulars," as they were known, controlled the Mississippi legislature, which had passed a series of laws making the registration process almost insurmountable. State law also forbade anyone from participating in a Mississippi party primary who did not agree with the principles of that party.

The only primaries that mattered were the Democratic primaries because Republicans were not then a viable party in Mississippi—they were, after all, the party of Lincoln, the party that had imposed the black vote, allowing blacks to be officeholders, in the brief years of Reconstruction. The Democrats had stated their position bluntly in their 1960 platform: "We believe in the segregation of the races and are unalterably opposed to the repeal or modification of the segregation laws of this State. . . ." In case anyone had missed the point, the party at its 1964 state convention reaffirmed its belief "that the separation of the races is necessary for the peace and tranquility of all the people of Mississippi and the continuing good relation which has existed over the years." Thus, as the Freedom Democrats later told the national party, "a Negro's mere belief in his own dignity and the United States Constitution makes him ineligible to participate in the political processes of Mississippi."[3]

Faced with the hostile attitude of the Democratic Party regulars, Fannie Lou Hamer and hundreds of other lifelong Mississippians set about registering black Mississippians for another mock election in 1964. But they also tried to participate in conventional electoral politics: Mrs. Hamer and Victoria Gray as well as MFDP candidates James Houston and the Reverend John Cameron had been on the June regular Democratic Party primary ballot for the U.S. Congress. They lost decisively, but they had tried to work within the framework of the Democratic Party. They had also supported the national Democratic platform, and they had talked about anti-poverty programs, Medicare, aid to education, rural development, urban renewal, and civil rights.[4]

In her race against incumbent Congressman Jamie Whitten, Mrs. Hamer voted for the first time. "I cast my first vote for my-self," she said, adding that it had been easier for her to declare her candidacy for the Congress of the United States than it had been to register.[5]

The regular Democrats resisted every overture from the black Mississippians. "We tried from every level to go into the regular Democratic Party medium," Mrs. Hamer said. "We tried from the precinct level. The sixteenth of June when they were holding pre-cinct meetings all across the state, I was there and there was eight of us there to attend the meeting, and they had the door locked at 10 o'clock in the morning. So we had our own meeting and elected our permanent chairman and secretary and regulars and alternates" and mailed the results to the local chairman of the regular party.[6] In other precincts, prospective black participants found the location of precinct meetings, but they still were excluded. In Hattiesburg, they were told that they could not participate without poll tax receipts, despite the recent constitutional amendment outlawing such re-quirements. Where blacks' attendance was allowed, their participa-tion was still restricted: they couldn't vote or nominate delegates or help count the votes. They proposed resolutions proclaiming loy-alty to the national party. In three cases, their resolutions were brought to a vote; they all lost overwhelmingly.[7]

After local meetings came county conventions June 23. The only blacks who attended were those who had been elected by the all-black precinct meetings that Mrs. Hamer described. In Madison County, Annie Devine and others who tried to attend were told that the meeting was that of the county executive committee, not the full convention; in Leflore County, potential black delegates were told their credentials were not in order; and so on.[8]

Few public voices of conciliation existed in white Mississippi. One was the *Delta Democrat-Times* in Greenville, which warned editorially that the regular party was electing as delegates "a combi-nation of John Birch–Citizens Council professional types" with no pretense of loyalty to the national party; at that rate, the paper said, the Freedom Democrats wouldn't have to work very hard to be seated. The regulars might do themselves what liberals had been unable to do for sixteen years—that is, drum Mississippi out of the national party.[9]

The advice was unheeded. "By the time the apex of the pyramid was reached—the state convention—there was not a single Negro delegate in a state with 435,000 Negroes of voting age," according to the MFDP brief submitted to the national convention. "The exclusion was complete. Furthermore, and possibly even more significant here, there was not a single delegate to the state convention, white or black, willing even to offer a resolution of support for the National Democratic Party."[10]

The Mississippi Freedom Democratic Party held its own precinct, county, and state conventions. Mrs. Hamer's district met in Greenville, and she was a dominant force, with a nod here, a well-placed word there. Volunteer Sally Belfrage described the scene: "In a church annex, a vast metallic quonset hut like an oven, they sat in sections marked off with placards: LEFLORE, PANOLA, HOLMES, COAHOMA, WASHINGTON, SUNFLOWER—and TALLA-HATCHIE, the toughest county of them all, whose delegation often received an ovation from some, the dazed open mouths of others.

"Mrs. Hamer stood at the front of the hall as the delegates assembled," Belfrage wrote, "greeting them, hugging friends, laughing. Volunteers who had never seen her before met her now and were instantly cowed with admiration."

Four delegates were to be selected, and when the gathering had heard all the speeches, the four best had been chosen. "People straight out of tarpaper shacks, many illiterate, some wearing a (borrowed) suit for the first time, disenfranchised for three generations, without a living memory of political power, yet caught on with some extraordinary inner sense to how the process worked, down to its smallest nuance and finagle," Belfrage added. Dewey Greene from Greenville, father of a young man who had applied unsuccessfully for admission to the University of Mississippi, received the most votes. He recalled that someone had shot into the Greenes' home after his son filed his application to enter Ole Miss. At that time, his son had been the only one active in civil rights. "I have seven children. When you shot in there, you got seven more [activists]. The white people of this state pushed me into politics, shot me into politics, and to get me out, they'll have to shoot me out."

Mrs. Hamer was elected as the Second District's representative on the MFDP executive committee. "She stood and in her booming voice spoke briefly on her theme: 'We are sick and tired of being sick and tired!' She told of the time they had shot at her, and 'my house was so full of holes it wouldn't hold water.' " Mrs. Hamer led the young people in the national anthem and in "We Shall Overcome," and "they sang with fight in their voices. The white students, sophisticated graduates of Ivy League political science courses, exchanged looks as they sang with the rest: they had received their first object lesson in politics, and not where they had expected to find it."[11]

Democrats' control of the state was such that they would be the only party challenged. Mrs. Hamer had already lectured young Ed Cole, who later became the first black person to head the Mississippi Democratic Party in 1987, about how pointless it was to be a Republican. Riding from Jackson to Ruleville early in 1964, Cole, then a senior majoring in political science at Jackson State, asked Mrs. Hamer why she was not involved with the Black and Tans, as the black wing of the Republican Party was often called in the South because of the color of its members. He already knew from his research that the Black and Tans' only role had been as patronage brokers when Republicans were in the White House. The long reign of Democrat Franklin Delano Roosevelt and his New Deal policies—plus the activism of Eleanor Roosevelt—killed what little influence the Black and Tans retained in Mississippi and elsewhere in the South. At midcentury, the Mississippi Black and Tans were run by Perry Howard, an attorney who lived in Washington, D.C.[12]

Essentially, Cole remembered, Mrs. Hamer's answer was that the Black and Tans were not an integral part of Mississippi. "They'd come to Mississippi every four years to hold a convention and once the convention was over, the few national Republican leaders would leave and go back to doing what they were doing and they would leave the people with the problems that they had."[13]

The Freedom Democrats moved forward in organizing their challenge against the regular Democrats, holding two weeks of precinct meetings in twenty-six counties in late July and early August. Thirty-five hundred people participated. Then came a week of county conventions in thirty-five counties at which 282 delegates were elected to go to the state convention in Jackson August 6. Ella Baker, who was setting up the party's Washington office, gave the keynote address. She spoke of the discovery of the bodies of the missing civil rights workers Chaney, Goodman, and Schwerner and told the delegates, "The symbol of politics in Mississippi lies in those three bodies that were dug from the earth this week."[14]

From among the people present, sixty-eight delegates and alternates were chosen to go to the national convention. It was a cross section of black Mississippi, rural mainstays of the movement and middle-class professionals. There were Fannie Lou Hamer and Hartman Turnbow, who had testified in Washington about being charged with burning his own house. There was Dr. Aaron Shirley, a physician then practicing in Vicksburg who had been denied hospital privileges even though Cubans who barely spoke English could admit patients. Among others were Lawrence Guyot, Charles McLaurin, and E. W. Steptoe, a farmer active in the NAACP who had been one of the first people with whom Bob Moses had worked in tough Amite County.[15]

Four members of the delegation were white, including Dr. A. D. Beittel, the president of Tougaloo College, and the Reverend Ed King, who had run with Aaron Henry in the 1963 mock election. King was chosen as national committeeman, while Victoria Gray of Hattiesburg was named national committeewoman. Chairing the delegation was Aaron Henry; Fannie Lou Hamer was vice chair. Annie Devine from Canton was the delegation secretary.[16]

Victoria Gray and Annie Devine became, with Fannie Lou Hamer, a triumvirate who worked together constantly in coming months. Strong women, they were hardly newcomers to the movement. Mrs. Gray was a dogged activist who bristled at the inequality she could remember from her childhood; she recalled the time that she and her mother had been told to leave a whites-only waiting room in a bus station in Louisville on a trip to Mississippi from a visit north. She "stopped riding the bus at a very early age because of the ugliness that the bus represented."[17] The wife of a plumber who could not get a license because of the couple's civil rights activities, she had attended Wilberforce College in Ohio. SNCC workers recognized early her leadership in her community of Palmers Crossing outside Hattiesburg. She taught in the SCLC citizenship education program and became its state director. When people from out of state sent food and clothing, she stored it in her home and organized a committee of women to distribute it.[18]

It was Mrs. Gray who, along with Ed King, held the news conference in Jackson in late July 1964 to announce the convention challenge and outline MFDP's tentative platform. She charged that the national party had known of the situation of black voters for years but had "stood silent while the all-white delegations from the Magnolia State have come to party conventions with no thought of contributing to the solidarity of the party behind a common platform."[19]

Annie Devine had taught school in Canton, where she raised her family. She commuted in the summers to Tougaloo to try to get her college degree, then switched to selling insurance for a black-owned company based in Jackson. "I was doing my insurance work, and I was asked if I would distribute materials for the two people who were running for governor and lieutenant governor" in the mock election. She put the materials in her black insurance bag and handed them out. She fought off an eviction threatened because of her civil rights activity, and she quit selling insurance to go work full-time for civil rights.[20]

These women would testify and lobby, argue and protest, at Atlantic City, playing a more politically active role than many women usually took in that era. Not for them the activities scheduled for women at the convention—not the round of brunches with the wife of the party chairman, nor Ladies Day at the Atlantic City Race Track, nor a tour of the Lenox china showroom or a fashion show at the Shelburne Hotel.[21]

Joseph Rauh, long active in the liberal wing of the Democratic Party, was the Freedom Democrats' lawyer. He had already traveled to Mississippi once during the 1963 mock election because he knew Aaron Henry through the NAACP. He met Mrs. Hamer then, but his first prolonged encounter with her was at the state convention. The meeting was held at the Masonic Temple, and, Rauh recalled, "Hell has no fear for me. This was without any doubt one of the hottest things I have ever been at. There was no air conditioning and it was one hundred in the shade outside. I don't remember exactly what the temperature was inside." Rauh had one of the seats of honor on the platform, and as he was arriving there was this "uneducated, large woman singing beautifully. Now I'm not a good judge on voices, [but] I thought it was beautiful." Mrs. Hamer was perspiring "like I've never seen perspiration. I couldn't see how this woman went on and on. I thought, gee, this is wonderful. I'd have to pay fifty bucks to hear this in New York, and I don't have to pay anything. It was the most wonderful thing I'd ever heard. Every time she'd sort of stop, the audience would make her keep going."[22]

Asked by one delegate whether he thought President Johnson would support a floor vote on the challenge at the convention, Rauh responded: "I think this is asking too much. I would be happy if the President would just remain neutral." Rauh had no doubt in his mind that if MFDP could get its challenge to a vote on the floor of the convention, it would win. "When states like New York, New Jersey, California and Illinois and many others have to put it on the line before those national television cameras, there's no doubt in my mind that they will go with us. Under these circumstances, I'm certain that we'll get at least two-thirds of the 5,000 delegate votes."[23]

Rauh spoke to the delegates about the strategy to get the MFDP challenge to the floor. "In substance, my speech was 'eleven and eight,' " he said. The credentials committee had one hundred ten members, and a vote of one-tenth of them—eleven—was needed to take the issue to the convention floor. Eight was the number of states needed to wave their placards to force a roll call vote. During his speech, Rauh recalled, "Mrs. Hamer started shouting, 'eleven and eight,' and the people started shouting 'eleven and eight.' "

Lyndon Johnson was furious about Rauh's role with the MFDP. He had come some distance from the senator who cast his lot with the South on civil rights legislation in the 1940s and 1950s. In office less than a year, the new president had twisted congressional arms to win passage of the civil rights legislation for which John F. Kennedy had provided only tepid backing. The 1964 Civil Rights Act that Johnson had signed July 2 outlawed discrimination in public accommodations such as restaurants and hotels. Johnson felt he was doing more for black Americans than any previous president had—and he *was*—but he wanted change at his pace, not theirs.

He also wanted no challenges, no demonstrations, to mar the convention at which he would finally win the presidential nomination in his own right. He was powerful and he was stubborn. He felt every person had his price and, Rauh added, the president evidently believed he had the two men who might know his. Angrily, he told Rauh's longtime political ally, Senator Hubert H. Humphrey, Jr., of Minnesota, and United Auto Workers president Walter Reuther, for whom Rauh worked on legal matters, to call their pal and straighten him out.

"Johnson had seen the television—Mrs. Hamer leading and the people calling back 'eleven and eight'—and Johnson called these two and told them in essence, 'You tell that bastard god damn lawyer friend of yours that there ain't gonna be all that eleven and eight shit at the convention,' " Rauh said.

Rauh came under intense pressure to abandon the MFDP to protect Humphrey's chance to become vice president. First, he got word through a Humphrey aide that White House insiders were saying that unless he stopped the Freedom Democratic Party fight, the Minnesotan wouldn't be vice president. Then he got a similar message from Reuther. Although one of the few union leaders who fought for his black members, Reuther had what he considered the greater goal of increasing Humphrey's influence and thus his impact on the nation's agenda. He made it perfectly clear to Rauh "that I was to blame for Hubert's not being vice president if he didn't get the job."[24]

In Texas, Lyndon Johnson had learned through political close calls to leave nothing to chance. Before the convention, he ordered the FBI to keep the delegation and the SNCC workers accompanying them, as well as some of the witnesses who would testify for them, under surveillance. On August 19, John Doar of the Justice Department asked the FBI for a name check on a number of MFDP leaders, including Mrs. Hamer.[25]

Operating under assistant FBI director Cartha DeLoach, agents tapped phones of key MFDP supporters as well as SNCC's storefront headquarters. They had an informant at the Gem Motel headquarters for the Freedom Democrats and at Union Temple Baptist Church, where MFDP held its meetings. In his book *Racial Matters,* author Kenneth O'Reilly said that whenever agents intercepted especially vital information, they telephoned Washington, where the material was typed and rushed to the White House by messenger.[26]

The FBI bugged the hotel rooms of Dr. Martin Luther King, Jr., and Bayard Rustin.[27] A Senate investigation of domestic spying on American citizens a decade after the convention revealed that this surveillance, launched under the Counter Intelligence Program (COINTELPRO) aimed at preventing possible disturbances, often produced information only tangentially related to that purpose. "From the electronic surveillances of King and SNCC," said the report of the committee headed by Idaho's Senator Frank Church, "the White House was able to obtain the most intimate details of the plans of individuals supporting the MFDP's challenge unrelated to the possibility of violent demonstrations. [White House aide Walter] Jenkins received a steady stream of reports on political strategy in the struggle to seat the MFDP delegation and other political plans and discussions by the civil rights groups under surveillance."[28]

Why would a man who went on to win a landslide victory over Barry Goldwater, an indifferent campaigner, have worried about a revolt among southern voters? What had so worried Lyndon Johnson that he called out the FBI, kept Hubert Humphrey dangling about the vice presidency, and cajoled seasoned politicians against letting the Mississippi issue get to the convention floor? And why did those same politicians worry so much that Johnson might not select Humphrey as his logical running mate to balance the ticket?

Johnson had just signed major civil rights legislation and feared he had lost the South for the Democrats for the foreseeable future. Naming a liberal—a man like Hubert Humphrey who had stood up to the segregationists at the 1948 Democratic convention—might only compound the ticket's problems in the South. Walter Reuther called Joe Rauh in a frenzy one day, telling him that if the Freedom Democrats persisted, he and Johnson both felt the Democrats would lose the election because of the backlash. " 'Either we're going to lose the Negro vote if you go through with this and don't win, or if you do win, the picture of your all-black delegation going on the floor to replace the white one is going to add to the backlash,' " Rauh quoted Reuther as saying. " 'We really think that Goldwater's going to be president.' "[29]

Even if Johnson had not feared that the election was at risk, he did not want a floor fight involving the sensitive issue of race; that could cost him the support of powerful congressional committee chairmen who, in those days when seniority carried heavy clout, were largely southerners. Johnson needed that support for the social programs he wanted to initiate. Publicly, he pretended the challenge from the Mississippi Freedom Democratic Party did not exist. His memoirs *do not mention it at all.* "Atlantic City in August 1964," he wrote, "was a place of happy surging crowds and thundering cheers. To a man as troubled as I was by party and national divisions, this display of unity was welcome indeed."[30]

In short, it was politics as usual versus the missionary message that the black Mississippians were bringing to Atlantic City. Trying to ensure that the rest of the country knew about that message, Mrs. Hamer spoke at a series of rallies along the East Coast. Ella Baker traveled with her, bolstering a relationship of respect between the two women. Baker, an intellectual and longtime activist, admired Mrs. Hamer's courage. She felt that the brutality that had been directed at her would have stopped a lesser person. "Even though you want to see things changed . . . it could change your mind, it could stop you from moving ahead, but it seemingly never stopped her."[31] The admiration was mutual. Asked whether she could think of a black leader who had made a real difference, Mrs. Hamer said there were many, but that Ella Baker was "a woman I respect more than I do any other living woman at this time for her role in civil rights."[32]

When it came time for the MFDP delegates to leave for the convention, the buses loaded in Jackson. James Forman of SNCC kissed Mrs. Hamer on the cheek, then watched as the bus pulled off on its 1,200-mile journey.[33] He remembered his speech that had roused her to try to register to vote and how much she had done since that day scarcely two years earlier. Mrs. Hamer and her fellow passengers had mixed sentiments as they rolled through the countryside. Some felt they could only raise the issue of Mississippi's injustices once again and show their faith in ultimate change. Others thought they might actually win their challenge against the all-white Democratic Party.

"I really thought we was gonna get seated," said Unita Blackwell from Mayersville, who had registered to vote and become active in the movement just that summer. "In a kind of way, I really did, because it was just so true," what she and her new political party were saying about life in Mississippi.

MFDP was led at Atlantic City by its chairman, Aaron Henry of Clarksdale, a small city less than thirty-five miles from Mrs. Hamer's hometown of Ruleville. Then forty-two, Henry had been active in the NAACP since a high school teacher, Miss T. K. Shelby, talked the whole senior class of 1941 into joining. He had served in the army from 1943 to 1946, becoming even more active in the NAACP chapters around the military bases where he was stationed. He helped organize the Clarksdale branch after graduating from Xavier University in 1950 with a pharmacy degree. Once while he was in school, he had been involved in a briefing that Hubert Humphrey, himself a former pharmacist, gave students about legislation to establish drug purity standards.[34] Henry had established his own drugstore, which he still ran decades later. His store windows had been broken repeatedly and his house bombed and set afire as well as shot into because of his civil rights activity. He himself had been registered to vote since the late 1940s. He said, however, that as long as the majority of his people could not vote, he did not think that situation was right, even though it accommodated him because he had had a little more academic training. Years later he would comment, "As far as I'm concerned, I got the right to vote in 1965, when my folks got the right."[35]

Eating soda crackers and drinking Cokes because they had little money for real meals, the Mississippians arrived in Atlantic City a few days before the sessions began. They slept four and five to a room in the Gem Hotel on Pacific Avenue, not one of the swank convention hotels. They lobbied arriving delegations and painted protest signs, sat on the hotel porch and fanned themselves, and sat in with hundreds of their supporters conducting a vigil of support on the Boardwalk.

What was arguably Mrs. Hamer's most famous singing—that captured in documentaries and run and rerun on national television—occurred at one of those demonstrations. "Go Tell It on the Mountain, to Let My People Go," she was singing, and the film showed a woman calling forth some inner vision of a political system that might—must—let her people go. There was Annie

Devine with her, holding a sign and singing, and Victoria Gray. And to Mrs. Hamer's left was young Bernice Johnson Reagon, singing alto.

Reagon, who had entered the movement through the bitterly resisted voter-registration campaign in Albany, Georgia, was one of the Freedom Singers.[36] In her eyes, Mrs. Hamer was a "fierce warrior." She would talk with young people, like those gathered in Atlantic City, about people shooting at her, yet she had an aura of peace and safety about her, Reagon added. "She looked like all of the black women I knew. She was hefty, she was short, she had a singing voice very much like the women who came out of our church. She didn't look like my teacher; she looked like the usher on the usher board. . . . She looked real regular." Remembering Mrs. Hamer with television interviewer Bill Moyers, Reagon recalled the clarity of her message. She was "so strong and insistent, and she was so mad and so loving. I really needed to meet a black woman like that."[37]

The MFDP demonstrations and lobbying—as well as the intense attention that had been focused on the grim search for the bodies of Chaney, Goodman, and Schwerner—started to have an effect. Eight or nine delegations, the giant contingent from California among them, had already backed the challenge. Like the other states, California had two delegates on the credentials committee. One was a black woman, Vera Canson. Her husband, who was president of the NAACP in Sacramento, reportedly was in line for a federal judgeship; she was being told he wouldn't get it if she went along with the challengers. MFDP geared up for action.

"I got Mrs. Hamer and Mrs. Devine, two of the most moving people, and the three of us went over, and we talked to Mrs. Canson at breakfast," said Mendy Samstein, who had worked with Mrs. Hamer in Ruleville.[38] "I just sat there, and Mrs. Hamer and Mrs. Devine did all the talking. The woman didn't have any question about what is right or wrong; she knew it was right. She was really moved by Mrs. Hamer and Mrs. Devine."

Party officials put the credentials committee hearing in a room just large enough for the panel members and witnesses, and not for television cameras. "Give [TV newsman] Sandy Vanocur the credit for opening that room," Joseph Rauh recalled. "He came to me in the middle of the afternoon and he said, 'Joe, they've screwed you.' I said, 'My god, already?' You could have heard me in the stars. He came back and put that on the air. He came back and said you and I have got this thing open. They're going to have television and cameras and everything."[39]

In the weeks before the hearing, Rauh and young attorneys Eleanor Holmes Norton and H. Miles Jaffe had prepared the brief from which Rauh would argue. He was proudest of one historical precedent he had found. In 1944, two Texas delegations vied at the convention to be seated. President Roosevelt, with Solomonic wisdom (and his renomination already assured), said seat them both. What's more, Lyndon Johnson had been on the dissident delegation. In Rauh's mind, the Texas precedent offered the seeds of compromise. If both Mississippi delegations were seated, Rauh knew the white regular delegation would not stay or pledge loyalty to the national ticket, whereas the MFDP would do both.

The hearing began at 2:55 P.M. on Saturday, August 22, with David Lawrence, governor of Pennsylvania, as credentials committee chairman. Mississippi's was the third case to be heard. The Freedom Democrats were seated directly opposite the party regulars, staring them in the face. "Some of the Freedom Democrats saw their plantation 'bosses'; some saw the women for whom they had worked as maids and cooks, and others, perhaps, saw some of their fellow townsmen," recalled MFDP delegate Leslie McLemore. Now the Freedom Democrats were in Atlantic City not to pay homage to their bosses, but to demand their bosses' seats and control of the Mississippi Democratic Party, he added.[40] The regular party delegation included, however, neither the state's governor, its two senators, nor members of the U.S. House of Representatives as it had in the past, even though they remained in close contact with what was occurring.

Attorney Rauh had one hour, and in that hour he set about showing "that the Mississippi Freedom Democratic Party is the loyal, legal and long-suffering body of Mississippi."[41]

First witness: Aaron Henry. Chairman of the MFDP delegation, Henry that summer was heading the Council of Federated Organizations, which was coordinating voter registration. He had become a prime target for violence from Mississippi's diehard segregationists after Medgar Evers had been killed. He and his sixty-seven fellow delegates knew when they left home that they might be arrested when they got back. The state attorney general had secured an injunction against their attendance at the convention because he said they were using the word *Democratic* illegally in their party name. "But, sir, if jail is the price that we must pay for our efforts to be of benefit to America, to the national Democratic Party, and to Mississippi," Henry told the credentials committee chairman, "then nothing could be more redemptive."

Stressing MFDP's support for President Johnson while the

party regulars turned their backs on the national Democrats, Henry said his delegation was concerned about the national image of America. He decried Mississippi governor Paul Johnson's description of Andrew Goodman and Michael Schwerner as "first generation aliens." He said Mississippi was so bogged down by racism that it stood last on many tables of economic or academic achievement. "The only reason we are not fifty-first is because we only have fifty states. . . . We seem to have an affinity for the bottom."

The next witness was Ed King, Tougaloo chaplain. A native Mississippian, King had been set upon and badly scarred for his civil rights efforts. "There are not many white people openly working this way in Mississippi," said King. "We have four white delegates in our freedom delegation here. There are more who would like to have supported us but could not do so for fear of their very lives. I know many Mississippians in the last several years, over one hundred ministers and college teachers have been forced to leave the state. This nation is being populated with refugees from the closed society in Mississippi."

Because of this fear, the Freedom Democrats had not been able to recruit delegates from every part of the state, King added. "We were not able to hold a county convention in Neshoba County or precinct meeting in Philadelphia because the church we wanted to meet in was burned to the ground. Three of our workers were murdered in Philadelphia. We do not apologize to you for not being able to hold a county convention in Neshoba County, Mississippi."

When King concluded, Governor Lawrence suggested that testimony be confined to election machinery, not "the general life of the state of Mississippi."

Rauh disagreed. "It is the very terror that these people are living through that is the reason that Negroes aren't voting. They are kept out of the Democratic Party by the terror of the regular party, and what I want the credentials committee to hear is the terror which the regular party uses on the people of Mississippi, which is what Reverend King was explaining, which is what Aaron Henry was explaining, and which is what the next witness will explain—Mrs. Fannie Lou Hamer."

Mrs. Hamer sat at the witness table before the 110 credentials committee members, the press, and the television cameras, and started to speak. Joe Rauh said he already knew her story by heart. He was a lawyer, and he knew a good witness. Mrs. Hamer spoke with special directness that day: "Somebody just wound her up," Rauh recalled.

Mr. Chairman, and the Credentials Committee, my name is Mrs. Fannie Lou Hamer, and I live at 626 East Lafayette Street, Ruleville, Mississippi, Sunflower County, the home of Senator James O. Eastland, and Senator Stennis.

It was the 31st of August in 1962 that eighteen of us traveled twenty-six miles to the county courthouse in Indianola to try to register to try to become first-class citizens. We was met in Indianola by Mississippi men, highway patrolmens, and they only allowed two of us in to take the literacy test at the time. After we had taken this test and started back to Ruleville, we was held up by the City Police and the State Highway Patrolmen and carried back to Indianola, where the bus driver was charged that day with driving a bus the wrong color.

After we paid the fine among us, we continued on to Ruleville, and Reverend Jeff Sunny carried me four miles in the rural area where I had worked as a timekeeper and sharecropper for eighteen years. I was met there by my children, who told me the plantation owner was angry because I had gone down to try to register. After they told me, my husband came, and said the plantation owner was raising cain because I had tried to register, and before he quit talking the plantation owner came, and said, "Fannie Lou, do you know— did Pap tell you what I said?"

I said, "Yes, sir."

He said, "I mean that," he said. "If you don't go down and withdraw your registration, you will have to leave," said, "Then if you go down and withdraw," he said. "You will—you might have to go because we are not ready for that in Mississippi."

And I addressed him and told him and said, "I didn't try to register for you. I tried to register for myself." I had to leave that same night.

On the 10th of September, 1962, sixteen bullets was fired into the home of Mr. and Mrs. Robert Tucker for me. That same night two girls were shot in Ruleville, Mississippi. Also Mr. Joe McDonald's house was shot in.

And in June, the 9th, 1963, I had attended a voter-registration workshop, was returning back to Mississippi. Ten of us was traveling by the Continental Trailway bus. When we got to Winona, Mississippi, which is Montgomery County, four of the people got off to use the washroom, and two of the people—to use the restaurant— two of the people wanted to use the washroom. The four people that had gone in to use the restaurant was ordered out. During this time I was on the bus. But when I looked through the window and saw they had rushed out, I got off of the bus to see what had happened, and one of the ladies said, "It was a state highway patrolman and a chief of police ordered us out."

I got back on the bus and one of the persons had used the

washroom got back on the bus, too. As soon as I was seated on the bus, I saw when they began to get the four people in a highway patrolman's car. I stepped off the bus to see what was happening and somebody screamed from the car that the four workers was in and said, "Get that one there," and when I went to get in the car, when the man told me I was under arrest, he kicked me.

I was carried to the county jail, and put in the booking room. They left some of the people in the booking room and began to place us in cells. I was placed in a cell with a young woman called Miss Euvester Simpson. After I was placed in the cell I began to hear sounds of licks and screams. I could hear the sounds of licks and horrible screams, and I could hear somebody say, "Can you say, yes sir, nigger? Can you say yes, sir?"

And they would say other horrible names. She would say, "Yes, I can say yes, sir."

"So say it."

She says, "I don't know you well enough."

They beat her, I don't know how long, and after a while she began to pray, and asked God to have mercy on those people.

And it wasn't too long before three white men came to my cell. One of these men was a State Highway Patrolman and he asked me where I was from, and I told him Ruleville. He said, "We are going to check this." And they left my cell and it wasn't too long before they came back. He said, "You are from Ruleville all right," and he used a curse word, and he said, "We are going to make you wish you was dead."

I was carried out of that cell into another cell where they had two Negro prisoners. The State Highway Patrolman ordered the first Negro to take the blackjack. The first Negro prisoner ordered me, by orders from the State Highway Patrolman for me, to lay down on a bunk bed on my face, and I laid on my face. The first Negro began to beat, and I was beat by the first Negro until he was exhausted, and I was holding my hands behind me at that time on my left side because I suffered from polio when I was six years old. After the first Negro had beat until he was exhausted, the State Highway Patrolman ordered the second Negro to take the blackjack.

The second Negro began to beat and I began to work my feet, and the State Highway Patrolman ordered the first Negro who had beat to set on my feet to keep me from working my feet. I began to scream and one white man got up and began to beat me in my head and tell me to hush. One white man—my dress had worked up high, he walked over and pulled my dress down—and he pulled my dress back, back up.

I was in jail when Medgar Evers was murdered.

There was a slight pause. Tears were welling in her eyes, but she went on. "All of this is on account we want to register, to become first-class citizens, and if the Freedom Democratic Party is not seated now, I question America, is this America, the land of the free and the home of the brave where we have to sleep with our telephones off the hooks because our lives be threatened daily because we want to live as decent human beings, in America?

"Thank you."

Someone took off her microphone. She dabbed at her eyes, picked up her purse, and left the witness table. Some of the seasoned politicians listening were in tears.

Rita Schwerner, whose husband, Mickey, had just been killed in Mississippi, was the next witness. She spoke about the treatment she received when she tried to see Governor Paul Johnson, who slammed the door of the Governor's Mansion in her face. Other witnesses included Roy Wilkins of the NAACP and Dr. Martin Luther King, Jr., of the Southern Christian Leadership Conference.

King had called the White House ten days earlier about seating the Freedom Democrats. Although he knew Goldwater might try to exploit the white backlash, King felt that some satisfactory adjustment to the Freedom Party issue had to be found or there might be even more racial protests that could hurt Johnson's prospects in November. He thought black votes could make a difference in a few states, especially Georgia and Tennessee, but if black voters felt the election was irrelevant, they might stay at home.[42] He asked the credentials committee: "Can we preach freedom and democracy in Asia, Africa and Latin America if we refuse to give voice and vote to the only democratically constituted delegation from Mississippi? The extension and preservation of freedom around the world depends on its unequivocal presence within our borders."

Then the regular Democrats presented their case: that there was only one lawfully constituted Democratic Party and that only its leadership could call precinct, county, and state conventions.[43] The MFDP was a rump group formed by a combination of nonresidents and dissident Mississippians, some of whom, the regulars claimed, had communist records. Victoria Gray and Fannie Lou Hamer had both had the opportunity to participate in the Democratic primary, the regulars reminded the credentials committee. Mrs. Hamer "received only 621 votes in the 23 counties in her district and there are over 1,500 qualified Negro voters in Washington County in that district alone," the regulars said, implying that the Freedom Democrats did not even speak for registered black voters—ignoring the fact that those voters may well have been intimidated and therefore did not cast ballots. "We submit, not by way of threat but as a matter of cold facts, even though we suspect our opposition to accuse us of threats, that there can be no surer way of forever killing the Democratic Party in the state of Mississippi than to seat this rump group who represent practically no one."

One of the regulars criticized Mrs. Hamer's testimony, calling it a "pitiful story" told by a woman who had, in fact, had a chance to participate in the electoral process. Hadn't she run against Representative Jamie Whitten in the primary? And the regulars still hedged on possible support for the party's nominee.

The hearing concluded with Rauh's rebuttal.[44] The regulars had contended that MFDP was a secret organization, like the Ku Klux Klan, and Rauh attacked that argument. Committee members were welcome to look at lists naming MFDP members, but, Rauh said, "We will not give them to the Mississippi people for the very simple reason—you heard Aaron Henry, you heard Mrs. Hamer, you heard the others say what would happen. A man's life is at stake if those are given."

Rauh said the regulars, including the governor, spoke one way in Mississippi, another before the credentials committee. In Mississippi they bragged about being independent of the national party. "Why does he want to come here if they are independent of the party? . . . I will tell you why they are here. They are here to warm the seats and keep the Freedom Party from them, because if the Freedom Party is once seated, Mississippi will change."

The regular delegates contended their meetings were open, said Rauh.

> I have got a stack of affidavits this high of people who were kept out of precinct meetings. Of course, Fannie Lou Hamer had the nerve to go there. She had the nerve to lay her life on the line, and you heard her here, the beating she took in that prison because she went to a voting school, and she had the nerve to go to a precinct meeting, and they say, "See, it is all open. Fannie Lou Hamer was there." Fannie Lou Hamer, who was beaten, lost her job and then was beaten for the privilege. They say we concocted these things. Do you think Aaron Henry concocted his story? Do you think Fannie Lou Hamer concocted her story? Do you think Edwin King, a reverend of the gospel, concocted his story? I don't believe you believe that at all.

The Democrats should not fight white backlash by surrendering to it, Rauh warned. "The Democratic Party has won over the years when it stood fast for principle. It cannot win this time by hauling down the flags. . . . What is worse than the fact that we won't win is that we won't deserve to win."

The hearing adjourned at 7:10 P.M. The MFDP members returned to the Gem Motel. There, Mrs. Hamer found out that her full testimony hadn't been on the air because President Johnson had called an impromptu news conference to preempt the hearing. She started berating Rauh. Suddenly someone yelled, "We're on." The networks replayed and replayed the testimony that night in prime time.

"Well, that ended her pain. She was on there in prime time Saturday night and could see herself, so this worked out fine," Rauh said.[45] Telegrams and phone calls started to pour in to the White House and to the convention in support of the MFDP. Newspaper articles reported the drama of the hearing. The *New York Times* profiled Mrs. Hamer, calling her testimony the most dramatic of a dramatic day. Interviewed by Nan Robertson for the profile, Mrs. Hamer mopped her brow as she sat in her stifling motel room and said she planned to stay in Mississippi.

"Why should I leave Ruleville and why should I leave Mississippi?" she asked. "I go to the big city and with the kind of education they give us in Mississippi, I got problems. I'd wind up in a soup line there. That's why I want to change things in Mississippi. You don't run away from problems—you just face them." She told the reporter that one thing had surprised her in the hearing the day before: State Senator E. K. Collins had testified that she received better than 600 votes in the primary that June; at the time she had been told her final count was only 388 votes. It made her suspicious. "They said that we could watch the ballot box but we had to stand across the street to watch it. There's no way of seeing through a concrete wall I know of."[46]

Joe Rauh and Aaron Henry, Ed King and Fannie Lou Hamer, held the moral high ground that day. But that was not the ground on which the decision would be made. It was hardball politics, as they quickly learned. People who might philosophically have been their allies were saying, Be realistic; we must elect Johnson. He will be far better for the cause of civil rights than Goldwater—don't stand in his way. Johnson himself was under enormous pressure from southern supporters not to let a floor debate occur that would injure his chances in the South, and their own standing as well. According to Rauh, some southern governors didn't mind "having other southerners who won't play according to the rules thrown out of the convention. The southerners do mind getting on the floor with a bunch of Negroes who were not part of the machinery."[47]

The credentials committee thus faced a dilemma no matter how it dealt with the challenge. It named a subcommittee headed by

Humphrey protégé Walter Mondale, then Minnesota's attorney general, to deal with the issue. Negotiators spent all weekend trying to shape a compromise. One suggestion was to offer the Freedom Democrats status as honored guests and seats in the balcony. Seats in the balcony? Just like a southern theater? Or the back of the bus? Forget it. "We can sit in the balcony and look on back in Mississippi," Aaron Henry told a rally Sunday night. "We won't settle for that in Atlantic City."[48]

Congresswoman Edith Green of Oregon floated a straightforward proposal that anyone who would take an oath of loyalty to the convention nominee should be seated. Green, a member of the credentials committee, felt that it was "absolutely indisputable" that blacks had been prevented from participating in the Mississippi Democratic Party in the selection of delegates.[49] She knew that the Mississippi regulars wouldn't take such an oath. Her proposal followed the 1944 precedent Rauh had found, and, indeed, many credentials' fights had been resolved by seating both delegations. Aaron Henry and Fannie Lou Hamer both said later that they had no doubt the MFDP would have agreed to that proposal.

Many established black politicians, dependent on the party for patronage, were of little help to MFDP. The evening after the credentials committee hearing, there was a secret meeting of all the black delegates to the convention. The MFDP wasn't invited, but some of its members showed up. As the dean of the black politicians, Chicago Congressman William Dawson, said, the word was, Nominate and elect Lyndon Johnson, follow the leadership, register black voters. "With that, a little woman, dark and strong, Mrs. Annie Devine from Canton, Mississippi, standing near the front asked to be heard," a SNCC worker recounted.

> The Congressman did not deny her. She began to speak. "We have been treated like beasts in Mississippi. They shot us down like animals." She began to rock back and forth and her voice quivered. "We risk our lives coming up here . . . politics must be corrupt if it don't care none about people down there . . . these politicians sit in positions and forget the people who put them there." She went on, crying between each sentence, but right after her witness, the meeting was adjourned.[50]

Hubert Humphrey, delegated by the president to defuse the crisis, surfaced Monday and began meetings with Rauh, Henry, and Bob Moses. Humphrey had made his reputation in the liberal community partly on the basis of his principled stand at the 1948 convention. As mayor of Minneapolis, he proclaimed the need for politicians to recognize the new day and open the door to people of all races. The southern Dixiecrats walked out over this issue of civil rights. Now, defeated in his bid for the presidential nomination in 1960, he wanted to be vice president to push the social programs he had long advanced.

Representative Charles Diggs of Michigan, a member of the credentials committee, called a meeting at the convention White House, the Pageant Motel. Present were Humphrey, Martin Luther King, Jr., Ed King, Aaron Henry, Joe Rauh, Representative Robert Kastenmeier of Wisconsin, Edith Green of Oregon, and Mrs. Hamer.[51] By her own account, Mrs. Hamer had heard about Humphrey and his stand for civil rights.

> I was delighted to even have a chance to talk with this man. But here sat a little round-eyed man with his eyes full of tears, when our attorney at the time, Rauh, said if we didn't stop pushing like we was pushing them and trying to get the . . . fight to come to the floor, that Mr. Humphrey wouldn't be nominated that night for vice president of the United States. I was amazed, and I said, "Well, Mr. Humphrey, do you mean to tell me that your position is more important to you than four hundred thousand black people's lives?"[52]

Ed King remembered a slightly different version. By his account, Mrs. Hamer told Humphrey,

> "Senator Humphrey, I been praying about you; and I been thinking about you, and you're a good man, and you know what's right. The trouble is, you're afraid to do what you know is right." She says, "You just want this job [as vice president], and I know a lot of people have lost their jobs, and God will take care of you, even if you lose this job. But Mr. Humphrey, if you take this job, you won't be worth anything. Mr. Humphrey, I'm going to pray for you again."[53]

With that upfront challenge of Humphrey, Mrs. Hamer was cut out of future meetings. "I was in one of those meetings when they spoke about accepting two votes, and I said I wouldn't dare think about anything like this. So I wasn't allowed to attend the other meetings. It was *quite* an experience."[54]

She was excluded, Bob Moses said years later, because she was unpredictable. She had not been processed through any part of the system that usually renders someone controllable, at least in the eyes of those in power. She wasn't a product of the educational system or a labor union or the political system. She owed nothing to no one. She was uncompromising.

President Johnson was squeezing everybody, and Rauh watched his support evaporate. One night he went to the convention floor and realized how weak the challenge was. Rauh asked Senator Paul Douglas of Illinois, a respected liberal, to speak for the MFDP; Douglas begged off, saying any speech would be perceived as anti-Humphrey.[55] Scores of liberals echoed Douglas's reaction. They agreed that Mississippi was a closed society. They agreed that the MFDP delegation should be recognized. But they wanted Humphrey as vice president more than they wanted to stand up to Johnson and support the black Mississippians. Their reticence underscored the gap many of the MFDP delegates and their allies saw between liberals' rhetoric and performance.

There would be no floor speeches, however, because Johnson telephoned Walter Reuther, who was in the middle of labor negotiations in Detroit, insisting that he go to Atlantic City to make sure that the protest was squelched. He went and met with Martin Luther King and Bayard Rustin, Bob Moses and Aaron Henry and Ed King; once again, Mrs. Hamer was excluded. Reuther hammered out what became the compromise proposal: The Freedom Democrats' delegation would be given two seats on the floor as at-large delegates; Aaron Henry and Ed King would fill those two seats, Henry because he was the chairman of the MFDP delegation and King because his presence would symbolize the hope for integrated delegations in the future; the rest of the delegation would be treated as honored guests of the convention; members of the regular party delegation who would pledge loyalty to the national nominee would be seated; and, henceforth, no delegations would be seated that did not guarantee full participation without regard to race, color, creed, or national origin. The party would establish a special committee to help fulfill that pledge.

"My God, half our delegation is sharecroppers," Rauh later told a top party official. "Aren't they to be represented?" The party leaders took a middle-class druggist professional and a white professor from a delegation of sharecroppers and, worse, made the selection themselves rather than consulting a group that prided itself on deciding its own representation. "Did that ever dawn on you guys?" Rauh asked the official.[56]

The word *compromise* is the word always attached to the report from the subcommittee, but compromise implies agreement between two sides. SNCC activist Stokely Carmichael did not believe that was the correct word: "The delegates of the FDP felt that it was not a compromise, but rather a decision which was handed down to them. If it was a compromise, then the FDP would have had a chance to save something. They were not consulted. The Democratic Party said, 'Here, take this; it's all we will give you.' "[57]

The MFDP delegation met Tuesday morning. It decided that under no condition would it accept less than the Green proposal to seat any Mississippians who would take the loyalty oath. National party leaders, however, still believed MFDP would accept the Reuther proposal.[58]

The leadership wanted the matter settled, and quickly. When the subcommittee's compromise proposal was made formally, the full committee did not give Joe Rauh time to find Aaron Henry and confer with him, much less to poll the MFDP delegation. Mondale presented the compromise, acknowledging the discrimination and intimidation in Mississippi but adding that the Freedom Democrats were not a political party and that the rule of law must be maintained by seating those regulars who would support the national party. The Freedom Democrats could, however, claim "a magnificent victory for the forces of civil rights. . . . We have spelled the end of discrimination in state parties."[59]

Rauh had a fight on his hands. SNCC workers remained suspicious of how hard he waged that fight because he generally felt at the time that the compromise was forward looking and would have advised its acceptance.[60] "I don't know if you've ever been in a lynch mob but this is one," he said of the credentials committee deliberations. "They started hollering vote, even while I was still talking." Rauh wanted a roll call but couldn't get one. "There was almost nobody for a roll call. I mean, the people leaving us didn't want a roll call."[61] Rauh thought he heard seven votes for his side, but he was short the eleven needed for a minority report.

Outside, Mondale and Rauh spoke to the reporters. The word went out that the proposal had been unanimously accepted.[62] Mrs. Hamer heard "unanimous," and Bob Moses heard "unanimous." If true, that would have meant Rauh, a credentials committee member from the District of Columbia, hadn't voted against the compromise. Rauh finally got on television and explained that wasn't true, that he and some others had voted against the compromise, but his comments came too late. The word was already out: unanimous.

Bob Moses called together another caucus at Union Baptist Temple. The proposal divided the delegation. Some said to take it and call it victory. Others said, no, who are they to say whom we should pick as our delegates, and why can't we all be seated? We are the loyal Democrats. The argument raged.

Troubled by the choices, Mrs. Hamer had gone to Moses and Ella Baker for guidance. "SNCC was the only one that didn't tell us what to do because I went to Bob, I was desperate. I asked him what in the world should we do?" She believed it was wrong to accept a compromise, she said, "but do you think we ought to accept it? He replied, 'You grown, you make your own decision.' "[63]

She did, and she became one of the most outspoken opponents of the compromise. As such, she was besieged by those trying to convince her that it was a victory, that politics was give and take. The more moderate civil rights leadership knew that if Mrs. Hamer could be convinced, she might help turn the rest of the delegation around. Roy Wilkins, executive secretary of the NAACP who had often been critical of SNCC's tactics, encountered Mrs. Hamer in the hall and challenged her stand on the compromise. " 'You people have put your point across,' " Mrs. Hamer recalled his saying. " 'You don't know anything, you're ignorant, you don't know anything about politics. I been in the business over twenty years. You people have put your point across, now why don't you pack up and go home?' "[64]

Aaron Henry felt that MFDP owed it to those who had helped them, people like Wilkins and Whitney Young and Martin Luther King, Jr., "to be advised by them and then make our decision. . . . I feel that if we had had time to talk this thing out, and listen to the people who had gotten us where we were," that the compromise proposal coming from the national party might have been changed.

> I would have perfectly been willing to accept the two seats if they had permitted us to fracture these votes, shall we say in 1/34ths, and give all of our delegates the same kind of rights to go on that floor and to take our seat and to participate in what was going on.
>
> I think we could have worked this thing out. I think that Bob [Moses] forced us into a hasty decision. I don't like to be critical of Bob, but I wonder really if he really wanted to win the situation. Now you know sometimes many of us feel more liberal everytime we lose a battle. And because of the pressure that Bob was putting on so many of the delegates . . . move now, not later, now, now, now, now, now, I wonder, you know, really if he felt that we might be able to work something out that would be amenable to the total delegation rather than to be panicked into an immediate decision. Certainly the two votes were completely unacceptable to me and to everybody else. . . . I don't want nobody handpicking me.[65]

Henry and Mrs. Hamer argued at the meetings because he wanted the group to listen to the leaders, who, he felt, knew more about politics than they did. When he said that, Mrs. Hamer retorted, " 'Tell me what leaders you talking about?' And he said, 'You know we got some great leaders,' " Mrs. Hamer recounted.

"I said, 'That's right, 'cause all those people from SNCC are some of the greatest leaders I ever seen. But now don't go telling me about somebody that ain't been in Mississippi two weeks and don't know nothing about the problem, 'cause they're not leading us.' "[66]

Andrew Young was one of the more fervent advocates that day for accepting the settlement. He felt then, and twenty-five years later still felt, that "power in the convention is meaningless if it doesn't help elect a President, and we felt that the most important thing for the civil rights movement was to get Lyndon Johnson elected. I think the Lyndon Johnson landslide made it possible to get the civil rights bills passed."[67]

Dr. Martin Luther King, Jr., said that Humphrey had promised him "there would be a new day in Mississippi if you accept this proposal."[68] Privately, he told Ed King that he thought that accepting the compromise would draw support for the voter-registration drive in the South. " 'So, being a Negro leader, I want you to take this, but if I were a Mississippi Negro, I would vote against it.' "[69]

Many of the speakers, Mrs. Hamer said, were people they had never seen before in the months they had been working and braving intimidation in Mississippi. They were telling the delegates they were gaining a moral victory. To that Mrs. Hamer retorted: " 'What do you mean, moral victory? We ain't getting nothing.' What kind of moral victory was that, that we'd done sit up there, and they'd seen us on the television. We come on back home and go right on up the first tree that we get to because, you know, that's what they were going to do to us. What had we gained?"[70]

Bayard Rustin, architect of civil rights statements for decades, made an argument for compromise as well.[71] He said the Freedom Democratic Party would be turning its back on its allies, that it was now in the world of politics, not protest, and that politics was the art of compromise.

No, thank you, no compromise, no condescension, the delegation said. "Them people had not been talking to us poor folks," said Unita Blackwell. "They had a certain clique that they'd talk to. The big niggers talk to the big niggers, and the little folks, they couldn't talk to nobody except themselves, you know. They just goin' to push the thing on through and have us there for showcase. But we tore that showcase down. That's for sure. We told them what we think."[72]

Among the voices that carried the day were those of several of the women. At Atlantic City, Fannie Lou Hamer "was the person more than anybody who established the bottom line. As much as anybody she carried the delegation. She was inflexible—not inflexible as in dogmatic, but as in knowing exactly who she was representing and why," said SNCC worker Bob Weil. She had a "rock-hard integrity and commitment to the people she had come from and she just never left them. She was unbreakable."[73]

Mrs. Hamer, Annie Devine, and Victoria Gray finally turned some of the waverers around. Mrs. Hamer rose and said they had come with nothing and they would go home with nothing.[74] She told the liberals who had just spoken that she understood why they thought two seats were better than none. But she thought they were wrong. She was near tears when she finished.[75]

Henry Sias, a sixty-nine-year-old farmer who was chairman of the Issaquena County Freedom Democratic Party in the western part of Mississippi, remembered that he had been for the compromise, as had Aaron Henry and Ed King, until Mrs. Hamer and Annie Devine shamed him out of it. "Now I seen Mrs. Hamer cry 'cause I got up on the floor; they wouldn't accept no two seats . . . I changed my mind right there. Those two women just shamed me right there. When they got through talking and whoopin' and hollerin' and tellin' me what a shame it was for me to do that, I hushed right then. See, I backed off and drew way back in that corner."

Those two women opened his eyes, Sias added. "I was just that dumb and when they opened my eyes, I was ashamed. That give us a chance to fight on."[76]

Victoria Gray told her fellow delegates what they had riding on their decision, "what it meant to us as opposed to some of the people who were pushing it. And two seats at large did not represent anybody so let's not fool ourselves . . . I spoke. Mrs. Hamer spoke. Mrs. Devine spoke. After we spoke, the vote was taken. And the answer was no."[77]

Aaron Henry still was not convinced. Mrs. Hamer remembered that he threatened to announce that the delegation would compromise. She insisted that he not auction people off like that, and he didn't.[78] Just as they went before the television cameras, she warned Henry that if he said that the Freedom Democrats wanted the compromise—any compromise—"you better stay in that convention hall, then, the balance of your life, 'cause if you come out I'm going to cut your throat." She had never carried a weapon, she said often afterward, but she swore she would have done it.[79] She was angry, and she remained steaming even when she returned to Jackson days later. "There was no singin' that day," recalled Jackson activist Henry Kirksey, shaking his head at the memory. "And it was the first time I had ever seen Bob Moses really angry and talking. Usually, he made you talk. But they had a meeting when they got back—without Aaron and without Ed King—over at the Masonic Temple. . . . Fannie Lou was angry. She was mad at Aaron and Ed King for wanting to accept those two seats."

But these internal arguments never saw the light of day in Atlantic City. They remained buried within the MFDP delegation. The full convention never knew that the MFDP had rejected the compromise. There was no debate, no floor fight. Governor David Lawrence presented the credentials committee report, and in three minutes, it was accepted. Mrs. Hamer and Bob Moses were enraged. The MFDP delegates, whose supporters had been staging vigils on the Boardwalk, rallied their allies and, television cameras and reporters in tow, headed for the convention hall. Most of the regular Mississippi Democrats had refused to sign the required oath of loyalty to the convention's presidential nominee. All but three, in fact—Douglas Wynn of Greenville, Fred Berger of Natchez, and Randolph Holladay of Picayune—had gone home.[80] (One of the three who stayed, Doug Wynn, was married to the daughter of one of the most powerful men in Texas, Edward A. Clark, who had long been Lyndon Johnson's attorney.) Wynn said he stayed out of loyalty to Johnson, and because Senator Eastland had called to urge the regulars to stay rather than let MFDP take the seats by default.[81]

Aaron Henry and Joe Rauh led the march down Pacific Avenue toward the convention hall with the delegation and hundreds of its supporters singing "We Shall Overcome." The credentials committee had given the MFDP delegates tickets as honored guests, and they were so angry that they decided to use those tickets to get onto the convention floor. At first, they weren't allowed in. The state police closed the gate, claiming the fire marshals had closed the hall because it was overcrowded.[82]

A few of the Mississippians had also been given credentials by delegates from other states. "You know how white liberals are. They still wanted to do something for us," Mrs. Hamer recalled.[83] The black Mississippians headed for the seats the regulars had left vacant. Michigan and North Dakota delegates offered some of them seats, and Fannie Lou Hamer, Annie Devine, and Ed King took them. Bob Moses and several MFDP delegates, all wearing photographs of President Kennedy around their necks, stood silently in a circle on the convention floor. For two hours, there was pandemonium around the Mississippi section as several sergeantsat-arms tried to remove the MFDP delegates. They finally gave up that effort; it could have created an even worse scene on national television than the debate just avoided.[84]

Interviewed by reporters during these protests, an angry Fannie Lou Hamer boomed, "We didn't come all this way for no two seats."

The vigil on the Boardwalk, the demonstrations in the hall, the whole summer of activity were winding down. Sally Belfrage described the scene at one of the protests after the compromise had been rejected. Mrs. Hamer, then Aaron Henry, then Hartman Turnbow spoke, and then the people sang. "The music grew huge, lost all restraint—the summer was over, the songs had to be sung with the most final volume and intensity." Later at the vigil people sang again, "We Shall Overcome," suspending "color, hate, recrimination, guilt—suffering," Belfrage said.

> The song begins slowly and somehow without anticipation of these things: just a song, the last one, before we separate. You see the others, and the instant when it comes to each one to think what the words mean, when each nearly breaks, wondering: Shall we overcome? The hands hold each other tighter. Mrs. Hamer is smiling, flinging out the words, and crying at once. "Black and white together," she leads the next verse and a sort of joy begins to grow in every face; "We are not afraid"—and for just that second no one is afraid, because they are free.[85]

The national Democratic Party leaders doubtless believed they had won. There had been no floor fight. Southern white voters did not have another excuse to rise in revolt. Neither MFDP nor the national party leaders knew it, but over the long term they had just opened the Democratic Party to greater participation by more Americans. But they had done it grudgingly and at no little cost in despair and disillusionment among black and white alike.

The Mississippi challenge had wide impact, positive and negative. It ultimately opened the state party to black participation and encouraged a different breed of white politician to seek office. The MFDP didn't want those two seats in 1964, but it opened many more seats at future national conventions. Its challenge was one more link in a chain of events that brought black Americans and then women, Latinos, and Asian Americans into fuller political participation. There had been civil rights debates at national conventions before, but this one reached directly into American homes because of the emerging power of television.

But there was disillusionment as well. When the nation failed to respond decisively to the challenge, the country lost many of the young crusaders who had gone to Mississippi. They went off in their various directions—to Africa, to soul searching and emotional upheavals, to black nationalism, to personal scholarship and fulfillment. Bob Moses, for example, changed his name soon afterward to Bob Parris, went to live in Africa, and for many years refused to associate with whites. Stokely Carmichael, jailed often across the South in civil rights protests, turned to Black Power, changed his name as well, and moved to Africa. In a few years, the Student Non-Violent Coordinating Committee would expel its white members, turn more radical, and ultimately fade from the scene. Who can know how American political life might have changed had the MFDP delegates been seated that August in Atlantic City?

On the other hand, some political analysts believe that Lyndon Johnson's civil rights efforts—despite his foot-dragging at the 1964 convention—hastened the day when Democratic candidates no longer could count on the southern vote. There were, of course, far more forces at work, including the transition of the South from an agrarian to a commercial economy and the failure of the Democrats to select consistently appealing candidates who dared explain to voters the importance of civil rights advances.

One thing is clear, however. The MFDP challenge, and especially Mrs. Hamer's testimony, had direct, personal effect on many young Americans. Johnnie Walls, now an attorney in Greenville, was but one. He was sitting in his family's home watching the challenge on the only television set in his Clarksdale neighborhood. Walls, about to enter Jackson State, recalled seeing Mrs. Hamer and Malcolm X on television. He had never heard his fellow black people stand up and talk like that. Of Mrs. Hamer and the MFDP challengers, Walls said: "Those were the people who caused me to be whatever I am now."[86]

CHAPTER 7

"I'm Going to Sit at the Welcome Table"

THE MISSISSIPPIANS were tired and frustrated. Earlier in their struggles when they had needed financial aid or support from visible people in the entertainment community, they had turned to singer and activist Harry Belafonte. Now, once again, he had an answer. Belafonte, who had gone to Greenwood himself and financially supported many drives by both the Student Non-Violent Coordinating Committee and the Southern Christian Leadership Conference, recognized burnout when he saw it. "They were saying silly things, and making silly moves. I saw this behavior as the expression of total exhaustion, including Fannie Lou," who he had thought would never wear out. He told them he had raised $60,000 to keep the voter-registration drive alive but that they could have it only if some of the leaders would get away for a while. "The leadership is too strung out," he had said. "This thing is taking its toll terribly on all of you, and I know you're making mistakes. You're fussing with one another, you're crabby at one another, you're coming to violence with one another and that's not where it should be at."

The SNCC leaders pooh-poohed his suggestion, but he was adamant. So they talked about going somewhere accessible. "I said, 'No, no, no. You don't understand. Y'all gotta go someplace where there's no chance for them to tap into you in any time soon. You're going to Africa.'"[1] Belafonte persuaded his friend Sékou Touré, the president of Guinea, to invite the civil rights workers to Africa. Touré's country had won independence from France in 1958, and he admired the young people who had braved police dogs and ridden blazing buses to try to win their rights.

Mrs. Hamer had never been out of the country. "I wasn't sure whether I would be frightened or what, because what little we had read about Africa or seen we thought everybody in Africa was just wild. . . . We really didn't know that they were our people."[2] Next to nothing was taught in American schools about African history. All Mrs. Hamer had learned was that the African people were "heathens," "savages," "downright stupid people."[3]

"Although we realized they [were] our ancestors, we didn't know how they act," Mrs. Hamer said. "I had never seen a black stewardess on a plane. When I saw a man come out of the cockpit who was black, right away then this meant that it was going to be different from . . . the way it had been taught to me."[4] When she returned, her neighbors told her the mayor of Ruleville said that "he just wished they would boil me in tar. But that just shows how ignorant he is, I didn't see any tar over there. But I was treated much better in Africa than I was treated in America."[5]

Guests besides Mrs. Hamer were SNCC officers or staff members: Bob and Dona Moses, Julian Bond, James Forman, John Lewis, Ruby Doris Robinson, Donald Harris, William Hansen, Prathia Hall, and Matthew Jones of the Freedom Singers. The group left September 11, 1964, and stayed three weeks as guests of Touré.[6]

"I can recall very well we flew from New York and we made a stop in Dakar in Senegal," said John Lewis, now a congressman from Georgia. "Mrs. Hamer was so excited—you know, we'd come through the Democratic convention in Atlantic City and to leave the United States and go to Africa, and to stop on our way in Senegal and for her to see black people, Africans, pilots—she made a lot of noise about that. . . . I'm not sure she kissed the ground or made some statement she *should* kiss the ground. . . . I really think she did."[7]

When the travelers arrived in Guinea, they were escorted to a villa that had been the home of the French ambassador before independence. They were told they would meet President Touré the next day at a reception, so Mrs. Hamer went off to take a bath. In less than an hour, Touré arrived unannounced, as was his custom, for a visit. He never showed up with a retinue; sometimes he had only a driver; sometimes he drove himself. "I had to go over to tell Fannie Lou Hamer that the president had arrived," Belafonte said. "It was the only time I could remember Fannie Lou Hamer getting totally rattled. She said, 'What, no, no, no, you all playing a joke. I'm having a bath. I'm definitely not ready to meet no president.' When she understood that we were telling the truth, she hurriedly dressed and came to the meeting."[8]

Belafonte said she was obviously rattled when she limped into the living room. "We had all been sitting around and the minute she walked in, the president stood up. And she looked at him and she at first went to just shake hands," and he swept her up in a big hug, enveloping her in the white African robe he was wearing. "She clearly, no question in my mind, was dumbfounded. I'd never known her to be inarticulate" before, but she was stunned. "He looked like a leader," as Belafonte described him, "in white against this very black skin and these gleaming teeth and these flashing eyes, this fez that he had on which was white. . . . He looked so storybook."[9]

After the meeting, Belafonte said,

> Fannie Lou started to cry and said that she didn't know quite what she would do with this experience. For so long, she and a lot of poor black folk had tried unsuccessfully to meet with the president of her own country, the United States of America, where we were citizens, and we could never see him. And here in Africa a head of state, President Sékou Touré, came to see her with great words of encouragement and hope and a declaration that this Africa was their home and its people their family.[10]

Touré "was one of the most fantastic guys I've ever met," Mrs. Hamer said, although she admitted she couldn't understand a word he said in French. She was fascinated with the way the president would seal his friendship with a kiss, with men and women alike. "He'd kiss them on each side—kiss them on one side and then kiss them on the other side," she said. "If a man would kiss a man here, you would hear all kinds [of things], but they pay it no attention. I really was proud to see that kind of honesty in men sealing the friendship of men."[11]

Mrs. Hamer hadn't anticipated that Africans would speak a different language. The Guineans spoke either French or local languages, and the visiting Americans spoke only English. "Most of us, faced with a language barrier, fall silent. That's a cultural response," said Bob Moses. "But it wasn't operating with her. Everyone she met, she talked and talked. She showed you could communicate despite language, that language was a vehicle for expressing feelings. She bonded with people."[12]

Music proved a strong means of communication for the travelers. The staff at the Guinean guest house declined to eat with their guests, out of a sense of propriety, Belafonte remembered, but whenever possible those workers were included as the visiting

Americans sat around and sang freedom songs. "I am quite sure that all of French Equatorial Africa heard her. Her voice was robust."

Guinea's political party was having its own convention, and the Americans were honored guests. Each evening they observed a cultural competition at an open stadium, watching everything from a performer imitating American rock and roll to local dancing. James Forman learned that Guinea considered this competition, which included dance, music, and theater, a key part of decolonization. "The Guineans had to win back their identity," Forman wrote, adding, "The fact that President Sékou Touré attended every performance himself from 8:30 P.M. to 1:00 A.M. indicated the political importance attached to these events."[13]

The Americans attended the opening of the new stadium, visited a printing plant, and saw people dyeing cloth. "They were doing it in a very primitive way," Julian Bond recalled. "They had vats and they would run the stuff through on rollers. I remember Mrs. Hamer getting into a very animated conversation with the people even though she didn't speak French." On another stop, they saw young women getting their hair done in cornrows. "It was the first time I had seen cornrows," Bond said, "and Ruby Doris got her hair cornrowed but Mrs. Hamer said, 'No, you're not doing that to me.' "[14] She was particular about her hair, and not about to experiment with it.

Guinea was worlds apart from Greenwood or Ruleville. "People dressed differently—bright clothing and cloths wrapped around their heads," Bond said. "Many were barefoot. The conditions outside the cities were primitive. That's third-world primitive as opposed to first-world primitive. So few people spoke English. There were palm trees instead of piney woods."

The experience moved Mrs. Hamer. "I had never in my life seen where black people were running banks. I had never seen nobody [black] behind a counter in a bank. I had never seen nobody black running the government in my life. So it was quite a revelation to me. . . . Because then I could feel myself never, ever being ashamed of my ancestors or my background." Africans had a sense of physical freedom in their artistic performances that Mrs. Hamer felt black Americans, particularly black Mississippians, had been forced to repress. After her evenings watching the African performers, she commented: "It's not unclean, it's just innocent people, you know, just pure innocence. . . . And that was really beautiful to me."[15]

A sweeping sense of relaxation enveloped the group as its

members enjoyed African hospitality after years of southern hostility. They finally had time to unwind at their villa overlooking the Atlantic Ocean. "The breakers would come in over the enormous patio," Bond recalled with his poet's memory. "Early in the morning you could look out and see the fishermen paddling out to sea—it looked like the ancient African war canoes with everyone paddling in unison, and then you would see them coming back in at night."[16]

The trip offered the group a chance to get to know each other better. It was also an opportunity to rethink what they were doing. Mrs. Hamer would say, "When we get back, we have to do this, we have to do that. If these people are controlling their country, *we* should be able to register to vote."[17]

Julian Bond and his friends were shocked when they saw in the windows of the U.S. Information Agency offices pictures of black Americans—judges, policemen—supposedly enjoying equal opportunity in the United States, pictures designed to make Africans who knew little about America think that those scenes were commonplace. "That's the worst kind of deceit," Bond said.[18]

"It was as though everything was okay in the United States, that we was happy and didn't have any problems," Mrs. Hamer said. "I saw a book—now, that was 1964—and this book had Bob Moses and another man sitting at a counter and that was showing how the South had progressed in integration. You wouldn't believe it, see, people be brainwashed there. I'm not kidding, they be brainwashed there like we've been brainwashed here."[19]

Underlying the wonder that these black Americans felt upon visiting an African nation was a deeper emotion, an almost primal tie to the people. "You say, 'I could have come from here, for all I know, Ghana, Guinea,'" said Julian Bond, "and the tragedy is, you will never know, never have any idea."[20]

Fannie Lou Hamer shared Bond's musings. She knew her grandmother had been a slave. "One thing I thought about while I was there . . . some of my people could have been left [in Africa] and are living there," Mrs. Hamer said. "And I can't understand them and they don't know me and I don't know them because all we had was taken away from us. And I become kind of angry; I felt the anger of why this had to happen to us. We were so stripped and robbed of our background, we wind up with nothing."[21]

She had only a general idea where in Africa her ancestors had lived. "Our foreparents were mostly brought from West Africa, the same place that we visited in Africa. We were brought to America and our foreparents were sold; white people bought them; white people changed their names . . . and actually . . . here, my maiden name is supposed to be Townsend; but really, what is my maiden name?" she asked. "What is my name?"[22]

Bigots would tell black people that if they didn't like America, they should go back to Africa. Mrs. Hamer retorted that she would not leave until Italians went back to Italy, Germans back to Germany, and so on. But she wished that, if Americans had to make slaves of her ancestors, they would have at least preserved a record of their background. "I have people somewhere there [who] might have been my real people."[23]

The African idyll ended abruptly when the SNCC staff got word that a meeting had been called to discuss the future of the voter-registration drive. Many of the summer volunteers had stayed in Mississippi, and their role was at issue—as was, more broadly, the role of whites and middle-class blacks in an organization that was becoming increasingly oriented toward the rural poor. James Forman came to believe that the trip to Africa, so necessary for individual revitalization, might have been a mistake in terms of keeping SNCC together and moving forward.[24]

So, in early October, most of the group returned quickly to Mississippi. That fall of 1964, they plunged into talks much like those before Freedom Summer. One side wanted the movement to remain integrated; the other wanted it to return to its indigenous black roots. Eventually, the emerging black consciousness would carry the day and whites would be ejected from SNCC, even those like Robert Zellner who had braved police dogs and billy clubs. By that time, Mrs. Hamer had moved on to other questions and felt SNCC had to do whatever it felt it should do. But she grieved nonetheless over dissolution of an organization she loved.[25]

Mrs. Hamer helped conduct that fall's freedom vote. She and Victoria Gray and Annie Devine decided to run against three of the Mississippi congressmen to help set up the Freedom Democratic Party's next challenge—against the state's delegation in the U.S. House of Representatives. The challenge required money, and Mrs. Hamer was one of the Freedom Democrats' most effective fundraisers. So she went on the road again and traveled to New York, where, in December 1964, she would encounter a figure who had an indelible impact on the American consciousness: Malcolm X.

Malcolm Little, an ex-convict who discovered Elijah Muhammad and his Nation of Islam while in prison, had changed his name to Malcolm X to drop what he called the stigmatic name of the slave owner. Preaching Elijah Muhammad's message around the country, Malcolm X voiced blacks' outrage at their enslavement, first under plantation masters and then under the American system that denied them equality and decent treatment. To Malcolm X, whites were devils, and only complete racial separation—and quite possibly violence against whites—would save black people. His was a harsh message, and he scared most white people, who excoriated him as a black racist. Few stopped to analyze the core of his message, the reasons it found a receptive audience.

Seeing that Elijah Muhammad did not practice everything he preached, Malcolm split with him in 1964, made a pilgrimage to Mecca, and traveled in Africa. By the time he and Fannie Lou Hamer met, he was stressing the interconnectedness of the black struggle. But he still scared white America, which, having virtually no media that covered the black community with any regularity or understanding, was unaware of the evolution of his message. Malcolm had no use for the nonviolence of Dr. Martin Luther King, Jr., but he was starting to form tenuous links with the civil rights movement. He appreciated its fieldworkers' acts of personal bravery. Only a few days before he was shot and killed while giving a speech in Harlem, he had visited civil rights workers in Selma, Alabama. He told them that he was the kind of threatening outsider with whom Selma's white establishment would have to deal if it did not bargain in good faith with people like King and the local black community.

Malcolm X and Fannie Lou Hamer appeared on the same platform twice on December 20, 1964. Charles Neblett, one of the Freedom Singers who was on the fund-raising trip, remembered that Malcolm "had tremendous respect for Mrs. Hamer. . . . He had tremendous respect for what we were doing."[26]

On these trips, Mrs. Hamer doubled as both speaker and singer. "We'd let her sing all the songs we did that she knew," Neblett said. She put her whole self into her singing, adding a power to the group. "When somebody puts their inner self into a song," as she did that day, "it moves people. Her singing showed the kind of dedication that she had—the struggle and the pain, the frustration and the hope. . . . Her life would be in that song."

First came a rally for the MFDP at the Williams Institutional Church in Harlem. About one-third of the audience was white. The Freedom Singers may not necessarily have agreed with Malcolm X's tactics or his philosophy, Neblett said, but "he was so brave and courageous. We all wanted to meet him."

The principal speaker at the afternoon rally, Mrs. Hamer had a new audience for her story of losing her job and enduring a brutal beating because of her voting rights efforts. She described the coming challenge, saying it would be difficult to unseat five entrenched members of Congress—especially five southerners. But she said that it could be done if other Americans lobbied their own members of Congress about the denial of political rights to blacks in Mississippi. If for any reason those members of Congress had not known of conditions in Mississippi before the events of Freedom Summer and the 1964 Democratic convention, she said, they surely knew now; they should be urged to support calling new elections to start changing the harsh conditions in the state.

The Freedom Singers performed several songs, including one about Kenya's number-two man, Oginga Odinga. Then Malcolm X spoke.[27] The song about Oginga Odinga had triggered thoughts about the Kenyan terrorist Mau Mau society. Malcolm insisted that Mississippi needed a Mau Mau, Alabama needed a Mau Mau, and Harlem needed a Mau Mau. Blacks needed to communicate with those in power in a language they understood; the Mau Mau, not the nonviolent, spoke that language. Like Martin Luther King, Jr., Malcolm X viewed men's role toward women as protector rather than as equal. "When I listen to Mrs. Hamer, a black woman— could be my mother, my sister, my daughter—describe what they had done to her in Mississippi, I ask myself how in the world can we ever expect to be respected as *men*, when we will allow something like that to be done to our women, and we do nothing about it?" Malcolm said.

> No, we don't deserve to be recognized and respected as men as long as our women can be brutalized in the manner that this woman described, and nothing being done about it, but we sit around singing "We Shall Overcome."
> We *need* a Mau Mau. If they don't want to deal with the Mississippi Freedom Democratic Party, then we'll give them something else to deal with. If they don't want to deal with the Student Non-Violent Committee, then we have to give them an alternative. Never stick someone out there without an alternative.

Malcolm's point was that independence had to be achieved through anger—not sadness, a passive condition. When people are sad, he said, they don't do anything; when they are angry, they aren't interested in logic or odds or consequences: "They bring about a change."

People had to speak the language of their oppressors, he said.

> The language that they were speaking to Mrs. Hamer was the language of brutality. Beasts, they were, beating her—the two Negroes,

they weren't at fault. They were just puppets. You don't blame the puppet, you blame the puppeteer. . . . I put the blame on that man who gave the orders. And when you and I begin to look at him and see the language he speaks, the language of a brute, the language of someone who has no sense of morality, who absolutely ignores law— when you and I learn how to speak his language, then we can communicate.[28]

Malcolm spoke a vastly different language than Martin Luther King or Fannie Lou Hamer: he urged his listeners to learn the language of the violent white racist.

If his language is with a shotgun, get a shotgun. Yes, I said if he only understands the language of a rifle, get a rifle. If he only understands the language of a rope, get a rope. But don't waste time talking the wrong language to a man if you want to really communicate with him. Speak his language—there's nothing wrong with that. If something was wrong with that language, the federal government would have stopped the cracker from speaking it to you and me.[29]

Malcolm also addressed the question of Mississippi's relevance to Harlem. "America is Mississippi. There's no such thing as a Mason-Dixon line—it's America. There's no such thing as the South—it's America. If one room in your house is dirty, you've got a dirty house. . . . You have authority over the whole house; the entire house is under your jurisdiction. And the mistake that you and I make is letting these *Northern* crackers shift the weight to the Southern crackers."

Then he addressed himself to the challenge at hand. "The senator from Mississippi is over the Judiciary Committee. He's in Washington, D.C., as Mrs. Hamer has pointed out, illegally. Every senator from a state where our people are deprived of the right to vote—they're in Washington, D.C., illegally." Congress, Malcolm said, is run by seniority and James O. Eastland and other southerners had the seniority to run the committees that run Congress. "Out of 46 committees that govern the foreign and domestic direction of this country," he added, "23 are in the hands of Southern racists. And the reason they're in the hands of Southern racists is because in the areas from which they come, the black man is deprived of his right to vote." If black voters had the ballot, Malcolm argued, the racists would be thrown out and there would be black faces and brown and yellow and red faces in Congress governing the whole country. "So, what happens in Mississippi and the South has a direct bearing on what happens to you and me here in Harlem."

The Democratic Party that most blacks supported was to blame because its foundation was in the South:

> The head of the Democratic Party is sitting in the White House. He could have gotten Mrs. Hamer into Atlantic City. He could have opened up his mouth and had her seated. Hubert Humphrey could have opened his mouth and had her seated. [Robert] Wagner, the mayor right here [in New York City], could have opened up his mouth and used his weight and had her seated. Don't be talking about some crackers down in Mississippi and Alabama and Georgia—all of them are playing the same game. Lyndon B. Johnson is the head of the Cracker Party.

Northerners were in Atlantic City as well as southerners. They belonged to the same party. "What did they do for you when you wanted to sit down?" Malcolm asked. "They were quiet. They were silent. They said, 'Don't rock the boat, you might get Goldwater elected.' "[30] Malcolm urged his audience to find out what stand Mayor Wagner and his powerful friends in the Democratic Party— local black powers as well—were going to take on the congressional challenge. "Make [Wagner] come out on the record without dilly-dallying and without compromise," he urged.

> So I say, in my conclusion, as Mrs. Hamer pointed out, the brothers and sisters in Mississippi are being beaten and killed for no reason other than they want to be treated as first-class citizens. There's only one way to be a first-class citizen. There's only one way to be independent. There's only one way to be free. It's not something that someone gives to you. It's something that you take. Nobody can give you independence. Nobody can give you freedom. Nobody can give you equality of justice or anything. If you're a man, you take it. If you can't take it, you don't deserve it.

When he finished speaking, Malcolm invited Mrs. Hamer to a rally of the Organization of Afro-American Unity at the Audubon Ballroom in Harlem that night. He wanted others to hear the songs about Oginga Odinga, Jomo Kenyatta, and Patrice Lumumba. It was snowing that night, but Mrs. Hamer and the Freedom Singers went to the Audubon Ballroom—the same ballroom at which Malcolm would be shot to death only two months later.

That night, Malcolm gave a more wide-ranging speech. The audience could not understand what was going on in Mississippi, he said, if they didn't understand what was going on in the Congo. "They're both the same. The same interests are at stake. The same sides are drawn up; the same schemes are at work in the Congo that are at work in Mississippi."[31] One way to foil the schemes in this country, Malcolm said, was to register to vote. "When you register your political potential, that means your gun is loaded. But just because it's loaded, you don't have to shoot until you see a target that will be beneficial to you. If you want a duck, don't shoot when you see a bear; wait till you see a duck. And if you want a bear, don't shoot when you see a duck; wait till you see a bear. Wait till you see what you want—then take aim and shoot."[32] Don't vote for any old dummy. Don't vote for a crook. Be nonaligned, he said; don't give away your bargaining power. Register as an independent.

Then he introduced "the country's number one freedom-fighting woman," Fannie Lou Hamer. "She's from Mississippi, and you've got to be a freedom fighter to even live in Mississippi." He added that he had asked the Freedom Singers to come to the meeting because "they sang one song that just knocked me out. I'm not one who goes for 'We Shall Overcome.' I just don't believe we're going to overcome, singing. If you're going to get yourself a .45 and start singing 'We Shall Overcome,' I'm with you. But I'm not for singing that doesn't at the same time tell you how to get something to use after you get through singing."[33]

Before the Freedom Singers performed, Mrs. Hamer told her story: The loss of job. The shots into homes in the black quarter. The beating. The rejection of the compromise at the Atlantic City convention. Each time she told her story, she added the latest indignity. She was never at a loss for new material.

Malcolm returned to the podium and reminded his brothers in the audience that Mrs. Hamer proved that "you don't have to be a man to fight for freedom. All you have to do is be an intelligent human being. And automatically, your intelligence makes you want freedom so badly that you'll do anything, by any means necessary, to get that freedom. And I want Mrs. Hamer to know that anything we can do to help them in Mississippi, we're at their disposal."

Then Malcolm introduced the Freedom Singers, who sang about " 'the Klansman who makes the sign of "K," Klansman, you're going to see your day,' " Charles Neblett said.[34] "It has a line about 'the devil who makes the K, devil, you're bound to see your day.'

"Malcolm said, 'Hey, you're talking like I used to talk.' "

CHAPTER 8

"Which Side Are You On?"

WHAT THE DEMOCRATIC PARTY had refused to do, Congress would now be asked to undertake—unseat white politicians. Fannie Lou Hamer, Annie Devine, and Victoria Gray, representing the Mississippi Freedom Democratic Party, challenged the seating in the House of Representatives of five white men from Mississippi. The Freedom Democrats said that since black Mississippians were effectively denied the vote, the election of the five congressmen in the fall of 1964 was illegal.

This radical challenge put House members on the spot even more than Democratic convention delegates in Atlantic City had been. On Capitol Hill, a politician could not blend in with his or her state's delegation. House members would have to make their own on-the-record vote either for their congressional colleagues—and thus against the civil rights movement—or for the black challengers—and thus against long-standing niceties in a chamber where people were routinely referred to as "the gentleman from Mississippi" or "the honorable" so and so. Compromise, this time, would not wash the issue away.

Mississippi had ensured this new confrontation by refusing to place on the November 3 general election ballot the names of four MFDP candidates: Mrs. Hamer, Mrs. Devine, Mrs. Gray, and Aaron Henry, who would have run for U.S. Senate. They assuredly would have lost, given their links with the movement and the few black voters who were registered. But Mississippi stuck rigidly to form, and the state election commission said the four didn't have enough signatures of registered voters on their petitions to get on the ballot. The prospective black candidates denied that claim, saying that the county registrars had refused to certify the signatures. The registrar in Mrs. Gray's county, for example, first refused to certify the petitions until the voters' names were arranged by precinct. Even then, he certified only a few of the signatures, saying that many of the other people, while registered, hadn't paid their poll tax. Told that poll taxes did not apply to federal elections, the registrar said that federal laws had nothing to do with these signatures.[1]

After the general election, Mrs. Hamer, Mrs. Devine, Mrs. Gray, party chairman Lawrence Guyot, and others met in Washington with several congressional aides and attorney Arthur Kinoy, who proudly called himself a "people's lawyer." In a packed career, he had represented, among other clients, the United Electrical, Radio and Machine Workers, then one of the largest trade unions, in union-busting and Red-baiting cases. Kinoy, a short, intense man, outlined for the MFDP members various procedures under which the five Mississippi congressmen could be challenged.[2] He also explained the urgency of organizing political support behind the upcoming challenge. Mrs. Hamer went up to him after the meeting and said people really had been listening to him. Then, Kinoy said, "she smiled and said something that I have often remembered in meetings or in courtrooms when I find myself slightly carried away by the occasion: 'You must have been a Baptist preacher in your other life.' "[3]

The women needed no convincing to be the candidates named in the challenge. "I've never been afraid to step out and to reach out and to move out in order to make things happen," Victoria Gray said. "Kinoy was telling about this law that they'd unearthed and I got caught up in that thing and all I needed to know was that it was on the books and I thought, 'My God, if it's there, let's use it. . . . Let's test it.' "[4]

Few lawyers had been willing to take the risks entailed in helping civil rights demonstrators in Mississippi, and SNCC and the Freedom Democrats valued those who had taken that risk. Thus, they had freely accepted attorneys affiliated with the National Lawyers Guild despite opposition from other allies. At a New York meeting to discuss the future of the Mississippi Project immediately after the Democratic convention, Joseph Rauh had pointedly said: "I would like to drive out the Lawyers Guild. I think it is immoral to take help from communists."[5] But Bob Moses, Lawrence Guyot, and others were miffed at Rauh for what they viewed, at their most charitable moments, as divided loyalties at the Democratic convention. As Kinoy put it, Rauh's connections "with Johnson and Humphrey and the national leaders of the Democratic

Party proved closer than his ties with Bob Moses and Fannie Lou Hamer and the leaders of the MFDP."[6]

So Rauh was out, and Kinoy and his law partner, William Kunstler, along with Ben Smith of New Orleans and Morton Stavis of New York, were in. They had already been in Mississippi, trying to keep Council of Federated Organizations workers out of jail or free them once arrested. In July 1964, Kunstler and Kinoy had filed a complaint concerning the disappearance of Chaney, Goodman, and Schwerner even before their bodies had been found. Using a Reconstruction-era federal statute, they charged Neshoba County sheriff Lawrence Rainey with failing to protect the three young men's civil rights and called for emergency appointment of federal commissioners throughout the state who would be empowered to arrest anyone violating civil rights laws. In legalese, the suit was known as *COFO v. Rainey*. Mrs. Hamer and the other COFO people mimeographed the complaint and sent it all over the state to show that they were the plaintiffs—that they were taking the offensive after several years in which all the cases had been initiated by the government. Mrs. Hamer was the one putting that notion forward in the sharpest way, Kinoy said, that "we must never be on the defensive and that was her fundamental theme, that we have to be constantly taking the offensive."[7]

Kinoy and Kunstler had represented Mrs. Hamer and Mrs. Gray before. When the two women lost in the Democratic primary in June 1964, they and several other defeated candidates, as well as blacks who had been denied registration, sued the state, the Democratic Party, and the registrars of Bolivar, Marshall, and Humphreys counties. In a sweeping suit filed in federal court in Greenville, they charged a conspiracy to deny political participation to black people and their white allies who supported civil rights. The suit also sought to block the party from going on with its convention delegate-selection procedures until black voters were better able to participate in those deliberations. *Gray v. Mississippi* offered a framework for doing through the courts what the Freedom Democrats tried to do at the Democratic convention.[8] Dramatic as it was, the suit never went to trial because time rendered its remedies moot.

Well before the congressional challenge, Arthur Kinoy had learned a valuable lesson in political organizing from Fannie Lou Hamer. He was arguing a case against Mississippi authorities in federal court in Jackson. "Argued all day long," he remembered, "and at the end of the day, Mrs. Hamer was in the courtroom. And she grabbed hold of me and she said, 'Arthur, you've got to come to the church with me now to give a picture to all of our people as to what happened today in the courtroom because it's so important.' I was exhausted. I was tired. I said, 'Oh, Mrs. Hamer. I don't think I can make it.'

"She said, 'Arthur, you've got to understand that this kind of a meeting is more important than anything that goes on in the courtroom.' " So Kinoy went and when he got to the hall, his face froze. Only three people were there. "Mrs. Hamer took a look at me and she grabs a hold of me and she says, 'Arthur, there is one thing you have got to learn about our movement. Three people are better than no people.' " The organizing drive had just begun, and a few weeks later the churches would be jammed. Mrs. Hamer "more than almost anyone else . . . understood that the legal struggles were in essence organizing tools for the people's movement," Kinoy said. "The question was not whether or not you thought you were going to win ultimately in the Supreme Court or any of the higher courts or whether the precedents were all against you—and most of the time they were—but whether this was an organizing tool."[9]

Kinoy, Kunstler, and Ben Smith had attended a two-day meeting of COFO workers in Oxford, Mississippi, in October to plot strategy for activity after Atlantic City. Bob Moses wanted to show the nation that MFDP was not a one-shot organization that would fade away. One of the COFO workers said that it was clear that Mrs. Hamer, Mrs. Gray, and Mrs. Devine would have more right to sit in Congress than five white men once they won November's Freedom Vote. Anyone eligible could vote in that election, conducted over four days just before the regular election; it was designed to show once again that black people would vote if given the opportunity. From that suggestion, Kinoy said, grew the idea of challenging the Mississippi delegation.[10]

The lawyers found that House rules permitted challenging members on the day they were to be seated; furthermore, they allowed challengers the subpoena power to gather evidence that the clerk of the House would have to print for the public as well as members of Congress. Then a House committee would decide the merits of the challenge, followed by a vote of the full House. The formal procedure for gathering evidence "seemed too good to be true," Kinoy said. "I could just see the expression on Sheriff Rainey's face as we slapped a federal subpoena on him 'commanding' his presence at a hearing of ours!" he wrote with his emphatic enthusiasm in his autobiography, *Rights on Trial*.[11] Gathering evidence could prove yet another organizing tool.

The MFDP Washington office, headed by Mike Thelwell,

started lining up congressional backing and mounting a national lobbying campaign. Thelwell had not been convinced at first of the merits of the case. "The [white] Mississippians were saying that this challenge was off the wall. 'These ladies were not on the ballot. They were elected by rules we [Congress] didn't set up.' Where the hell is this challenge coming from? I myself thought that in purely legal terms, it didn't exist. But Kunstler and Kinoy said it's really political. Congress can seat them if they really want it to happen. And we have to make it happen."[12]

On December 4, a month before Congress would convene, Bill Kunstler met Mrs. Hamer, Mrs. Devine, and Mrs. Gray in Washington. They went to the office of Clerk of the House Ralph R. Roberts and filed the formal challenge. Ben Smith was in Mississippi making sure the notices were served on the congressmen.[13] Mrs. Hamer, for example, charged that Jamie Whitten was elected by 70,218 votes out of a total of 306,463 people of voting age, "an electorate from which Negroes are regularly and systematically excluded." She acknowledged that she had run against Whitten in the primary and had lost, 35,218 to 621, and then had been denied a place on the November ballot. But she felt the Freedom Election that fall gave a more accurate picture of her support. In that balloting, all citizens could vote "without intimidation or discrimination as to race and color," and Mrs. Hamer said she got 33,009 votes and Whitten only 59. More than 52 percent of the adult population of the Second District, which Whitten represented, was black; only 2.97 percent of those people had been permitted to register to vote in regular elections.

The women's legal papers gave a history of the disfranchisement of black voters, with particular attention to the 1962 package of voter-registration statutes that further reduced blacks' chances to register. They outlined efforts to intimidate black voters and civil rights workers, concluding that Mississippi had violated the agreement under which it was readmitted to the Union in 1870. Therefore, the November 1964 elections were invalid and each woman held that she should be seated instead of the congressmen who were being challenged.[14]

Under the MFDP strategy, once the Speaker of the House was sworn in on the opening day of Congress, a member of the House would get the speaker's attention just before the rest of the representatives rose to be sworn. He would challenge seating the Mississippians; those members challenged would have to stand aside while the rest were sworn in. "If we could do that," Thelwell recalled, "we felt it would be symbolic if only for five seconds.

. . . Our strategy was to find a congressman who would at least challenge the seating. But those we approached said no [because] we didn't have candidates who had really been on the ballot." The Freedom Democrats answered the hesitant members of Congress by saying theirs was an unusual challenge. "We had a fairness resolution. We were looking for a strategy to embarrass [the Mississippi congressmen]. We were saying nobody should be seated until Congress has a thorough investigation. Hold the seating in abeyance. Even that didn't play very well."

At last a popular congressman with a safe seat—William Fitts Ryan, who was in his third term from Manhattan's Upper West Side—said he would offer the challenge. Although not MFDP's first choice, because he was considered a maverick, Ryan was the only one who was prepared to step forward.

MFDP wanted others to stand with him so that Speaker John McCormack could not ignore the challenge. President Johnson's landslide election victory helped MFDP; his coattails had carried several dozen new members into Congress, including John Conyers, a black congressman from Detroit. "They were so new. Compared to them, we were pros," Thelwell said. "So we would try to get to them. They had to have an orientation because they were such a huge class. So we would find out where the briefing sessions were. . . . We did have some name recognition because of Atlantic City. So we sent out invitations and rented the room next door." Ryan briefed the freshmen, and about five said they would join him. "There was some white-haired guy from upstate New York who stood up and said his district had been Republican ever since the end of the Civil War. He said, 'I don't expect to be back in two years. I guess I might as well do some good while I'm here.' "

As opening day of the session neared, MFDP's leadership calculated that it had perhaps fifteen or twenty members who would stand with Ryan. "We hoped really to embarrass the Mississippi legislators. Just to get the issue raised. But to get that we had to survive certain key procedures. That was made hard because the liberal establishment—the people logically expected to carry the ball, like Rauh and the United Auto Workers and Clarence Mitchell [NAACP's chief lobbyist]—the whole liberal establishment who wasn't talking to us said it was 'just a quixotic plan by Kunstler and Kinoy, who are radical and reds anyway.' "[15]

The Americans for Democratic Action (ADA) put out a position paper in December opposing the challenge; Mike Thelwell considered it "a political hatchet job." Others would consider it a principled stand for democratic procedures. ADA said, "The contention that the Mrs. Hamer, Devine and Gray should be seated in Congress is without legal support and has dangerous implications. Their greatness as civil rights fighters is unquestioned; but the Congressional challenge they have been persuaded to make is something wholly different." ADA's executive committee advised its local chapters that the women's "illegal exclusion from the ballot is not a substitute for their election on the ballot." ADA warned that if this

> undeniable moral and emotional basis of their claim were sufficient to warrant seating them in Congress, some day an emotional but immoral claim might equally sweep the nation. For example, a right-wing movement claiming to represent the majority of voters in various areas might seek to blast its way into Congress on a wave of emotional hysteria against liberal principles. Legal processes afford protection to democracy; liberals can hardly support their destruction.[16]

ADA asserted, misleadingly, that "the vast bulk of the civil rights movement" opposed this challenge. True, middle-of-the-road black leaders like Roy Wilkins were not well disposed to the challenge. But MFDP had enthusiastic backing from Dr. Martin Luther King, Jr., James Farmer, and John Lewis. Furthermore, MFDP pointed out that anyone, "whether claiming the seat or not, is entitled to file a challenge." Congress could throw out the regular election without sustaining the women's claim to be seated, as it had in the past, the MFDP said.[17]

The Freedom Democrats were indeed ambivalent about precisely what they wanted: whether they wanted the congressmen ousted and new elections called or also wanted the three women seated. For example, the *Freedom Primer No. 3*, issued by the party in late 1964 or early 1965, said in no uncertain terms that Mrs. Hamer, Mrs. Devine, and Mrs. Gray "are going to Washington to tell Congress that they are the *real* representatives from Mississippi. . . . They are going to ask Congress to let them sit in the seats for Mississippi and talk in Congress about the things *you* want."[18] Mrs. Hamer's brief also stated that she should be seated, but despite that, she herself said the challenge was misunderstood. "We're not asking to be seated now in lieu of the five Congressmen," she told reporters. "We're asking that no one from Mississippi be seated until Congress has a chance to investigate the real story of voting in the state."[19]

As the positions were being argued, lobbying continued.

MFDP was trying to hold those members of Congress who had said they would stand with Ryan and perhaps add a few more. "What really turned it was we had Mrs. Hamer, Mrs. Devine, and Mrs. Gray going to meetings, trying to explain about the fairness resolution because the press was writing that what we wanted was to seat these three women," which was not the case, Thelwell said. "But then when people came up to talk to House members, there were sharecroppers, farmers, maids, cooks, a few teachers but mainly working people. Their presence for two or three days made a difference. What finally swung it—what gave us enough to force a roll call vote—was that some of the more influential liberals started to come over."[20]

On January 4, 1965, the Eighty-ninth Congress opened its session. Hundreds of people traveled by bus from Mississippi, having raised money for the trip with fish fries, cake sales, and pie suppers. Before going to Capitol Hill, the challengers held a briefing at a local church. Lawrence Guyot told the group that once again America would have brought to its attention "the repression and intimidation under which Mississippi's Negroes live and die." Then Mrs. Hamer set the tone when she said, "We are here for our own people—and we are here for all the people."[21]

On Capitol Hill, Kunstler and Kinoy escorted the women to the door of the chamber of the House of Representatives. The chief of the capitol police, Carl Schamp, and several other officers met the women at the door. They were told that only newly elected members could enter. The women showed Schamp affidavits that they were contesting seats. "You may not enter here," Schamp said quietly.

"But we are attempting to enter as contestants," said Victoria Gray.

"You cannot come on the floor of the House. You do not have floor privileges."[22]

An American Nazi dressed as a minstrel with black face slipped into the House chamber at the same time but was quickly hustled out. That night at a rally, Mrs. Hamer asked, "How could twelve policemen block us but could not see that man in the black-face?"[23]

Mrs. Hamer had supporters mobilized at home as well as in Washington. Three hundred people demonstrated that same day by marching around the Sunflower County courthouse in Indianola, shouting, "Uhuru"—meaning "Freedom"—and carrying signs saying, "DOWN WITH JAMIE WHITTEN," "GET RID OF EASTLAND," and "WE WANT FANNIE HAMER." Fifty people also tried to register but were denied admittance to the registrar's office.[24]

As the swearing in was about to begin at the Capitol, there were too many people, too few passes, to seat all the Mississippians in the gallery. Because it was winter, members of Congress would be walking inside through the tunnel from their office buildings to the chamber in the Capitol Building. A silent line of black people greeted them in those tunnels, one person standing about every ten yards: maids, farmers, a few teachers, but mainly people who worked with their hands and their backs. "They had no signs. That wasn't allowed. They just stood there," Thelwell said. "It was very impressive. It was very intimidating—I don't mean in a physical sense but in a moral sense. You could see it having an account."[25]

Said one congressman: "When I started into the tunnel, I knew I was going to vote to seat the [white] Mississippians. The farther I got, the more I weakened. Finally I had to say to myself, 'What kind of person are you?' " He got to the floor of the House and told majority leader Carl Albert, "I'm sorry—I'm not going with you on Mississippi. I can't vote against those people out there."[26]

The session started. Speaker McCormack was sworn in. The minority leader, the gentleman from Michigan, Gerald R. Ford, praised McCormack, who pledged cooperation with the Johnson-Humphrey administration. "According to the precedent," McCormack then said, "the chair is now ready to swear in all Members of the House. The members will rise."

Ryan rose first. "Mr. Speaker!"

"For what purpose does the gentleman from New York rise?"

"Mr. Speaker, on my responsibility as a Member-elect of the 89th Congress, I object to the oath being administered to the gentlemen from Mississippi [Democrats Thomas G. Abernethy, Jamie L. Whitten, John Bell Williams, and William Colmer, and Republican Prentiss Walker]. I base this upon facts and statements which I consider to be reliable. I also make this objection on behalf of a significant number of colleagues who are now standing with me."[27]

There was literally a groundswell. About seventy members stood with Ryan. "I almost started shouting up there in the gallery," Thelwell recalled. "I thought we would get maybe fifteen people."[28] Kinoy and the challengers were excited as well. Victoria Gray leaned over to the attorney and whispered, "We did it. Even if just for this moment, we did it."[29]

All but the challenged members were sworn in. Then Majority Leader Carl Albert of Oklahoma, acting on a request he had received from Speaker McCormack, offered a resolution that the Mississippians be sworn in. Any question involving the validity of their election should be dealt with under standard procedures for contested elections: that is, through a House committee. Albert had already told Ryan that the full weight of the Johnson administration would be thrown against the challenge.[30]

Edith Green of Oregon, who had supported the black Mississippians to the end in Atlantic City, asked for a roll call vote: 276 yeas, 149 nays, one present. The Mississippians then stepped forward and were sworn into office. "It was easy to see why most Congressmen didn't want a roll call," columnist Drew Pearson reported. "For it showed such avowed champions of civil rights as Manny Celler of Brooklyn, author of the civil rights bill, voting against the Negroes of Mississippi." Several other New York civil rights advocates voted with Celler, "thereby demonstrating the alliance between big city machines and the conservative South when it comes to personal backscratching."[31]

Despite the setback, Ryan pushed on. He reminded his House colleagues that "the terror, violence and murder perpetrated last summer upon those who attempted to help their fellow citizens exercise their right to vote focused national attention upon the fact that Mississippi tramples upon the U.S. Constitution by denying American citizens the right to vote." He reiterated Mississippi's legislative steps to control black voting, adding, "laws are apparently not enough, for there is also economic reprisal, threats, intimidation and violence," not only toward blacks who try to vote but also toward their white allies. "According to the Justice Department in McComb, Miss., alone, there were from June to October 1964, 17 bombings of churches, homes and businesses; 32 arrests; 9 beatings; and 4 church burnings as a result of voter registration and civil rights activity." Continuing with damning numbers, Ryan said that the Justice Department had already sued twenty-seven of Mississippi's eighty-two counties. In seven cases so far, courts had found a pattern or practice of discrimination.[32]

Supporting Ryan, Congressman James Roosevelt of California said the Mississippi members of the House claimed their constituents would have no representation if they were not seated. "But their constitutents will not have representation if we do seat them. We must say to them that they cannot run a society like Soviet Russia and then claim seats in the American Congress; that they cannot 'win' elections with a system based on murder and then claim the right to govern."[33]

Because of the usual courtly standards of House debate, no one ever touched on the manner in which the five Mississippians represented their constituents, nor would any of the members do so when the matter came to the floor again the following fall. Roosevelt's allusion to lack of representation for a substantial number of

Mississippians—black Mississippians—was the closest anyone would come to discussing this sin of omission of which many of them might be guilty. The Freedom Democrats were not so shy. Mrs. Hamer often referred to Jamie Whitten's vote against a program that would have retrained farm workers, a move that would have benefited black Mississippians left unemployed by mechanization. MFDP's Washington office prepared a nineteen-page report on the congressmen's records, showing, for example, that the four long-term officeholders consistently voted against programs that would benefit poor people, such as rent control, farmworker protection, low-cost public housing, federal aid to education, or food stamps. MFDP also pointed out that Walker, a Republican who had just been elected, "celebrated his victory for the party of Abraham Lincoln by making his first public appearance after the election before the Americans for the Preservation of the White Race in Brandon, Mississippi, on November 24, 1964."[34]

After the vote, the three women and their lawyers were briefing supporters waiting outside the Capitol. James P. Coleman, attorney for the challenged congressmen and a former governor of Mississippi, handed each woman a formal-looking legal document. What was of more interest than the documents denying voting discrimination was the envelope in which the response to Mrs. Hamer's challenge was contained. "On its rear side were a series of hatch marks penciled by Coleman as he had made his unofficial count of the vote on Albert's resolution," Kunstler wrote. "It was quite obvious that the ex-governor, at least, was taking the challenges very seriously indeed."[35]

Now came the next stage: informing the public about the challenge, lobbying Congress, organizing support around the country and at home in Mississippi. Although they functioned as a team, the three women, in fact, had distinctly different personalities. Victoria Gray (now Adams) explained the nuances of these roles. Mrs. Hamer was the orator, the one who took the message to the people, she said, while she herself would think about the tactics they should use. "And Mrs. Devine supplied the wisdom. . . . She could discern and focus. . . . I might get carried away [looking at some aspect of strategy], and Fannie Lou might be flying, you know," and Mrs. Devine would say, " 'Now wait a minute. Let's examine this.' We had a little apartment that we shared there [on Capitol Hill] and we had great times together, but whenever there was a task to be done, there was never any argument. Each person knew what it was."[36]

Northerners had heard most about Mrs. Hamer because of her credentials committee testimony. "People begged to have Mrs.

Hamer stay with them. That was a whole technique," said Jan Goodman, who worked in the MFDP Washington office. "Let me say this: if we could have brought Mrs. Hamer up [from Mississippi] every time, we would have," Goodman added. "So wherever we could, not so much to send her to the congressional delegations, but for fundraising and rally-type things, wherever we could get Mrs. Hamer, we would, but she was much harder to get than the others because it just wasn't her priority."[37]

The scene shifted from Washington back to Mississippi, both because MFDP lawyers were gathering statements there about discrimination against black voters and because the MFDP leaders had lives to lead and chores to do that took them home. Mrs. Hamer's priorities then, as almost always, involved organizing her neighbors at home in Sunflower County and trying to spend as much time with her family as her travel schedule permitted. Her daughter Dorothy Jean became pregnant that year, and her first child, Lenora, was born October 29, 1965.

Mrs. Hamer, who cared deeply for her daughter and later adopted Lenora and her younger sister, Jacqueline, when Dorothy died, rarely spoke publicly about events within her own family, so little is recorded about her innermost feelings. But she did comment that one of her white friends in California had told her, "me traveling, it might affect my reputation for her to have this child at home, and why didn't I send her off? And I told them I would stick as close to her as I could. So I kept her at home."[38]

In addition to family concerns, Mrs. Hamer's health was not good—and would not be for the rest of her life. After the initial vote in Washington, she had gone to a New York hospital for more treatment for ailments caused by the Winona beating.[39]

Mrs. Hamer was learning that movement activists did not have the luxury of concentrating on one campaign at a time. That same spring, black tractor drivers and other field workers in the Delta were organizing the Mississippi Freedom Labor Union, and she spoke out in their behalf. She was not especially a strategist in their ranks, but she could get press attention for their cause. A dozen tractor drivers and their families struck for higher wages on the A. L. and W. B. Andrews plantation at Tribbett, near Greenville, and Andrews retaliated by evicting them.[40] The strike leaders brought in Mrs. Hamer to shore up their nerve. First, she spoke at a Cleveland church at a meeting to discuss a potential strike, then she rode south to the dusty front yard of the Bogue grocery store near the Andrews' farm. Introduced as one who "started as a cotton chopper and will end as a Congresswoman," Mrs. Hamer assured the twelve strikers that she wouldn't go back into the fields to break their strike and declared that no one else should.

"We got to stop the nervous Nellies and the Toms from going to the Man's place," she shouted, as perspiration dripped down her face on that hot June night. "I don't believe in killing, but a good whipping behind the bushes wouldn't hurt them."[41] Mrs. Hamer didn't like other people—white people—messing with black people, but she didn't mind telling them off herself. She wanted the black community to understand that the actions of each affected others.[42] In her fiery speech, Mrs. Hamer scored "chicken-eating preachers" who supported neither civil rights nor farm workers' efforts, adding, "These bourgeoisie Negroes aren't helping. It's the ghetto Negroes who are leading the way. . . . I admire you for quitting before you got fired."

Because she had worked in the fields herself, Mrs. Hamer may have been more interested in the labor union than many of the other movement leaders. She believed that for the black people of rural Mississippi, jobs with living wages must accompany freedom, that there could not be one without the other. As years went on, this would become a growing concern and lead her to develop the Freedom Farm cooperative. But despite her support, the farm union, a largely unstudied phenomenon, soon dwindled away, plowed under by the planters' machines and the indifference of other labor unions.[43] There was no Cesar Chavez in Mississippi.

Closer to home, people in Ruleville busily distributed food and clothing to those who had little income because they had lost their jobs as a result of either civil rights activity or increasing farm mechanization. They were building a community center, with northern groups paying the construction costs. The COFO staff canvassed the town thoroughly to build support for the congressional challenge. Ruleville was divided into three precincts that each had weekly meetings about the challenge or about voter registration. There were mass meetings every Friday night as well.[44] Mrs. Hamer was deeply involved in all these activities. For example, she told some of the young people they had a right to use the local library, which had always been segregated. And so they integrated it.

"Ruleville is a pretty well organized town," SNCC volunteer Linda Davis reported. "Local people are taking responsibility for just about everything. The problem here is the despair and subsequent apathy of some people who have been working hard for over two years and don't see any change. Some people have been down to register 15, 18, even 23 times."[45]

That winter and early spring, a deposition detail of some one hundred fifty lawyers was deployed to collect evidence for the congressional challenge. The attorneys traveled through Mississippi churches and courthouses in thirty-three counties to gather fifteen thousand pages of testimony from six hundred witnesses. They heard from black people who had been denied the right to vote. And they had the power to compel testimony from the state officials responsible.[46]

The basic pattern of the testimony was the same across the state. In Batesville, for example, Robert Miles, then fifty, who had been an MFDP delegate in Atlantic City, testified about the cancellation of all his insurance after his first attempt to register, of a threat to kill him, and of the reprisals that had always stopped black voter registration.[47] Miles's house had also been bombed twice during the summer of 1964 and shot at many times. Not long after he testified, Miles and several hundred other Batesville citizens were set upon by local whites while waiting to learn how a local court would rule in a case involving several civil rights workers and black residents charged with parading without a permit. Miles fought back and was arrested. A few days later someone fired a shotgun through the window of Miles's front door. The pellets narrowly missed two young white civil rights workers who were staying with him.[48]

In Jackson, many state officials, including four of the challenged congressmen, attended the deposition sessions. There the lawyers, and many black residents of Jackson, heard testimony from a former governor, the Mississippi secretary of state, and the state's attorney general. Asked what he had done in support of blacks' rights to register and vote, Attorney General Joe Patterson said, "I haven't done anything." The audience clapped and hooted, and Patterson threatened to get a federal marshal to clear the room. MFDP attorney Morton Stavis reminded him that he was not in charge. Later, a group of young blacks quietly entered the room to watch; former Governor Coleman, representing the challenged congressmen, said he hadn't known the hearing was going to provide entertainment for a local audience. "So I am going to take it upon myself to lock the door. Those people have no interest in this," Coleman said.

"Just a moment, Mr. Coleman," Stavis said. "This is a group of 20 to 25 people, vitally interested in the proceedings, and they are quietly standing and listening. As long as these proceedings remain orderly, we will insist that the doors remain open. We will not tolerate the exclusion of any citizen of Mississippi."[49]

"We learned a lot from the testimony of the state's witnesses," MFDP attorney Kunstler said.

Attorney General [Joe] Patterson, for example, admitted that in the five dozen voting suits filed against county voting registrars by the federal government, he had sprung to the defense of the attacked officials without investigating their guilt or innocence. Director [Erle] Johnston of the Sovereignty Commission conceded that he had dispensed hundreds of thousands of dollars from the state treasury to help the White Citizens Council maintain racial segregation. One of his investigators revealed that it was part of his job to spy on Negroes trying to register.[50]

Despite edginess at these hearings, the challengers' attorneys noticed new willingness to cooperate among state officials. Governor Paul Johnson had attended the presidential inauguration in Washington and realized that the challenge was serious business: The whole delegation might be ousted. *New Orleans Times-Picayune* correspondent William F. Minor, who provided some of the most accurate coverage of the movement, reported: "Johnson saw fit to tell the people that they should be on their best behavior in preserving the peace so that no incident would mar the chances of the state holding its congressional seats." Officials in counties where no blacks, or only a handful of elderly blacks, were registered had the law laid down to them that qualified blacks had to be registered.[51]

Soon after Governor Johnson returned from Washington, he received a letter from state senator Hayden Campbell, a State Sovereignty Commission member, about "the threat of radical groups to unseat our Congressmen." He urged that the Sovereignty Commission, established ostensibly to preserve states' rights in the face of school desegregation orders, provide money to "help defray the cost of opposing these efforts to rob a sovereign state of its duly elected members of Congress."[52]

Governor Johnson, not noted for racially moderate views, called off a special session of the state legislature that had been planned to denounce the 1964 Civil Rights Act. Once he had called for Mississippians not to obey that law; now he told five hundred bankers and business leaders meeting in Jackson, "Law and order is going to prevail, particularly for the next six months."[53]

But law and order were not prevailing in Selma, Alabama, where SNCC volunteers had been working for some time with local leaders like Amelia Boynton to increase the number of black registered voters. In Selma, the civil rights efforts met brutal resistance from Sheriff Jim Clark. Local authorities tried to head off violence by asking the Justice Department to intervene to prevent Dr. King, who had just been awarded the Nobel Peace Prize, from joining the crusade. But King went to Selma, and the protests escalated. Soon the nation's major papers carried photographs of Clark shoving Mrs. Boynton with his billy club.

Malcolm X also went to Selma, where he told an audience at Brown's Chapel, staging ground for many of the protests, "If the white people realize what the alternative is, perhaps they will be more willing to hear Dr. King."[54]

King was arrested and jailed, a young protester named Jimmy Lee Jackson was killed, and pressure mounted on President Johnson for a voting rights bill that would, as King told the press, "end the necessity for any more voting rights bills."[55] Finally, with King away from Selma, on March 7, 1965, demonstrators started a march toward Montgomery to take their case to the state capitol. Led by Hosea Williams of SCLC and John Lewis, the marchers got only as far as the Edmund Pettus Bridge on the edge of town, where state troopers charged them, flailing billy clubs and firing tear gas canisters.

The spectacle galvanized America, and hundreds of out-of-state demonstrators poured into the city to join King to complete the Selma-to-Montgomery march. The Reverend James Reeb, a Unitarian minister from Boston, was clubbed to death by whites, and Viola Liuzzo was shot and killed by Ku Klux Klansmen while driving to Montgomery to pick up prospective marchers. The violence, the deaths, and the perseverance of the living finally convinced Congress to pass the landmark Voting Rights Act of 1965.[56]

With national attention diverted to Selma and with a leisurely timetable for Mississippi's challenged congressmen to respond to the evidence being gathered against them, the Freedom Democrats were finding it difficult to keep up their momentum. In late April, the MFDP called a meeting of the civil rights movement, unions, and churches in Washington to plan the next phase. Four hundred people attended and heard speeches by Lawrence Guyot, Mrs. Hamer, Mrs. Devine, and Mrs. Gray. Mrs. Hamer worried that the voting rights bill moving through Congress was an attempt to choke off the congressional challenge.[57] Congress, like the Democratic Party, seemed much more inclined to prohibit future discrimination rather than act against past, especially when its members feared the precedent that ousting the Mississippi representatives might set.

Back in Mississippi, some of the MFDP workers wanted their "congresswomen" to speak more around the state. But Mrs. Devine reminded them that this was not a party of a few people but of many. She told an MFDP meeting in Jackson that "unless local people took up their load and went to work and stopped depending on [the] Congresswomen, the party would have already failed."[58]

On May 17, the eleventh anniversary of the Supreme Court

decision outlawing school segregation, the Freedom Democrats submitted their depositions to the clerk of the House. Dr. Martin Luther King, Jr., James Farmer, and John Lewis took the opportunity to renew their support for the MFDP challenge. King was particularly critical of the Senate because it had just dropped abolition of the poll tax from the proposed Voting Rights Act. King said that that action "makes it absolutely imperative that the House of Representatives does not waver in its obligations" to unseat the Mississippi congressmen.[59]

Governor Johnson called the Mississippi legislature into session to expunge requirements that voter applicants must read and understand the state constitution. But at the same time, the legislature passed laws restricting demonstrations near public buildings; the city of Jackson, where the legislature met, enforced its own tough ordinances against distributing leaflets without a permit. So MFDP took to the streets, sending hundreds of people out to protest that summer. The demonstrators contended that the legislature was acting to thwart the intent of the pending federal voting rights bill. They also argued that, because blacks still could not vote freely, the legislature was illegally constituted.[60]

The first day of protests, June 14, 482 people were arrested in Jackson. Then 204 the next. By June 30, the Justice Department had recorded 1,028 arrests.[61] Police first hauled the arrested demonstrators to jail, then, when the jail was filled, to the fairgrounds, where they baked in the late June heat. The arrests stopped after the federal court of appeals blocked the city from enforcing ordinances requiring permits for parades and handbill distribution.

During these demonstrations, Mrs. Devine was arrested for the only time in her life. She was working in the MFDP office in Jackson and knew someone had to stay out of jail. But she looked out the window and saw armed policemen blocking the street.

> I rushed downstairs and there was an old broken down car sitting there on the lot—a vacant lot right by the café—and [I] jumped up on top of that car. . . . I said, "Why do they come with those billy clubs in order to beat us down? But we're not going to be beaten down." And before I could get through with what I had to say, one of them said, "Arrest that woman in blue." And so here they come to get me down off that car. I said, "I can walk." So they handcuffed me and put me in the wagon.

She stayed in jail about five hours. The white policemen didn't care about black women who were demonstrating, Mrs. Devine said, but it killed them when they saw white women marching. They arrested one white girl who walked with a cane, she said, then picked her up and dropped her in the van, hard. "Like animals."[62]

In Washington, House clerk Ralph Roberts refused to print all the testimony gathered in Mississippi. After negotiations, he agreed to print some of the documents, then backed off again, saying the documents were not properly certified. MFDP supporters from around the country soon swamped him with letters and phone calls. Writing in *The New Yorker,* Richard Rovere said that the party's lawyers, "many of them men of enormous skill and varied experiences, did their legal work atrociously"; there were "so many procedural oversights that the clerk was able to say that their failure to conform to established standards made it impossible for him to order their printing."[63]

Exasperated, Mrs. Gray led a delegation to try to see the House clerk. On the first visit, Roberts was away. The group sat down and began to sing, "We want justice, Lord, come by here. / Oh, Lord, come by here." Roberts's assistant then gave Mrs. Gray an appointment with the clerk the following morning. That morning, another assistant told Mrs. Gray that Roberts wasn't there because he had to attend a funeral. Complaining about broken promises, the group sat on the marble floor outside the clerk's office. They would wait until Roberts returned, they said. The police arrived and closed off the corridor to the public.[64] When the group refused to leave the Capitol at closing time, police arrested ten people, who spent the weekend in jail. "As one having gone to jail in the South, I was really appalled at the difference in spite of everything," Mrs. Gray said. "First of all, I had never been relieved of my clothes. I was shocked. To me that was much worse than being jailed in Mississippi."[65]

In July, the case went to trial. The government dropped the charges after House speaker John McCormack intervened upon learning that the defendants had apparently acted in good faith.[66] Roberts relented and at the end of July sent three 1,000-page volumes to the speaker of the House. The printing furor was important because MFDP wanted to ensure that each member of Congress saw the weight of the evidence supporting its argument that the 1964 election was fraudulent.

In the meantime, Congress was focusing on the proposed Voting Rights Act. How far should it go in opening the voting rolls to blacks? The 1964 Civil Rights Act had sidestepped voting, dealing more with public accommodations. Selma and its violence had created a moral imperative for Congress to act (although Mrs. Hamer believed, rightly, that those demonstrations diverted attention from the congressional challenge[67]). The Freedom Democrats strongly favored an even tougher voting rights bill than ultimately passed, one that would order new elections after voter registrars were sent into an area so that local officials who were symbols of brutality could be removed from office quickly.[68]

President Johnson had gone before Congress to urge passage of the legislation, closing his speech by proclaiming in his Texas drawl, "And we *will* overcome." The resulting Voting Rights Act, signed on August 6, suspended literacy tests and other discriminatory registration practices, directed the Justice Department to file suits to strike down poll taxes, provided that federal examiners be sent to help sign up voters in many southern counties, and required that changes in voter laws in many states be cleared through the Justice Department before taking effect.

Now Congress had landmark legislation on its side. See, its members could say, we acted. The MFDP challengers may have been victims of their own success. The Freedom Democrats, along with John Lewis and Amelia Boynton and the other demonstrators in Selma and across the South, had kept the issue of denial of the right to vote before the American people and their representatives in Congress. But now passage of the Voting Rights Act would undoubtedly kill whatever hope there was, however unrealistic, of ousting the Mississippi congressmen. There was now the legitimate means to prevent injustices in the future, but members of Congress were unwilling to correct the illegalities of the past. Then they, too, might be held accountable.

President Johnson was, however, sending mixed signals to Congress. In June, at the height of debate on the voting bill and at a point when the congressional challenge awaited consideration, Johnson nominated the Mississippi congressmen's lawyer, former governor Coleman, to the U.S. Court of Appeals. While more moderate than, say, Ross Barnett or Paul Johnson, Coleman was still considered a stout segregationist.

In mid-August, the MFDP stepped up the pressure for action on the challenge, bringing in a lawyers' lobby and then a clergymen's lobby seeking a vote. Congressmen Edwards, Conyers, and Ryan urged the chairman of the subcommittee considering the challenge to take action.[69] Dr. King sent a telegram to the Leadership Conference for Civil Rights calling for an emergency meeting for September 10 and urging it to make a clear statement of support for the challenge.[70]

At the end of August, the Mississippi congressmen asked that the challenge be dismissed on grounds that the MFDP members had not been on the ballot and therefore were not proper people "to contest said election." Accordingly, the chairman of the House Subcommittee on Elections, Democrat Robert Ashmore of South Carolina, scheduled a September 13 hearing not on the challenge itself but on the congressmen's motion to dismiss. The hearing would be closed.

"It is difficult to understand what might be said in these hearings that must be kept secret," Mrs. Gray said. "Some 600 people from Mississippi who are vitally concerned with these challenges are en route to Washington. This issue affects their lives and constitutional rights, and I cannot understand why Mr. Ashmore should want to bar them from the hearing. What can occur in these hearings that must be kept from the press and the nation?"[71]

The hearing was set for room H-329 of the Capitol, a small room reached by an elevator few knew existed. Only the challengers, the challenged, and subcommittee members would be present. The press was not allowed on the third floor to wait for the hearing to break up. Unlike in Atlantic City, the closed doors stayed closed. But there was a congressional stenographer present. Ashmore said later that he had closed the hearings because the case was built entirely on "racism and emotionalism" that the press wanted to exploit and because he needed to prevent crowds of demonstrators from taking over the hearings.[72]

The hearing began on Monday morning, September 13.[73] The atmosphere was testy from the outset. Kunstler objected to the closed hearing. "People have come from Mississippi to witness all stages of this challenge, and the press is interested in the challenge," Kunstler said, noting the presence of police all around the Capitol and the elaborate identification procedures needed for even the participants to get into the hearing. "We think it is a mistake to hide these hearings."

"Your motion is noted and overruled," said Ashmore.

Congressman Colmer, dean of the Mississippi House delegation, summed up his colleagues' position by pointing out that "a self-styled 'Freedom Democratic Party' group held what they were pleased to term 'freedom elections' in three Congressional districts"—what he called "nothing but mock elections, tantamount to straw votes . . . held without any sanction of law." The challengers had been selected in those elections, which were not valid under Mississippi law, and were not on the official November ballot. "In order for there to be a legal contest in the House of Representatives, there must be a legal, bona fide contestant," and these challengers did not fit that requirement, Colmer said. He noted that the chal-

lengers' "scattergun attempt to make a case" was based on the
theory that Mississippi's election laws were illegal in that they violated the agreement under which the state was readmitted to the
Union after the Civil War. "If this contention be justified," Colmer
told the subcommittee, "then it is common knowledge that every
state in the Confederacy—Virginia, North Carolina, South Carolina, Georgia, Florida, Alabama, Louisiana, Texas and Arkansas as
well as Mississippi—are in the same position."

Mrs. Hamer and the other challengers knew that Colmer was
trying to reduce their moral claim to an absurdity—and to throw the
fear of subsequent challenges into all other southern members of
Congress. On strictly legal grounds, he was right. The women had
not been on the ballot. They had taken their case to Congress to try
to demonstrate once again the futility blacks faced when they tried
to work within the political system in Mississippi. They were enraged by their opponents' attempts to use passage of the Voting
Rights Act—which all the Mississippians had voted against—as
another argument against the challenge. And they were angry about
the secret hearings. " 'With the people, for the people, by the people,' " Mrs. Hamer complained. "I crack up when I hear it; I say,
with the handful, for the handful, by the handful, 'cause that's really
what happens. . . ."[74]

Then the challengers presented their case. Victoria Gray
quoted the words of the last black member of Congress from Mississippi, John Roy Lynch, as he argued for (and won) a seat in the
House. The black people of the South had remained loyal to the
U.S. government during the Civil War and asked no special protection, Lynch had said. "They feel that they purchased their inheri-
tance when upon the battlefields of the country they won the
freedom of liberty with the precious blood of their loyal veins. They
asked no favors. They demand what they deserve and must have,
an equal chance in the race of life."

Asked whether she had been a contestant in the fall election,
Mrs. Gray recited the difficulty getting the Forrest County circuit
clerk to certify the signatures on her petition. She was also asked
whether she knew of any attempts that Congressman Colmer had
personally made to prevent blacks from participating in the election. She said she did not, adding that the challengers had made no
such claim. She concluded that Congress must not allow the history
of disenfranchisement to repeat itself, "that time is short, the hour
is late, the matter is urgent."

Annie Devine testified that she, too, had tried to get her name
on the ballot but the county registrar once again refused to certify

the names of qualified voters on her petition. When asked if she knew whether Congressman Walker had been a party to any exclusion of black voters, she said: "Mr. Walker knows about 56,000 people in the Fourth District had nothing to do with his election." Fifty-six thousand black people. Mrs. Devine said she couldn't answer whether Walker personally had excluded anyone, adding: "Maybe I should ask a question. Who is responsible? We come to the Congress of the United States."

Two other witnesses testified,[75] then Mrs. Hamer spoke. Black people in Mississippi, she said, do not feel safe going to "what are called police officials or state highway patrols" to be protected.

> I am standing here today suffering with a permanent kidney injury and a blood clot in the artery from the left eye from a beating I got inside of the jail in Winona, Mississippi, because I was participating in voter registration, and these orders was ordered by a county deputy, a state highway patrol. I want to say something else. When we go back home from this meeting here today, we stand a chance of being shot down, or either blown to bits in the state of Mississippi. . . .
>
> You gentlemen should know that the Negroes make up 58 percent of the potential voters of the Second Congressional District. This means that if Negroes were allowed to vote freely, I could be sitting up here with you right now as a Congresswoman.

Mrs. Hamer said that federal examiners had just been sent to Leflore County, where Greenwood is located. In just a few weeks, more than three thousand blacks had registered to vote, reflecting "the eagerness of the Mississippi Negro to participate in the elective process." But Mississippi was retaliating through lawsuits to try to keep newly registered voters off the rolls and through renewed violence and threats. "Sweeping this challenge under the rug now and dismissing this challenge, I think would be wrong for the whole country because it is time for the American people to wake up. All we want is a chance to participate in the government of Mississippi." With all the violence and people killed, she added, no one had been convicted for these crimes and no one had served any prison time for them.

> It is only when we speak what is right that we stands a chance at night of being blown to bits in our homes. Can we call this a free country, where I am afraid to go to sleep in my own home in Mississippi? I am not saying that Mr. Whitten or the other congress-

men helps in that, but I am saying that they know this is going on. . . . I might not live two hours after I get back home, but I want to be a part of helping set the Negro free in Mississippi.

In the evenings as the subcommittee was considering the challenge, Mrs. Hamer spoke at rallies at a nearby church. She told the crowd about all the police outside the hearing room and about telling the Mississippi congressmen, "I don't know if you did it, but I do know you know what went on in Mississippi—the shooting, killing and burning. It's time for America to get right." One night Mrs. Devine spoke about how disgusting she found the hearings. The Republicans asked the best questions but still seemed unwilling to irritate their southern colleagues, she said, adding that the Mississippi congressmen's attitude was that their slaves had been taken away from them and they still couldn't forget it.[76]

The subcommittee recommended dismissing the challenge. On September 15, the full House Administration Committee also voted, nineteen to five, against the challengers. The committee, headed by Texan Omar Burleson, did not deny that there was discrimination against blacks but rather adopted the contention of the congressmen that the challengers were not certified candidates. Its recommendation to the full House included a warning that the House would "carefully scrutinize" future elections for racial discrimination.[77] A minority of committee members dissented. Led by Congressman Gus Hawkins of California, the dissenters wanted the committee to hold public hearings on the challenge. When a person could not register or get on the ballot, then requiring an individual to be a candidate before he could contest an election was meaningless, they said.[78]

The full House would debate the measure on Friday, September 17. The civil rights leadership, belatedly in some cases, swung into action, trying to win the challenge on the floor. The group, organized by Dr. Robert Spike of the National Council of Churches, argued that no public hearings had been held on the challenge, and the evidence gathered by the challengers had not even been made available to all the House members. Dr. Martin Luther King, Jr., pointed out the civilized nature of the Freedom Democrats' challenge. "They have not rioted. They have destroyed neither person nor property in their pursuit of justice," King said in a telegram to Congressman Ryan. "They have, instead, sought diligently to apply the statutes of our Constitution."[79]

Thursday, September 16, the day before the House vote, was filled with more lobbying, a quiet vigil across from the Capitol, and a special prayer meeting at the National Cathedral. One man, talking to others about the challenge, was told to stop making a political speech. "I'm not making a political speech," he replied. "I'm talking about democracy."

Once again as the lawmakers opened their session, black Mississippians stood in vigil before the Capitol. The galleries were full. Speaker John McCormack had invited Mrs. Hamer, Mrs. Devine, and Mrs. Gray to sit on the House floor during the debate. Some of the black congressmen felt that would hurt their cause, and Representative Adam Clayton Powell of New York suggested to the women that they not accept McCormack's invitation. "Do you know who I am?" Powell asked Mrs. Hamer in what one onlooker called "the tone of a man who felt himself God's gift to Negritude."[80] In turn, Mrs. Hamer described some of the frightened black congressmen when the challenge came up for a vote as "standing there shaking in their boots, stripped of all their manhood."[81]

"I was not concerned with the outcome," Victoria Gray said. If the women's presence on the floor was going to affect the way some people voted, it would affect it. "I was concerned about the people up there in that gallery that day. I knew what price they had paid to get there."[82] What would those people say if the challengers did not appear?

Then Congressman Ryan, sponsor of the challenge, and California lawmakers Philip Burton and Don Edwards escorted the three women into the chamber. They were the first black women ever seated on the floor of the House, and the first black Mississippians since 1882. Just as Victoria Gray had whispered to Kinoy in January, now Lawrence Guyot exclaimed, "We did it. We did it."

The women gripped the arms of their chairs as the debate began. They sat at the back, on the Democratic side, neatly dressed, virtually motionless.[83] "The first thought that came to me was—I was looking at our own Congressmen and I was looking at those people who had helped us get that far—I was grateful to be there," Mrs. Devine said. "To me, the purpose was different but it was just as exciting as maybe the March on Washington. It was better for me. Like some people, I wasn't at the March. Some people could say, you know, 'We sat there and we dipped our feet in the water.' It was just a lovely get-together day. But this is the day when you are sitting and looking at these people that you're challenging and you're free to sit here. You're free. This is what you wanted to do. It was a remarkable feeling."[84]

Ashmore, as chairman of the elections subcommittee, spoke

first. On the challengers' contention that they had been dis-criminated against, even if that were true, Ashmore said, "My friends, how can you, or I, or the members from Mississippi, know of, or control, these officers back home when we are attempting to attend to our duties here for 10, 11 or 12 months out of the year?" Moreover, Ashmore said, the Voting Rights Act of 1965 was by then law, and, in the future, similar practices that the challengers complained about would violate that act. Ashmore did not allude to the fact that he had voted against the law.[85]

Those who would dismiss the challenge repeated this argu-ment: that the Voting Rights Act would now prevent the kind of behavior about which Mrs. Hamer, Mrs. Gray, Mrs. Devine, and the Freedom Democrats were complaining. Their backers said the evidence that Mississippi had discriminated against black voters was uncontradicted. If that "is not sufficient to serve as the basis for a proper challenge," asked Congressman Hawkins, one of the senior black Democrats, "then what evidence shall suffice?" Oth-ers joined Hawkins by arguing that the hearings were too brief and should not have been held in secret. Nor, said James Roose-velt of California, should Congress allow people to continue serv-ing who had been chosen by "a perversion and misuse" of elective processes.

Then Ryan put the question plainly: whether the House of Representatives would stand by the Constitution and the Fifteenth Amendment, which provides, "The right of citizens of the United States to vote shall not be denied or abridged by the United States, or by any state, on account of race, color or previous condition of servitude."

Once again, the Mississippi congressional delegation defended itself by charging that Mrs. Hamer, Mrs. Devine, and Mrs. Gray had not been on the general election ballot and were not therefore qualified challengers. Jamie Whitten took it one step further, saying that this was the start of a well-financed campaign to create dissen-sion and turmoil in Congress. "It might be well to note that any individual or any group, conservative, radical, or otherwise, Com-munist or non-Communist, could create the same situation with regard to any delegation; and if the House of Representatives went along with any such efforts it would, in effect, cause the House to destroy itself from within."

The debate ended. Then the House voted on the motion to dismiss the challenge: yeas, 228; nays, 143. Ten people voted pres-ent, including the five Mississippians; fifty-one members did not vote. The challenge had lost, in the sense of an up-and-down vote.

In organizing terms, the terms the challengers used, it won because it kept their issue alive, and it drew more black people into the political process. Once again, the challenge marked the Mississippi Freedom Democratic Party as a unit that would force politicians to make choices. Mrs. Hamer, Mrs. Devine, Mrs. Gray, and the rest of the MFDP were considered uncompromising purists by the politicians in Washington; they considered themselves practical realists at home, knowing better than anyone what they were up against and how they simply could not bend as Mississippi still attempted to break them.

Some of the moderate voices approved what had happened in Washington. Mississippi had reformed its voting regulations into some of the most lenient in the nation, the *Delta Democrat-Times* editorialized; through the Voting Rights Act, the means was now at hand to rectify whatever voting inequities still existed. The ballot was the way to get rid of undesirable representatives, and the "new legislation now insures the ballot is available to every Mississippi resident." As a result of both federal and state action, the *Democrat-Times* said, "Challenges of debatable value and ill-defined legality have become superfluous. . . ." The MFDP challenge, if approved, "could only have increased Mississippi's existing problems."[86]

In part, the *Democrat-Times* was correct. The challenge had started a turnaround among Mississippi politicians. "The counsel for the state of Mississippi, Governor Coleman, he was a very smart man," Morton Stavis said. "And I think he was the one who told the Mississippians, 'You can't do it that way anymore.' "[87] To be sure, the Mississippi legislature, seeing that it now had to let black people register, threw up roadblocks to hinder effective use of this new voting power. And there was still violence in the cities and on the backroads. But Mississippi business leaders had recognized that change was necessary; voices of moderation no longer were automatically suppressed.

The outcome of the challenge deepened resentment within the MFDP. "I guess the thing that hurt the most was the disillusionment on the faces of the young people. That hurt. That really hurt because many of them thought that when faced with the truth, . . . our officials will do the right thing," said Victoria Gray. "That is what I spoke to when we were interviewed there on the grounds outside . . . the tragedy of what was happening to many of the young people. Once again, there was an opportunity to lead ourselves, and we turned our back on it."[88]

After Congress concluded its debate on the challenge, the press caught up with Mrs. Hamer to ask her opinion. Before she could finish speaking, she broke down in tears. She asked, "What kind of country is it that is afraid to let the people know the truth? Why is the white man so afraid to let the people know?"[89] She went on: "I'm not crying for myself today, but I'm crying for America. I cry that the Constitution of the United States, written down on paper, applies only to white people. But we will come back year after year until we are allowed our rights as citizens."[90] She pledged to continue to run for office "if there was anything left to run for."[91]

After the vote, the challengers and their backers went again to the Lincoln Memorial Church. There Mrs. Hamer repeated what she had said: "It ain't over yet. We're coming back here, again, and again, and again." On the way out, she grabbed Kinoy and a few others and urged them to keep fighting. " 'We showed them we're for real,' she said. 'And now we have to build solidly in the state. Let's take the challenge right to them in Sunflower County elections this November.' "[92]

CHAPTER 9

"Freedom Is a Constant Struggle"

SIGNIFICANT AS THE CHALLENGES were to the Mississippi delegation to the 1964 Democratic convention and to the House delegation in 1965, they neither defined Fannie Lou Hamer's life nor limited her role. She remained a poor woman who lived with her family on a side street in the black quarter in a small town in the Delta. She shelled peas as she visited with her neighbors. She cooked huge meals for visitors. She traveled to raise money for causes in which she believed, enduring her husband's complaints because she was away so much. When she returned, she often gave away money she raised to people who then disappeared when she needed them, leading Pap Hamer to warn her constantly about overgenerosity. She went into the fields to urge people to vote. She challenged Sunflower County to allow more of those people to register and then to conduct its elections fairly. And she endured personal tragedy.

In the years after the congressional challenge, the Mississippi movement's leadership changed. The Student Non-Violent Coordinating Committee was falling apart. The NAACP, although active in the early days when no other civil rights organizations existed, had rarely taken the bold positions that Mississippi organizers felt necessary as their movement accelerated. The Congress of Racial Equality and the Southern Christian Leadership Conference had never been as strong throughout Mississippi as they were in some other states. White students, increasingly unwelcome in black-led organizations, were turning to organizing in northern cities and at colleges, directing their energies either toward fighting urban poverty, protesting campus policies, or opposing the escalating Vietnam War. It fell increasingly to the Mississippi Freedom

Democratic Party, to the civil rights attorneys representing them, to individuals like Mrs. Hamer and Unita Blackwell of Mayersville and other local people to do the work at hand at home.

Two years after the Justice Department had filed a voting-rights suit against Sunflower County, a federal district court had ruled in April 1965 that the county registrar, Cecil Campbell, had discriminated against black citizens by denying their right to register to vote. The court found that whereas 80 percent of the 8,785 white residents of Sunflower County who were of voting age were registered, only 1.1 percent of the 13,524 eligible black persons were. Federal Judge Claude Clayton ordered the registrar to make it no harder for blacks to register than it was for whites.[1]

The role of Mrs. Hamer, other Ruleville activists, and SNCC worker Charles McLaurin is evident when one looks at the case the Justice Department presented against Campbell. Sixty-two of the sixty-seven Sunflower County people who said that Campbell's office had discriminated against them were from the Ruleville and Doddsville areas.[2] Their willingness to document discrimination was a tribute to the skill and patience of community organizers.

After Clayton's decision, the MFDP conducted a crash registration program; within three weeks, 306 blacks had registered in the county for the first time. "I'm hoping we get some good people elected mayor and sheriff around here the next time elections come," Mrs. Hamer said. "Right now we got to get at least twenty people a day from this little town down to that courthouse, even if it means we got to stay up all night doing it."[3] But these new registrants still couldn't vote in local elections that spring because Mississippi law required that they be registered for four months before a general election and that they had paid poll taxes for the last two years. Meeting those conditions was next to impossible. Most blacks also couldn't run for office because the state set restrictive requirements for candidacies. As a result, the black people of Sunflower County faced four more years of rule by people they could not vote for or against, and could not oppose as candidates themselves.

Although she was already pressing the congressional challenge in Washington, Mrs. Hamer was willing to put her name on a lawsuit challenging this continued disfranchisement. She never helped bring frivolous lawsuits but she also never shied from being on point. The civil rights lawyers working with her knew that she would not back down under pressure and would use the cases in which she was involved to help educate the community on the issues at stake. In this case, she and four other Sunflower County residents sued the county on April 23, 1965—two weeks after the court decision in *U.S. v. Campbell.* They asked the court to delay their local municipal elections until more blacks had a chance to register and to suspend the poll tax. Mrs. Hamer said she had wanted to run for mayor of Ruleville that spring.[4] She knew, of course, that with only one percent of black voters registered, she had a snowflake's chance in hell of being elected, so she had not formally tried to run. But when it came time to file the suit, she also knew that an example of black people's frustration must be given. The legal conflict must be joined not just in theory, but with real candidates who had been deterred from running, so people could understand the opportunities they were being denied.

Just home from a SNCC benefit in New York organized by Julie Belafonte and Diahann Carroll, Mrs. Hamer traveled to Oxford to testify before Judge Clayton on April 29, 1965, about how many black residents of the county wanted to register. "I never will forget that day," Mrs. Hamer said, "because the assistant attorney general of the state asked me did I think if these elections was held up that I could represent the Negroes. I told him that I wouldn't only represent the Negroes, I would represent him, too, if he was in my municipal election district."[5]

Clayton denied the requests made in this suit, *Hamer v. Campbell,* on technical grounds. For example, he ruled that Mrs. Hamer had been registered long enough that she could have become a candidate had she wanted. A federal appeals court would later back Clayton's ruling on her individual argument, although it overturned much of the rest of his decision.[6]

Voter-registration workers still had to fight resistance on many levels, not just in the courts. The same day Mrs. Hamer testified in Oxford, a front-page column in the Indianola newspaper advised white people that blacks were registering all over Sunflower County without having to pass any tests. "Now, are we going to allow apathy on our part to turn this decision of electing our city and county officials over to the colored race because they are more interested in who will run cities and counties in the future?" the newspaper asked, shouting in print: "DON'T LET THIS HAPPEN."[7] The Indianola Chamber of Commerce hired a person to check registration books so that qualified whites who had not signed up could be encouraged to do so. From August 1965 to February 1966, 810 whites were registered, as opposed to only 725 blacks.[8] In addition, civil rights workers were still being arrested for minor traffic infractions. And that spring, the Freedom House in Indianola was firebombed, as was the store of Oscar Giles, an MFDP executive committee member. A firebomb severely damaged the home of a woman who had housed civil rights workers, and the house of a man active in civil rights was destroyed.[9]

Mrs. Hamer was shuttling across the country, raising money for the congressional challenge, going back to take care of her family, staying active in registration activities. She was often exhausted, her large eyes and her weary limp showing her fatigue. One evening, attorney Morton Stavis, who was involved in both the congressional challenge and the Sunflower suit, showed up at her house in the middle of the night after driving in from Memphis. "We came in and she's in bed with her husband. We had to be in court at ten o'clock [the next morning], and I said, 'I have something to talk to you about.' I'll never forget this. She looked so tired. She threw the bedcovers off. She said, 'Man, you've come all the way down from New York to help us out. I can at least get out of bed and talk to you.' "[10]

Despite their effort, MFDP activists were unable to block the local Sunflower County election, which took place as scheduled. Mrs. Hamer and her attorneys appealed to the Fifth Circuit to try to get the results tossed out. Meanwhile, they moved on other legal fronts as well. One month after Congress voted against ousting its Mississippi members, the Freedom Democrats challenged the way the state had drawn its congressional district lines. This suit was called *Connor v. Johnson* because Peggy Connor, a Hattiesburg beautician who was an MFDP officer, was the lead plaintiff in the case against Governor Paul Johnson and the state of Mississippi; it became the longest running permanent floating redistricting case in the country and ultimately resulted in the drawing of fairer political lines. The case demonstrated how Mississippi's activists and their lawyers led in the fight to try to prevent the newly obtained black vote from being diluted.[11]

In March 1966, Judge Clayton's decision in the Sunflower County case was overturned in a historic opinion: A federal appeals court for the first time threw out an election because black voters had not had fair opportunity to participate. The U.S. Court of Appeals for the Fifth Circuit, sitting in New Orleans, sent *Hamer v. Campbell* back to Judge Clayton to set a date for new elections in the small town of Sunflower and any other communities where similar circumstances had occurred. Writing for the court, Judge John R. Brown cautioned that the decision did not necessarily mean the court would set aside other elections where substantial numbers of people had been denied the right to vote. It was acting in this case, he said, because Mrs. Hamer and the others who had appealed had tried to block the election, "and failing where they should have succeeded," they had acted diligently to try to have the failure reversed before the election.[12] Later in the year, after the U.S. Supreme Court denied Mississippi's appeal, Judge Clayton set new elections, to be held May 2, 1967, in the towns of Sunflower and Moorhead.[13]

Sunflower County organizers then faced the work that came with their victory. Sunflower was a plantation town with seven hundred residents, 70 percent black, most of whom worked in the fields when they could or as maids in white people's homes. Robert Analavage, who covered Mississippi in the 1960s for *The Southern Patriot,* said Sunflower "resembles, in miniature, all the black communities in the rural South: the dusty, unimproved roads, the dilapidated shacks, the rundown churches. It has a few grocery stores, a couple of gas stations, a five-and-ten. There is a railroad running through the center of town; no train ever stops."[14] Moorhead was about twice as large as Sunflower. As Mrs. Hamer put it, "You can drive right through those towns and not even know you've passed them."[15] The town of Sunflower was not far from Senator Eastland's plantation, and Eastland and his allies had a grip on Sunflower County politics, making the confrontation all the more significant in the eyes of Mrs. Hamer and the other black activists.

"We have enough strong people to do this," Mrs. Hamer said. "For peoples to win this election, it would set a precedent for other counties in the state. Peoples need a victory so bad. We've been working here since '62 and we haven't got nothing, except a helluva lot of heartaches."[16]

But the federal government sent no registrars to help, as Mrs. Hamer felt they should do under the Voting Rights Act. A month after the federal appeals court decision ordering new elections, thirteen members of Congress asked the attorney general, Nicholas Katzenbach, to dispatch registrars. Katzenbach said he had received no complaints from Sunflower County.

"Is there need for a complaint, when only 13 percent of eligible Negroes are registered in this county, while about 85 percent of the eligible whites can vote there?" Congressman John Conyers of Detroit asked him. Replied Katzenbach, according to an account written by columnist Drew Pearson: "As long as state registrars make it possible and convenient to vote, we do not like to send in federal registars."[17] But Sunflower County continued to conduct registration in only one location, requiring poor people without transportation to make in many cases a fifty-mile round trip to the county seat in the southern end of a long, narrow county. It also kept its registration office open only during weekday working hours.

Katzenbach was asked by Congressman Charles Diggs of Detroit whether Sunflower County had no registrars because Senator Eastland lived there.

"Oh, is that his home county?" deadpanned Katzenbach.[18]

The organizing drive that would follow represented a major effort within Mississippi. But it could have been far more nationally significant had not the attention of many in the movement been diverted by internal schisms: among those who demanded increasing militance, even violence, and those who persisted in nonviolence; among those urging black separatism and those focused still on integration; and among those who were moving on to other issues—opposition to the Vietnam War or organizing in the nation's cities or on its university campuses—and those who chose to stay in the rural South. The "beloved community" was fracturing.

As *Hamer v. Campbell* was winding its way through the courts, James Meredith, the maverick who had become the first black student at the University of Mississippi, embarked on a "March against Fear" from Memphis to Jackson to encourage blacks to register and vote. On June 6, 1966, he was shot and wounded near Hernando, in northernmost Mississippi, by an unemployed hardware clerk. Civil rights leaders like Dr. Martin Luther King, Jr., and Floyd McKissick of CORE felt they had no choice but to complete Meredith's march, and thus his mission, even though they had not originally supported his idea. Mrs. Hamer joined the marchers as they moved from Sunflower to Indianola, leading one hundred people to hear King speak and chanting, "We Shall Not Be Moved." The summer heat was intense, and sweat trickled down her face as she and Dr. King and Andrew Young walked along with scores of marchers snaking along behind them. She did not stay with the march long, both because marching was physically too hard on her and also because she, like many others, felt the time for marching had passed and the need to organize at home was more pressing.

But while she was there, she spoke to reporters about "black power." Led by Stokely Carmichael and Willie Ricks, angry young blacks on the march made "Black Power" into a virtual war cry against whites, and the march therefore marked a critical turn in the militance of the movement. Mrs. Hamer put her own spin on black power, saying that she wanted a voice for blacks in government rather than wanting a black government.[19] Black power, she often said, could coexist with the power whites already had. Hers was a far more benign interpretation of black power than most fretful whites were hearing.

SNCC itself was changing in the face of this militance, and the young people who might in the past have come to Sunflower and Moorhead were now divided among themselves. SNCC had voted to expel its white field secretaries, including veteran Bob Zellner, in December 1966. At that meeting a few separatists even belittled Mrs. Hamer, who had opposed the firings, saying she was "no longer relevant" or not at their "level of development."[20]

The eyes of the nation thus were turning away from Mississippi and onto black ghettos in the North, where riots had been erupting, starting with Watts in Los Angeles in the summer of 1965. Mrs. Hamer went on the road again to try to recapture the nation's attention to raise money for voter registration and the campaigns in Sunflower and Moorhead. The effort was national in scope, coordinated by Sandra Nystrom and Eleanor Holmes Norton at the National Committee for Free Elections in Sunflower, headquartered in Manhattan. Typical of her trips was a visit to Westport and Norwalk, Connecticut, early in 1967. Mrs. Hamer stayed with her friend from Freedom Summer, Tracy Sugarman, his wife, June, and their two children. She had been in their home earlier to help raise money for a community center in Ruleville.

"When she came here to our house," Sugarman said,

> it was something to watch. Here was this badly educated, wonderful woman who was able to communicate at a most comfortable level with people who were infinitely more educated than she, more traveled than she. . . . Our kids were then in high school and junior high school and the two of them were at her feet, soaking it up. She was funny, and she was loving. She was a very endearing person. Everybody felt special about Mrs. Hamer. Everybody had that connection with her, and she obviously gave it back to you. She gave it to you and she got it right back. It was that kind of love connection that was her trademark.

She appeared comfortable in any setting. It didn't matter whether she knew which fork to use or was served food she had never eaten before—although she was quick to say, " 'You know, we don't eat lamb in the South, June,' " June Sugarman recalled. "She did not sit and act like, 'Oh, I should be liking this lamb.' " Her focus was elsewhere. "I have never been in the presence of someone where I felt that person was so connected to her faith and that was her stability."

Her schedule was always a heavy one when she went north, and there was little time for small talk. She did miss her family when she was gone and occasionally took her teenage daughter, Vergie, with her. She always would wonder how Pap was doing while she was gone, the Sugarmans said. When there was time, she would talk with the Sugarmans about whether she was doing the right thing with Head Start or the community center or local politics, as well as worry about what was happening with SNCC. "She was conflicted, in our experience with her, I think, when SNCC came apart, the whole schism, because she had enormous love and affection for a lot of the kids who had come down and worked with her and continued to support her," Tracy said. "She thought it was the sweetest thing she'd ever seen. It was beyond her wildest dreams. [She never] thought she would live to see whites and blacks working in concert because there was nothing in her experience to prepare her for that." She understood the cries for black power and rationalized the split within SNCC, he added, "but she sorrowed a great deal."[21]

Traveling from Manhattan to Connecticut to speak before the Sunflower elections, Mrs. Hamer saw northern prejudice firsthand. "This problem is not Mississippi's problem. This is America's problem," she told her audience. When she got on the train and walked through the coach, she spotted one seat. "I asked the lady, which was some white woman, was this seat taken? And she said yes. [Later] I looked down again and nobody was there, and a little while later another white woman came in and said, 'Is this seat taken?' " It wasn't, and she sat down. "So I said to myself, 'It's here, too.' "

Mrs. Hamer reminded her audience that violence in the South had not ended. A week before her appearance in Norwalk, a black leader in Natchez, Wharlest Jackson, had been blown up in his truck. A month before that one of the biggest churches in Grenada, Mississippi, had been burned after an announcement that Mrs. Hamer would speak there. Intimidation remained rampant, and Sunflower County activists had once again asked the Justice Department to send voter registrars to oversee their efforts. "They have had federal registrars in Bolivar County that adjoins Sunflower County from the west, federal registrars in Leflore County that joins Sunflower County from the east, federal registrars in Humphreys County that joins Sunflower County in the south and federal registrars in the north of Sunflower, but there has not been one federal registrar sent to Sunflower County," Mrs. Hamer stormed, "and you know the reason as well as I do—because of the stronghold of Senator James O. Eastland, one of the biggest segregationists of the century."

Eastland had had to campaign in the November election for the first time, Mrs. Hamer said, pointing out that he had both Republican and black opposition. The Republican accused Eastland of being a liberal, "so you know what we're caught in the midst of," she told her audience with a disgusted laugh.

Her voice remained quiet, then rose as she got to her point: "For Sunflower and Moorhead, the second of May is a very important day in our lives because we have worked very hard and we haven't actually won one major victory in Sunflower County. . . . We know now that we have a chance not just to prove something but we're in there to win." Enough people were registered so that black candidates could win if all those voters turned out, Mrs. Hamer predicted. "What this will mean—people is going to be cut off welfare. There is going to be all type of reprisals. Whatever you can do to support us will keep people going for these two elections. It's very important to me because the case was called *Hamer v. Campbell* [that set up the elections]. Whatever you give," she concluded, "it's not only to free me in Mississippi, but it's also to help to free yourselves because no man is an island to himself. And until I'm free in Mississippi, let's not kid ourselves, you're not free in Connecticut."[22]

Mrs. Hamer's trips generated money and television and press exposure. Her ten-day visit to New York and Connecticut in March—two months before the Sunflower elections—brought in more than $7,000, not lavish by today's megabuck fund-raiser yardsticks but enough to go a long way in small Mississippi towns. She spoke at house parties and at a reception put on by a group of young black women at the home of African drummer Babatunde Olatunji. She appeared on the Mike Wallace television show and other radio and television broadcasts and held a press conference with Manhattan Borough president Percy Sutton, who would later travel to Sunflower County to encourage blacks to vote.[23] At the news conference, Mrs. Hamer issued a challenge to Ramsey Clark, who had succeeded Katzenbach as attorney general, to prove he was a liberal southerner. "Will he bow to Eastland, too? Or will he live up to his reputation as a strong defender of civil rights and civil liberties? We say to Ramsey Clark he will have to show us before May 2 by sending in federal registrars, examiners and poll watchers. Before May 2, Mr. Clark."[24]

The Freedom Democratic Party was starting to become a potent force, Mrs. Hamer told the reporters.[25] "We've grown up a lot since the summer of '64," she added. "We may still be political babies, but we are beginning to know how to deal. We know how to get people out to welfare hearings. We make sure there is a turnout when there is a civil rights commission hearing. We'll never go back to the way we were before."[26]

With the election only days away, Sunflower County remained without federal voter registrars. So again, on April 26, 1967, Congressman William Ryan of New York and Bayard Rustin led a delegation of civil rights supporters to ask Clark and Assistant Attorney General John Doar, head of the civil rights division, for the registrars and for Justice Department observers on election day to prevent intimidation.[27] The Freedom Democrats especially wanted election day observers to prevent the kind of irregularity—more votes being cast in the town of Sunflower than there were actual residents—that they claimed had occurred in the November 1966 election just past.[28]

"By the end of 1965, after the Voting Rights Act was passed, 43 percent of eligible Negroes in counties having federal registrars were registered," according to a statement issued by the delegation that visited the Justice Department. "By contrast, only 15 percent were registered in counties without federal registrars." In Sunflower County, they said, only 24 percent of black people eligible to vote had registered while 85 percent of whites were on the rolls. "After so many decades of hardened resistance to Negro registration, Sunflower can better accommodate federal registrars than its Negro citizens the slow travail of registering to vote under present conditions."

For the delegation's presentation, Mrs. Hamer had prepared a list of Sunflower County people who had not registered out of fear: One woman felt harm would come to her family, one couple feared eviction from their plantation home, another couple worried that harm would come to their children. And there were more. All said they would sign up with a federal registrar. "Some people who work," Mrs. Hamer said, "would register to vote on Saturdays, but the circuit clerk's office closes on Friday." She mentioned talking to a group in Rome, Mississippi, about going to Indianola to register

and they all walked away. The word "register" frightened them. If federal registrars could come to where the people are, many more people would vote. They would then feel that the federal government is behind them, and that the Voting Rights Act is not just a paper law.

Because of the absence of federal officials in Sunflower, we must canvass for voters on back roads in the middle of the night and take our chances. The people wonder about the absence of federal men in the county, when all surrounding counties have not been left ignored the way we have. The people look at Eastland's 5,800-acre plantation right here in Sunflower, and they know why we have to canvass in the middle of the night.[29]

In the town of Sunflower, the white power structure felt Senator Eastland would be embarrassed to have a black government in his own backyard. Those in office knew they had to take steps to keep themselves in power. Sunflower's mayor called MFDP's local vice chairman, Lela Mae Brooks, to tell her the town had raised $2,000 to pave streets in the black community. "They used to tell us that they didn't have enough money to make street repairs," Mrs. Brooks said. "Now all of a sudden they found the money. They trying to get friendly with us."[30]

Mayor W. L. Patterson, who had held office in Sunflower for twelve years, said he had a good record of working with both black and white and that he was pitching his campaign to both. He said he hoped to get some black votes. "I have to, or I will be in bad shape," he told the *New York Times*.[31]

At a four-hour meeting at the Baptist Grove Church in Sunflower, speaker after speaker urged black voters to stick together. Mrs. Hamer was joined by Percy Sutton, by New York state assemblyman (later Congressman) Charles Rangel, and by MFDP chairman Lawrence Guyot. Mrs. Hamer told the group, "We are going to put some folks in there that know what is happening."[32]

The ticket Mrs. Hamer backed was headed in Sunflower by twenty-one-year-old Otis Brown, candidate for mayor. Unemployed himself, he wanted to help create jobs for blacks and poor whites, install a sewage system, construct a recreation center for the town's children, and try to help people with welfare and Social Security problems. "I will also try to get a doctor, which is of greatest necessity for this town," Brown said. "I have hired a lawyer who is trying to find out what poverty programs can be brought to the town of Sunflower."[33]

Annie Mae King, whose home had been burned in 1964 because of her civil rights activity, was running for alderman. She had joined Mrs. Hamer in suing to bring about the new elections. "If I win, I want to work for all people, not just the colored," Mrs. King said. "But I think we're going to have to win a majority just to show the white folks what we can do." Lonnie Echols, a farmer and candidate for alderman, addressed the basic need to have police

JOHN HOLBERT AND WIFE

WHO MURDERED PLANTER JAMES EASTLAND AT DODDSVILLE

ARE BURNED AT THE STAKE

Bruised and Battered Almost Beyond Recognition ; Bleeding From an Hundred Tortures ; With Ears Shorn From Their Heads.; Palsied Limbs and Fingerless Hands—More Dead Than Alive— They are Led to Their Horrible Doom.

In the usually quiet little village of Doddville, just over the line in Sunflower County, close beside a negro church, just across the road from the scene of the crime, a thousand or more enraged citizens gathered on last Sunday evening to avenge the murder of Mr. Eastland.

Early Sunday morning the news reached Doddville that the murderers had been captured and that they were then on their way to the scene of the crime. It had already been announced that the negroes were to be burned at the stake, hence the news spread rapidly that the event was to take place. By Sunday at noon the crowd had swelled well up into the hundreds. At three o'clock in the evening it is estimated that not less than a thousand people were present. The mob went about its work in an orderly manner. Several wagon loads of inflammable wood had been prepared and a roaring fire was soon kindled. Holbert and the woman were dragged to the scene. Several citizens who realized the enormity of the offense which was about to be committed mounted a stump and tried to dissuade the mob from its purpose, but the of the orators were drowned organized cries of the spectators.

"Burn them !" "Burn them that could be heard.

The leaders of the mob consultation. It was decided woman be burned first. She if she desired to pray, to which plied that she had already been pray

FIRST DETAILED REPORT OF THE HORRIBLE AFFAIR

The Commonwealth today contains the first detailed account of the capture and burning of John Holbert and wife at Doddville last Sunday evening.

which the two men paid $50 each to Luther Lloyd, the sixteen-year-old boy who located the negroes.

To a reporter of THE COMMONWEALTH Mr. Lavender related the details of the capture with becoming modesty. He is a clerk in the store of Clark Bros. at Brent. Mr. O'Neal is the manager of the Se___ bert plantation, and happened in the store late Saturday eve___ n Luther Lloyd came in and ___nspicious negroes which he ___ the woods a short distance ___ boy said that both of them ___d suggested that they might ___ devilment. Lavender armed ___th a 38-calibre Smith & Wes___ er and O'Neal secured a Win___fle and the boy went with ___e spot where he had seen the Holbert and his paramour ___g down when approached, and ___ffort to escape. Mr. Lavender ___t he was satisfied as soon as he ___d at the suspects that there was

of Holbert, and accompanied them to O'Neal's.

The two Eastland brothers afterward arrived, and Mr. W. C. Eastland wrote a check for $1,200 which he turned over to Messrs. Lavender and O'Neal. The two negroes were then securely bound and dumped into a wagon in which were a number of blood hounds, tired out by the prolonged chase, and the crowd moved off toward Itta Bena. From Itta Bena the negroes were carried to Doddville.

Holbert's Possessions.

On the person of Holbert, in addition to the gun and pistol before mentioned, search revealed a gold watch and $285 in money. His parramour carried two razors.

Holbert's Crime.

The crime for which John Holbert paid the horrible penalty of his life at the stake is one or the most revolting chapters in the criminal history of Mississippi. James Eastland was a prominent planter residing in the vicinity of Doddville, where he had inherited large interests from his father. He was a young man and popular throughout this entire section. The negro had been a servant of the family for years, having come from Forest with Mr. Eastland when he moved to Sunflower County. He was a trusted servant of the family until a few months ago, when he became unruly and was ordered to leave the place. It was this order that enraged the negro and finally resulted in the murder of Mr. Eastland. A son of the

A climate of fear permeated Sunflower County decades after lynchings such as this one in Doddsville, occurring after planter James Eastland, uncle of the man who later became a U.S. Senator, was killed. Newspapers as far away as New York reported the pursuit of the Holberts, which lasted three days and stretched across two counties, through dense swamps and seepy marshes. MISSISSIPPI DEPARTMENT OF ARCHIVES AND HISTORY

Fannie Lou Hamer marched in a voter-registration demonstration outside the Forrest County Courthouse in Hattiesburg, Mississippi, in 1963. MATT HERRON

Charles McLaurin, a Student Non-Violent Coordinating Committee worker in Ruleville, rode with Mrs. Hamer to the Sunflower County Courthouse to try to register and worked closely with her for years afterward. STEVE SCHAPIRO/BLACK STAR

SNCC's Hollis Watkins, left, discussed Mississippi's Congressional districts with summer volunteers, and Bob Moses, right, led an orientation session in Oxford, Ohio, in June 1964. STEVE SCHAPIRO/BLACK STAR

James Forman, SNCC's executive secretary, helped train summer volunteers, including Andrew Goodman (in dark T-shirt) at Oxford. Goodman, Michael Schwerner and James Chaney disappeared June 21, 1964. STEVE SCHAPIRO/BLACK STAR

The missing civil rights workers had gone to Longdale, Mississippi, to investigate the burning of the Mt. Zion Methodist Church, where Schwerner had urged parishoners in the all-black community to register to vote and allow their church to be a freedom school. STEVE SCHAPIRO/ BLACK STAR

Two days after the workers disappeared, their burnt-out car was found at Bogue Chitto in Neshoba County. Bob Moses told volunteers still in Oxford he had to assume the three were dead. STEVE SCHAPIRO/BLACK STAR

ABOVE: Perry "Pap" Hamer trimmed a neighbor's hair as summer volunteers prepared for their work in Ruleville. STEVE SCHAPIRO/BLACK STAR

RIGHT: Summer volunteer Len Edwards, right, urged Ruleville residents to register to vote. STEVE SCHAPIRO/ BLACK STAR

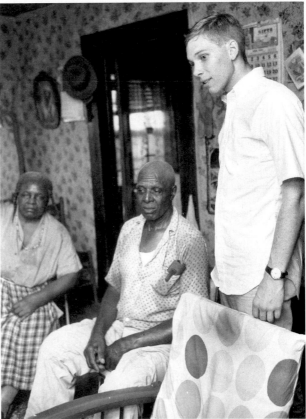

"I question America," Fannie Lou Hamer told the credentials committee at the Democratic National Convention on August 22, 1964. Her dramatic testimony centered on how she had lost her job and had later been beaten because she wanted the basic rights that black Americans were being denied in Mississippi. AP/WIDE WORLD PHOTOS

Joining Mississippi Freedom Democratic Party delegation chairman Aaron Henry, left, and Mrs. Hamer in demonstrating outside the Atlantic City, New Jersey, convention hall were Anne and Nathan Schwerner, Mickey Schwerner's parents. Ed King, who also testified, is in the center, rear. UPI/BETTMANN

Women rallying MFDP supporters on the Atlantic City Boardwalk were Fannie Lou Hamer, Eleanor Holmes Norton, center, and Ella Baker. GEORGE BALLIS

New Jersey state police put up a blockade to keep MFDP members out of the convention hall, confronting Aaron Henry, center, and Mrs. Hamer. Television reporter John Chancellor (in glasses) was next to Henry. UPI/BETTMANN

RIGHT: Fannie Lou Hamer walks toward the entrance to the convention hall, where she was finally admitted. Later, some convention delegates gave their floor passes and seats to MFDP members. UPI/BETTMANN

BELOW: Mrs. Hamer spoke frequently in churches across Mississippi as she ran against Representative Jamie Whitten in the fall 1964 Freedom Vote. BERN KEATING/BLACK STAR

Three Mississippi women—Fannie Lou Hamer, Victoria Gray, center, and Annie Devine, right—stood up against the entrenched Mississippi Congressional delegation in 1965. They charged that since blacks faced extreme discrimination in voting, the five representatives had been elected illegally. AP/WIDE WORLD PHOTOS

"We'll come back year after year until we are allowed our rights as citizens," Mrs. Hamer told MFDP sympathizers outside the Capitol in Washington after the House of Representatives rejected the challenge to the Mississippi congressmen September 17, 1965. AP/WIDE WORLD PHOTOS

RIGHT: U.S. Senator James O. Eastland (with cigar), a powerful plantation owner from Sunflower County, controlled appointments to the federal bench in his role as Judiciary Committee chairman. UPI/BETTMANN

BELOW: Dr. Martin Luther King, Jr., center, in hat, picked up James Meredith's march through Mississippi after Meredith was wounded in an ambush. With aide Andrew Young, hatless at right, and Mrs. Hamer, second row, to the left of Young, King led marchers through rough Yalobusha County on June 12, 1966. UPI/BETTMANN

Wherever she went, Fannie Lou Hamer restored demonstrators' spirits with her singing, as she did during a break on the Meredith March with Robert Greene, center, Andrew Young and Dr. Martin Luther King, Jr., far right, at the Enid Dam Campsite. CHARMIAN READING

Field workers watched as the Meredith March passed near Itta Bena in Leflore County. Marchers held voter-registration rallies as they traveled. UPI/BETTMANN

LEFT: Credentialed at last, Fannie Lou Hamer spoke from the podium of the 1968 convention in favor of black Alabamians who sought seats. Anti-war protests in the streets of Chicago and police reaction overshadowed the seating of an integrated Mississippi delegation. UPI/BETTMANN

BELOW: Using MFDP as an example and backed by Mrs. Hamer, Julian Bond, right, shaking hands, led an integrated delegation that successfully challenged the Georgia delegation handpicked by Governor Lester Maddox at the 1968 Democratic convention. Activist Bayard Rustin was behind Bond, far right. FRED WARD/BLACK STAR

Fannie Lou Hamer listened as MFDP chairman Lawrence Guyot, who had been jailed with her in Winona, spoke at the Holmes County Courthouse and urged a strong turnout for elections in Lexington, Mississippi, in May 1969. SUSAN (LORENZI) SOJOURNER

Charles Evers and Fannie Lou Hamer didn't always agree on matters political, but they were in harmony at this point at a state political gathering in 1971. PETE DANIEL/NATIONAL MUSEUM OF AMERICAN HISTORY

Fannie Lou Hamer relied on young people in the North for help raising funds for her cherished Freedom Farm cooperative. She praised Debra Jean Sweet of Madison, right, for her work on a 1971 Hunger Hike. MILWAUKEE JOURNAL PHOTO

Announcing that she intended to run for the state Senate and then challenge U.S. Senator James O. Eastland, Fannie Lou Hamer participated in the founding meeting of the National Women's Political Caucus in Washington, D.C., in July 1971 with, from left, Betty Smith of the Wisconsin GOP, Dorothy Haener of the United Auto Workers Union, and feminist leader Gloria Steinem. UPI/BETTMANN

Poor people in Mississippi needed meat in their diets, Fannie Lou Hamer explained to a visitor, and that was why she had begun a "pig bank" with the help of the National Council of Negro Women. FRANKLYNN PETERSON/ BLACK STAR

Honored by several universities for her civil rights work, Fannie Lou Hamer received a degree as doctor of humane letters from Howard University and its president, James Cheek, in Washington, D.C., on June 3, 1972. GERALD MARTINEAU/ WASHINGTON POST

ABOVE: "None of us would be where we are now had she not been there then," said UN Ambassador Andrew Young as he preached Mrs. Hamer's eulogy at services in Ruleville on March 20, 1977. She was fifty-nine when she died. UPI/BETTMANN

LEFT: "I'm sick and tired of being sick and tired," said Fannie Lou Hamer, and that motto was chosen to mark her grave in a field not far from Williams Chapel Church where she first raised her hand and vowed to try to vote. Her husband, Perry, who died May 19, 1992, is now buried next to her. KAY MILLS

enforce the laws. "In the colored community," he said, "whites speed through at 50 miles an hour and there's kids playing in the streets. That's got to stop."

What the MFDP candidates basically wanted was jobs and equitable treatment. Aldermanic candidate Elvin Gibson, 69, said there had never been any light industry in town because no one ever spoke up for it. "The white folks don't want no factory 'cause they want to keep us all field hands and domestic. They work a man like a mule here, then turn him loose to die. Worked me hard all my life, and that's the way they did me." Gibson said he paid taxes and all his money went to the white section of town. "If I pay taxes, let me see some good come of it."[34]

More blacks than whites were registered in Sunflower so the MFDP ticket seemed to have a better chance there than in Moorhead, where Jimmy Douglas, a twenty-four-year-old wholesale grocery worker in Indianola, was running against the incumbent, Mayor W. I. Upchurch. Blacks outnumbered whites in Moorhead, but not among registered voters.[35]

Mrs. Hamer hammered the point that the election was important not just to these black candidates; not just to the residents of Sunflower and Moorhead, black and white; but to people throughout the country. At another news conference in New York, Manhattan borough president Percy Sutton, back from a trip to Mississippi, joined her in making that point. "What is the connection between the Delta land of Mississippi and the urban cities of the North and Midwest?" Sutton asked rhetorically.[36] Thousands of sharecroppers who had been evicted or left jobless by farm mechanization had become "the immigrants of the late 60s," arriving in northern cities with no skills. If the Freedom Democrats were successful, Sutton reasoned, then more industry would flow into the South and displaced blacks could be absorbed "by the South in the South under conditions of respect and cooperativeness." Thus, said Sutton, "all New Yorkers have an interest in the May 2nd elections in Sunflower County, Mississippi"—in addition to the altruistic aim of seeing Mississippi reject a system that impoverished children and evicted their parents because they tried to vote.

On the day of the balloting—May 2, 1967—MFDP's political allies and a press contingent converged on Sunflower. Sutton returned with Rangel and former New York City councilman Paul O'Dwyer. Walter Rugaber was there from the *New York Times*. That morning, some Sunflower voters received anonymous circulars warning that their homes and property were at stake in the election. "You have a chance to vote for a good town or a bad town in the election. The choice is yours. If you are smart, you will not be misled by paid racial agitators who would promise you everything and give you nothing but misery if they succeed in fooling you into following their leadership."[37]

The Sunflower town hall was roped off. Only voters and officials could go inside. Across the street beneath a cottonwood tree on the post office lawn, Rugaber reported, several dozen black people stood talking quietly, and on the opposite corner a handful of white farmers lounged around a pickup truck. The scene was similar in Moorhead.[38] Mrs. Hamer was watching the activity in Sunflower, and as the flag was raised at the post office across the street, she said, "Yes, that's the country's flag. And this is the first day it's been ours, too." She turned to the crowd, saying: "Remember the song we used to sing: 'If you don't find me in the cotton fields, and you can't find me nowhere, / Come on over to the City Hall; I'll be voting right there.' Well, this day is what that song was all about."[39]

Robert Analavage of the *Southern Patriot* described one scene as the police chief, "a small rotund man who constantly puffs on a cigar, stationed himself right by the door a person would have to enter to cast a vote. At the exit, groups of local whites clustered. A black person would have to pass that chief of police and walk through that knot of white folks."[40]

In Sunflower, Mayor Patterson beat Otis Brown, 190 to 121. Patterson got some black votes because black registration—and black votes that day—outnumbered white. Patterson said he hadn't campaigned for any votes from the "radicals" of the Mississippi Freedom Democratic Party, but he did campaign among the "good niggers." In Moorhead, Mayor Upchurch swamped Jimmy Douglas.[41] The white slates for alderman in both towns also won. One of the aldermen reelected in Sunflower proclaimed, "I think we have enough sensible Negroes in this community to realize these foreigners are not the ones to lead them in their politics."

The black candidates had financial, legal, and moral support from outside the state. They had Fannie Lou Hamer and other prominent civil rights leaders drawing attention to their cause. They had mass meetings and workshops on how to cast votes and what issues were at stake. No black community in the state had been as well organized. The black candidates surely lost some votes because of outright fraud. They doubtless lost because some blacks were intimidated by the rifles in the pickup truck windows. And they lost because whites cast their votes in a bloc while some blacks voted for whites; for example, in Moorhead, some blacks who worked with the local government in the anti-poverty program voted against the MFDP candidates. And they lost, said one lawyer, because the other side had better candidates, at least in the eyes of the voters.

What happened in Sunflower would happen in many other areas when black candidates first ran: Black voters did not reward civil rights activism at the polls and sometimes found black candidates' backgrounds wanting in comparison to those of whites. Accustomed to whites running government, they could not believe blacks could do it—unless they were flawlessly educated and impeccably dressed, maybe not even then. For black candidates, it was not enough to get on the ballot, to get people to register and to vote: they were going to have to gain education and economic standing to win elections in Mississippi.

The Freedom Democrats rallied after the results were announced. They were angry, and they were frustrated. Analavage described it as "one of the bitterest and angriest meetings in the history of the Southern freedom movement. . . . People wept. People cursed. People stared dumbly as they listened to speakers trying to explain what happened."

Lawrence Guyot, MFDP's state chairman, exploded. "People in the Delta have got to decide how they're going to fight for the first time in their lives. We are going to run an all-black slate in November and stay the hell out of the goddamn Democratic Party." And an angry Mrs. Hamer sounded weary of it all. "There was nothing symbolic about this election," she said. "I'm sick of symbolic things. We are fighting for our lives."[42]

The Freedom Democrats challenged the results in court, charging that illiterate black voters had not had the opportunity to seek help in the polling booth from the one black aide available, Joseph Harris. MFDP also charged that election officials maintained segregated lines of voters waiting at the polling places and showed preference to whites. Once again, Mrs. Hamer was the prime plaintiff as she had been in the original suit that won the elections.[43]

This time when the case went to court, Mrs. Hamer would lose. Judge Clayton found that the election was conducted objectively and that the results represented the will of a voting majority. Writing for a sympathetic appeals court, Judge John Minor Wisdom said in the face of the Sunflower loss, "It is easy to understand the feeling of the Negro candidates and their supporters. They felt there must have been skullduggery at the polls. Indeed, with reason, they could and did say that the Board of Election Commissioners should have shown more consideration for the uninformed, often illiterate, Negro casting his first ballot." Nonetheless, Wisdom said, "On the record as a whole, we cannot say the district court erred." The Voting Rights Act required that voters be told of their right to assistance, "not that they be induced to accept it," and in those terms Sunflower officials had obeyed the law, the appeals court would rule. "On the cold record before us, the attitude of Sunflower's Election Commissioners may have been shoddy," Wisdom wrote, but he added that that shoddiness did not justify the drastic procedure of throwing out a state election. Such measures, the court said, should be reserved for serious violations of voting rights of the sort that had led to the new elections in the first place.[44]

Anger soon transformed itself into energy, and the next campaign began. MFDP fielded scores of candidates for the fall elections. Other black candidates ran as independents. Civil rights patriarch A. Philip Randolph appealed to his labor-union brothers and sisters for money for the Sunflower County candidates. The Justice Department had finally certified Sunflower County for the appointment of federal registrars on April 29, 1967, three days before the local elections. But six weeks later none had been sent, and the August party primary and November general election still lay ahead. All the county clerk would have had to do to prevent dispatch of the registrars was to open offices in Ruleville and Drew one day every two weeks and let people know about the changes. But only one unpublicized registration day was held in Drew; no office was opened in Ruleville. Only when Mrs. Hamer learned about the clerk's visit to Drew did any other local people hear of it.[45]

White resistance was dogged. Mrs. Hamer complained that the Drew police chief, Curtis Floyd, was still harassing registration workers and the people they visited about voting. On May 29, the policeman stopped Pap Hamer to check his driver's license, and the next day he arrested him for speeding. He had been driving a car filled with white student workers from Georgetown University. Instead of giving Mr. Hamer a ticket, the chief took him to the city jail. Trial was set for the next morning before Mayor W. O. Williford, also the local justice, who told Mr. Hamer he needed a commercial license to drive that many people.

The Hamers sued. *Hamer v. Floyd* became the first lawsuit under the federal Voting Rights Act brought by private parties to try to block a state court prosecution. The Hamers considered the arrest as harassment of their voter-registration activities. The case was heard June 7 in Federal District Court in Oxford, where Judge Clayton was asked to issue a restraining order against Mayor Williford so that the voter-registration work could continue.[46] Judge Clayton denied the injunction the Hamers sought, and they did not appeal.

The week after this newest *Hamer* case was heard, Bayard Rustin, John Lewis, and Eleanor Holmes Norton again asked the Justice Department to send federal registrars to Sunflower County. "We would very much appreciate an explanation as to how it is possible officially to certify a county for registrars and observers without thereafter sending them in."[47]

The deadline for registration before the primary election was approaching. Still no registrars. And still more harassment. Mrs. Hamer called national attention to continuing intimidation by police in Drew and by the new circuit clerk. Two workers handing out flyers about voter registration on a farm near Senator Eastland's plantation were told by a white man to leave or he would kill them. Mrs. Hamer herself received two threatening telephone calls. "The first caller threatened to take her in front of her house and tar and feather her. He said 'dirty' things to her and called her names," according to a letter to John Doar of the Justice Department. "The second caller (who could have been the same person) told her she had better get flowers (implying her funeral) and asked when she would make an integration speech. He also called her names."[48]

Despite Mrs. Hamer's efforts, registration in the county was still conducted from 8:00 A.M. to 5:00 P.M., Monday through Friday. Field hands were at work by 6:30 in the morning and worked until dark. Earning only $3.50 to $4.00 a day, they couldn't afford to take time off. Still no federal registrars were sent.

Black candidates, however, made small but significant gains across the state in the Democratic primary on August 8. Fifteen black candidates won in races that would not be contested in November, and one candidate would face Republican opposition. There were new justices of the peace, constables, county supervisors, a coroner, and a chancery clerk. Twenty-two black candidates faced runoffs; all of them lost. The greatest gains were made in the southwest part of the state, in Claiborne County and in Jefferson, Charles Evers's home county. Evers called the runoffs "outright robbery" and suggested that "instead of sending observers to Vietnam to guarantee free elections, President Johnson ought to send them right here to Mississippi."[49]

Mrs. Hamer had wanted to run for the state Senate that fall. She was denied a place on the ballot because of a new state law that barred anyone who had voted in a primary from running as an independent in the general election. She had, however, drawn up a platform that, as matters evolved, foreshadowed the program that she would pursue in the remaining ten years of her life. It called for increased hiring of black workers in welfare policymaking positions and legislation to allow counties to receive federal money for housing for the poor and the elderly. To improve blacks' access to voting, she wanted a change in registration laws to allow people to sign up to vote up to one month before an election and to lower the voting age to eighteen. She also sought mobile registration for applicants' convenience.

Turning to education, Mrs. Hamer wanted black history taught in all Mississippi schools, increased teacher salaries and job security so that teachers wouldn't fear helping the black community, better bus transportation and school equipment, and special remedial courses. She also advocated better health and nutrition programs, a concern to which she was increasingly turning her attention. Finally, Mrs. Hamer also urged uniform tax rates so that plantation owners and big businessmen would have to pay their fair share of taxes.[50]

Mrs. Hamer's proposed platform illustrated how she viewed her work as evolving beyond, but still including, voter registration. She was constantly goading her Sunflower County neighbors to go beyond even whatever seemingly bold step they had just taken. Her stand on taxes, for example, revealed one of the reasons—quite apart from upholding strict segregation—that Senator Eastland might have objected to the increasing numbers of black candidates and to their positions. Suppose, speculated Victor Ullman, writing for *The Nation* that fall, that the Sunflower County tax assessor were to be replaced by a black tax assessor. How would the new officeholder treat Eastland's property tax assessments? Ullman pointed out that Eastland's cotton land was assessed for an average of $3.14 an acre in the county tax assessor's office although it would sell for between $400 and $500 an acre at the time. His personal property value was set at $750, even though that included mechanical pickers that would cost $15,000 to replace. And his cotton gin was valued for tax purposes at $8,400: "that includes everything, plant and machinery, equipment, offices." Furthermore, suppose black officeholders were selected and insisted that the federal government shift its money from crop subsidies to retraining of field hands or improvement of local schools? Or making all those other changes Mrs. Hamer and other MFDP candidates were calling for? Perhaps, Ullman concluded, the MFDP and the Delta Ministry and these other groups were subversive, but hardly in the way about which Eastland consistently complained.[51]

Accordingly, the Sunflower County Democratic Party, headed

by its campaign committee chairman, Jack Harper, Jr., the influential chancery clerk, sent the following letter "TO OUR SUNFLOWER COUNTY NEGRO CITIZENS." Harper appealed for support primarily for Democratic Party nominees but encouraged black voters to associate themselves on a permanent basis with either the Republican or Democratic Party and reject "the so-called Freedom Democratic Party." The regular parties had prestige on the local, state, and national levels, while the FDP and like-minded groups "will soon pass away since they exist principally for the purpose of raising money and building up a fund to support self interested out-of-state lawyers and persons concerned with neither you, Sunflower County, nor good government."[52]

Notwithstanding constant pressure against their activities, the Freedom Democrats that fall ran thirty-two independent candidates in eight counties for offices such as county supervisor, justice of the peace, and sheriff. A team of lawyers went to Mississippi to advise local MFDP representatives and to check the accuracy of voter rolls. The twenty-five lawyers and fifty-six law students also served as poll watchers.[53] The Freedom Democrats had high hopes for their candidates. Robert Clark, a teacher, was running for the state legislature from well-organized Holmes County, and Unita Blackwell, by then working for the National Council of Negro Women, was running for justice of the peace in Issaquena County. Clark won election to the previously all-white state legislature by one hundred sixteen votes. Mrs. Blackwell lost by twenty-six. In all, six black candidates won, bringing to twenty-two the number elected in state and local elections in August and November. Twenty-six other black candidates lost decisively. One black candidate was elected as a Bolivar County supervisor, but no black candidates were elected in Sunflower County at any level. The Mississippi general election also saw the Republican gubernatorial candidate, Rubel Phillips, who lost, campaign for black votes on a platform of improving economic and educational conditions for both races.[54]

Robert Clark, thirty-seven, had beaten James P. Love, a sixty-five-year-old planter who had held the seat since 1956 and who was chairman of the education committee in the state House of Representatives. Holder of a master's degree from Michigan State University, Clark was running a local literacy program when the board of education refused to sponsor a work-experience program that would have helped 240 poor families. He decided to run so he could work on changing state laws that allowed local authorities too much control over poverty programs.[55]

Holmes County may have voted to send him to Jackson, but

that did not mean that Jackson—and the state legislature—had to like him. First, his defeated opponent challenged his seating, claiming that Clark had not filed his nominating petitions in all the places he was supposed to file them. Love withdrew his challenge a few weeks later. Then insurance companies indicated that they might require higher bonds for the new member. Mrs. Hamer swung into action. She called the secretary of state. She called the press. "She told them if I weren't seated, she and Aaron Henry would lead a march on the state capitol from the north and Charles Evers would lead a march from the south," recalled Clark, a large, affable man.

> Now, that came at the time that [the state legislature] had been not seating Julian Bond in Georgia and they had made a hero out of Julian Bond. Mississippians were not about to let that happen. It could have been covered up and they would have given me the run-around except for the national attention. They knew [Mrs. Hamer] was a national figure. They knew she could command attention. The papers here were blacked out. But she could get attention. Without that attention they probably would have kept me out.[56]

Once Clark was seated, Mrs. Hamer called him. He thanked her for her help, and then she warned him that she expected him to speak up for black people's concerns. She said, "Young man, I called those white folks. We got you there now. And if you don't do right, then I'm going to march down on you just as hard as I would those white folk."[57]

Clark was sworn in on January 2, 1968, the first black legislator in seventy-four years in Mississippi. Before entering the chamber, Clark passed a statue of U.S. Senator Theodore G. Bilbo, a staunch segregationist, in the capitol building lobby. When he went in to the chamber, nobody showed him where to sit, but finally another legislator from his district shook his hand and guided him to his place. No one wanted to sit beside him. "A vast majority of the members, of course, would prefer that the membership had remained all-white," wrote William Peart of the *Delta Democrat-Times*. "Many of them will never reach the speaking stage with Clark."[58] Clark outlasted many of them, winning reelection year after year and continuing to serve into the 1990s. He ran unsuccessfully for Congress in 1982 and 1984, setting the stage for Mike Espy's successful bid in 1986.

The year 1967 proved a watershed one for black electoral politics in Mississippi. More and more black candidates would be elected in years to come, and eventually Mississippi could claim the most black elected officials in the United States. It would still take nearly twenty years before anyone black went to Congress, and no black has yet won statewide office. Few blacks hold the powerful countywide offices in the Delta.[59]

It was also a pivotal year for Fannie Lou Hamer. She would still advocate black political independence and work on voter registration, but the political platform that she had not been able to use that fall became the platform of social concern from which she increasingly worked. She devoted more and more of her attention and her diminishing physical energy to the needs of her neighbors for housing, food, and health care.

She also had two babies to care for because, within weeks after the spring elections in Sunflower and Moorhead, tragedy had struck the Hamers. Their daughter Dorothy, who had given birth to her second child, Jacqueline, on September 22, 1966, began hemorrhaging. Medical care for black people in rural Mississippi was poor under the best of circumstances, and many hospitals would not admit black patients. "We couldn't get a doctor to attend my daughter and she died as we were driving her 127 miles to Memphis," Mrs. Hamer said. "A few months later, they carried her husband home from Vietnam disabled. He's not able to take care of his own children."[60] Mrs. Hamer grieved deeply, and she sought counsel in her church and from her civil rights ally, the Reverend Harry Bowie. Mrs. Hamer, nearing fifty, and her husband, a few years older, soon adopted Jacqueline and her sister Lenora.

CHAPTER 10

"This Is a Brand New Day"

THE MAN FROM the U.S. Department of Agriculture was announcing with obvious pleasure that the government would now charge people with very little income only 50 cents, not $2.00, for $12.00 worth of food. He thought the poor rural women gathered at an Indianola meeting in the spring of 1967 would approve. But he was greeted by absolute silence.

"What do you do if you have no income?" asked one woman. Sixty-two years old, she had not found any work since she registered to vote, and there was no record of any money ever having been paid into her Social Security account.

"That could be a problem," said the Agriculture man. "You may not have cash but you must have some income."

"I wonder where mine is hid," the woman replied. "I can't find none."

The Agriculture Department man had just surveyed one hundred fifty families in that area of Mississippi and said he had found only one with no income.

"Well, Mister, you have just found yourself another."[1]

The setting for this confrontation between those who governed and those who were governed was the Travelodge Motel in Indianola in June 1967. The sponsor: the National Council of Negro Women. The local organizer: Fannie Lou Hamer.

President Johnson had declared war on poverty, but even the best of the foot soldiers in the war did not always know the true conditions and aspirations of the poor. In Mississippi, they had the added disadvantage that many in government disapproved of their programs. Sharecropping had died, and those who had had little before had less now. For example, in 1959, there had been sixty-five thousand jobs for hand picking cotton in Delta fields. In the main harvesting months of 1966, before this meeting in Indianola, there were fewer than three thousand hand pickers in the fields.[2]

The Indianola session to discuss anti-poverty programs, a model of its kind, was the product of an unlikely trio: a fearless local woman, Fannie Lou Hamer; the shrewd, almost regal president of the National Council of Negro Women, Dorothy Height; and a well-connected woman from New York City, Polly Cowan. Height and Cowan had cemented their relationship in a unique undertaking between northern and southern women in their own freedom summer of 1964.

Polly Cowan is one of those overlooked figures of American history: those who bring people together to try to solve problems but who stay out of the limelight themselves. A member of the wealthy Spiegel catalog family, she had graduated from Sarah Lawrence College and married Louis Cowan, who later became president of CBS. In October 1963, she had gone to Selma, Alabama, to look into the way women and children were being treated when they were jailed in ongoing civil rights protests. Dorothy Height also went. Afterward, Cowan suggested that caravans of women go into the South to show their concern for the women there, black and white.[3]

The following March, Height brought together in Atlanta a group of black and white women from eight southern cities undergoing the worst racial tensions. For many, it was their first time in an integrated setting. The women discussed their fears and the support they felt they needed from outside. From that conference came a plea from a Jackson, Mississippi, woman for a "ministry of presence" from women outside to women inside the South. Women, having neither financial nor political power, had to act as shock absorbers as the system underwent change. To do that, said Dorothy Tilly, a fighter of renown against the Ku Klux Klan and founder and director of the Fellowship of the Concerned of the Southern Regional Council, women of North and South should build on "the common ground of their always present concern for the welfare of children."[4]

Thus was born Wednesdays in Mississippi. Almost every week during July and August of 1964 and 1965, a handful of black and white women would board airplanes in northern cities—first New York, then Boston, Washington, Baltimore, Chicago, and Minneapolis—and fly to Jackson. Forty-eight women visited Mississippi the first year. The black women met with black women around the state to bolster their morale. The white women sought to reach moderate white women in Mississippi and convince them that social change was necessary and good. They wanted the Mississippi women to know that leading women across the North supported the civil rights activities, that the swarm of young people coming into their state were not unwashed hordes of hippie kids bent on sex and drugs but rather, in the main, informed and dedicated young people. These were their children, in some cases literally so. For example, Polly Cowan's sons Paul and Geoffrey were working in Mississippi during Freedom Summer, 1964.

The teams of women would arrive in Jackson on Tuesday, meet that night, travel to an outlying community to visit a Freedom School or voter-registration project on Wednesday, and return to husband and family Thursday. Thus the name: Wednesdays in Mississippi. The routine may seem tame today, but it occurred at a time when the mere sight of blacks and whites together could ignite violence. Tensions ran so high that first summer that not only could white and black staff members not live together, but often when Susan Goodwillie wanted to meet with her black counterpart, Doris Wilson, she had to sneak through the crepe myrtle in back of the swimming pool at the Sun and Sands Motel near the edge of the black community and then walk to the YWCA in that neighborhood. The first two white staff members who went to Jackson, Goodwillie and Diane Vivell, billed themselves as cookbook writers. They carefully displayed gourmet magazines on the coffee table at their Magnolia Towers apartment in downtown Jackson. A sympathetic local white minister told them theirs was the dumbest cover story he'd ever heard. If they were really writing a cookbook, he said, they'd be talking to black women, not white women.[5]

The black women from out of state were surprised at the problems they encountered. "The middle-class Negro woman [in Mississippi] was terrified, was not interested, was afraid she'd lose her job, etcetera, etcetera," Polly Cowan recalled. The northern black women found that they had as much of a sales job to do for civil rights with some black women as the northern whites had with southern whites.[6] "Fear blocks well-meaning citizens on both sides from identifying with the struggle," added Flaxie Pinkett, a Washington, D.C., real estate and insurance executive who traveled to Jackson and Meridian.[7] Convincing the white women to meet openly with outsiders, no matter how distinguished, was tough slogging, too. Some of the white women in Jackson would draw the drapes when the out-of-towners arrived for tea. Others reneged on pledges to open their homes for a meeting, saying they couldn't risk ostracism at church. Slowly they realized they were not free, either.[8]

Covering all bases, the women kept the White House and the

Justice Department aware of their mission in Mississippi. Theirs was a prominent and sophisticated group. From New York there were Marian Logan, wife of Dr. Arthur Logan, who was the chairman of HARYOU-Act, a jobs-and-education program, and active in the Urban League, and Jean Benjamin, herself active in United Nations work and wife of the chairman of United Artists; from Boston there was Laya Wiesner, wife of President Kennedy's science adviser. And among others were Pearl Willen, president of the National Council of Jewish Women; Helen Meyner, wife of the former governor of New Jersey and herself later a member of Congress; and Dr. Geraldine P. Woods, national president of Delta Theta Sigma, the influential black sorority. The women visited Hattiesburg, Canton, Meridian, Vicksburg, and Ruleville in addition to Jackson that first summer.[9]

On the trip to Mrs. Hamer's hometown, the group left Jackson at 6:30 in the morning in two cars, and, as the women drove by fields of cotton in bloom or ripening, one of them thought the green expanse looked peaceful. "One could well imagine how the South acquired its romantic reputation," Trude Lash, executive director of the Citizens Committee for Children of New York and wife of author Joseph Lash, wrote in her notes.[10] Mrs. Hamer met with the women and made sure they saw the Freedom School classes. The women of Ruleville laid out a big lunch, "obviously a matter of great pleasure and pride to them, but it was difficult to eat because the children, and adults too, looked on so hungrily," Lash noted.

"Mrs. Hamer was the 'big cheese' at this affair," according to one participant. She told how she lost her job when she tried to register, then was beaten because she tried to register other people. She quoted the Bible, then she led the group in freedom songs. "As I participated," the woman wrote later, "I thought of those white ladies at the coffee the day before who likewise are convinced their point of view can be defended biblically."[11] One of the guests spoke to Mrs. Hamer that day about the attitude of the local whites, and she replied that they had tried unsuccessfully to intimidate her. "They can do what they can," she told the woman, "but I'll never give in again."[12]

After lunch, the group met with the Ruleville Student Action Group, which complained about serving on cotton-picking details during school hours. "I was struck by the utter contempt these children had for their teachers and principal (all of whom were, of course, Negroes)," Lash wrote. "They seemed to be sure that any promise made would not be kept, that they would have to picket the school in the end and that it would be closed."[13]

Flo Kennedy, a wisecracking black attorney from New York,

went to Ruleville that day. At moments Kennedy was scared during the drive to Ruleville, she recalled, because at times they were obviously being followed. But she knew the pursuers must be afraid as well. "Maybe not as much [as we were] but they are also afraid. Everybody's scared for their ass. There aren't too many people ready to die for racism. They'll kill for racism but they won't die for racism."[14]

"Many women who had felt completely alone in their thoughts discovered through our efforts that other women were like-minded and that it would be possible for them to work together," Polly Cowan concluded. "We, in turn, were able to make it clear that we came into Mississippi in inter-racial teams to learn more about the problems of the South, but at the same time that we consider desegregation and integration a national learning process in which we, too, are deeply involved. . . .

"Even the most hostile Southern woman has been impressed by the honesty and sincerity of team members, and the presence of Northern women of such respectability plus a quiet and dedicated approach did modify many of the most antagonistic attitudes," Cowan said in a report at the end of the first summer. "There is a special sign of hope in the fact that we have finally been able to arrange for white team members to stay in southern white homes. No matter how much emphasis one feels should be placed on this as a breakthrough in white attitudes, the intimacy—and the necessarily polite exchange of ideas—of a host-guest relationship will provide an ideal atmosphere for establishing a dialogue between our team members and these influential white leaders."[15] The hope was that the women, now questioning some of their old values, might help change their husbands' attitudes, too. "We knew that the men would never move as fast as the women," Polly Cowan said. "Women do see the issues at a different level and they do think about their children in a different way, and they do think about the school system."[16]

Did Wednesdays in Mississippi change attitudes? Yes, and "once it happens, it doesn't unhappen," said Patt Derian, one of the white Jackson residents who cooperated with the project. For some, she added, it was just one more grain of sand that may ultimately produce the pearl. Others were given courage. "Every experience, especially a dislocating one like that, changes you."[17]

The Mississippi women asked the northerners to return a second year. The project evolved into Workshops in Mississippi, sessions at which women talked about specific community needs and programs that could meet those needs. In November 1966, some sixty women met in Jackson, where they talked about wanting better housing, more community centers, and free school breakfast and lunch programs. That session led to another in Oxford the following January. Annie Devine was a co-chair of the program that brought together federal officials and specialists from several Mississippi universities to help forty-three black women learn to write grant proposals for day care centers, school breakfasts, community centers, and programs for impoverished young teenage girls. Gone was the front-page drama of protests and pickets; the movement for change in Mississippi was evolving into quiet organizing around economic and educational issues. Mrs. Hamer attended the Oxford meeting. She stood up and said she hoped the next time there was such a session, she could bring "some of our poor white people from Sunflower County. We have some poor white people that feel exactly like we feel."[18]

Although the black women benefited from the information they received in Oxford, it became clear that the government officials needed help, too. An Agriculture Department home economist, informed ahead of time that she would be speaking to poor black women, nevertheless arrived complete with flannel-cloth visual aids with an illustration of a white middle-class family. Her talk "was not only inappropriate," it was also "nearly disastrous," said Polly Cowan. "It left the women convinced that Agriculture had nothing to offer them. Their real question—'how do you feed a family without enough money to buy sufficient food?'—was consistently answered by the advice that they go on welfare." Cowan considered the performance insensitive and went to Washington with a tape to play for department higher-ups. The tape proved "an articulate example as it played back the words of a roomful of grumbling, angry women."[19]

As a result, the National Council of Negro Women (NCNW) suggested a meeting between government officials and black women. The government would treat the black women as equals by considering them "consultants." Communications would therefore be two-way. The Agriculture Department and the Office of Economic Opportunity selected Sunflower County as the site for the meeting because NCNW had developed contacts there, especially Mrs. Hamer. She had had frequent conversations with county anti-poverty officials in which she was critical of the lack of representation of poor people in planning programs ostensibly designed to help them. These local officials were not, then, overjoyed by her role in the forthcoming meeting and complained to an Agriculture Department official in Washington. He replied that if Mrs. Hamer didn't attend, "we might as well not have the meeting."[20]

The National Council of Negro Women, as sponsoring organization, received a modest grant from the Office of Economic Opportunity to pay the women picked to attend. But there was a catch: NCNW had to have approval for the grant from the governor of the state in which the meeting would be held, and Governor Paul Johnson vetoed the grant. Word was that it was not only the content of the program that caused the veto, but also Mrs. Hamer's participation.[21] The governor considered the conference another sign of federal intrusion in state affairs.

Arriving in Indianola and learning of the veto, Cowan said that "to have called the workshop off at the last moment would have meant letting down the very people we were trying to help." The organizers had finally gotten federal and local officials to meet on the women's terms, despite the veto, and they didn't know when that opportunity would come again. "We couldn't have looked at ourselves in the mirror if we hadn't gone. So we took the chance and decided we could raise the funds after we had figured what money we owed, what the deposit would come to. It was more than worth the gamble."[22]

The day came, June 27, 1967, less than two months after the major election battle in the two small towns nearby, Sunflower and Moorhead. Mrs. Hamer had started lining up people three months earlier; in all, thirty-one women attended, as did fifteen members of federal, state, and local agencies and nine staff members from the local community action program, called Sunflower County Progress, Inc.[23] The anti-poverty agency chose eleven of the women who attended, Mrs. Hamer twenty. The women ranged in age from their twenties into their seventies. Most had worked either as domestics or as field hands. Some had recently volunteered as Head Start aides. Some of the women never showed up.

Mrs. Hamer was accustomed to people's living with fear, but the list of women attending remained in constant flux up until the last minute because of the threat of reprisals—reprisals for a meeting with government officials sanctioned by government officials. When Mrs. Hamer had told the local women about the workshop months before, they were delighted; later, tensions rose. They forgot. The baby was sick. They didn't have the right clothes. Or whatever. Few Indianola women would attend because the workshop was held too close to home—everybody knew them, and there might be retaliation.[24] One woman, though, attended despite being sick and bedraggled. Mrs. Hamer said she shouldn't have come in such bad health, but she wanted so much to participate that Mrs. Hamer didn't have the heart to say no. The woman hesitated in signing for her stipend for attending the conference, and finally one of the aides realized she couldn't write. They let her make an X, and Polly Cowan wondered, "How many of these people are there for whom Mrs. Hamer asked us for adult literacy training?"[25]

Driving up to a motel that had previously only had white guests, registering—then staying there—created enormous fear among some of the women. But it was overcome by the desire to "find out." Coping with private worries was part of the process. As a postscript, when the conference ended and the women prepared to leave the Travelodge, two of them held up their room keys and asked Polly Cowan: "What would you do if we said we were not going to return these?" They were joking, but they were telling her "they had never had it so good, that they had enjoyed every moment of the comfort . . . polite treatment by the white people who ran the hotel, privacy . . . and all the other things that more privileged people take for granted as part of a civilized, industrialized nation."[26]

The first morning of the session, Mrs. Hamer stood to speak about the governor's veto of the grant. Governor Johnson "wanted to know was I going to be here, so it must be political," she said. "The meeting is going to be held, and that's what's important. If we didn't get $6 a day, we'll still have gained a chance to talk and discuss our problems. This shows you the governor is not really concerned about poor people." Then she turned her guns on the local officials. She said that at anti-poverty board meetings the politically powerful Chancery Clerk Jack Harper did all the talking. She called him "nasty" and "not tolerant of civil rights people." The community action agency was hiring people who were economically better off, who had cars, she said. Eleven members of one family held jobs in the poverty program, she added indignantly. Poor whites and poor blacks don't benefit, and the "top folk look down on the bottom folk."[27]

Dorothy Height had given some of the women the confidence to speak up. "No one can divide us at this meeting," Height had said. "When we make a point with the government people, we make it as 'we'—the women in this workshop. No one will put us on the spot. We stand together."[28] So, after Mrs. Hamer spoke, the women bombarded the Agriculture Department representative with questions. How do you pay $58 for $100 worth of food stamps if your income is $30? Why does money go abroad when people are starving in Mississippi?

One woman said that when people visited her in her old cabin during rainstorms, they usually thought she was preparing to go outdoors because of the way she had to dress just to stay dry indoors. "I put on my rain hat, my coat and boots, and I put a number 3 tub on the chiffonier to catch some of the leaking water." Another woman topped that story. "When my family goes to bed" in the wintertime, she told the group, "we all look as though we are going for a walk. It's so cold most of the winter that we put on our hats, scarves and coats and anything else we can find to keep us warm before we dare to lie down. . . ."[29] A third woman spoke about her dilapidated house: "There is no place in the house from which you can't see the outdoors. You can sit just anyplace and look out."[30]

The women and the government officials ate two meals together at the local Bel Grove Baptist Church. Said one woman: "We've learned here we can better understand each other when we talk together. We've learned we can work together and even sit together. And to go a step further, we can even eat together. Maybe we can learn to live together and die together."[31]

When the day's sessions concluded, the planners got together that evening in a motel meeting room. Mrs. Hamer was clearly in a better mood after seeing that what the local woman were saying had registered on some of the officials. "What's beautiful to me," she said, was having the chance to "tell people what's really happening. [We've] never in our life really had a chance to express these feelings to the people in charge."

Dorothy Height and Fannie Lou Hamer, both formidable women, each in her own way, had talked only in a formal, how-do-you-do setting before this session. In Polly Cowan's notes, she stressed that Mrs. Hamer knew only that the National Council of Negro Women had held the Oxford workshop she had attended in January, and that her friend Annie Devine was working with the council. "Mrs. Hamer was round-eyed at Miss Height's ability to talk to the white people of Mississippi in a straightforward manner which, though never skipping or pussyfooting on the issue, still did not offend these men whose notion of the Negro woman was as uncomprehending as though they did not live in the same land."[32]

Chancery Clerk Harper, who ran the county, had initially seemed to Polly Cowan to be angry at having to attend. Someone at one of the workshops asked about women's being sterilized without their knowledge, and Harper reacted violently, "Who said that?" He feared that the people in charge would put false charges in their report and carry tales back to Washington. Cowan explained that that was not the point, that the conference organizers wanted instead to try to help the women state their needs and the government officials understand them and communicate with them.[33] Harper also questioned breaking up into small groups because he didn't want to miss what anybody might be saying. "Is this the way you *insist* on working?" he asked Cowan and Height.

The second day the group shifted to the Sunflower County anti-poverty offices. The chairs were arranged in the stiff, row-after-row arrangement so common at every meeting everyone has ever attended. The conference staff quickly rearranged them so that people could talk more comfortably. And the questions began. What about emergency hospital services for poor people in Sunflower County? Poor people had to travel partway across the state to charity hospitals in Jackson or Vicksburg. What about Social Security? Employers had been saying they were taking it out of a field hand's pay, then never wanted to know the worker's Social Security number. Were they being cheated? What about cutbacks in aid to dependent children? Why does one part of society consider some children "illegitimate" when another treats a child simply as a child? Why don't food stamp officials know more about how the poor really live? Why don't they understand that the poor cannot always come up with cash when they have bills for the rent and the doctor and limited money with which to pay them? Why don't people who run job training programs understand that pride sometimes stands in the way of learning? Why don't they know that people don't like to be laughed at because they aren't used to learning new things, or that they sometimes don't have the right clothes to wear to a training session?[34]

The auditorium filled up as people from other county agencies came in to listen. Dorothy Height was always impressed that no matter what he had thought of the conference at the outset, Harper—she referred to him as Colonel Harper, after his World War II rank—stayed and listened. When the sessions concluded, she thanked everyone and said: "We may not get all the answers, but none of us will ever be quite the same. For we have, in this day, been trying to hear one another." Then Harper stood up and praised Height and the staff, saying they had put on "a most objective meeting." He had heard civil rights leaders and he had heard the Ku Klux Klan. "I've never heard them be objective. No one could have done it as well as you did."[35]

Harper said he would not have predicted that such a session would be held, Dorothy Height recalled. " 'This is the first time I have heard Mrs. Hamer talking like this. We have had real communication,' [he said]. And from that moment forward, our best friend that we had was Colonel Harper."[36]

Then "Mrs. Hamer went up to Colonel Harper to thank him for saying what she and all of the women had wanted to say, and for saying it so well," Cowan reported. "He told her to sit down;

made her sit on the bench next to him, and they fell into earnest conversation. These leaders from Sunflower County, Negro and white, male and female, conservative and radical, each of whom had always talked about each other with total scorn!" Harper had known very well that the sterilization story came from Mrs. Hamer. But nonetheless the conference seemed to change his outlook. One day he had talked about something she said as a total lie, "and at the end of the second day they are able to have a conversation in ordinary tones without death and destruction in their manner."[37]

Harper said years later that he recognized Mrs. Hamer as "an aggressive, hard-hitting type of person who was asserting her rights . . . a natural leader because of her ability to rally people around her. I don't think there was any question but what she's entitled to be referred to as the leader in the transition from a no-rights to full-rights kind of situation."[38]

From the Indianola sessions emerged a cooperative program through which Sunflower County officials developed housing for poor people. Unita Blackwell developed many of the proposals for NCNW. From it also emerged a tie between Mrs. Hamer and NCNW that would lead to a unique "pig bank" to supply meat for some of the people of Sunflower County. From her own thoughts about hungry people and land ownership, Mrs. Hamer would bring forth Freedom Farm cooperative. In itself the two-day session did not yield great advances—if it had, Sunflower County would not still be in the sorry economic condition that it is today. The conference did open doors, although many in the community still resisted helping people through those doors.

The Indianola conference illustrated Mrs. Hamer's talents as an organizer. She delivered. She prodded people to take an extra step, to think for themselves about their own problems, as she did in organizing the Indianola workshop. Women played this role over and over again in the civil rights movement, as Mrs. Hamer's friend and fellow organizer Hollis Watkins, pointed out.

> If it hadn't of been for Ella Baker, there wouldn't have been any SNCC. When you looked at Sunflower County, you had to look at Fannie Lou Hamer. There was Victoria Gray in Hattiesburg and Annie Devine in Canton. When you looked at the Jackson movement, you had to look at Hazel Palmer. When you are talking about important roles, you have to ask which person has the most important role—the one who speaks or the one who got the people there?[39]

Fannie Lou Hamer could do both.

CHAPTER 11

"Do What
the Spirit Says Do"

HOW DOES A preschool program enter the realm of politics? Through the door opened by civil rights activities. When the poor people of Mississippi confronted those who governed them, a major source of friction was over who would run the new preschool programs known as Head Start, and, therefore, *how* they would be run. Working with the summer volunteers in 1964, people across Mississippi had set up Freedom Schools to help prepare their children to get a better education. For the youngest children, these schools were precursors of the Head Start program, run at first in Mississippi by ordinary people—black people, by and large, a fact that exasperated the white establishment.

Whites in Mississippi government at first misjudged the influence that programs like Head Start could have. They never dreamed how much federal money would be invested. They let that money, and control of the programs, slip from their grasp momentarily. Eventually, they wrestled control away from grass-roots organizations like the Child Development Group of Mississippi—known as CDGM, for short—but not without a horrific fight that split communities and reduced the influence of rural black people. A similar bruising battle occurred in Sunflower County; Fannie Lou Hamer was deeply involved—and accused of selling out—as a county agency outlasted her organization. The battles were bureaucratic, but they went to the core of this question: Would government help the poor change their own lives, or would government try to make the changes by itself?

Head Start does just what its name implies: it gives young children basic skills that they need to begin school. Perhaps more important for poor children, Head Start also gives them health and dental care they may never have received and helps them to enter the world outside their homes, to deal with new children and adults in their lives. Head Start in Mississippi began because local black parents, often with little or no education themselves, badly wanted their children to have what they had not had. The Child Development Group of Mississippi was established as their statewide umbrella organization.

In the summer of 1965, CDGM received its first federal grant of $1.4 million, funneled through a small black junior college to avoid the veto of Mississippi Governor Paul Johnson.[1] After setting up a network of parents who decided what programs their children needed and who helped teach the children, CDGM received a $5.6 million federal grant in February 1966.[2]

Senators John Stennis and James Eastland looked at the millions of dollars flowing into black communities and charged that federal money was being mismanaged. Under the rules governing anti-poverty projects, the programs had to have "maximum feasible participation" by the poor. Doubtless, some of the money was improperly managed because the poor, by definition, weren't used to managing money. But what was more offensive to white leaders in Mississippi was the fact that Head Start chiefly benefited black children and gave jobs to many blacks. The programs would have welcomed white children, but their parents were under enormous pressure not to enroll them. CDGM also offended because it wasn't run by white school boards.

The battle for control of Head Start in Mississippi concerned more than just who would help educate children, important as that was. As poor black people started speaking up about what they thought should be done to prepare their children for school, they also started asking questions about other aspects of their lives. Why, once their children completed a Head Start program, did they have to go to school in dilapidated old buildings or to segregated schools a decade after the Supreme Court had said segregation was unconstitutional? Why, since their children got sick because they drank foul water collected in rain barrels, didn't they have any running water in their neighborhood when white neighborhoods did? Or paved streets? Or street lights? Or other services? Their children were hungry, yet the government was paying huge subsidies to local planters not to use their fields to grow food. They wanted to know why. Why should special credentials be needed to teach children when, as one woman said, "Everybody know how to raise their children—they done raised up all the white children"?[3] Ultimately would come the question, Why can't *we* change those conditions by electing one of us?

Initially preoccupied with voter registration, Mrs. Hamer had mixed feelings about Head Start and other anti-poverty programs. Mary Tucker, who had invited Mrs. Hamer to her first mass voter-registration meeting in August 1962, said her friend fought her "like a dog would" against establishing Head Start.[4] MFDP wanted attention to remain on political action, which, it believed, could force other change. Anti-poverty programs, some Freedom Democrats believed, would drain efforts away from this political action. They considered them an attempt to curb black militancy and buy people off before real social changes were made. With anti-poverty money came rules about what people could and could not do. But others argued that by changing conditions for children, society itself would start to change. These arguments, however, occurred within the movement, which remained united when attacked from outside.

Head Start was not only a program for children; it benefited adults as well. L. C. Dorsey, whose family had sharecropped on Delta plantations, had had difficulty finding a job that paid decently or allowed her any pride until she started working for Head Start. She had heard her six children cry themselves to sleep because there was no money and no food in the house, and she swore that she would never go through that again. As a result, "I didn't see the Head Start program the same way everybody else saw it. I saw it purely as an economic opportunity for black folks who was oppressed not because they couldn't vote, dammit, but because they didn't have control over food for their kids. The job offered some money that white folks in the state didn't control."[5] Mrs. Hamer, she said, eventually became interested in Head Start more because of her love for children than for this economic reason.

When she did get involved, Mrs. Hamer was a pivotal figure because her name was known in Washington. Amzie Moore, the local man who helped SNCC get a foothold in the Delta, and Charles McLaurin contacted Mrs. Hamer and others about organizing a local anti-poverty program that was not part of the Sunflower County government.[6] "We felt kind of foolish sitting down and writing up a two-page proposal calling for $100,000 of federal money for our pre-schools," Mrs. Hamer said. "There wasn't maybe 12 years of schooling together among all of us folks who were struggling to write the proposal."[7]

Four Sunflower County women—Cora Flemming, Alice Giles, Thelma May, and Annie Mae King—had already gone to Jackson for the first CDGM organizational meeting and training. Cora Flemming became the director of this grass-roots group as it set up a preschool program. Every day during the summer of 1965, the women had to take the children who enrolled in their program out of Sunflower County to a rented church in Leland because Sunflower County people feared letting them use their buildings. That October, they were finally able to open four centers in people's homes in Indianola.[8]

At first, they operated on whatever money they could raise themselves, then with help from the statewide CDGM. Then, as white politicians started tightening the screws, the grass-roots group had its federal money cut off, even though it had 400 children enrolled in Indianola and another 168 in Ruleville. Senator Eastland had reportedly said that federal money would support CDGM efforts in Sunflower County over his dead body.[9] Annie Mae King felt her group held its own despite the cutoff of funds because it was not working for money alone. "We were working for freedom and to be able to govern our own affairs and our own businesses and to teach our own children." Everyone learned from the program, she added. The adults wanted to let the children "know to be free and don't have white people over them every time they turn around."[10]

To the white power structure in rural Mississippi, the only political fear greater than black advancement was the unity of poor blacks and poor whites. A few poor white people who had seen that Head Start might help their children, too, enrolled them to the program. "The other people in town tried to get them to take their children out," Mrs. Hamer said. "The poor whites just told them no. You never did nothing for my child. You're not going to get him now."[11]

Local officials, waking up to the federal dollars coming into their communities, decided that they should control that money. During the winter of 1965–1966, Sunflower County had set up a community action program, in part because Chancery Clerk Harper told the local authorities that if they didn't do it, less responsible people would. A World War II veteran, Harper had been recalled to duty during the Korean War and had served with blacks in an armored artillery group.

> I could see the world was changing. I could see that the federal government which was representing all of us . . . was beginning to provide for them and I could see the questions mounting. I was trained as an attorney and . . . knew what the Constitution said. I knew what the government was going to be doing, and I felt like I owed it to myself and to my family to position myself on these matters that were coming up in a way that I could live with.[12]

The agency, Sunflower County Progress, Inc., was headed at first by Indianola's former police chief, Bryce Alexander. Because he had broken up voter-registration meetings and arrested civil rights workers in Indianola, Mrs. Hamer and her allies saw his appointment as a mockery of the program.[13]

The grass-roots Head Start program in Sunflower County was surviving without government money because people volunteered their time; they donated fruit that they had canned or meat from their hogs to feed the children. When the rival Sunflower County Progress board was set up, Cora Flemming went to the board chairman and asked that the two programs be combined because her program was already up and running but desperately needed financial support. "He said definitely not, this was to be a new program, the right kind," Mrs. Flemming said. "We asked if theirs would be integrated. He said definitely not." Asked why there had been no public meeting before the board was selected, "he said he'd meet with two or three of us, but he didn't want no public nigger meeting." At another session with R. J. Allen, the board chairman, he kept using the word *nigger,* Mrs. Flemming told Polly Greenberg, a CDGM staff member who later wrote a deeply personal account of the organization. "We kept interrupting him, and asking him not to. Then he would turn red, and a minute later forget, and use it again."[14]

In March 1966, Walter Gregory, a young black graduate of Mississippi Valley State, was hired as assistant director of the county anti-poverty program. Soon he invited the community to meet with the government program's board at the American Legion hall. There had never been such a meeting before, so, despite one day's notice, a number of people turned out. None of the black board members attended because chairman Allen had asked them to stay home. He explained that "people of the community would feel more free talking to me instead of the Negro members."

Cora Flemming asked why. "Why did you tell the CAP Negro board members to stay home, are they children?"

Allen complained that outsiders were attending the meeting, that is, people from outside Indianola. "You mean to tell me the [community action program] board is set up for Sunflower and we are not a part of it and you consider us an outsider?" asked Mrs. Hamer. She and her allies accused the Sunflower County Progress board of not representing poor people, and they wanted an election. They had a point: the white members of the board included a planter, a grocer, a banker, and a physician, and the black members included two ministers, two teachers, two principals, a farmer, and a laborer.[15] "These were not poor, illiterate militant agitators," one historian said, in a monument to understatement. "They were individuals who already had well established communications with the white leadership."[16]

After Mrs. Hamer's complaint, Chancery Clerk Harper recalled that he told board members, "I don't see any reason why y'all don't elect Mrs. Hamer. Invite her on in. Put her on there. . . . Let's all talk about the same thing together instead of being divided." Mrs. Hamer was put on the board but, Harper said, she never attended a meeting. People were so at odds that there even was disagreement over why she wouldn't attend: she said the meetings were closed; the agency said they were open.[17]

Relations between the grass-roots and the government groups disintegrated even more two weeks later when Mrs. Flemming and thirty other people showed up for a meeting at city hall to which they had been invited. Police with billy clubs blocked the door and yelled at them to keep out. Police also drove several times past the church where Mrs. Flemming's group met after it left city hall. Walter Gregory went to that meeting and asked Mrs. Flemming to return to city hall, but she and the others were too frightened and refused. Later that evening Mrs. Flemming talked on the telephone with Polly Greenberg, and they composed a telegram to Sargent Shriver, director of the federal Office of Economic Opportunity, pointing out that police with blackjacks and riot helmets had driven the poor people from the meeting site. "Request clarification," their wire said. "Is this consistent with [Community Action Program] guidelines concerning maximum feasible participation of the poor?"[18]

In autumn 1966 the powers-that-be set up a new statewide organization—Mississippi Action for Progress, or MAP—as a politically more moderate grant-seeking rival to the Child Development Group. Its leadership included white and black moderates like Hodding Carter III of the *Delta Democrat-Times,* and Aaron Henry, the NAACP leader from Clarksdale. The board chairman was Owen Cooper of Yazoo City, president of the Mississippi Chemical Company and of the Mississippi Economic Council. "Wooing and winning [Aaron Henry] was the key that made it possible for OEO to get away with MAP. Aaron was a longtime symbol of the new-world Negro in Mississippi," wrote Polly Greenberg. "Shriver knew that liberals in the North, seeing Aaron's name on a list of board members for MAP (picked and controlled by the three chartering whites), would automatically believe MAP to be the good-guy group."[19] Because of his participation in this group, Greenberg argued, "Wow is he in trouble with thousands of articulate CDGM-type Negroes! They are absolutely livid with rage at him. . . . As far as they are concerned, he's a quisling."[20]

For his part, Henry saw nothing wrong in the federal government's requests for regular financial accounting or reports on use of automobiles. "We had to take the pressure off of Shriver, because Stennis and Eastland and the whole damn gang" wanted to cut off money for child development programs.[21]

With MAP waiting in the wings, the Johnson administration cut off CDGM's money in the fall of 1966. The Office of Economic Opportunity was so eager to turn to other groups to run Head Start programs that it gave a startup grant to Rust College in Holly Springs—not allied with CDGM—even before Washington had received the college's formal application.[22] Mrs. Hamer traveled to the Jackson State University campus for a rally at which she flayed the federal anti-poverty agency for backing down in the face of senatorial pressure. "I feel sorry for Sargent Shriver because he ain't ever had a mess like the mess he's going to have when all of us sit down in front of his house," she told a crowd of three thousand people. "People from Harlem, people from Watts are saying, 'Tell us when, honey, and we'll come with you.' "[23]

In April 1967, Sunflower County Progress, Inc., held elections for board membership.[24] Mrs. Hamer ran—even while busy raising money for the landmark elections in the towns of Sunflower and Moorhead. She was defeated, 105 to 84, by Miles Foster, a black man from Ruleville who was supported by whites. Mrs. Hamer filed a protest, but two federal examiners said that the election was properly conducted.[25]

Mrs. Flemming and Mrs. Hamer's group, Associated Communities of Sunflower County, still wasn't getting federal money, and Mrs. Hamer was mystified. She testified before a congressional hearing on the anti-poverty program in Jackson in April 1967. ACSC had one thousand children going to school every day, "and we haven't been able to get a dime."[26] Answering questions from Senator Joseph Clark of Pennsylvania, Mrs. Hamer said there remained great hostility to letting poverty-stricken people run their own program. "I am not convinced at this time that the landowners that's on the board, the people have cause us to be *in* poverty, is going to get us *out of it.*"[27]

Later the same day, Senator Jacob Javits of New York asked the black people of Mississippi who had come to testify at the hearing which anti-poverty program they thought most important, given limited resources of the government. Mrs. Hamer replied that

Head Start was one of the most important "because not only does it give the children a headstart but also it will give the adults a headstart."[28] Her friend Unita Blackwell told the senators what Head Start had meant to people with few skills when they left plantations in the mid-1960s. They learned that "they could make some decisions," she said. "They brought dignity to people, they also argued—like they do in Washington—on committees and these kind of things. They learned that they could argue with one another and try to reason and find out that they could make some decision for themselves." CDGM, she said, was so beloved because "it's the only program that ever reached down to where the poverty-, poverty-, poverty-stricken folks is."[29]

Officials of Sunflower County Progress protested Mrs. Hamer's appearance before the committee; they felt her testimony gave the senators a distorted view. In a telegram to Senator Clark, Colbert Crowe, SCPI's executive director, characterized the group that Mrs. Hamer represented as numerically insignificant, adding that it "consists of Negroes only." Mrs. Hamer had made a mistake in her testimony, Crowe said, in talking about a highway project that was not part of the anti-poverty program. "I would like to make the observation at this point that had Mrs. Hamer attended the meetings of our Board of Directors, she would know one program from another." Elsewhere, he said that OEO's Atlanta office had tried to mediate so that his agency and Mrs. Hamer could work together. "To this time, Mrs. Hamer has not demonstrated any interest in working with anyone in Sunflower County unless she is 'running the show.' "[30] It was clear that Mrs. Hamer annoyed Crowe intensely. She was domineering, and her interests and his clashed repeatedly.

Survival was a day-by-day matter for Sunflower County's grass-roots program. It finally managed to win a new federal grant to run its Head Start centers under the county anti-poverty agency—as what was called a delegate agency—for six months, July through December 1967. Sunflower County officials didn't like that idea, but OEO said it would withdraw its support for the whole county unless the Hamer-Flemming group got its money. As one senior OEO official in Atlanta said at the time, community action agencies were supposed to nurture, not obstruct, grass-roots organizations.[31]

But the poor were losing ground steadily in Washington and across the country. President Johnson, distracted from his war on poverty by the war in Vietnam, decided not to run again. Martin Luther King, Jr., was killed in April 1968 while in Memphis to lead marches by striking garbage workers, and the one champion of poor blacks to whom white America might listen was gone. After his death, the Poor People's Campaign foundered in the mud on the mall in Washington, D.C. Mrs. Hamer spoke on May 5, 1968, to marchers, led by a mule-driven wagon, as they pulled out of Marks, Mississippi, for the encampment in Washington. She said that a fair housing bill that had just passed promised her that she could eventually move into a white neighborhood, "But I can't find $16 to pay the rent where I live right now."[32] The moment for poor people was passing.

By that August, Sunflower County Progress cut off money for the grass-roots ACSC, claiming that it was not properly managing its programs, and the fight for remnants of control went on. Mrs. Hamer led protesters outside the county agency's offices in Indianola. They urged the anti-poverty program to borrow money to pay back wages to ACSC staff members who had been volunteering rather than see their program die. The county employees left the building, so the demonstrators moved inside out of the 90-degree heat. "Mrs. Fannie Lou Hamer, titular head of the group, took a seat at the receptionist's desk. From behind an 'information' sign, she occasionally broke the silence to answer reporters' questions," wrote Bob Boyd in the *Delta Democrat-Times.* " 'We just plan to sit here,' she said. 'We got plenty of time and this place is more comfortable than home for most of us. . . . The ACSC started Head Start in Sunflower County. Now the power structure is trying to take it away from us. We seen [Head Start] was something could lift people up by their bootstraps. The boot is being taken away from us and the strap, too.' "[33] Mrs. Hamer, Mrs. Flemming, and their allies had asked OEO to stop all salary payments to workers in both groups until their Head Start program got its own money. That made the black employees of the county program angry, and they blamed their rivals—not their own white-dominated board—for the cutoff.

The Sunflower Head Start programs also got caught in cross fire over school desegregation. Mississippi governor John Bell Williams was maneuvering for more lenient desegregation guidelines. For leverage, he vetoed Head Start grants in four counties, including Sunflower County, in February 1970. Health, Education and Welfare Secretary Robert Finch overrode the governor's veto and gave money to both Sunflower County programs. Mrs. Hamer's connections continued to pay off, and national civil rights leaders soon convened hearings in Jackson to let the poor tell their story. "We outnumber whites from five to one to nine to one and they use all kinds of tricks, every trick in the book to destroy Head Start programs ever since it has been started," Mrs. Hamer testified. It was not Governor Williams alone who sought to destroy local control over Head Start, she added, but rather a conspiracy of whites in the local counties as well.

"What they're saying now is, 'If we are going to have to deal with these niggers, *we've* got to determine how we're going to deal with them.' This whole thing is again using us for political footballs. We're not going for that mess. We have been pushed far enough and our voices are going to be heard," Mrs. Hamer said, adding that "the poor whites are seeing the same thing that has kept me behind the eight ball has kept them behind the eight ball." The programs would be worthless if taken out of the hands of the local people running them. And the trouble was not new, she said. "We have been in trouble with this program ever since Head Start started because all these politicians, they know as long as they control the program they are going to control the folks, and we ain't going to have it."[34]

By 1971, the federal government finally directed that there be only one Head Start program in Sunflower County and that the county run it. Rather than merge with the county program, the grass-roots ACSC held its six hundred children out of the county program and operated again on a volunteer basis.[35] Anti-poverty law provided for appealing federal decisions, and ACSC took its case to the OEO office in Atlanta. "To the best of my knowledge, that was the first hearing that had been held in Atlanta" on this kind of issue, said Walter Gregory, Sunflower County Head Start director.[36] Even though the government had said no, Mrs. Hamer and Mrs. Flemming wanted to prove a point: that people had a right to challenge government decisions, he added.

At the Atlanta hearings, Mrs. Hamer took the position that the grass-roots ACSC should continue to exist. But she was starting to see that a merger was inevitable. Pascol Townsend, a white attorney from Drew who was helping with the county government's response, traveled to Atlanta for the hearing and remembered how effectively Mrs. Hamer put her point across. She said, "You know if I would hit you with this finger, it wouldn't hurt," and she held up one finger and then another and another, saying each time, "If I were to hit you with this finger, it wouldn't hurt." But then she formed a fist and said, "But if I hit you with all fingers, it would hurt, like this."[37] The only way anti-poverty programs could work effectively, she was saying, might be as one program.

The federal government officials decided that all programs

should be operated through the community action agency, but that the grass-roots ACSC people should be involved. That proved easier to say in Atlanta than to do in Indianola. Mrs. Hamer was agreeable. She said that if her group could get acceptable, recognizable positions, it should merge with the county agency. The job of assistant Head Start director was created for Cora Flemming, said Walter Gregory, but she refused it. She was still simmering at the white employees of the government-run program, whom she had accused of "making their living from black people while they separate their [own] children from black children" by putting them in private schools.[38]

Mrs. Flemming, who had worked so hard and so much more directly with the program than Mrs. Hamer, was furious. Mrs. Hamer and several others "had joined forces behind our backs. They just sold out. It was the most horrible thing I ever saw. I hope I never go through anything like it again. When I got to the meeting [appealing the merger order], she said the meanest things to me. She called me everything but a child of God. She was just as vicious on me as she was on those chicken-eating preachers she was always after. . . . She knew better."[39]

The weeks after the Atlanta hearing on the Sunflower County Head Start program were a time of enormous stress on both sides of the dispute. Each group thought it was doing the right thing to achieve the same end of helping the children. Walter Gregory offered this explanation:

> Mrs. Hamer was not a self-centered selfish individual. Mrs. Hamer was concerned about the progress of the low-income black community. Mrs. Hamer saw this as an avenue to elevate some of the black residents of Sunflower County. Other persons on the outside, influential people outside, advised her that this was the right way to go. She wasn't hung up on the identity that "we want to keep ours." The differences between Mrs. Flemming and Mrs. Hamer really did not surface until we came back [from Atlanta] and we started working out the merger.

The fight over Head Start "created divisions between the races—not only between the races but among the races. People were divided between SCPI and ACSC in their loyalties—even down to families being divided. When I look back, I don't think that was good for the community."[40]

As tension escalated, someone threw a pipe bomb at Mrs. Hamer's house on January 28, 1971, but the bomb didn't explode. No one was ever prosecuted. No one can say for sure that the incident was connected with the Head Start dispute, although Mrs. Hamer told FBI investigators that she was convinced the people responsible were associated with the ACSC program. She had had some threats from people who believed she had sold out, she said. She said that it hurt her tremendously "to think that people of her own race, blacks, would attempt to harm her" or her family.[41] Mrs. Hamer used to say, only half in jest, that she knew white people didn't make the bomb, because if they had, it would have exploded.[42]

She was torn over which side was the right side and caught in an unwinnable exercise with the power of federal, state, and local governments arrayed against a grass-roots organization. "The ACSC still tried to lean on high visibility types to bail them out of an administrative problem," Jack Harper said, and Mrs. Hamer couldn't do it. "I think she concluded it would be better for her people if everybody came together. And then she set out to get an arrangement whereby everybody in that organization would be in a transition and brought in and taken care of and the children would be taken care of." Many of the ACSC people did go to work for the county program, but there were still bad feelings. "I think Mrs. Flemming was getting bad advice," said Harper; others felt Mrs. Hamer got bad advice.[43]

Mrs. Hamer was the key to outside support that the grass-roots group felt it needed. "Each side would try to get some prominent individual to side with them," recalled David Rice, who ran the statewide program that succeeded CDGM. Mrs. Hamer "got sucked in that way, and it may have been better not to get involved."[44] Telling Fannie Lou Hamer not to get involved, however, was like telling the pope to renounce Catholicism.

Speaking of the bitterness and of the charges of sellout, Unita Blackwell had an explanation. "Mrs. Hamer was a big piece of that community and everybody leaned on her," she explained. "It's a bad way to be. . . . When everybody's looking to you . . . then whenever a decision is made, you're wrong."[45]

Mrs. Flemming and Mrs. Hamer later made peace while Mrs. Hamer was ill in the hospital. For a long time, Mrs. Flemming said, she had not wanted even to hear Mrs. Hamer's name. "It took a lot of prayer, a lot of talking to other people, a lot of prayer. Finally the Lord began to soften the innermost hatred I had for her." By the time of the hospital visit, Mrs. Flemming said, "I had forgiven her a long time ago. I imagine I said too much. When you get down to the nitty gritty, we all said too much." Even with this intense personal conflict, Mrs. Flemming said she had learned from the long battle. "I learned how it didn't take all the harshness, all the animosity. It took a coming together of black and white. It was a new era and we couldn't expect it all to happen overnight, but we could do things if we worked together. [Mrs. Hamer] taught me how to give and take. She taught me how to love—how to dislike your ways but love the person."[46]

Children's education proved not to be the main issue in this fight; the divisions centered on how adults were involved. The children "were going to get nutrition services in any event, they were going to get social services in any event, they were going to get educational services in any event," said Greenville attorney Robert Buck, who directed the educational program for the grass-roots ACSC from 1969 to 1971. "Now, it depended on one's point of view when it comes to education, but I think in terms of provision of basic services, either program was capable. Now that the dust has settled and the disagreements have somewhat died down, you could say the children are being served. But a lot of people got shut off—but we're talking about adults."

Adults had not only held jobs under ACSC but had also started to question the conditions under which they lived. "It was key as I saw it," Buck added, "to get people registered, to get people organized, to get people educated because the whole idea of participation in the political process was very new to black folks at that time. This was the vehicle. That was of course not the official purpose of the organization—but I saw that as a purpose of the program." Thus, the local white officials were right to be concerned. "They recognized clearly—they were not mistaken" about its impact, Buck added. "The people from the civil rights movement put the picket signs in the back room and put on a tie and went to work with children. The anti-poverty program as originally conceived was a nightmare for the local power structure. But it was a springboard for people."[47]

Head Start was not Fannie Lou Hamer's cause of choice. She was far more motivated by the issue that had caused her own life to change: voting. But she became involved because the fight over control of Head Start in Mississippi and in Sunflower County was intensely political. It went to the root of what politics is all about, what politicians and the press so often forget: that in a true democracy, people are politically active not to achieve celebrity or money but to change their own lives. The fight over control of Head Start also was a classic contest of us-against-them, and Mrs. Hamer was a scrapper. That the battle made adversaries of people who should have been allies was the community's loss.

CHAPTER 12

"Every Rung
Goes Higher,
Higher"

WHAT THE NATIONAL Democratic Party refused to do in 1964—seat the challengers from Mississippi—it finally did with relative ease in 1968. A common misperception exists, however, that it was the Mississippi Freedom Democrats, joined by liberal whites, who were officially recognized at the Democratic National Convention in Chicago. In fact, Aaron Henry, Fannie Lou Hamer, and a few others belonged to both the 1964 and 1968 delegations, but it was not MFDP that was seated in 1968. Cries of black power and the fear that slogan generated among many established politicians guaranteed that the predominantly black MFDP, acting alone, would never have been seated.

The 1968 delegation from Mississippi was instead a coalition representing the NAACP, AFL-CIO, Young Democrats, MFDP, the black Prince Hall Masons, and the black Mississippi Teachers Association. Although the delegation was far more liberal than those from most other states and decidedly to the left of the one sent by the regular Mississippi Democratic Party, it was not guided by the principles of radical reform that MFDP espoused. Its core group had, all signs indicate, been established to undercut the MFDP militancy. Nonetheless, its seating, the result of long and patient effort by a handful of lawyers and activists of varying political stripes, did cap years of effort by MFDP, the Student Non-Violent Coordinating Committee, the NAACP, and hundreds of individuals working to force the national Democratic Party to recognize the rights of black southerners to participate in political affairs.

Their achievement did not get the attention it deserved. Violent protests against the Vietnam War swirled through the streets and parks of Chicago. Television cameras and print journalists focused outside the convention hall, not inside, as police and protest leaders alike seemed intent on escalating the confrontation. No delegation would have been more likely to be in the streets with the demonstrators in any other year than this new crew from Mississippi. Mrs. Hamer and the MFDP members of the delegation were already clearly on record as opposing the war—and had been since well before Dr. Martin Luther King, Jr., made his own public declaration. Mrs. Hamer had questioned the war in speeches before the 1964 convention. She later sent President Johnson a telegram asking him to bring the troops out of Vietnam "where they have no business anyhow, and bring them to Mississippi and Louisiana because if this is a Great Society, I'd hate to see a bad one."[1] Mrs. Hamer's frequent appearances at anti-war rallies marked her as one of the individuals about whom the FBI was filing its COINTEL-PRO reports. Despite their natural sympathies, however, these delegates stayed in their places inside the convention hall because they had put their lives in jeopardy and built a detailed case to get there.

Fannie Lou Hamer remained the member of the delegation whom others most wanted to meet. She generated concern among establishment politicians that she might transform an already volatile convention with an emotional speech. But she had had to be persuaded to attend the convention in the first place because she felt blacks were being muscled aside.

Maneuvering for the 1968 convention had begun almost as soon as the 1964 convention was over. The national Democratic Party named a commission, headed by former Pennsylvania governor David Lawrence, chair of the credentials committee in Atlantic City, to draw up rules for selecting delegates to the 1968 convention.

The national party's requirement that every state Democratic Party open its ranks to full participation by blacks might as well have been beamed to outer space as far as Mississippi was concerned. The state's regular Democratic Party conducted business as usual, either thinking the national convention would once again prove spineless or, more likely, knowing that they retained local political control and would continue to retain it. They were playing out their drama for consumption from Holly Springs to Biloxi, not for Washington.

White Democrats with mixed loyalties—local and national—found themselves torn. Douglas Wynn, the Greenville attorney who had stayed at the 1964 convention when the rest of the regulars walked out, wanted Mississippi to find favor with the national party but opposed the militant leadership that had provided the muscle behind the 1964 challenge. Wynn was married at the time to the daughter of Lyndon Johnson's political ally in Texas, attorney Edward Clark, and was a guest at the LBJ Ranch immediately after the 1964 convention. Returning to Greenville after that visit, he told the *Delta Democrat-Times* that civil rights was not discussed at the ranch. It was "a dead issue and will probably never be a campaign issue again," he said.

"I think whatever else is said about the so-called Freedom Democratic Party, the actions of its members in Atlantic City exposed the group for just what it is . . . an extra-legal lawless bunch of hooligans, people who do not have the ability to abide by any legal precepts," Wynn added. He hoped its supporters would work within the framework of the two established parties. The oath of loyalty to the presidential candidates required by the Democratic convention was "onerous and uncalled for," he added.[2]

Wynn kept after the White House and the national Democratic Party over the next few years to reduce MFDP strength by supporting more conventional groups in Mississippi. "I have gotten together a group which fairly represents current leadership among the loyal Democrats," Wynn wrote to presidential aide Marvin Watson in November 1965, "and believe that we can really go places with this group, provided we are given a little assistance." Wynn also wrote to the White House on judicial appointments, White House invitations, and federal anti-poverty programs in Mississippi. His letters on Mississippi politics vis-à-vis the national party are relevant because he would become an attorney for the 1968 challenge delegation. He was the only person from Mississippi actually seated at both the 1964 convention—as a regular—and at the 1968 convention—as a Loyalist challenger. The letters represent only one source of opinion on Mississippi politics, but they moved through a White House channel to which the Freedom Democrats had no access.

Wynn's letters contained no opinions about individuals such as Mrs. Hamer. Decades later, he had come to regard her as "a woman of great integrity," although "not a political realist up until just about the very end." She "supported her convictions with every ounce of energy that she had, and my God, that woman had some energy."[3] But his letters to the White House did characterize the entire MFDP, of which she was a leader, along with the Student Non-Violent Coordinating Committee, as "the extremist civil rights organizations presently active in the State of Mississippi . . . they support neither the Administration, nor the efforts of the local citizens to arrive at a peaceful and equitable solution of racial problems. Their aim is racial disharmony rather than racial harmony."[4]

Both Aaron Henry and Fannie Lou Hamer, chair and vice chair, respectively, of the Mississippi Freedom Democratic Party delegation in 1964, had in fact campaigned for Lyndon Johnson. Henry took the month of October to travel in support of Johnson and Hubert Humphrey.[5]

Wynn again wrote to the White House in August 1966, urging strongly "that a repetition of the public hearings at the 1964 convention in Atlantic City should be avoided at all costs."[6] Through those hearings, the American television audience had seen the unfiltered view of black Mississippians concerning the obstacles to voting and other political participation they faced. But at this juncture, Wynn was hardly alone in his view that MFDP was immoderate. The NAACP increasingly distanced itself from the Freedom Democrats because of their rhetoric and their anger at Aaron Henry. Many Democrats nationally were wary of MFDP's unpredictability. And national newsmagazines were elevating the more moderate Martin Luther King, Jr. (until he came out against the war) and sniping at the MFDP. During the 1964 convention, *Time* magazine had huffed that MFDP members spent "most of their time shouting into ever-ready television mikes." *Newsweek* fumed that the "undisciplined, mistrustful Freedom Democrats" did not understand that they had won a victory, then "frittered away its psychological impact by treating it stubbornly as a defeat." Later, *Newsweek* took on Mrs. Hamer directly, reporting that black moderates said that "Fannie Lou Hamer, the Freedom Democrats' leading mouthpiece, is showing disturbing demagogic tendencies— attacking middle-class Negroes and whites, American policy in Vietnam, and Martin Luther King."[7]

The Democratic Party's Special Equal Rights Committee was setting about its work writing the rules for the 1968 convention. Headed by New Jersey governor Richard Hughes after David Lawrence died, the committee was considering a proposal requiring each state to meet specific quotas for black representation within its delegation. The proposal was drafted by Joseph Rauh, who had been named special counsel for a Hughes Commission subcommittee; by Mildred Jeffrey, an ally of the black Mississippians and Democratic national committeewoman from Michigan with strong ties to Walter Reuther and the United Auto Workers; and by Aaron Henry. Under their plan, the 1968 credentials committee could have decided that discrimination existed in state party processes if a delegation had less than 10 percent black representation from a state with more than 20 percent black population. Top state party officials would also have had to pledge support for the 1964 Civil Rights Act and the 1965 Voting Rights Act, pledges many southern Democrats were unwilling to make at that point. But the panel shelved this proposal when it generated a stormy reaction and decided instead in mid-July 1967 that the convention could deny seating to a state delegation that had failed to grant "full participation" to black people. This meant that all public party meetings at all levels had to be open to all Democrats, regardless of race; the meetings also had to be publicized in advance and held in large, accessible halls. There could be no party membership tests that required supporting racial discrimination, as there had been in Mississippi. And the party at all levels must support broad voter registration, again without reference to race. The rules were imprecise, and it was still unclear how they would be put into play at the convention the following year. But by that October, all but two states had pledged to send racially representative delegations to that convention. Mississippi and Alabama were the holdouts.[8]

Meanwhile, in Mississippi two new groups emerged to assuage fears within Lyndon Johnson's White House that blacks and their reform-minded white allies might be reaching too far too fast toward both economic and political change. The first group appeared in the fight over Head Start, that is, the group known as Mississippi Action for Progress. The other, featuring somewhat the same cast, called itself the Loyal Democrats of Mississippi, or Loyalists. Its leaders included Aaron Henry, newspaperman Hodding Carter III, NAACP official Charles Evers, Jackson activist Patt Derian, attorney Wes Watkins of Greenville, and Doug Wynn. There was talk that this was a "Third Force" established to undercut the Freedom Democrats. There was no conscious plan that he knew of, Hodding Carter insisted in a 1968 interview, but "having said that, I want to say very candidly that I believe totally in that approach." He agreed with many of MFDP's goals, he said, but unless they could work in a coalition, "no matter how ideologically distasteful it may be on both sides, we are going to be absolutely powerless in the face of whatever conservative group may exist in Mississippi."[9]

As the 1968 convention neared, the Loyalists carefully monitored activities of the regular Democratic Party, documenting its exclusion of black people. They conducted their own precinct, county, and state nominating conventions, then challenged the regulars in Chicago. In Mississippi, there had never before been an integrated political force like the Loyalists; in 1968, it was still an act of political courage for whites to ally themselves publicly with blacks. This was a state that had elected its first black legislator since Reconstruction only one year earlier.

The regular Democratic Party made the Loyalists' job easy. For example, at a meeting of the white-controlled regular Democrats, Donald Franks of Booneville tried to place the party record as having "no objection" to participation by blacks, but his resolution failed when Governor John Bell Williams said such a statement would damage the organization.[10] Franks believed the party had to "solicit the Negro vote in counties where Negroes dominate," but the party leadership disagreed.[11]

The Loyalists drew up a legal brief for their challenge that detailed how these regulars thumbed their noses repeatedly at the idea of "full participation" by anyone other than themselves. For example, in Coahoma County, home of Aaron Henry, no black convention delegates were elected even though blacks made up 70 percent of the population. In one precinct, three hundred or four hundred blacks showed up for a meeting at the community's small health center but couldn't get in. "There were six or seven white men inside and a couple of colored folk," John B. Hollins, who was active in voter-registration work, told a reporter. "Pretty soon they came out and told us who was going to be chairman, the delegate and the rest. That was it. When we complained, they went back inside."

In Holmes County, 72 percent black, the regulars announced in the local paper that their meeting would be held at the courthouse. But the meeting was actually held at city hall, where a small group of whites picked the delegates while blacks and a few whites gathered at the courthouse, waiting futilely for the session to begin. In Leflore County, regulars controlled the convention and ignored blacks. In nearby Sunflower County, however, Chancery Clerk Jack Harper, Jr., led a convention that selected a more racially balanced delegation than the one the Loyalist faction chose later. All the black delegates were people with ties to the white leadership: that is, teachers, preachers, or merchants.[12] Harper later unsuccessfully challenged the Loyalist delegation from his county.

In defeat, the black participants were building their challenge case. Before attending the regular party meetings, they studied the rules and drilled on how to participate in political caucuses so the regulars couldn't outsmart them. Wes Watkins, one of the Loyalist attorneys, remembered that he and Doug Wynn conducted workshops all over the state. "We did a lot of role-playing—usually Doug and I would play the sheriff and just give 'em hell and we'd just do it over and over again until, at some caucuses, the blacks just turned the [regular] whites inside out. The whites didn't know shit about Roberts Rules of Order but the blacks . . . knew the magic words, and we made just a hell of a record out of those caucuses."[13]

A few Loyalists, such as Charles Evers, were elected to attend the regular party convention in Jackson starting in late June 1968. It would pick twenty-four at-large delegates to go to Chicago along with twenty delegates already selected at caucuses around the state. The regulars' convention was historic for two reasons: it was the first integrated party session since Reconstruction ("integrated" meaning that about 10 percent of the delegates were black), and it was the first time the convention, meeting in a Mississippi summer, had ever been held in an air-conditioned hall.[14] Three blacks were among those elected locally—Evers, Dr. Gilbert Mason of Biloxi, and Dr. Matthew Page of Greenville. Loyalists tried to get a more open process and failed. They tried to win agreement to an oath of loyalty to the national ticket and failed again. No blacks were elected among the twenty-four additional delegates. Evers withdrew in protest.

After the convention, Governor John Bell Williams promised that the regulars would comply with national party guidelines yet remain true to their principles, a contortionist act virtually impossible to perform. Yet he also proclaimed that his party did not plan to comply "to make ourselves guinea pigs for social theoreticians, dreamers and planners trying to restructure the world to conform to their preconceived notions of idealism."[15]

The conduct of the regular party's state convention made a challenge imperative. The Loyalists held their own conventions in all but about ten of Mississippi's eighty-two counties in the last week of July 1968. In Sunflower County, the Loyalists held precinct and county conventions the same night. Only two of the 125 people present were white. Mrs. Hamer led a field of seven black delegates, including her friend Mae Bertha Carter from Drew, and two whites.[16]

The next step was the congressional district convention. That meant Mrs. Hamer had to return to Winona, where she had been jailed and beaten in 1963. She went unquestioningly, and she and Hodding Carter were among the delegates selected at a meeting August 7 at the Haven Methodist Church. "It was in a black church," Carter recalled. "It was, as always, hot. It was, as always, a little scary underneath." It was clear to Carter that if anyone was going from that district, it would be Mrs. Hamer.

"What divisions there were, were on what you were going to

the convention for—whether it was opposition to the war, support for a particular candidate or as a fifth column to change the party," Carter said. The Loyalists conducted their entire delegate-selection process, including this Winona meeting, in a ritualistically formal manner to ensure compliance with national party guidelines. It was obviously a fragile coalition, however. "There is nothing like a lack of power to create division," Carter said, so there were "ferocious fissures."[17]

A tug-of-war for the soul of the reform movement was under way in Mississippi. Would Mrs. Hamer and Lawrence Guyot and others who sought a restructuring of the society keep the momentum gained in 1964? Or would others who thought the MFDP far too radical ever to prevail in Mississippi gain the upper hand? Doug Wynn of the Loyalists said he worked with MFDP that year although he still opposed it. He felt the MFDP had been a divisive influence in Mississippi in 1964. The Freedom Democrats had "alienated . . . an awful lot of white people" by their mock election race against Governor Paul Johnson in 1963, which Wynn said contributed to Lyndon Johnson's failure to carry Mississippi in 1964. But Wynn was also concerned about MFDP's economic positions. "They seemed pretty Marxist to me. I think they had some people that . . . genuinely had from a socialist to a Marxist economic outlook."[18]

Because of the need to articulate a strong black point of view, the Freedom Democrats had decided to join the challenging coalition even though it was more conservative than the MFDP would have liked. One district meeting, for example, faced a vote on Vietnam. The more conservative element suggested not giving the national party any directives on the war until the Loyalists were seated. "FDP on the other side was saying well, hell, the only reason for going is to be able to speak to the issues that people are concerned about," said the Reverend Harry Bowie, one of the MFDP strategists. "And if you violate that [commitment to speak out] in the effort to get seated, then you don't go with integrity. . . ." The MFDP members spoke out firmly on the war and carried the vote on that issue in the caucus.[19]

The dilemma for Mrs. Hamer was her fear that the political structure of Mississippi would be changed without altering the relationship of the poor to that structure. She did not want to replace "a totally bad political structure with one which is nice perhaps, more benevolent, but still not necessarily . . . fully responsive to the needs of the poor," Bowie said.[20]

The blacks who had been associated with the 1964 convention

challenge were not alone in recognizing the gulf between the militants and the moderates. Ed King, the former Tougaloo chaplain and one of the only whites in that 1964 MFDP delegation, wrote: "To many radicals in the movement, the wrong style is a most serious offense, punishable by everlasting distrust. What one does is not nearly so important as how one does it. Since [Hodding] Carter does everything in Southern, aristocratic fashion, all the fine editorials that he may write can never commute his sentence."[21] To many in the MFDP, white liberals of Carter's stripe, though sympathetic to their cause, at best were seen as guilty of paternalism and at worst were viewed as part of the ruling establishment.

There are those who have said that the MFDP was submerged in the 1968 Loyalist delegation. Lawrence Guyot has adamantly insisted that was not the case, that the MFDP was better organized in more regions than the Loyalists thought, and that it had elected many of its people in precinct and county conventions before the Loyalists knew what had happened. "We had 50 percent of that delegation. Harry Bowie and myself went around the state and organized the nominating committees and we sat down with Hodding Carter and Charles Evers. . . . They were prepared to laugh at us. They said, 'What've you all got?' " Guyot named the MFDP-backed delegates. "They couldn't believe it."[22]

Engineering a balanced delegation, in which all segments of the coalition felt they had a voice, was a delicate operation. Hodding Carter, Charles Evers, and Aaron Henry were bringing aboard more whites than some of the black civil rights workers wanted. Recalling a meeting before the convention, Owen Brooks, who had gone south from Massachusetts to work after hearing Mrs. Hamer speak at a rally, said that the leaders pulling together the delegation had one clear goal: They wanted it 50 percent black, 50 percent white. Brooks questioned the controlled atmosphere. "I said, 'Aren't we being as bad as white folks have been to us all these years? We shouldn't really be creating this delegation like this.' " By Brooks's account, Charles Evers jumped up and said, "Owen, you don't understand us black Mississippians. We aren't going to be as bad to white folks as they have been to us."

"Charles," Brooks replied, "ain't no white folks going to vote for Hubert Humphrey in the state of Mississippi. Why we got to give up half our delegation to white folk if we know they going to vote for you-know-who in 1968?"[23] You-know-who was Governor George Wallace of Alabama, who appealed to southern whites fearful of integration.

Faced with these moves, MFDP struggled to ensure that the

platform of the new party would reflect its own goals. "A lot of the principles of FDP did get lost in the shuffle, which was predictable, given who was in charge of the party at the time," Brooks said.[24] But MFDP "really had no choice" in 1968, he added. "With the guidelines the national party had laid out, it would not have been seated" acting on its own.

Brooks had a reputation as a tough negotiator—Loyalist attorney Watkins, smiling at the memory of it, called him "the great destroyer." He made consensus difficult, Watkins recalled, but added, "Thank God for those guys because they scared the whites so goddamn much that they were willing to deal with us [the Loyalists], and it couldn't have happened without them. But at the same time, it made a very prickly sort of marriage."[25]

The Loyalists held their statewide convention in Jackson on August 11. The convention delegates called for a negotiated settlement of the war in Vietnam, recommended lowering the voting age to eighteen, pledged support for the national ticket, and announced that they would indeed challenge the seating of the regular Democrats. They selected a delegation that would be balanced racially. This time, Vice President Hubert Humphrey supported the challenge, sending Walter Mondale, who had succeeded him in the Senate, to Jackson as his representative.[26]

Creation of the Loyal Democrats did not immediately end the influence of the Mississippi Freedom Democrats. MFDP continued to force Mississippi to confront itself. MFDP suits eventually produced fairer district lines for the state legislature and contributed to a landmark Supreme Court decision broadening interpretation of the Voting Rights Act's clause on clearing election laws through the Justice Department. MFDP, and Mrs. Hamer, thus helped break the back of official southern resistance to black political participation.

The Freedom Democrats had to be part of the challenging coalition, said Annie Devine; the coalition's leaders had no choice. Political activists across the country knew who had brought the 1964 challenge, knew who had forced the change in national party rules. They knew that without the former sharecroppers and other working people, this 1968 delegation would lack legitimacy. If the public remembered anything about the 1964 convention, it was Mrs. Hamer's testimony at the credentials committee hearing. "The challenge was FDP's from the beginning," Mrs. Devine said, and FDP had to be there in the end or outside support might dry up.[27]

Mrs. Hamer's was an especially vital presence. Locked out

again, she would have been very vocal, possibly saying that the Loyalist Democrats still did not represent Mississippi and that therefore the Freedom Democratic Party was still needed. "Mrs. Hamer and a lot of other people didn't want to have anything to do with [the Loyalists], initially from the outset," said former SNCC worker Hollis Watkins. "They felt that it truly did not represent the constituency and the masses of poor black people. And when you look at what has happened over the long run, you can say now in retrospect that that was the correct position."[28]

Mrs. Hamer had to have her arm twisted to go to Chicago but finally decided to give the coalition a chance. In an interview before the convention, she said that she and MFDP allies had to go to prevent others "from going up there saying they represent the people of Mississippi 'cause they don't. Whole lot of us they are not representing, and we have to be there to say they ain't representing us; we are here to represent ourselves."[29] Ninety percent of the delegation should have been black, she felt; blacks were the ones who had begun the fight when few would join them. "Now I don't mind giving the whites what they got, but don't give them over what they got 'cause they never give us nothing.'" In her more suspicious moods, which came and went in later years, she voiced the notion that whites had become involved because they thought a black delegation might be seated in 1968. That would be "too much recognition for a bunch of niggers. So why not step on the bandwagon and take it over?"[30]

Unita Blackwell summed up the feelings of some MFDP delegates about their new allies with her characteristic bluntness: "These is some of the same folks that's in the coalition now [that was] asking what in the hell was we going up yonder for in 1964." Blackwell did not expect to be seated but added that she now understood what the system was doing to black people. "I won't leave there upset in a kind of a way like I was in 1964. I really won't."[31]

Once again, Mississippians presented a challenge before the national party's credentials committee. This time, however, the challengers had the party's own declaration of 1964 on their side. They could ask whether the state party had done what the national party said must be done: that is, assure black voters the opportunity to participate fully in party affairs. "The irrefutable answer is *no!* They have not," the challengers said.[32] The Mississippi Democratic Party had continued to run the state of Mississippi, continued to control all three branches of government and continued to fill every single one of the 1,245 party offices with "regular" whites.

Mississippi also continued to engage in threats of violence and economic sanctions. Reprisals against black candidates and voters continued. Vernon Dahmer of Hattiesburg and Wharlest Jackson, both black men active in civil rights, had been killed. Night riders shot into Charles Evers's home in 1968. And Mississippi legislators had introduced thirty bills to dilute the black vote in the 1966 session; twelve of those bills passed. Election officials still refused to assist illiterate blacks at the polls in some counties; in the Delta, officials sometimes located polling places in plantation stores where black voters could be easily intimidated by the landowners.

Party regulars might argue that they had no control over local election officials—which was not true—but they did govern internal party affairs. The regular Democratic Party never responded, as required, to the report of the Democratic National Committee on opening up state parties to minorities. During this period the regular party never held a nondiscriminatory voter-registration drive and, the challengers said, they in fact fostered many local drives aimed at signing up only white voters. Governor John Bell Williams's right-hand man, Brad Dye, Jr., directed the selection of at-large delegates and alternates to the national convention, and no blacks were selected. "The governor showed his true colors," the Loyalists said, "that he did not want to comply with the mandate of the national Democratic Party in having a broadly representative delegation."[33] Even the three blacks selected as regular party delegates had been elected locally because of black-led efforts, not selected by the party.

In their brief presented to the credentials committee, the challengers outlined a history of disloyalty by regular Mississippi Democratic delegations. They pointed out that, in their contempt for the national party, neither the governor nor lieutenant governor was attending the 1968 convention, nor was either of the Mississippi senators or any of its members of Congress. It was another "Joe Doakes" delegation. As in 1964, "the delegation contains no one who can give a binding pledge to the national convention to ensure loyalty by the state 'regulars,' " the Loyalists pointed out.

Loyalist chairman Aaron Henry knew it did not matter how good his delegation's preparation was or how meticulous its legal brief. Once Democrats gathered at their Chicago convention site, politics, not legalisms, would determine who won. That summer he told a meeting of political activists that if the national Democratic Party leaders "think they can get more votes out of the country by supporting us, then they'll support us. If they can get more from John Bell Williams, they'll support him."[34]

On Monday, August 19, the credentials committee held five hours of discussion. Loyalist attorney Douglas Wynn reminded the panel that "if the regular delegation is seated, they will go home after the 1968 convention just as they did in 1964 and work for the third party candidate or a Goldwater." Wynn was careful to add that the Loyalists did not represent themselves as a separate party but used the name Loyalist to distinguish themselves from the regulars.[35]

Speaking for the regulars, Jack Travis, Hinds County district attorney, said that decent people in Mississippi deplored the violence directed at civil rights workers but that these wrongs could not be blamed on the party. "I am a loyalist and many people in the delegation are loyalists," he insisted. "We have answered the call to this convention which said an effort must be made. We have made progress. You kick us out and the Wallace crowd will have their arms open and catch a lot of people. . . . They'll flock to Wallace. . . . We'll be out and the Republicans will be in Mississippi and all over the South."[36]

The Loyalists rejected a last-minute compromise. Emissaries of New Jersey governor Richard Hughes, chairman of the credentials committee, asked Aaron Henry and Wes Watkins to seat eight members of the regular delegation in addition to all the Loyalists. The eight would have been chosen from the three so-called clean counties in which discrimination against black party participation was minimal or nonexistent.[37] Hughes sent a young black staff member to Henry with the request, a young man who was clearly uncomfortable in his mission, Watkins recalled. "The kid swallowed and said, 'The governor has told me that you will accept it or he will force it on you.' And Aaron was speechless, and I said—I don't know where I got the guts to say it, 'You tell that son-of-a-bitch we'll see his ass on national television in the morning if he tries it.' And Aaron smiled and agreed with me and the kid was so happy. He asked if we wanted it repeated just that way."[38]

At the credentials committee meeting, Governor Farris Bryant of Florida also tried unsuccessfully to win a compromise. He wanted to rebuke—he called it "punishing"—the regular party for failing to do enough to end discrimination rather than unseat its delegation. Then Geri Joseph, committee member from Minneapolis, moved to unseat the regular delegation. She said the move was necessary to "remedy longstanding injustices."[39]

It was clear that sentiment was with the challengers. Millie Jeffrey, who was on the credentials committee, said, "We knew going into '68 that Mississippi [challengers] would be seated." It was the black challenges against the Georgia and Alabama delegations that provided the controversies. Georgia, for example, had far less documentation than the Mississippi Loyalists, who had been working meticulously on their case. "They knew their state rules, they knew their party rules. No, they were in good shape. There wasn't any contest," Jeffrey added. "I think the black movement [in Mississippi] had turned to the political process much more so than in Georgia."[40]

Jeffrey herself was "the fairy godmother of the Loyal Democrats of Mississippi," said Wes Watkins. "She singlehandedly had as much to do with us getting out of the credentials committee as anybody. . . . She twisted arms and kicked ass for three days."[41] At a closed door session Tuesday night on the top floor of a Conrad Hilton Hotel tower, eighty-four committee members voted to oust the regular delegation, with ten nos and thirteen absences or abstentions. The vote to seat the insurgents was eighty-five to nine, with fourteen absences or abstentions.

To Hodding Carter, interviewed after the convention, it was "another symbol that there are victories that can be won by people working together. This shows that the promise unveiled by the Freedom Democrats in '64 was fulfilled by the Loyal Democrats in '68, so it is not yet time to abandon the political process." Winning in Chicago was not the same as holding power within Mississippi. But it was closer than the MFDP could have gotten alone, and Carter was quick to point that out.

> We are now the county Democratic executive committee. To be a member of the county executive committee of the Freedom Democratic Party simply means that you've created something that has no standing in the political process right then in that particular county. This way, you name the poll watchers, you do this, you do that, and this is important. This is why the apparatus is important. You don't have to put up extra money to get the candidate on the ballot.

He added, "I'm realist enough to know that until we show power, we are not going to have power."[42]

But Fannie Lou Hamer and Unita Blackwell and others whose loyalties lay with the poor, the rural blacks and whites, felt otherwise. They rejoiced at their seating at the national party convention, but they felt pushed aside. Unita Blackwell said that Mrs. Hamer felt that the challenge "lost the truth. It lost the real and basic feelings of the grassroots. Because all the guys was in again—the big wheels and the ones from Mississippi and all these guys that you see [who] now jumped up on the back of this and became big famous people."[43]

The Mississippi challenge settled, the full convention turned to other challenges to delegations from segregated states. Mrs. Hamer and her fellow members of the newly seated, integrated Mississippi delegation had a chance to vote to oust the regular Georgia delegation, making them unique among southern delegations in voting for Julian Bond's group.[44] Mrs. Hamer had already become involved in the Georgia fight. On a trip before the convention, she stopped in Atlanta, where she spoke out against the Vietnam War; she also criticized six black Georgia delegates selected to go to the convention by segregationist governor Lester Maddox. They should resign their posts because the delegation was unrepresentative of true Democrats, she said. "If they were in Mississippi, they would know they would not be representing us," she said.[45] The Georgia challenge delegation—composed of people both urban and rural, black and white—charged that blacks were systematically excluded from the state's Democratic Party and that Maddox and his allies were disloyal to the national party. The challengers ultimately were awarded half the delegation seats and benefited from the groundbreaking work of the Mississippi Freedom Democratic Party in 1964 and the thoroughly documented Loyalist case in 1968.

In 1964, Fannie Lou Hamer had been the outsider trying to win seats for her delegation. In 1968, with her credentials on a chain around her neck, she spoke from the podium at the convention in support of an unsuccessful challenge to the Alabama delegation brought by a group headed by John Cashin, a black dentist from Huntsville.[46]

Mrs. Hamer also spoke to the platform committee the Saturday before the convention began. Along with Lawrence Guyot, she presented the Freedom Democrats' ideas for dealing with rural poverty; theirs were not words to make Delta planters sleep easy.[47] The Freedom Democrats wanted outright grants of free land—take it from the land "now being subsidized to lie unused"—along with government advice and long-term, low-interest loans for farm cooperatives. MFDP also wanted a guaranteed annual income, fair representation for the black and the poor on all state agencies receiving federal funds, expanded day care, free and complete medical care for every person from birth to death, expanded federal food programs, and free higher education. The Freedom Democrats knew few of these dreams could be achieved without an end to the war in Vietnam, and they also sought an end to compulsory military service. They wanted a halt to arms shipments to the Middle East, resumption of diplomatic relations between the United States and Cuba as well as the United States and China, and an arms embargo against South Africa.[48]

Mrs. Hamer was not alone in espousing many of these ideas. The new Mississippi delegation clearly was more liberal than the average. As one member, John Garner, a physics professor at Tougaloo, wrote to friends later that year, the delegation generally supported the seating challenges. "It voted overwhelmingly for the minority report on Vietnam which was the dovish position. The votes for President were scattered among all the nominated candidates, with Humphrey receiving a plurality. . . . As far as I know, the delegation took the strongest stand of any delegation about Chicago police and National Guard treatment of demonstrators at the convention."[49]

Bob Kochtitzky, another of the delegates, typified the kind of white activist willing to get involved at this stage of Mississippi racial and political development. He had been heading a nonprofit organization called Layman's Overseas Services and had helped form one of the first groups in which blacks and whites met regularly for breakfast in Jackson. More a populist than a politico, Kochtitzky found the convention a heady experience. One moment he was being congratulated by folk singer Theo Bikel for the liberal Mississippi votes, and another he was being photographed talking to actress Shirley MacLaine on one of her visits to the Mississippi delegation.[50]

Despite its centrifugal energy, the Loyalist delegation held together, perhaps because each delegate could go his or her own way on issues like Vietnam, or even on the presidential nominee, as long as there was absolutely no wavering in the commitment to an integrated delegation and to the ultimate party nominee. About 90 percent of the delegation had originally supported Senator Robert F. Kennedy's candidacy, but that unifying force disappeared with Kennedy's assassination.

Even though she was let down by MFDP's loss of ideological clout in the delegation, Mrs. Hamer was excited to be part of the action. "She was always crackin' jokes and having a show," Robert Clark remembered. "On the bus going to and from the hotel at the 1968 convention, she had the floor, telling jokes. Maybe Charles Evers or Aaron Henry would try to tell her something and she'd say, 'Who are you to be telling me somethin'? Perry Hamer is the only one who breathes on my face at night, and he's the only one who can tell me something.' "[51]

She loathed what she saw in the streets near the convention. Invited to a rally of Jesse Jackson's Operation PUSH, she and Unita Blackwell rode through Chicago and were stunned by the police brutality. Police and anti-war protesters clashed around convention hotels, and the message of what the integrated Mississippi delegation stood for became a casualty, almost a lost symbol of an earlier day.

Mrs. Hamer remained dissatisfied with the potential presidential nominees. She wanted a candidate who she felt would be more in touch with poor people, one who would distance himself from President Johnson's conduct of the war, which Hubert Humphrey had been unwilling to do. One day she announced that she was going to the podium to nominate Teddy Kennedy. "Mrs. Hamer, if you do that," Hodding Carter recalled, "you will catch holy hell, but if you want to do it, I'll go with you." They moved toward the podium and then Carter said, "You know, you really should call Teddy and ask him if he wants this." They couldn't reach Kennedy, but they got Steve Smith, Kennedy's brother-in-law and political confidant. He said, "For God's sake, don't do that," as Carter recalled. Hearing that warning, Mrs. Hamer slumped in the phone booth in disappointment, Carter said.[52]

With a single speech Fannie Lou Hamer could have stampeded the already skittish delegates, so she was followed by someone at every turn. "When she went to the bathroom, they followed her," Lawrence Guyot said. "She was never *not* considered a threat."[53] It was never clearly established who gave the orders to follow Mrs. Hamer, but she knew she was being followed and decided to have some fun with her pursuer.

"I watched this guy while he be watching me and . . . I put this dodge to him. They must have told him, 'You better not let her get out of your sight,' because this little man had some of the saddest little blue eyes. He'd be ducking through that convention and I'd be standing off laughing, and after I would let him go through total hell, I would step out where I could see him and you could just see him relieved."[54]

To add to Mrs. Hamer's discontent, men held all the key posts within the convention delegation. "She was quite angry about the male domination," said Jeanette King, then married to Ed King and present as an observer.[55] No one today can quote a line or a word from a fiery speech she made to the delegation on the subject, but many remember that she spoke her mind.

Wes Watkins said her speech made a believer out of him. "My most vivid impression of Mrs. Hamer was and will always be . . .

[that she was] the first person who ever read me the riot act about women's rights, and she did it to the whole delegation in private caucus. . . . She did one of her impassioned, incredibly cogent, right-to-the-point, tough, righteous" speeches, Watkins said. The men were on all the committees, and she unloaded on them. Many of the delegates made the commitment then and there that four years later women would be in more jobs—and they were.

> Fannie did that, with that one speech. Not that it might not have happened anyway, but Mississippi was the only absolutely totally, completely, by-any-judgment balanced [delegation] at the '72 convention; I personally feel that on an emotional level, at least, it was Fannie that did it in that one diatribe. I couldn't quote you a single phrase from it, but I will never forget it. That little spherical powerhouse sitting there and with what she did better than anybody I ever heard was that barely controlled rage. She was speaking in a very calm voice but you knew she was furious. It made a feminist out of me.

That, said Watkins, crystallized Fannie Lou Hamer for him. "She was about justice. She was not just about black. She was about justice wherever it came down, and she was able to voice it that way—that it was a matter of justice."[56]

When Fannie Lou Hamer spoke, the delegates listened. Not so for Willie Brown of California, then a state assemblyman, later Assembly speaker. During the convention, Brown approached Aaron Henry. He wanted the newly seated Mississippi delegation to walk out of the convention over the platform's plank supporting President Johnson's conduct of the war in Vietnam. Brown was "skinny as a rail, an elegant little devil," Watkins recalled. "He walked into our delegation and jumped up on a chair and started haranguing Mississippi to walk out over the war, and Aaron reached up and grabbed him and pulled him off and said, 'Get your ass out of my delegation. I've been trying to get seated for 20 years and you want me to walk out?' "[57]

At moments the violence outside could be ignored. "There we were at the convention," Patt Derian wrote later, "duly seated, charmed with our victory, gamboling through our caucuses, voting on the issues, beguiled by democracy, its responsiveness to us and our participation in it. We simply looked about and saw others doing the same, debating, deciding, voting. Mrs. Hamer declared after our presidential vote (everyone nominated had an advocate among us), 'Mississippi had *the* most democratic vote I ever heard of.' We smiled and were moderately happy." But the anti-war demonstrations in the streets, not the civil rights victories inside the hall, had captured the nation's attention. "Returned home," Derian added, "we find those we left behind . . . 'unutterably sad.' They had watched it all on television and called it ghastly and filled with danger. The reality was a flickering shadow, in living color, on 20 million, 21-inch screens. It was we who had missed it, because we were there."[58]

The human stories of a Fannie Lou Hamer or an Ed King had dominated the 1964 challenge. The lawyers carried the day in 1968. The only surprise was that Mississippi's regular Democrats let it happen. In Doug Wynn's view, a politician like Senator Eastland saw that segregation was dying and did not want to be drummed out of the party—did not want to lose his seniority as John Bell Williams had when, as a congressman, he had supported Goldwater in 1964. Therefore, said Wynn, Eastland would not be averse to seating a more moderate delegation than the MFDP had represented in 1964.

Despite the violence in the streets, there was cause to celebrate. Black and white Mississippians had come together at a time when such an alliance was still not popular. There they were, on the convention floor as official delegates and alternates. The Clarksdale druggist whose house had been shot into and whose store windows had been broken because he wanted black people to vote. The Ruleville sharecropper who had been fired for trying to register to vote and beaten for wanting to help others to vote. A woman from Laurel who wasn't sure where she would get money for nylons was sitting in the same delegation with the planter from Coahoma County, the law professor from Mississippi State, and the newspaper publisher from Greenville.

The coalition would soon fray. At a Loyalist meeting in Jackson after the convention, Robert Clark was the only person backed by the MFDP who was elected to the Loyalist executive committee, which picked Aaron Henry as chairman. MFDP had wanted Clark named national committeeman, and Charles Evers knew it. But Evers orchestrated a demonstration for his own candidacy, and his ally, the Reverend Allen Johnson, gave a nominating speech for Evers that swept even Clark's supporters into tears.

Early in 1969, the MFDP held its own state convention with 350 delegates from thirty-two counties. Mrs. Hamer spoke angrily about the preachers and teachers joining the ranks now that it was safe. "We knowed when we left Mississippi, we had some house niggers with us. As soon as the FDP walked through the valley of the shadow of death, they hopped on the bandwagon."[59]

Lawrence Guyot, leaving his post as party chairman to attend law school, said MFDP had to "continue to be unpopular and deal with issues of poor people and attack every unacceptable institution" or it would not survive. He urged continuous challenges. After Mrs. Hamer was elected MFDP vice chairman, Julian Bond closed the convention with a speech about the need to organize "if we are going to survive these next four years."

These younger people had begun the effort in the early 1960s, and Mrs. Hamer followed them. Now many had left the state. She remained, organizing on issues close to home, ignored in large measure by both national press and national party, frustrated by the inattention when she thought there was hard work yet undone.

CHAPTER 13

"Every New One Makes Us Stronger"

IN THE LATE 1960s and early 1970s, Fannie Lou Hamer and the civil rights movement struggled to consolidate their gains. They lost key leaders; others who had been active in the voting rights movement were shifting directions. The year 1968 was a pivotal one with the assassinations of Martin Luther King, Jr., and Robert F. Kennedy, whom Mrs. Hamer had looked to for leadership even as she recognized their personal and political frailties.

Often ill and frustrated, Mrs. Hamer seemed almost out of step with her times, even though she was ahead of those times in her thinking. Nonetheless, she stayed active. Voter registration remained a staple of any political conversation with Fannie Lou Hamer; she constantly walked into the fields to urge people to help change their lives by voting. Mississippi continued resisting change by making people reregister in many parts of the state, including Sunflower County, and so Mrs. Hamer ran Voter Education Project drives into the 1970s.

But just as Martin Luther King had been moving his focus in his last years toward jobs that he hoped would ensure freedom, so, too, Mrs. Hamer was shifting her emphasis. She contended, in fact, that King did not really become a threat to the power structure until it recognized that he was concentrating on organizing the poor for economic change.[1] She had been organizing poor people in Sunflower County for years, and she stepped up that effort in the late 1960s. "If what the politicians have done to the poverty program hasn't taught us anything else, it has taught us that we are not going to get much help from the politicians," she wrote. "And it has taught us that we are not going to get any serious useful help from the government, to deal with problems we have because we are poor and because we are black."[2]

Music remained a significant means for her to communicate her message. Before she would give a speech, she would sing, joined often now by a group of singers that she founded in 1968, the Hamernettes. Charlene Rogers played the piano for the group, which performed around the state, appearing, for example, at the Jackson Urban League Guild's dinner at the Masonic Temple. "Mrs. Hamer came up with the idea of forming a group," Rogers said, "because she loved singing."[3] The group remained together for several years until Mrs. Hamer's health dictated that she reduce her travels.

At the same time that she was fighting the Sunflower County authorities over their handling of the Head Start program, Mrs. Hamer was also concentrating more on all aspects of education than she had in the past. She knew that better education would be required for people to get better jobs. She took her message to university campuses, she helped local college students organize, she pressed local officials to hew the line of fairness in school desegregation, and she rebuked officials who sought to penalize black women in a backlash against that desegregation.

A few weeks after the election of 1968, Mrs. Hamer traveled to Harvard University, invited as a result of black students' protests that Harvard had too few blacks and that their history and culture were not represented in the courses they took. Because of the student protests, Harvard had asked Alvin Bronstein, a former civil rights lawyer in Mississippi then teaching in Cambridge, to help organize a series of seminars as part of an American history course. Bronstein brought to the Cambridge campus some of the people prominent in the civil rights movement: Vernon Jordan, then with the Voter Education Project; Andrew Young of the Southern Christian Leadership Conference; Whitney Young of the National Urban League; George Wiley of the National Welfare Rights Organization; Mrs. Hamer; and others.

The guests would speak to the history seminar, meet with black students, and have lunch at one of the student houses. Bronstein recalled taking Mrs. Hamer to dinner at the Signet Society's richly paneled quarters—"as stuffy as you might imagine at stuffy Harvard." Senior staff and a dean were there, none of them women. But because a woman was the guest, some faculty wives were invited. "I remember her bowling them over. She would be commenting on the food—saying, 'I'm eating these greens but I don't see any fatback; how do you keep the greens moist without any fat?' Down-home one minute and very wise and philosophical the next."[4]

One day during her visit, she took her message about grass-roots organizing before a group of students at Lowell Lecture Hall. "The country is sick and Americans are on the critical list," she said, using a familiar metaphor. To heal the divisions that she had seen at the 1968 convention and throughout the country, she said that blacks and poor whites had to organize together at the local level. The country could not long endure without such cooperation to bring about fundamental change. The United States "must give blacks the respect they deserve, which it hasn't done. America is substituting cries of law and order for plain respect for blacks as blacks." People would say to her, " 'Fannie Lou, you must be with the Left group,' " she said. "I'd answer, 'Yes, I've been left four hundred years.' " Left *out*.

Churches remained low in Mrs. Hamer's estimation. "The most disgusting hour in the country is 11:00 A.M. Sunday morning when hypocrites from all walks of life converge on our churches for the sake of paying the minister's way to hell and theirs, too," she told her Harvard audience. Churches must translate their ideas into practical action. "If Jesus were here now, he'd be called a militant because he was where it was at, right down with the grass roots." The Reverend Jesse Jackson's Operation Breadbasket in Chicago, which was trying to win jobs for black people, was in her mind a good example of the church in action.[5]

In Mississippi, some churches were at the heart of the action. Spend a Sunday, spend a life of Sundays, in a black Baptist church in Mississippi and see the respect granted the preacher and the power with which a preacher can move his congregation, if he is so moved. But in the toughest days of the sixties, many were not so moved. Again and again, Mrs. Hamer blasted "chicken-eating preachers" and other educated hypocrites. Called in to shore up a black boycott of schools and white businesses in the small town of Leland in 1969, she said, "I'm here tonight to support your boycott and to warn the old people that the things that happened fifty years ago just don't happen anymore. The young people are not going to tolerate it; they're doing what the rest of us should have done a long time ago." Some ministers, she told the gathering at Ebenezer Baptist Church, were "selling out for the big Cadillacs." So were some educators: A college degree "makes some people who are teaching our children turn up their noses at their brothers," she added.

Many were unwilling to participate in the boycott. People were scared; they wished the civil rights people would go away and let life be peaceful—if poor—the way it had always been. They might have nothing, but they still felt they had something to lose. Mrs. Hamer took direct aim at them: "God sees you when you try to slip uptown, and your brothers see you, too."[6] If Fannie Lou Hamer was hated, if she was feared, it may have been as much among the faint-hearted among her black neighbors as among bigoted whites. She made them face an unambiguous moral choice in an amoral world; she would not let them off the hook, and many still felt they had too much too lose to join her.

Where she found support, however, was among restive black students at Mississippi Valley State College near Itta Bena, just off the highway between Indianola and Greenwood in the Delta. Their academic elders were sending them the message that the limit of their aspirations should be buying that big Cadillac and getting modestly paid jobs. The students rebelled against the narrow horizons that they felt were laid out for them by J. H. White, the college president. Mrs. Hamer, in contrast, reminded the students what young people had already done in bringing about change in Mississippi and urged them to do more.

Valley State's student government leaders differed with the college president on the role young blacks would play in the life of their state. The student government had encouraged students to be involved in community affairs; some of them had worked with Mrs. Hamer on voter-registration drives and on picket lines in small-town demonstrations. Black students ought to be pushed toward higher achievement, she said, and in no uncertain terms she felt J. H. White, who was also black, was failing in that mission. It was a time when students felt that they should be audacious and assertive, yet White was saying, "Be a good little Negro boy and Negro girl and don't buck the system," recalled Wilhelm Joseph, student body president at the time of the protests. "When the [all-white] board of trustees would come to campus, he would even put on his apron and serve them like a servant. We felt that was very demeaning." One big donor visited the campus and referred to the students as "niggers." Some of the students walked out of the building-dedication ceremony at which the man was speaking. Joseph recalled that White apologized for the donor, saying he was old and didn't know better.[7]

By February 1969, the students were fed up. They boycotted classes, demanding more black studies courses, permission to wear African clothes or hairstyles, improved remedial programs in math and English, more scholarships, and an end to the requirement that outside speakers be approved by the school administration. The students also objected to strict supervision of women students and penalties for such "infractions" as couples walking across campus holding hands.

"The time is out for the kind of compromising we have had to do for the last 350 years," Mrs. Hamer thundered in a speech to the students—delivered off campus. She had just returned from a visit to Duke University with comedian and activist Dick Gregory, and the comparison of the quality of the schools was obvious. "The kind of education you are getting here at this college prepares you to teach black children only in the state of Mississippi because if you leave Mississippi, you have got to get a mop doing a dust job 'cause you cannot qualify to do anything else. The fact is, people, that here at Mississippi Valley State College, you get a fairly decent *high school* education."[8]

At the height of the demonstrations, the college president sent many of the students home to Jackson by bus, thinking their parents would be so upset that their children had been involved that they would support the school administration, Joseph said. "But Mrs. Hamer spoke to the students and the press reported it. She was on the side of the students. It helped to turn the parents in our favor and against White. Mrs. Hamer carried a lot of credibility in the community," added Joseph, now head of a Legal Services program in New York City. "She spent many hours in my room talking about what was happening and what we should do. She had a good understanding of what was wrong with that institution. I didn't have to educate her that much; she knew."[9] The day after Mrs. Hamer spoke to the students, an agreement between the students and the faculty helped end the Valley State boycott. Most of the students' demands were met.[10]

Separate and inferior education was also the rule in Mississippi public schools. The Supreme Court had issued its ruling that school segregation was unconstitutional in 1954; Mississippi, whipped on by Senator Eastland, led the South's massive resistance effort. By the middle 1960s, Mississippi had moved little beyond what it euphemistically called "freedom of choice" plans—black students could choose to attend previously all-white schools, but they were not encouraged to do so. Mrs. Hamer's friends, Matthew and Mae Bertha Carter, for example, had enrolled their seven youngest children in the white school in Drew. Over the next months, the Carters were forced off the plantation where they had lived and worked, could not get jobs, and could not even find a place to live. The children stayed in the Drew schools, often treated unfairly by school officials. Ultimately, the family, very much alone in the black community as well as shunned by most whites, sued the school system, which even today operates under the results of the *Carter v. Drew* lawsuit.

Mae Bertha Carter did not feel that white children were any

better than her children. She sent her children to school with them because she knew that the white schools were the only ones to which white community leaders paid any attention; thus, they were the only schools at which her children had a chance of getting a decent education. The Carters did not want their children to pick cotton as they had throughout their lives.[11] All seven Carter children not only completed Drew public schools—all seven graduated from the University of Mississippi.

By 1967, the Justice Department filed suits across the state to try to force school desegregation; most districts still resisted.[12] In 1969, the Supreme Court ruled that freedom-of-choice plans were unconstitutional. The court said that the 1954 *Brown v. Board of Education* decision ordering desegregation with "all deliberate speed" meant *now*, not next year, not next century. Some school districts then desegregated smoothly; others had problems but gradually worked them out. Still others saw massive white flight as private academies opened and public schools were left to the black and the poor.

Arsonists who had burned churches in the mid-1960s turned now to a school in Tchula, in Holmes County. But rights leaders pledged a fund-raising drive to rebuild the school. Speaking from the back of a pickup truck near the burned debris, Mrs. Hamer blamed the loss of the school on hate. "Hate have never built; hate have destroyed. If hate didn't destroy, that building would still be standing." She urged blacks not to let whites escape integration. "As many black children as there are in this state and as many of us as there are, we're going in to those schools you call private, too."[13]

Sunflower County was not immune to the fight over school desegregation. In Indianola, and in the county as a whole, school authorities tried to close what had been the black public schools, moving their classes to white schools and threatening to fire or demote many of the black teachers and principals. Black students and their parents periodically boycotted public schools in Indianola as a result. Mrs. Hamer and Carver Randle of the NAACP in Indianola decided that boycotting alone was not enough: that they needed the power of the federal court behind their attempts to win fairness in the public schools. On May 17, 1970, Mrs. Hamer filed a class-action suit in the federal district court in Greenville, arguing that the Sunflower County school officials' plan was not effective in desegregating schools and that black teachers and principals were not adequately protected against losing their jobs.[14]

Hers was not the suit of an idle bystander. In the fall of 1968,

the Hamers sent their fourteen-year-old daughter, Vergie, to Ruleville's previously all-white grade school. Four families enrolled their
children. Mrs. Hamer felt that she had always been brave, but she
quivered a bit when she found that she and her daughter were
surrounded by whites. "When we got almost to the door, Vergie
walked ahead a little and said: 'Come on, mama.' That's hard when
it's your child. But she's not afraid."[15]

Education was the key to the future, Mrs. Hamer and her 104
fellow plaintiffs knew. The same day's newspaper that announced
their suit carried a story from the Agriculture Department that
Mississippi farm workers were among the nation's lowest paid at 93
cents an hour, and even these'jobs were dwindling.

The suit's name—*Hamer et al. v. Sunflower County*—could
have summarized the battle that had been occurring for the better
part of a decade on the political, economic, and now education
fronts. The suit charged that the county and the Indianola school
districts maintained a dual school system in violation of the Fourteenth Amendment. The suit asked the court to order the defendants to establish and maintain one racially open school system and
prevent them from closing formerly all-black schools.[16] Sunflower
County and the city of Indianola were already operating under
federal court orders to desegregate as a result of suits brought by the
U.S. Justice Department. Judge William Keady of the U.S. District
Court in Greenville had appointed James McCullough of Mississippi State University as a special master to oversee desegregation.
Part of his charge from the judge was to confer with a biracial
committee from Sunflower County that Mrs. Hamer headed.[17]

Charging bad faith in negotiations with the school board, Mrs.
Hamer's committee drew up its own desegregation plan with district lines placing more more black children in school with whites.
It paid particular attention to Ruleville. There, hitherto all-black
public schools were threatened with closing as a result of enrollment
declining because segregated private academies had been opened.
The Hamer committee proposed that the white school house some
grades, the black high school some others; thus, neither system
would suffer all the lost classrooms and jobs. At the heart of the
Hamer committee proposal were its suggestions protecting black
teachers and administrators. If there were to be any reduction in the
number of principals, teachers, or teacher aides, then nondiscriminatory standards had to be used. Any vacancies had to be filled
by people of the same race as the person being replaced. There was
thus no gain, from any anti-integration perspective, in firing black
teachers or principals.[18]

Sunflower County and Indianola officials acknowledged that there had been a dual school system and insisted that they wanted to establish one system. If there was a discriminatory system, they said, it was being maintained by the federal court, not by Sunflower County or by Indianola. But they rejected combining the districts in the fashion the Hamer committee suggested. They argued that the plaintiffs, many of whom in fact had children in the public schools, lacked legal standing to bring the case.[19]

Thus were the sides laid out before William Keady, chief judge of the northern district of Mississippi. One of the lesser known members of the federal judiciary outside the state, he handled many civil rights cases in a difficult era. Almost from the day he took the bench, Keady heard emotion-laded cases involving school desegregation, prison conditions, free speech, and reapportionment. He was named a federal judge in March 1968. Then the U.S. Supreme Court abolished freedom-of-choice plans and told school boards to adopt other ways to desegregate at once. "Had I known the *Green* [*v. New Kent County School Board*] decision was just around the corner, my eagerness for the federal bench would have been considerably diminished," Keady wrote candidly in his autobiography. He would receive blunt letters from people throughout the Delta who told him that it was one thing for the Supreme Court to make its rulings on schools, quite another for a son of Mississippi to help enforce them. Eventually, he had judicial oversight over twenty-six public school districts, including Clarksdale, Indianola, Greenwood, and Oxford, and in Sunflower, Bolivar, and thirteen other countywide districts.[20]

Keady knew what it was like to be an outsider. The son of Irish immigrants whose bar business was wiped out by Prohibition, he was born without his right forearm and hand. He did not attend law school in Mississippi, and, although he had been chosen president of the local and state bar associations, he was not of the Delta aristocracy. Keady had lost his Washington University scholarship when he married and never forgot the townspeople who helped him with the money to finish law school. He valued his establishment contacts, represented businesses and railroads, loved his Cadillac, and lived up to the nickname "Cash," earned because he insisted on payment in advance in divorce cases. Named by President Johnson to succeed Claude Clayton, who had been promoted to the appeals court, Keady insisted that people be aware that he had been selected by Senator John Stennis, himself a former judge, rather than the senior senator, Eastland. Of Eastland, whom he acknowledged as "once the single most powerful individual, politically speaking, in our state," Keady wrote discreetly in his autobiography that "though I voted for him on most occasions, I disagreed with some of his positions."[21]

Keady "was the most patriotic person. He owed everything to the United States," said Allan Alexander, a Greenville native who was his first female law clerk in 1978. "His favorite day used to be Americanization day when new citizens would be sworn in."[22] He "thought that the courtroom was the most important place for citizens to redress their rights," Alexander, now an Oxford attorney, recalled. "It was a sacred thing." He was also a canny judge who didn't want to be reversed, and he recognized the evolution of civil rights law, especially as read by the Fifth Circuit, which would hear any appeals from his court. Keady was particularly solicitous of people who had the nerve to appear in court to say what they had to say about discrimination they faced at the hands of powerful people. Thus, he would listen intently to Mrs. Hamer, who appeared several times in his courtroom.

Working with Mrs. Hamer was like having your case "served to you on a silver platter," recalled John Brittain, then with the North Mississippi Rural Legal Services in Oxford. "In most cases, you would have the normal steps of finding people willing to put their names on a desegregation suit. You'd have an organizing meeting and you'd get some names. Then you'd have a few days of seeing who would stick because the bossman would come around, and you'd have someone say, 'Jim can't do it' because his job would be at stake." When Mrs. Hamer worked on a case, that didn't happen. "I can distinctly recall Mrs. Hamer—rather stout, sort of short"—in those meetings to determine who would testify, Brittain said.

> The men would have on coveralls, and the women would be modestly dressed. I would be going over the particulars of what we needed to do. And she would just say, "This is what we have to do," and she always was right. When she said it was so, you could count on it, that it would be produced.
>
> We would get in the car—I remember this distinctly—and we would go out to visit people. We'd roll into the driveway or through the dirt and the chickens and we'd go into these little rural shacks. The people would say, "Hi, Mrs. Hamer." And she'd say, "Now, Bill and Amy, we want you to be plaintiffs in this school case because it's the right thing to do for our people." And they'd say, "Yes, Mrs. Hamer." She'd ask them to sign the court papers and they'd sign. And they'd be there to testify.
>
> Then [in court] the white attorney would ask them, "This isn't something you wanted to do, is it?"

And they said, "Yes, suh."
And he'd say, "Somebody came and made you do it?"
"No, suh."

The school attorney would try to shake their story, asking insistently: "And 'You don't understand why you're doing it?'

" 'Yes, suh, I understand' " would come the reply. "Then there'd be some simple statement like, 'My kid hasn't been getting the kind of education I think he should be getting.'

"I've been burned with other people and other cases, but with Mrs. Hamer, you knew the people would be there and you knew they would say the right things. With other cases, I might just put my head in my hands [in frustration] but not where she was involved."[23]

With a new school term approaching, the case of *Hamer v. Sunflower County* moved rapidly. On June 15, 1970, Judge Keady ordered Sunflower County to merge schools so that there would be one public school system starting that September. Much of the language in his decision came directly from the Hamer report. For example, Keady ruled that when a teacher was dismissed, that vacancy could not be filled by someone of the other race. The Fifth Circuit Appeals Court affirmed Keady's decision in August, saying that the judge had "demonstrated a fundamental grasp of the situation presented. His order is clear, concise, and is in accordance with the decisions of the Supreme Court and this court." Desegregation was going to be difficult because almost 86 percent of the students in the school district were black, but that factor did not alter the requirements of the law. " 'Deliberate speed' is no longer a viable principle in school desegregation cases," the appeals court said.[24]

Judge Keady had so readily accepted the citizens' plan "basically because it was the only thing you could do," Brittain said. "When it came to the question of merging the two systems, the practice had been to close the all-black schools. But we managed to keep some of the black schools open, and then they had Title I [of the Elementary and Secondary Education Act] money to try to spruce up some of the grounds to try to make them attractive to white students."[25]

Mrs. Hamer had long objected to educated blacks looking down on "the nitty gritty people"—what she called "the ruralest of the ruralest, the poorest of the poor USA." She saw a change in their attitude when teachers' and principals' jobs were threatened under desegregation plans; then they understood that they needed the support of community people.

I told Judge Keady, "We've seen these desegregation plans and how they work all over the state of Mississippi, and if you think we're going to watch you take the man with a master's degree and put him down as a janitor's helper, you're wrong." We got to have the same black principal that we've been having. We held that position. Rule-ville Central High is one of the few schools in the whole state of Mississippi that has a black principal because the community fought for it.[26]

That principal, Henry R. Smith, was the same principal of whom the Ruleville students had been so critical during the summer of 1964. The same principal with whom Mrs. Hamer had tangled over participation in civil rights activities. A graduate of Alcorn A&M, Smith went to Ruleville as principal in 1955 and retired in 1984. "It was because of Mrs. Hamer's efforts that we retained the high school because we were about to lose all our students," Smith said. "We didn't see eye to eye on some things. I felt that what with the students, I couldn't get out there and do some of the things. The students would see you and lose their respect. They would think they were the same as you. I didn't get out there and march with them. But we did work together to get the school saved."

On occasion, Smith took some heat in Mrs. Hamer's behalf. The white superintendent in his district had always told Smith that he was in charge of the school, that whatever he scheduled there was all right. But after a 1970 program was planned honoring Mrs. Hamer, whose group was even then organizing the suit against the Sunflower system, the superintendent called Smith and said, "You know, you're not supposed to have a program for Fannie Lou Hamer." Smith replied: "I thought you said I could do what I felt was right at the school. They're not going to eat the school. I'll be right there with it."[27]

That "Fannie Lou Hamer Day and Banquet," held March 29, 1970, at the high school had been instigated by leading black activists in the state. Representative Robert Clark, relatively new then in the state legislature from Holmes County, was the principal speaker. The Hamernettes performed. That such an event could happen in Ruleville showed how much had changed since those days in the early 1960s when there had been a curfew for black citizens, when civil rights workers were arrested, and when Mayor C. M. Dorrough asked the Sovereignty Commission to investigate Mrs. Hamer's work. Now, in 1970, the mayor wrote Mrs. Hamer a letter of tribute on her day of recognition. So often such letters are boilerplate, but Ruleville had seen too much, Dorrough and Mrs.

Hamer had been through too much, for this letter to fall in that category.

"You have put up a valiant fight for those things you truly believe in, and you have obtained results that you should be recognized for," the mayor wrote.[28]

> Many people have been publicly commended and decorated for battles won, where they actually were not exposed to the real dangers and rath [sic] of the enemy. This is not the case with you, for you have carried your fight straight into the camp of the opposition. The results of your battles are now a matter of public record, and more benefits are coming each year. If more Americans gave of themselves as you have for the things they believe in, ours would be a better nation.
>
> I trust that those you have helped and befriend will give credit where credit is due, and remember you as a champion for their cause. The history books of tomorrow will record your efforts and the results, but I am sure you are more interested in the tangible things around your own community that speak of a better, more comfortable way of life for those you love. May I add my commendation for you and the job you have done for those around you.

The letter was signed, "Sincerely, C. M. Dorrough, Sr., Mayor."

Despite this tribute in her hometown, Mrs. Hamer remained in more demand for public appearances out of state than in Mississippi. She was often on the road. In January 1969, she had spoken at Seattle University; in February 1969, at Duke; in March she went to Carleton College in Minnesota, then in April to Tougaloo, outside Jackson. Her speeches addressed both long-range issues and the concerns of the moment. In Seattle, she was asked, as she often was, what "black power" meant and whether she was a black separatist. This question remained prominent in many people's minds, black and white, ever since the words rang out at the Meredith March. Black power was what each individual thought it was. It could mean voter registration; it could mean political power. It could mean keeping white cops out of black neighborhoods; to some, it could even mean killing white police officers or other whites. It could mean blacks' owning their own businesses, or boycotting white businesses that discriminated against black people. It meant solidarity with people of color around the world, or it could mean separatism from others of any different color. Far more complex than any one paragraph could summarize, it stemmed from disillusionment with white society and an attempt to rally black pride.

Mrs. Hamer's view of black power was more practical than ideological. She was proud of being black, and she could not understand why people became tense when they talked about black power. "I was very puzzled when everybody got shook up at the scream of blackness," she told a Seattle writer. "Everybody in this country we have dealt with since we got off the slave ships dealt with us as black people, but when we said to ourselves 'black,' everybody got shaken up." But she would add that she was not a black separatist. "What I am trying to tell you is that I am not fighting for an all black world, just like I am not going to tolerate an all white world."[29]

Black power hovered over discussions of education, politics, and economics in Mississippi and elsewhere in the late 1960s. Black power made white university administrators reluctant to have a short, stocky incendiary arrive on their campuses. Not long after the Mississippi Valley State demonstrations, the political science honorary society at the University of Mississippi invited Mrs. Hamer to speak on the Oxford campus. As at Valley State, the Ole Miss administration had to approve campus speakers. The administration vetoed Mrs. Hamer's appearance, as it had the Young Democrats' request to have Charles Evers speak on campus. Ultimately, the administration relented.

Mrs. Hamer's presence on a campus gave a charge to black students, who did not often hear their point of view forcefully spoken. Appearing April 19, 1969, on a panel with prominent law school faculty members at the University of Mississippi, Mrs. Hamer listened as they spoke in their gray, legalistic way. The topic was "Law Enforcement Crisis in a Changing South."[30] Johnnie Walls, then a law student, recalled that Mrs. Hamer said that when whites talked about police and law and order, they were talking about being protected. But black people don't look at the law the same way, she explained. When blacks think about police, she said, they see people coming after them with billy clubs, bent on denying them their rights. After her presentation, Walls said, the few black law students in the audience were proud that someone had come there to talk about life as they understood it and had so dominated the discussion. She was the one everybody clustered around at the program's end.

Even by the late 1960s, however, some black people, as well as whites, remained at odds with Mrs. Hamer. The antipathy in some quarters stemmed from her message, in others from the uncultured way she delivered it. She butchered grammar, so much so that when she was invited to receive an honorary degree at Tougaloo College in June 1969, some of the middle-class "bourgeoisie" blacks who had graduated from that school objected because they considered her unlettered. But she received the degree, as she did from Howard University three years later. Unlettered she was, so much so that she told people that Martin Luther King's widow, Coretta Scott King, had not wanted to appear on the same platform with her on one occasion. "I may not have all the education but I do have common sense, and I know how to treat people," Mrs. Hamer said.[31]

Mississippi school leaders had their own ideas of how to treat people—in this case, those who were fighting for desegregation. They would punish the black people who worked in the schools to try to get their leaders to back off, and one such attempt would result in another education-related court appearance for Mrs. Hamer.

In May 1969, a federal court had ordered the desegregation of the Drew schools, north of Ruleville, in the ongoing case brought by the Carter family. Two years later, Drew school superintendent George F. Petty issued a rule that no one with an illegitimate child could teach in his district's schools. Katie Mae Andrews, a graduate of Mississippi Valley State University who was certified to teach in any Mississippi public school, and Lestine Rogers, a Drew High School graduate hired as a teacher's aide in the district, were both barred from employment as a result of Petty's rule. Three other black women—one a substitute teacher and the others teachers' aides—were also denied reemployment in Drew. Petty applied the ruling to cafeteria operators, dieticians, librarians, gym teachers, nurses, principals, even PTA presidents. But he didn't include janitors and school bus drivers because, as he later acknowledged in court, it was "easier to find an unwed mother than an unwed father . . . because the unwed mother is stuck with the result."[32] The women sued.

Victor McTeer, then a Legal Services attorney who had met Mrs. Hamer when he was a law clerk, represented the women in a case heard before Judge Keady. McTeer brought in several expert witnesses to counter the school district's argument that these unwed mothers, if allowed to teach, might corrupt their students' morals. Among them was Dr. Kenneth Clark, who had been an expert witness in the Supreme Court's deliberations on *Brown v. Board of Education*.[33] McTeer then turned to Mrs. Hamer to inject some life into his case. She was always motherly toward him and "sensitive to the problems of the young black man in the South," McTeer said.[34] So she pushed black lawyers to handle cases that in the past had been handled by the white lawyers who trained them. He asked her to talk about "the sociological and political thoughts of black people in the Sunflower County region," that is, whether it bothered the people of Drew whether someone teaching their children had a child but was not married.

Mrs. Hamer testified in Judge Keady's court in March 1973. First, McTeer asked her about her civil rights activities, then about the honorary degrees that she had received. She had been honored by Columbia College in Chicago as well as by Tougaloo and Howard. She had also taught black contemporary studies classes at Shaw University in Raleigh, North Carolina. Then the Drew attorney, Champ Terney, rose to question Mrs. Hamer's qualifications. Terney was Senator Eastland's son-in-law and represented Sunflower County in many cases. Had she ever, Terney wanted to know, had much direct contact with parents or students in Drew schools?

Yes, she replied, she had worked on voter registration in Drew. "I know quite a few people in Drew because part of my family is in Drew."

"Now, voter registration was back in, what, 1962?" Terney asked.

"But I still go to Drew," Mrs. Hamer replied. "I go to church in Drew, I know people in Drew, I go to Drew now."

"How much time do you spend in Sunflower County now?" Terney asked. "Most of your time?"

"Most of the time."

"Haven't you in the past traveled a good bit?" Terney said.

"Yes, I did do traveling," Mrs. Hamer said, about to summarize her credo for the rest of her life. "But I would be at home, and I was always at home when I was needed in Sunflower County. All they had to do is to tell me when I was needed and I was right there. Because that's home."

The black community, Mrs. Hamer told Terney, agreed "that these young womens are not really on trial. You are trying all of us. Because when you say we are lifting ourselves up and you tell us to get off of welfare, then when peoples try to go to school to get off of welfare to support theirselves, this is another way of knocking them down. So we are here because we really don't like what's happening."

Keady qualified Mrs. Hamer as an expert witness, "a sociologist from the black point of view." She was asked how the black community felt about unwed mothers. Her answer foreshadowed her opposition to abortion:

It's quite a few people, black people in Sunflower County that have young people that's not married with children. But these are still our children. And we still love these children. And after these babies are born we are not going to disband these children from our families, because these are other lives. . . . God breathed life into them just like he did into us. And I think these children have a right to live. And I think that these mothers have a right to try to support these children in a decent way.

McTeer asked Mrs. Hamer whether she thought the black community and the white community had different views about the children of unwed parents. She replied that she had worked in white people's kitchens "and I know what's going on. And if justice was really done, it wouldn't only be black women in here, it would be a whole lot of young white folk in here, too. . . . This would almost be funny to me if it wasn't so serious."

Judge Keady asked Mrs. Hamer whether there was any morality issue in the black community in having an unwed child. "After a child is born," she replied, "I don't think the people should be treated like a outcast."

"No, that is not the question," Judge Keady said. "But in becoming a parent out of wedlock, is that frowned on, looked down on, or is it encouraged and approved?"

"It's not encouraged," Mrs. Hamer answered. "But people are not looked down on."

Mrs. Hamer testified that she thought the whole state would suffer "a terrible blow" if people trying to lift themselves up could then lose their jobs because they had had children without being married. The children, too, would feel that they were considered unfit. "And you know, when I think of this—may I say this, Judge Keady? I think about the story of Jesus Christ. I think of what would have happened to Virgin Mary if she walked into Drew Separate School [District], what would have happened if Christ had been born in that school? What would have happened?"

McTeer asked Mrs. Hamer why this case affected her. "I had two children, adopted children, Vergie and Dorothy Jean," Mrs. Hamer responded, telling how, while she was traveling around, Dorothy Jean, twenty-one, became pregnant. One of her friends had suggested that she send her away rather than risk hurting her own reputation. She had refused to do that. "She died in 1967, my daughter did. And if I had mistreated that child of my daughter, I would have never forgiven myself. I don't think that we have the authority to forgive man. Only God got that power. Man is not to judge man. We don't have that kind of power."

When Terney started questioning Mrs. Hamer, he asked her if schools employed people who had had illegitimate children, might not students think that type of behavior was being condoned and might not that increase the problem of teenage pregnancies? She disagreed.

"You know what you have to do if that's what you are going to deal with?" Mrs. Hamer asked, her voice rising. "When you get back to Drew this evening, lock up the doors. There won't be any school."

"Why is that?" Terney asked.

"The moral conduct. Nobody would teach."

"All the teachers?"

"All of them. It might be two not fall out of the sack if that's what you call moral. Two. Lock it up."

"You don't have much confidence in the faculty?" Terney asked.

"I'm just calling a spade a spade," Mrs. Hamer replied, her voice now barely controlled.

> You know what, Mr. Terney? If this was a young white woman with this same problem, I would come here and fight you the same way, because I would fight for her rights as a woman, as a person fighting for her child, just like these young womens are fighting for the right to take care of their child. You always tell us, we go through this thing with the welfare or we have got so many kids on the welfare roll, "Why don't you get up and do something?" And then when we start doing something, "You don't have any business being that high."

Said Terney: "You realize that this rule is not racially motivated. In other words, this is enforced equally against whites and blacks. You understand that, don't you?"

"I don't understand that," Mrs. Hamer replied. "Because to save my life, is no way on earth that I could believe that every white teacher in Sunflower County is single that there hasn't been a child involved. I don't believe that."

"We are talking about Drew now," Terney said.

"I'm talking about Drew," she retorted. "If there's more than two teaching there single."

As Mrs. Hamer's court appearance drew to an end, she tangled once more with Terney. He asked her whether the black community drew a distinction between prostitution, that is, sexual intercourse for pay, and voluntary sexual intercourse outside marriage without pay.

"See, you know, I think, Attorney Terney, this is ridiculous," to be asking that kind of question, Mrs. Hamer replied. To her, the real issue was that a woman who had tried to lift herself up in life by getting an education so she could support her child decently should be allowed to work in the schools. "And that's what we are talking about."

Judge Keady ruled for the teachers. He held that the policy of barring people from working in the public schools solely because they had had an illegitimate child had "no rational relation to the objectives ostensibly sought to be achieved by the school officials and is fraught with invidious discrimination." The federal appeals court upheld Keady's decision, as did the U.S. Supreme Court in September 1975.

The Andrews case represented a small investment of Mrs. Hamer's time. But the attention paid to her in a federal courtroom, the fact that, despite her own ill health, she was willing to stand up for several teachers from a small town tucked away in the Mississippi Delta, typified her life at the time. She had forced the segregated society of the Delta to take notice of her, then nudged it along toward justice.

CHAPTER 14

"Got My Hand
on the Gospel Plow"

BLACK MISSISSIPPIANS lived with hunger and died of hunger. Mothers listened as their children cried themselves to sleep. Fathers left home because they could not provide for their families. Economic conditions, as much as discrimination at the polling place, conspired to keep black people in Mississippi in their historic place: poverty. Yet "if you talked too much economics in the fifties and sixties, you were called a communist," said Andrew Young. "So we clearly avoided the economic issues, I mean deliberately. . . . When we got around to taking them up in the Poor People's Campaign [in 1968], that was the time that the war in Vietnam had hit." Little money was left for anti-poverty efforts. Voting rights, integration of lunch counters, desegregation of schools: "none of those cost the society any money. In fact, they saved the society money when you could run one school system instead of two," Young said.[1] Tackling the structural woes of the economy was—and still is—quite another matter.

But Fannie Lou Hamer did not shy away from economic issues. She was poor herself. She stressed the ballot box as a tool for eradicating that poverty. She testified before U.S. Senate committees, and she attended the White House Conference on Hunger. She appeared in a nationally televised documentary on hunger. She worked, as usual, on two levels: nationally, helping put the question before the public and the politicians, and locally, trying to put meat and vegetables on people's dinner tables. "You can give a man some food and he'll eat it. Then he'll only get hungry again," she said. "But give a man some ground of his own and a hoe, and he'll never go hungry again."[2]

She dreamed of cooperatively owned farms on which black

and white alike could produce food for themselves and their neighbors; she hoped to create organizations that could also help people deal with government agencies and obtain better education for their children. Her dream failed. The pig bank and farm cooperative that she started did not outlive her; they were among her major accomplishments, and her worst heartbreaks.

In her work on economic development, she continued to receive help from northern liberals, as she had since her earliest civil rights activity. She remained a conduit for northern interest, a speaker who could stir liberal passions and open liberal pocketbooks. As she moved from the Freedom Democrats to Freedom Farm, Mrs. Hamer forged a key North-South link with the liberal community in Madison, Wisconsin, home of the University of Wisconsin. In 1965, a group calling itself Measure for Measure had been organized by people from Madison who had made contact with rural black communities in both Mississippi and Arkansas. Mrs. Hamer had visited Madison in 1966 for a training program sponsored by the federal Office of Economic Opportunity and met some Measure for Measure members. By 1968, the organization was concentrating its aid on farm co-ops in Bolivar and Sunflower counties.

In April 1968, members of Measure for Measure traveled to Ruleville with 3,500 pounds of clothing. Mrs. Hamer asked them to focus their attention next on food for the people in her area. The U.S. Department of Agriculture had stopped distributing surplus food and started selling food stamps to poor people, who were then to redeem the stamps for more than face value at grocery stores. "What good are the stamps if folks haven't got money to buy them? At least with commodities, folks got something to eat. Now there's nothing. There's starvation," Mrs. Hamer said.[3] "Who ever heard of having to pass a test to feed hungry people?" she would ask angrily.[4]

Hunger was emerging as a front-burner issue in American politics. The civil rights workers who had gone into the South had come back and told of the hunger and poverty they had seen. Robert Coles, a child psychiatrist with Harvard's University Health Service, and Raymond Wheeler, an internist from Charlotte, North Carolina, and executive committee chairman of the Southern Regional Council, had gone to Mississippi, where they found children "weak, in pain, sick; . . . suffering from hunger and disease and directly or indirectly they are dying from them."[5] Mississippi doctors like Aaron Shirley had taken the press to see hungry children, children whose only drinking water came from a barrel in which rainwater was collected. And Dr. Jack Geiger of Tufts University, who had started the Delta Health Center in Mound Bayou, was documenting health problems as well.

Then a Senate manpower subcommittee headed by Joseph Clark of Pennsylvania—and including Senator Robert Kennedy of New York—went to Mississippi. They heard from Mrs. Hamer and Amzie Moore, who talked especially about gains brought by Head Start. Once the hearings were completed, Clark and Kennedy traveled to the Delta to see Mississippi poverty and hunger for themselves. Writer Nick Kotz described the visit Kennedy and Clark made to a shack in Cleveland during which Kennedy tried for five minutes—"talking, caressing, tickling, poking"—to get some response from a listless, badly malnourished two-year-old girl. "The baby never looked up." Outside, Kennedy told a companion, "I've seen bad things in West Virginia, but I've never seen anything like this anywhere in the United States."[6]

Kennedy and Clark put pressure on the Agriculture Department to start more food programs in Mississippi. In so doing, they ran up against Mississippi congressman Jamie Whitten, the powerful chairman of the agricultural appropriations subcommittee. At the end of World War II, Nick Kotz reported, Whitten had killed a study that would have anticipated the economic problems of black soldiers returning from war. "By opposing all studies exploring the effects of a changing agriculture upon people, Whitten helped insure that Agriculture Department farm policy would never seriously include consideration of the effects of its programs on sharecroppers or farm workers."[7]

Whitten's power stemmed not only from his seniority[8] and control over the appropriations process but also from his complete understanding of Agriculture Department budgets that have long received little national press scrutiny. In the 1960s, 0.3 percent of the people in Whitten's district received $23.5 million in farm subsidies. The 59 percent of the constituents who lived below the poverty level received $4 million in food relief funds.[9]

Mrs. Hamer wanted to help correct that imbalance. Early in 1968, she appeared on a public-broadcasting documentary called *Hunger—American Style,* filmed in Sunflower and Tallahatchie counties.[10] Reporter Kotz, then with Cowles Publications, remembered that Mrs. Hamer especially helped him in finding people from Senator Eastland's plantation to interview. The documentary stressed that Eastland, like the Agriculture Department and other members of Congress, served two constituencies: "the producers of food, and those who consume it—or would like to." In Eastland's county, the film's narrator said, more than half the families fell under the federal government's poverty level, yet the Agriculture Department also paid the county farmers more than $10 million in supports, "eight times the amount spent on food for the poor." The result of this imbalance—hunger among the poor—contributed to an infant mortality rate in Mississippi that was the highest in the nation. Those children who did survive might be raised on milk alone, with no iron; they would become anemic and succumb when a bad cold became pneumonia.

Eastland was an inviting target. Mrs. Hamer peppered her speeches with references to him, saying, "We plan to really work on that man" to unseat him, or charging that "because of Senator Eastland's power, you can't register in Sunflower County."[11] The hunger documentary reported that Eastland earned almost $170,000 the previous year in price supports for not planting cotton. He had publicly declared that seventy-eight black families currently living on his plantation, working or not, had a "home for life." But his generosity had a hollow ring for Mrs. Hamer: "Senator Eastland has never done nothing for nobody poor, not in this county. 'Cause the people on Senator Eastland's plantation is just as poor as I am. And he hadn't done anything for them and he hadn't done anything for nobody else that's poor in Sunflower County. And I've been right here in Sunflower County since I was two years old."

Black soldiers returning to the Delta from Vietnam could not get decent jobs, housing, or food. "When I think about that and how hungry people are in the South, then it makes me a little sick to say, how can they spend all that much money in another country and really not doing nothing at home? See, I think charity begin at home and then spread abroad."[12]

Participation in government food assistance programs had dropped sharply when Sunflower County switched from commodities to food stamps: 18,540 people received commodities in March 1966, and 7,856 were getting food stamps in October 1968.[13] When Mrs. Hamer's friends from Measure to Measure visited Ruleville in 1968, she explained the problem to them, and that spring they raised $5,000 that Mrs. Hamer used to help people buy food stamps.[14] That Christmas, Measure for Measure members collected presents and cooked turkey dinners for children at Head Start centers in Bolivar and Sunflower counties. Mrs. Hamer told the people from Wisconsin that she thought blacks' only hope lay in acquiring land for cooperative farming and housing. The state wanted black people out of Mississippi, and the federal government "considers us surplus," she said. "We must buy land immediately or our people will die forgotten." The Madison organization started raising money to help buy the land that would become Freedom Farm, a cooperative designed to share ownership and work, produce and profits, among black former field hands. Poor white families were welcome to participate, too.[15]

Measure for Measure had already contributed money to develop a co-op in northern Bolivar County. It estimated that in those two counties virtually all of the black population earned less than $900 a year and that most of the people, black and white, lived in poverty. A telling 75 percent of the houses lacked running water, 80 percent had no electricity, and 90 percent had no indoor toilet. With little health care, poor sanitation, and poor diet, many infants were dying; in a very short time, the Delta Health Center in Mound Bayou reduced that mortality rate.

Meanwhile, another fund-raising drive was getting under way in Cambridge, Massachusetts, at Mrs. Hamer's instigation. Harrison Wellford and Lester Salamon, both teaching fellows in Harvard's government department, had been on a research trip to Mississippi when Mrs. Hamer pleaded with them for help to raise $1,300 to hold an option on forty acres of land for Freedom Farm. She told them the co-op would help blacks not only by raising food but also by protecting them from economic vulnerability so they could participate more freely in political life. Of 31,000 black people in Sunflower County, only 71 owned any land.[16]

Harry Belafonte joined the effort with a fund-raising letter in May 1969, urging contributions to Freedom Farm as an "example of initiative, racial cooperation and political militancy worthy of the support of all decent Americans."[17] Belafonte had often been called upon to help, and Mrs. Hamer was sensitive to the fact that she frequently went to him with money problems. "She didn't want me to think that our relationship had been reduced to just being the fat cat for the movement, that every time she had to pick up the phone or say hello, it was just to say, 'Give me some more money,'" Belafonte said. "She then began to call and try to develop a deeper social relationship that went out beyond the need for funding." They talked most about the movement, about whether she was needed to speak somewhere, but also about her husband and children. "She was tenacious on making sure that I and others understood that as desperate as the need was within her own family group, that not one dime of movement money would ever go to satisfy any of those needs."[18]

Land was not enough: people needed meat as well. Joining with the National Council of Negro Women, Mrs. Hamer bought thirty-five gilts (females) and five boars (males) in 1968 to create a Pig Bank. Gilts were loaned to local families, who could keep the dividends, in the form of piglets, and return the principal, mama pig, to the pig bank. Thirty-five families received the pigs the first year; they in turn would lend a pregnant gilt to other families the next year. By the third year two thousand or three thousand new pigs had been produced; at least three hundred families had meat on the table.[19] Mrs. Hamer loved to joke when she took people on tours about how the male pigs were kept busy. That one "just knocked hisself out," she said as visitors walked through a barnyard.[20]

Mrs. Hamer always insisted on laying out a feast for her guests. Mr. Hamer might withdraw if there were too many guests he didn't know, but she would cook and fuss over everyone. One consultant went to check on the pig bank for the NCNW and raved about the turnips and greens Mrs. Hamer had prepared "along with fried chicken, corn bread, sweet potato pie, lemon pie and pound cake. I had forgotten," he added, "how delicious fresh greens were until that time."[21]

In 1969, Mrs. Hamer bought the first forty acres of Freedom Farm. The small-town South is the kind of place in which yesterday's enemy can be today's ally, people's lives so overlap. It should, therefore, be noted that much of the legal work for Freedom Farm was done by Pascol Townsend, Jr., who as city attorney in Drew had complained bitterly in letters to the White House about the civil rights workers who had come to his community in 1964. "The young whites that came—they were living with the blacks—of course, we had never seen that before," Townsend explained later.[22] He favored more gradual change, he said, and he didn't always agree with Mrs. Hamer. They were an odd couple, the courtly white southern lawyer and the stout, black former sharecropper, but Townsend found that he could talk to her, and she turned to him for help with the farm's legal business. Townsend also represented her and Mr. Hamer when they adopted Dorothy's daughters, Lenora and Jacqueline, in 1969.

The connection dumbfounded civil rights attorney Alvin Bronstein when he heard of it. Townsend, who wanted to be a federal judge, knew his name was being put forward by Senator Eastland, whose Ruleville law office he had used when he first left the navy after World War II. So he called Bronstein, asking him to use whatever influence he had to prevent Senate liberals from blocking his nomination.[23] Bronstein said he'd have to check with Mrs. Hamer before he would say anything to anyone, and she vouched for Townsend, just as he had said she would. Townsend didn't get the nomination—his views were considered too conservative—and William Keady was named instead.[24]

At first, the main crops on Freedom Farm's land near Ruleville were butter beans and collard greens. After high school students across the North raised $120,000 for Sunflower County in a series of "Walks against Hunger," Mrs. Hamer bought farm machinery and another 620 acres. To raise money to pay taxes, salaries, and other expenses, the co-op planted most of the land in cotton and soybeans but left 150 acres for food such as corn, peas, beans, okra, and collard greens. The co-op fee was $1 a month, although only 30 families could afford even that. "Another 1,500 families belong in name," Mrs. Hamer said. Anyone who needed fresh vegetables could help harvest the crop. That was an altruistic concept, and people often helped themselves to food but did no work to keep up the farm.

In the Delta, the plantation system had ended and no safety net of meaningful government assistance had ever existed, so people needed cash as well as food. Mrs. Hamer's organizing efforts helped establish regular payrolls for some black workers in Sunflower County through Freedom Farm, Head Start, and the Fannie Lou Hamer Day Care Center, which the National Council of Negro Women also helped finance. The day care center was started to care for the children of the women working at a small garment factory in Doddsville that Mrs. Hamer also helped establish.[25]

Nationally, concern was mounting about the persistence of hunger in America. In December 1969, President Richard Nixon convened a White House Conference on Food, Nutrition and Health, and Mrs. Hamer attended. The conference, largely a gathering of academics, scientists, food industry representatives, and public policy types, was chaired by nutrition expert Jean Mayer. It was designed, at least from the White House point of view, to allow Nixon to contrast his commitment to the repeated rejections of food aid reform during the Johnson administration. Nixon addressed the four thousand delegates assembled at the Sheraton Park Hotel in Washington and said he not only accepted the responsibility for putting an end to hunger: "I claim the responsibility."[26]

At a taping of *Town Meeting*, a public television program, before the conference opened, members of the audience, including Mrs. Hamer, talked about hunger in their own communities.[27] Mrs. Hamer could be counted upon throughout the conference to draw on her own experience to illustrate what hunger meant for people in Mississippi. However, she used the conference more to express her opinions on abortion, speaking out forcefully on that question several times.[28] She always held that human life was sacred, that if young women did become pregnant, they should be helped to raise their children, not encouraged to terminate their pregnancies. She had raised other people's children, as had many in the black community, and she felt that children, properly educated, were the hope of the future.

The conference itself was a "pressure cooker," wrote *Washington Post* reporter Spencer Rich: "3,000 people stuffed into meeting halls, caucus rooms and the huge grand ballroom of the Sheraton Park Hotel, endless press conferences and lists of demands by the radical groups; hundreds of meetings of panels and task forces as they worked to refine and revise their recommendations."[29] To dramatize the hunger issue, some of the delegates began a fast in protest of the $18 price of conference meal tickets. They contrasted that with the school lunch program that only provided 58 cents a day per child.[30] The protesters attempted to draw Mrs. Hamer into the fast—or persuade her to eat only beans instead of the regular meals, recalled L. C. Dorsey, who had traveled to Washington with Mrs. Hamer. "They had all these good meals and those of us who had known malnutrition were just bellying up, and so when they asked Mrs. Hamer to eat pork and beans, she said, 'Chile, I have eaten enough beans. I know what beans tastes like and I am going to eat this food.' "[31]

When the conference ended, the participants drafted a five-point proposal topped by a request that the president "free funds to feed all hungry Americans this winter." Although President Nixon met the day after the conference with several of its delegates, the poor again went home mainly with promises. The basic pledge that Nixon had delivered that the moment was at hand to end hunger in America remains unfulfilled to this day.

Early the next year, writer Paule Marshall visited Mrs. Hamer to report for a women's magazine on the efforts to feed people. She came away as taken by Fannie Lou Hamer as many others had been. "To be in her presence, to sense her special force, is to know the Black heroines of another time," Marshall wrote, comparing her to Harriet Tubman, who helped fellow slaves escape, and to abolitionist Sojourner Truth. Mixed with this image of Fannie Lou Hamer as fighter was Marshall's portrait of her as "a universal aunt. . . . When word of her arrival at a house gets about, that place begins quietly to fill up with people come to warm themselves on her spirit."

On Marshall's visit to Ruleville, she tapped into Mrs. Hamer's anger at the injustices lingering within the system. White Ruleville, Mrs. Hamer told the writer, was built on the backs of black Ruleville. "You see those houses over there?" she said, pointing to the white section of Ruleville across the U.S. highway, "We paid for them. Me, my husband, my daddy, and his daddy before him. All the Black people working in these cotton fields for next to nothing all these years paid for them. They belong to us."[32]

Poor whites, too, had been left out of the economic equation. Some were beginning to lose their fear of working with blacks, if only in desperation at first, and then with the understanding that their poor black neighbors lived with the same holes in the roof, the same threadbare winter clothing. Some realized that poor blacks understood their hunger better than the white town officials or bankers. In 1971 a white family moved onto Freedom Farm. The man had gone to Mrs. Hamer and said, " 'I got five children and I got nowhere to live,' " she recalled. " 'I don't have food. I don't have anything. And my children, some of them, is sick.' And we gave this man a house."[33]

To combat the desperate housing situation, "we decided to organize everybody who lived in a shack—which was most of us, and teach them how to take advantage of low-cost FHA and farm mortgages," Mrs. Hamer said. "Once we got started, we found that so many people wanted to take part that we didn't have time to give the organization a name. We just call it The Co-op."[34] The program started slowly, with Freedom Farm Corporation first buying three houses in Ruleville and reselling them to the people who lived in them. That way, the money the people had been paying for rent would go toward home ownership.[35] Then, at Mrs. Hamer's instigation, construction was begun on new housing for low-income families. By 1972, seventy new homes had been built and occupied—including a modest one-story yellow-brick bungalow on a side street into which the Hamers moved.[36] Freedom Farm's original investment in housing resulted in release of more than $800,000 in Farmers Home Administration mortgage money for Ruleville, a large amount for such a small town in that era.

Mrs. Hamer could hear her neighbors exclaim on the benefits of the new houses on chill winter mornings. "You'll see two men walking out their front doors. One will kind of stop, look around and say, 'Phew! I didn't realize how cold it was outside!' Every place they ever lived in before, it was always just as cold inside as it was outside."[37]

Important as these projects were, it was Freedom Farm that consumed Mrs. Hamer's energies in her later years, bringing her joy and then sorrow. In the ongoing fight to maintain the farm she had the support of groups like Measure for Measure that did more than just raise money. Once, Freedom Farm needed a large water tank, and a Wisconsin volunteer saw an unused tank on a farm outside Madison. He talked the farmer into donating it, then rented a pickup truck and drove it to Mississippi.[38] By 1971, Measure for Measure could report that infant mortality had been almost cut in half in the Freedom Farm area as people started eating better food, as well as receiving more health care.[39] Mrs. Hamer often said that January 14 of that year was a "great day in Sunflower County" because young people had raised money that helped put a down payment on 640 acres of land. "For the first time in our lives, we will have a chance to control our destiny," she told an audience in Madison. Whites could participate in the program, too. "The cry of hunger is the cry of hunger whether it comes from black, brown or red."[40]

In May 1971, young people staged an International Walk for Development, of which Fannie Lou Hamer was honorary chairman. The walks, a program of the American Freedom from Hunger Foundation, were held in fifty-one countries as people pledged contributions for each mile the youths walked. Freedom Farm was among the beneficiaries, and Mrs. Hamer visited walk groups around the United States before the event. Flush with a little success after the fund-raising efforts, Freedom Farm planners hinted at things to come, plans never realized for more clothing factories, more land purchases, a heifer bank, and, harbinger of the 1990s, a catfish pond.[41]

Measure for Measure remained a consistent source of funds and moral support for Freedom Farm as the years went on. The organization's archives contain letters back and forth between Measure for Measure and Mrs. Hamer about donations ranging from $40,000 in mid-1971 for a major land purchase to small monthly stipends as the farm encountered problems. Mrs. Hamer traveled often to Madison to raise money and to report on the progress of Freedom Farm. She formed close friendships with many of the families there, staying in their homes and getting to know their children. One of those young people, Debra Jean Sweet, had helped organize the hunger hikes and then, invited to the White House to receive a Young America Medal of Honor for her work, had told President Nixon she could not believe his sincerity unless he got the nation out of Vietnam. Several months later, Mrs. Hamer sat next to her at a dinner for the people who had organized the walks. "Debbie Sweet is my kind of woman," Mrs. Hamer told the audience. "What you said to President Nixon, you said for all of us. There are a lot of concerned people in the United States. You keep being critical. . . . You keep speaking out."[42]

On her trips north, Mrs. Hamer, a gifted mimic, also loved to prick the pretensions of her Sunflower County neighbors, either uppity whites or chicken-eating preachers. "Last Wednesday, I met a little white lady—she was very old—at the washer," she told her friends on one visit, her voice filling with mischievous glee.

> She was talking about me but she didn't know it was me [she was talking to]. And she was telling me about "some of the work that Fannie Lou had been doing."
>
> So I asked at that point did she know Fannie Lou, and she said she did. So I went on to further questions. I asked her how did she look? She said, "She's a very small, real light Negro." I said, "Is *that* right?"
>
> So I propped against the washer and I said, "You know something?"
>
> She said, "What's that?"
>
> I said, "This is Fannie Lou Hamer."
>
> She said, "Oh, nooooo."
>
> I said, "Oh, yeaaaahhhhh."
>
> We went through that a while with little dialogue and finally she told me she was going to meet me at the washer again this coming Wednesday, and we'll talk some more. So I see the change. She said, "You know, there's a lot of people won't want to know I've been talking to you."
>
> I said, "That's right."
>
> "But I sure would have thought you was a little bright woman!"
>
> "No, I'm a big black woman." She said, "I see." I'll be meeting her again this coming Wednesday, and we'll be talking together.[43]

She constantly used humor to illustrate a point or to break tension. One of her Madison friends, Jeff Goldstein, said that was what he remembered most. "Laughing like hell. Me calling her. Her calling me. We'd spend a lot of time on the phone together," he said, remembering one time "when we picked up the phone and said hello, we heard about eight or nine tape machines all click on. And we both started to laugh. We didn't have to say nothing. And then she said, well, if they want to listen, they can listen." The humor, the booming voice, stayed with Goldstein. "I can still hear her saying things like, 'Well, Jeff, the hate's going to destroy us. We've even got to love Eastland.' And on and on. And then she'd make some terrible face and crook her fingers like she was stranglin' him."[44]

Freedom Farm may have had generous financial support from northern groups, but its southern banks would only carry it so far. Like many farm operations, Freedom Farm had difficulty paying its debts. Food crops that people picked and took home didn't pay the bills. In 1972, Freedom Farm's emphasis switched to crops that could be sold—cotton and soybeans. The farm managers predicted a profit of $21,750. "However," they had to report, "the weather didn't cooperate with any of the farmers in the Delta during 1972 as more than 40 percent of a record crop was left in the fields during the harvest season due to early rains" that continued through the winter months of 1973. All Delta farmers suffered. "The anticipated profit turned into bank debts that couldn't be paid."[45]

The banks wanted their money, but even an anti-establishment type like Jeff Goldstein never felt the bankers were out to get Mrs. Hamer. "I think there was a lot of respect for her, especially when she started working with white folks and the word got out that she didn't give a damn who you were, if your children were hungry, you could be involved."[46]

Freedom Farm was reorganized in 1972 to try to achieve more professional management. The farm managers separated social service projects from farm money so that any farm profits could be plowed back into retiring the debt incurred to purchase the land. From then on, the ambitious social-service ideas—everything from helping people untangle welfare payments to providing six $300 college scholarships to Sunflower County high school graduates—would have to be self-supporting. Generally, that meant those projects were dropped.[47]

In December 1972, a close friend with whom Mrs. Hamer often stayed in Madison, Martha Bucy Smith, traveled to Mississippi from Madison to check on the co-op. She found that the farm had $50,000 in unpaid bills, including an $11,000 land payment due that month. If Freedom Farm couldn't raise the money, it would lose its land. There was also no money set aside for seed for the 1973 crop. "The weather has been a major drawback this year," Smith reported to Measure for Measure.

Freedom Farm has $20,000 worth of cotton and soybean crops out in the fields still which they can't get in to get until the weather dries off, and it just keeps raining. . . . Another aspect of the problem is that there are none left who know how to pick cotton. In renting cotton pickers and trailers to haul the cotton, [Freedom Farm is] the bottom of the totem pole, for the whites see to it that their crops get in first, and the blacks are the last to get their cotton to the gin."

When the crop needed picking, Freedom Farm people spread the word and local residents gleaned the crop. "The farm lost a lot of corn," Smith reported. "People just tramp around on the plants, and they would tear back the husks on the corn to see if it was ripe, leaving it if it wasn't to their liking. Those cobs of corn then dried up and were not usable later."

But the greatest problem seemed to be management:

> The bookkeeping system at Freedom Farm is almost non-existent. They have no breakdown on their spending. They don't know where the money went to. They have a more accurate estimate of how much they owe. They don't know, however, which Walks for Development they got money from in the past. A lack of long-term planning is characteristic of Freedom Farm and other black co-ops. At Freedom Farm they have no tool shed and no barn, so expensive equipment just stands out in the rain.
>
> They have no organized way of contacting people when they need help in the fields; no training sessions for potential workers on how to pick the vegetables. They have no office where planning can go on. Fannie Lou has little long-range planning ability or organizing how a business should be run. She is a champion grant getter, however. [Farm manager] Joe Harris hasn't been paid yet, and doesn't know when he will be. He was good at getting housing built, but he doesn't know much [about] farming.

Along with these problems, Smith concluded, "is a general lack of concern on the part of the black people. They live for today, see little reason to plan for tomorrow because they have been disappointed so often about tomorrow. Fighting white harassment is a bad enough problem, but to also have to overcome black apathy is almost overwhelming."

These two women, one white, one black, were old friends by then, so the northern visitor would also ask Mrs. Hamer about her health and financial needs. There had been improvement since a trip to Ruleville two years earlier. "Fannie Lou is now in much better shape. They live at the edge of town and there are 70 houses now built—prefabricated which they have bricked on outside, with lawns and all, which now are owned by black families. They are '235' houses," so named for the federal program under which they were built. Two years earlier, about 75 percent of the people had had no running water; by this visit, that figure was down to 35 percent. That fact alone could make an enormous change in people's lives: it meant that water was safer to drink, that no one had to pump water outside in the chill before dawn, that no one had to heat water on a stove, that people didn't have to use outdoor privies. Two garment factories had come to town; although they paid only minimum wage and had no unions, "it is a job, and it is having an effect, for plantation owners now have to improve the homes which black folks live in in order to keep them on the plantations."

Martha Smith also visited the North Bolivar County Farm Co-op, which she found much better off than Freedom Farm. It had steel buildings and a tool shed; it had an office; it had a manager from a three-generation Alabama black farm family, Ron Thornton. "More people seem to know something about how to manage things."[48] She asked Thornton, who had come to Mississippi in the fall of 1972, to help with Freedom Farm and help Measure for Measure raise money for it in Madison. He worked with Miles Foster, of the farm's staff, and Pap Hamer on getting cotton seeds and chemicals.

Freedom Farm made only the smallest, temporary dent in the Delta's economic blues. But to individual families, the co-op could make a major difference. By 1973, for example, the corporation was reporting that it had helped thirteen families who did seasonal work to catch up with mortgage payments. It had helped fifty-seven families apply for welfare and Social Security. More than eighty families had received clothing from donors in northern states, and twenty-five families got assistance in obtaining food stamps. The farm provided jobs for a manager, a secretary-bookkeeper, and four full-time laborers, plus part-time work for thirty-five people. But the financial problems mounted.[49] In January 1973, Paul Silverblatt, whose firm held the deed on the Freedom Farm land, indicated that the note had to be paid, with the interest, within ten days or foreclosure proceedings would start. Joe Harris sought help from Mississippi Action for Community Education—MACE, a community development group based in Greenville—and borrowed $6,000 to forestall foreclosure. By August the farm was delinquent on paying off that loan.

That summer, Mrs. Hamer went to Harry Belafonte again for help. In June he mailed another fund-raising appeal, citing the need for money because "changing weather in the Delta has brought the corporation to the brink of disaster." He recited the story of drought, followed by rain at harvest time, followed by flooding in the Delta, all of which reduced the cash-producing cotton crop. "Will you join me once again in supporting the efforts of Fannie Lou Hamer to prove that poor people of all races can live together in harmony and pride?" Belafonte concluded. "No person has worked harder than Fannie Lou to make Mississippi a better place to live."[50] In June, the New York Foundation gave Freedom Farm $5,000. Measure for Measure also sent out a fund-raising appeal, pointing out that "Fannie Lou's health is poor and she cannot make any more fund raising trips that once generated money for the farm."[51]

Debt, weather, and human indifference conspired against the success of Freedom Farm. There was too much to do, and too few people to do it. Rivalries may have played a role as well. "There were powerful (one-time) SNCC people in Mississippi but they wouldn't help Freedom Farm," Ron Thornton said, "because they did not like the management." He especially criticized Delta Foundation for not helping.

> If [the] poor North Bolivar [co-op] had co-signed for cotton seeds and Measure for Measure had sent money for fuel, wages, repairs, etc., surely Delta Foundation, which tapped . . . a lot of foundations funds could have co-signed for some nitrogen fertilizer. In short, nobody would help Freedom Farm when it was in a real tight spot but North Bolivar and Measure for Measure. Delta Foundation was hoping to get the Freedom Farm in the background. Maybe that's why they didn't come forward in the summer of 1973.[52]

"Freedom Farm didn't have to go," L. C. Dorsey once told an interviewer.

> There was a time when [Mrs. Hamer] was desperately looking for money and she went to some of the groups like [Charles] Bannerman at Mississippi Action for Community Education and who had the foundation money by that time. Foundations were not giving money to individuals but giving to the Delta Foundation, who would give money to needy groups. They didn't want to help her on her terms. That would allow her to still maintain ownership and exercise self-determination and she refused to allow them to take it over in her name.

Dorsey said there was also no cooperative spirit in the Farmers Home Administration or the Federal Land Bank. "They didn't try to help any of us during those times. . . . So there was no help to be coming forward from the federal government where there should have been."[53]

Charles Bannerman had provided help in the past for Freedom Farm to make its land payments. On March 12, 1973, however, Mrs. Hamer and farm manager Joe Harris wrote to Bannerman for help consolidating their debts into one loan for $155,910.54 over seven years. Bannerman replied on March 20 that $156,000 was too much to ask, that his organization wanted to provide jobs, not farm financing.[54]

North Mississippi Rural Legal Services in Greenwood stepped in to help. Victor McTeer, whom Mrs. Hamer had helped in the case of the Drew schoolteachers, worked with MACE and the Emergency Land Fund in Jackson, headed by another former civil rights worker, Jessie Morris, to set up a new schedule of payments for Freedom Farm. For the moment, the farm seemed back on course. But its benefactors were starting to ask questions. In August 1973, Measure for Measure president Bunny Wilkening wrote a long letter to Joe Harris. "This is awkward to ask," she wrote, "but it is a constant question now being asked us by potential and past contributors to Measure for Measure. We are asked for an accounting from Freedom Farm of the use the money we send down is being put to. . . . As I've said before, we are finding it harder and harder to raise any money from the community, and especially churches, without a clear picture" of how the money was used. Specifically, she questioned the budget items of $2,400 for scholarships, $5,000 for food stamps and clothing, and $7,500 for land options. "People in the churches need to know why these are in your budget request."[55]

Harris sent Measure for Measure a detailed look at finances, explaining that the scholarships, food stamps and clothing, and land options were part of Freedom Farm Corporation's overall program.[56] In the face of need surrounding her, Mrs. Hamer could not stop helping people, even with the farm itself at stake.

But soon she had to stop. She had not been well for several years, had never fully recovered from the Winona beating, and in January 1974 suffered a nervous breakdown and was hospitalized in Ruleville. Increasingly, Pap Hamer would have to care for Lenora and Jacqueline, who were now school-aged. A few weeks later, Mrs. Hamer was home from the hospital, reporting to her friends that "she felt better than she had in years."

At the same time, Freedom Farm lost 640 acres to creditors, settling out of court rather than lose all by being sued. "All that remains in Freedom Farm's possession is 40 acres, a tractor, a combine, wagons and the houses and their lots being supported under HUD 235," Harris, who had gone on part-time status, told the farm's supporters in Madison. Money remained to farm the 40 acres Freedom Farm still had. Meanwhile, the better-managed North Bolivar Farm Co-op was still working 760 acres.[57]

In June, several Measure for Measure leaders went south and

were shocked at what they found. Mrs. Hamer's sense of well-being
had not lasted long. She was, they reported, "in the worst health
ever, heavily medicated for pain and dependent on Pap and a
neighbor" to keep the household going. Trying to help his wife out,
Mr. Hamer, who was also driving a Head Start bus, had become the
farm manager. He had found the farm's equipment in bad shape
and was trying to overhaul it when he had time. "Seeds were left in
the planter last year which subsequently molded and rusted in the
machine." Ron Thornton was trying to plant the North Bolivar
cotton and help out Freedom Farm when he could. Both farms
were waterlogged, and their staffs were "praying that the sun shines
steadily to dry out the fields." Crops badly needed cultivation.[58]

On July 12, 1974, the Hamers celebrated their thirtieth wedding anniversary. Mrs. Hamer had been ill, off and on, for months
and had not accepted any speaking invitations since October 1973.
Head Start employed Mr. Hamer only nine months a year. Money
was tighter than usual. Their needs were small—less than $300 a
month for medical bills, telephone, electricity and gas, water, and
food.[59] But, Measure for Measure members learned, they did not
even have that. The anniversary celebration was held at the Elks
Auditorium in Greenville, and the Reverend Harry Bowie, ally
from the 1960s, led the Hamers in repeating their wedding vows.
Joe Harris, who had planned the party, had a heart attack and was
in intensive care in a hospital in Cleveland. Despite Mrs. Hamer's
own poor health, she stayed up late partying. The special appeals
for a cash gift to help the Hamers yielded $1,500, much of which
went to pay medical bills.

Mrs. Hamer had high blood pressure, diabetes, and fluid re-
tention. Medications, which included tranquilizers, plus doctors'
fees, cost the Hamers around $100 a month. Friends from Madison
who had gone to the anniversary celebration found that "there are
days Fannie Lou can't get up." Mrs. Hamer was applying for a
disability pension, her husband for Social Security to try to get
some cash for monthly living expenses.[60]

Pap Hamer, then sixty-two, was working twelve hours a day.
He ran Freedom Farm with one hired tractor driver, a woman.
Heavy rains had stunted the small cotton crop being grown on the
farm's remaining acres; then the summer was extremely dry, so Mr.
Hamer chopped cotton on someone else's land for $1.50 an hour.
"Much of the Freedom Farm equipment is standing around in the
open. [Former employee] Miles Foster did not keep the equipment
in good repair," Measure for Measure members reported. "Pap has
spent a lot of time trying to get the farm machinery back in shape.
The cotton picker seems to have been vandalized."[61]

On August 5, 1974, Joe Harris, still a relatively young man, died. Come 1975, and there was more rain, more crops to get in. Head Start closed its doors until January, leaving 1,400 children uncared for and 200 employees, including Pap Hamer, out of work. By November, Mrs. Hamer asked Measure for Measure for personal help: "The girls need coats very bad."[62] Despite ill health and other hardship, Mrs. Hamer still dreamed that Freedom Farm could outlive her. In December 1976 she asked friends and former co-workers to revive the corporation. It never happened.

There is no shortage of assessments of why Freedom Farm failed. Ron Thornton, the former North Bolivar co-op manager, provided the most eloquent:

> In short, Freedom Farm failed because of the plantation mentality. The people off plantations and sharecropping can't make good quick economical decisions when they try to farm on their own. See, the farming itself carries a nomadic cyst of slavery in it for the black man. Furthermore, the plantation boss never let the black sharecropper or wagehand make a single decision. . . . So they could not come off the plantation in 1965 or out of slavery in 1865 and make a decision. All they could do was stand and wonder (like the Russian farmer today) and wait for the other one to move.[63]

L. C. Dorsey, who was running the North Bolivar County Farm Cooperative much of this time, remembered that Mrs. Hamer

> really was all heart and all love and so often people took advantage of her. And I'm not saying that this was done maliciously or as a conspiracy to keep her from doing things, but they would just come to her with their problems and she would try to help them. Pap talks about this: how when she'd wake up in the morning, there'd be people there with problems and how in the evening when she'd come home, they'd be there with their problems. She just tried to address those problems.

In Dorsey's view, there were two principal reasons Freedom Farm did not last. "Farming is very sensitive business and one of the things that Mrs. Hamer did was she decided she didn't want any government money, so she didn't go after grants and things because she didn't want any strings attached." She didn't want the federal government "dibbing and dabbing." Timing was the second problem. "Freedom Farm was developed during a period when the people had been kicked off plantations that they hated," and Mrs. Hamer was trying to find people work using the skills that they already had—yet people were trying to get away from that back-breaking work. Freedom Farm

> didn't represent glamour. It didn't represent steady income. It was more of the same backbreaking work that they'd been doing all that time, and it really didn't make any difference if you told them, "You're working for yourself, you're not working for the plantation owner. This is yours." It didn't sink in because how can anything be mine that I haven't sacrificed for? How can anything be mine that I share with 700 other families or 200 other families or 40 other families? It was a totally foreign concept. Co-ops had never been part of this society in the sense that black folks or poor whites could participate in. So the concept was very foreign.[64]

Farming is risky in the best of circumstances and requires professional management. Freedom Farm lacked such management because Mrs. Hamer wanted to use local people, some of whom she trusted more than she should have. Black farmers in Mississippi also testify that state and federal programs are not geared to help them survive. The question is not so much why Freedom Farm failed but how it managed to operate as long as it did, especially when run by someone who was not in good health and when financed largely by gifts from the North when the North was turning its attention toward its own problems. Fannie Lou Hamer was not an administrator; that was not her calling. There was no remaining central civil rights movement organization, no group like the Student Non-Violent Coordinating Committee, that was both attuned to her gifts and able to support her in areas in which she was weak.

CHAPTER 15

"Sisters, Brothers, All"

FEMINISTS PROCLAIM that the personal is political. White women may have needed consciousness raising to see how their private worlds could be changed by collective political action, but Mississippi had already provided all the consciousness raising Fannie Lou Hamer needed. She approached the emerging women's movement not as someone critical of men—although she could criticize men with the best of them—but as one who wanted to be sure that this new movement did not forget black people.

"We've had a special plight for 350 years," she said, pointing to the history of women and slavery in the United States during a speech before the NAACP Legal Defense Fund Institute in New York City in May 1971. She had some uncles and aunts who were as white as anybody, she said, and her black grandfather wasn't responsible. But she said she was almost sorrier for white women than she was for black women because they had been caught up in feeling special. They had worked her grandmother, they had worked her mother, and then they tried to work her. "You thought that you was *more* because you was a white woman, you had this kind of angel feeling that you were untouchable," she said. "There's nothing under the sun that made you believe that you was just like me, that under this white pigment of skin is red blood, just like under this black skin of mine."

In working around white people's homes, "one thing that would make me mad as hell, after I would be done slaved all day long, this white woman would get on the phone, calling some of her friends, and said, 'You know, I'm tired, because *we* have been working,' and I said, 'That's a damn lie.' " White women had been put on a pedestal, and blacks were "whacking like hell for the

273

pedestal. And when you hit the ground, you're gone have to fight like hell, like we've been fighting all this time."

Furthermore, as she often said, Mrs. Hamer was not "hung up on this about liberating myself from the black man. I'm not going to try that thing. I got a black husband, six feet three, 240 pounds, with a 14 shoe, that I don't *want* to be liberated from. But we are here to work side by side with this black man in trying to bring liberation to all people."[1]

Despite her own independence and forcefulness, Mrs. Hamer had views on relations between the sexes and about abortion inconsistent with those of many women in the emerging feminist movement. "I am a woman, strong as any woman my age and size normally, but I am no man," she said. "I can think but I am still a woman and I am a mother, as are most women. I can carry the message but the burdens of the nation and the world must be shouldered by men. Decisions concerning life, comfort and security must finally rest in the hands of men. Women can be strength for men, women can help with the decision-making, but men will ultimately take the action." She would, however, publicly and privately bemoan the fact that black men did not take more active roles. Warning black men not to "accept second-class citizenship and inferior positions in the name of integration," she said that too many people had given their lives to end the evil of segregation for them not to be more forceful. "So stand up, black men, this nation needs you, mothers need you. In your hands may lie the salvation of this nation."[2]

Her position was unequivocal on abortion. She herself would have liked to have borne children, and she did not want young women who became pregnant to have abortions. "The methods used to take human lives, such as abortion, the pill, the ring, etc., amounts to genocide," she said. "I believe that legal abortion is legal murder and the use of pills and rings to prevent God's will is a great sin," she said in one 1971 speech.[3] In another, she said that once black women had been bought as slaves because they were considered good breeders. "Now they talk about birth control and abortion for blacks. If they'd been talking that way when my mother was bearing children, I wouldn't be here now."[4] After that "narrow escape to be here," she said she would fight for other kids, too, "because if you give them a chance, they might grow up to be Fannie Lou Hamer or something else."[5]

Despite her differences in personal history and political perspective from the white women who launched the contemporary women's movement, it was natural for Mrs. Hamer to get involved in founding a new organization for political women. In July 1971, three hundred women from twenty-six states met at the Statler Hilton Hotel in Washington to form the National Women's Political Caucus. They wanted to place more women in elective and appointive offices to make the political system more responsive to the concerns of women about credit laws, violence toward women, educational opportunity, and health issues. There were at that time only twelve women in the House of Representatives and one woman in the Senate. Sandra Day O'Connor's appointment to the U.S. Supreme Court was still years away. There were no female governors, and few women were mayors of big cities.

The first NWPC meeting attracted more than a few giant egos. A professor at the University of Wisconsin, Kay Clarenbach, was asked to preside over some of the sessions because she was such a good mediator among the women contending for leadership. Bella Abzug, the flamboyant member of Congress who had already made a name for herself opposing the Vietnam War, was one of the leaders at the first caucus session, as was Betty Friedan, author of *The Feminine Mystique,* the book that helped many women see their own powerlessness. Writer and activist Gloria Steinem, soon to help found *Ms.* magazine, was also among the leadership. Women of color were also represented: Congresswoman Shirley Chisholm, California civil rights activist Myrlie Evers, National Council of Negro Women president Dorothy Height, National Welfare Rights Organization vice president Beulah Sanders, Native American rights leader LaDonna Harris, and Fannie Lou Hamer.[6]

The meeting's theme was clear. "Would a Congress with adequate representation of women and other groups allow this country to rank 14th in infant mortality among the developed nations of the world?" Bella Abzug asked in a speech to the group. "Would they allow a situation in which millions of kids grow up without decent care because their mothers have to work for a living and have no place to leave them—or else that condemns women to stay at home when they want to work because there are no child care facilities?" Would women in political office vote for missiles instead of schools, weapons instead of decent housing or health centers? "And does anyone think they would have allowed the war in Vietnam to go on for so many years, slaughtering and maiming our young men and the people of Indochina?"

Abzug insisted that female political leaders must also represent the diversity of America:

> It is certainly not my purpose to replace or supplement a white, male middle-class elite with a white, female, middle-class elite. I believe very deeply that the hope of an effective women's political

movement lies in reaching out to include those who have been doubly and triply disfranchised—reaching out to working women, to young women, to black women, to women on welfare. . . . I am not elevating women to sainthood. Women have screamed for war. Women, like men, have stoned black children going to integrated schools. Women have been and are prejudiced, narrow-minded, reactionary, even violent. *Some* women. They, of course, have a right to vote and a right to run for office. I will defend that right, but I will not support or vote for them.[7]

Would the fledgling caucus support the candidacy for Congress of Louise Day Hicks of Boston? Hicks was a prominent female politician, a member of the Boston school board, but she opposed school integration. Given the civil rights agenda of the group, it could not support her.[8] But policy lines were unclear. Would the caucus support men who supported women's issues? And what ranked higher, concern over sex discrimination or ongoing racial discrimination? Myrlie Evers, widow of slain Mississippi civil rights leader Medgar Evers, pointed out that black men needed all the support they could get. Mrs. Hamer underlined the point: "I'm not fighting to liberate myself from the black man in the South, because he's been stripped of being a citizen," she told the group.[9] But she also knew that there were issues that concerned her intimately that the young men of the civil rights movement, of whom she was very fond, did not take as seriously as she did. She spoke up repeatedly, for example, about the inhumanity of sterilizing black women, yet that had never been on the Student Non-Violent Coordinating Committee agenda.

Attending the caucus meeting in obvious physical discomfort, Mrs. Hamer nonetheless continued to hammer home her points.[10] If the white women there thought they had problems, Mrs. Hamer said, "then they should be black and in Mississippi for a spell." She had taken with her to Washington the mother of Jo Etha Collier, a young woman slain on the night of her high school graduation in Drew. If there were more women in power in the United States, Mrs. Hamer said, young people like that wouldn't be dying, young people might not have died at Kent State and Jackson State, and young people might not be dying in Vietnam. "If you think about hooking up with all these women of all different colors and all the minority hooking on with the majority of women of voting strength in this country, we would become one hell of a majority," she said to an ovation from the audience. "This is something that should have been done for a long time. Because a white mother is no different from a black mother. The only thing is they haven't had as many problems. But we cry the same tears. And under the skin, it's the same kind of red blood."

The next time a white man asked her for her vote in order to bring change, she said, "I'm going to say, 'If you want to see this, you can support ME because I'm going to be the next one running, baby.'"[11]

"Fannie and I attempted in a very assertive manner to tell the ladies that they had to pay attention to the concerns of women of color," recalled Shirley Chisholm with only a trace of understatement. "Many of the ladies were quite surprised at what we had to say." The white women were trying to obtain a "liberation of the spirit," the former congresswoman said, but she and Mrs. Hamer told them that they, as "sisters," had a double concern: "Not only were we women but we were not white," and overcoming racism was of greater concern to them. Other black and some Hispanic women had criticized them for attending: How would they know that the white women would be any different than their white men? "But we felt it was important to be there and identified with the development of this organization so that our ideas would flow over the sisters," said Chisholm.

At the time, the former congresswoman said, few women of color had any power or influence. "Shirley Chisholm was one," she said of herself.

Fannie Lou Hamer was another. They needed women that were respected, that had a certain amount of influence. At that point, I had a certain reputation as a black woman who had gone to Congress, who had dared to say she would run for President [in the coming 1972 campaign]. What Fannie did on the other hand—she was trying in her own inimitable way to caution these women that black women would never join their organization unless they understood the particular depth of our concerns. It was kind of harsh. I remember it was a hot meeting. Fannie "told them off," and I put that in quotes. We were both quite militant in our different ways. A lot of women could not understand what is Fannie Lou Hamer railing about? They were stuck on the word "sisters," and they thought we were all sisters. What we were saying is that sisters had different agendas. It was a revelation to some of those women. I remember a lot of the women who were there, they never had had any relations with black women. They didn't know how to. This was an experiment on their part. But they knew, or someone behind the scenes told them, that if they expected to start a women's organization, they should have Fannie Lou Hamer and Shirley Chisholm there. We were both known to be fearless.[12]

Although the caucus founders were all women of accomplishment, Mrs. Hamer had a particular moral cachet because of the physical suffering she had endured trying to win a right that many of the others present could take for granted: the right to vote. Former White House aide Liz Carpenter remembered that first encounter. "She was five-by-five, wearing a cotton smock, her passion and her commitments." Her emotions played openly on her face: "sympathy, anger, indignation, determination, faith in the Lord. And her voice—my God, her voice—spoke out from the soul. She could quote the scripture or burst forth with a hymn. She made Billy Graham look like amateur night."[13]

Peace advocate Benjamin Spock was hissed when he addressed the caucus. The famous baby doctor, Spock had written that women's place was in the home with their children. He admitted that he had been a sexist and had written some "foolish and unwise things," but Gloria Steinem said many women had given up on Spock. His books created guilt among huge numbers of American women, and in that context Steinem said she did not see the women's behavior as discourteous.[14] Mrs. Hamer did. When the women interrupted Spock, she rose from her chair. "I'm ashamed of you," she lectured her white sisters. "I know what it is to be harassed." Her words had a quieting effect. She spoke only occasionally, but people knew who she was and listened.

In contrast to Spock's reception, loud cheers greeted Mrs. Hamer's announcement that she would run not only for the state Senate that fall but also against U.S. Senator James O. Eastland the following year. She predicted she might win and said she was fighting "for the liberation of all people, because nobody's free until everybody's free. . . . I've passed equal rights; I'm fighting for human rights."[15] At the close of her remarks, Mrs. Hamer quoted the biblical story of Esther saving her people. "Who knows," she concluded, "but that I have cometh to the kingdom for such a time as this?"[16]

Mrs. Hamer did run for the state Senate; she was not well enough the following year to take on Eastland. She would lose that 1971 state Senate race, but her candidacy was, once again, an example of the constant attempts made by blacks to open the political system to wider participation. She would be helped by some of her friends from the National Women's Political Caucus.

Mississippi lawmakers had continued to resist black gains, and Mrs. Hamer had to fight even to be listed on the ballot. She had wanted to run for the state Senate in 1967 but ran afoul of a law passed in 1966 that no one who had voted in the primary, as she had, could run as an independent in the following general election.[17] The law also substantially increased the number of signatures needed to qualify to run and created earlier deadlines than previously set for independents to file nominating petitions. The provisions made participation in the political process more difficult at just the time black candidates were starting to try to get involved. These new laws came on top of blatantly discriminatory redistricting by the state, as well as new legislation allowing counties to elect supervisors in at-large races that favored white candidates. While the laws themselves did not expressly deny blacks the right to participate fully in elections, nobody in the state capital had any illusions about their intent. White Mississippi was worried: At the time of the last congressional elections—1964—fewer than 7 percent of Mississippi's eligible blacks had been registered to vote. By 1966, about 34 percent of the eligible blacks had signed up.

The restriction on voting in primaries meant that blacks had to make an unenviable choice. They could try to work within the system by casting ballots in what were Mississippi's most important elections—the primaries—or they could run themselves in the general election if they felt, as they usually did, that their interests would not be served by the Democratic Party primary winner. They could not do both. In 1967, Mrs. Hamer and more than a dozen other candidates were denied places on the ballot by the state election commissioners, who cited this law. These would-be candidates then joined an ongoing lawsuit, *Whitley v. Johnson,* named after the Reverend Clifton Whitley, a Freedom Democratic Party activist from Holly Springs, who had wanted to run as an independent for the U.S. Senate in 1966.

Represented by the Lawyers Constitutional Defense Committee in Jackson, the candidates argued that the 1965 Voting Rights Act intended to protect all citizens' rights to cast votes effectively. Toward that end, the act required federal clearance of any changes in election laws. That meant changes in laws affecting not only voters' qualifications but candidates' qualifications. A three-judge federal district court panel, including Senator Eastland's ally Harold Cox, ruled, however, that the Mississippi statute under attack did not affect individuals' voting rights and therefore did not require clearance under Section 5 of the Voting Rights Act.

The Supreme Court heard the case in the fall term of 1968. In their brief, attorneys Armand Derfner, Alvin J. Bronstein, and James A. Lewis argued that the Mississippi law was

no more than an inventive means of maintaining white political supremacy in Mississippi which has resulted from denying Negroes the vote for many years. Yet because the statute does not say in so many words that former slaves may not vote or that the state voting registrar may register whomever he pleases, it is claimed that this statute does not deal with a voting practice or procedure. . . . [Mississippi] should not be allowed to thwart Congress by the devious expedient of calling a spade a shovel and saying they are different.[18]

The Supreme Court was hearing several cases involving Mississippi's fight against the Voting Rights Act and combined them with a Virginia case involving fair treatment of illiterate voters. The principal issue in all the cases was how broadly Congress intended the application of the federal preclearance section of the Voting Rights Act. On March 3, 1969, the Supreme Court ruled for the black candidates. It suspended all new voting laws passed since 1964 by Mississippi and the other southern states involved unless they could prove those laws did not discriminate against blacks. The court did, however, let stand the elections that had been held under those laws. Exultant Mississippi Freedom Democratic Party officials cautioned Congress that these cases clearly demonstrated that if the Voting Rights Act were not extended, Mississippi would be free of its provisions—and the court's restraints—by August 6, 1970.[19]

Surveying the cases years later in his book *Black Votes Count,* attorney Frank Parker wrote that the Supreme Court's 1969 decision was a landmark, "the *Brown v. Board of Education* of voting rights, critical to continuing black political progress throughout the South. For the first time . . . the Supreme Court recognized and applied the principle of minority vote dilution—that the black vote can be affected as much by dilution as by an absolute prohibition on casting a ballot." The decision established the precedent for challenging the legality of this "second generation" of disfranchisement devices, he added.[20]

Whitley v. Johnson remains a centerpiece of the MFDP legacy in Mississippi politics. The black activists showed a recalcitrant state that the force of national opinion was on their side, as well as the power of Congress and the U.S. Supreme Court. Black votes did start to count—not so much in electing black candidates immediately as in electing candidates less hostile to black concerns. Ultimately, the black vote may have made itself felt most strongly in those small local elections for constable or even county sheriff; when white law officers had to face substantial numbers of black voters, law enforcement started to change. Would the law officers in Winona, required to face any substantial number of black voters regularly, have felt as free to arrest and beat Mrs. Hamer and her companions on transparently discriminatory charges in 1963?

What would have happened to Chaney, Goodman, and Schwerner had local officials known they would face substantial numbers of outraged black voters demanding retribution?

In this changing political climate, Fannie Lou Hamer decided to try again for the state Senate. She was encouraged in these efforts by Charles Evers, who had emerged as one of the most persistent black office seekers in the state. In 1968, he had run for Congress, receiving the most votes in the primary against six white opponents but losing in a runoff. By 1969, he was elected mayor of Fayette, in the southwestern corner of the state near the old Natchez Trace; Evers became the first black mayor in a Mississippi town, with the exception of all-black Mound Bayou. By 1971, Evers decided to up the ante and run for governor. He wanted to see black candidates run anywhere there was a black voting population of 45 percent or better. It fell to Ed Cole, then working for Evers and today the state Democratic Party chairman, to find the candidates. This time, Mrs. Hamer got on the ballot.

Black citizens of Sunflower County prepared to take on the county hierarchy. More than a dozen planned to run, challenging the state senators from Sunflower and Bolivar counties, a state representative, the Chancery clerk (Jack Harper), the superintendent of education, the coroner, the county supervisors, and several constables. Throughout Mississippi, there was occurring, as Vanderbilt University political scientist Lester Salamon put it, "the most comprehensive political challenge to white power in Mississippi since 1871. . . . Black leaders in Mississippi were confident that the hour had indeed come to redeem the dream of the early movement, the dream of substantial black political power in the heart of the rural South. Over 300 blacks declared for political office in this crucial state and local election."[21]

In Sunflower County, Cleve McDowell, who had been the first black student to attend the University of Mississippi law school, and Carver Randle, an NAACP leader in Indianola, were running for the state House of Representatives. Randle, a heavy-set attorney whose office is now diagonally across from the Sunflower County courthouse in Indianola, shared election rallies in local churches, parks, and recreation centers with Mrs. Hamer. "I was always impressed with her bravery," he recalled. "I was impressed with her openness and frankness no matter who was in attendance." Mrs. Hamer was especially hard on the educated people in the black community, he remembered, "because she believed they were much better equipped to do what she was doing, yet they didn't have the fortitude to do it."[22]

Mrs. Hamer and Randle campaigned on a platform that urged

that state and local governments hire more minorities for jobs previously held by whites; they also wanted more minorities in appointive government positions and on school boards. And they wanted respect. That was Carver Randle's motivation: he had become active in the Indianola NAACP, which he headed for a decade starting in 1965 after his graduation from Mississippi Valley State, because of what he called the "overall disrespect of whites for blacks." There were no black clerks in the stores, and the white clerks would never call black customers "Mister" or "Missus" when they went into the stores. "These are things that seem little," Randle said, "but were so important then." The two candidates were concerned about the schools as well. Black students predominated in the public schools because the whites had gone to "seg academies," private schools set up expressly to circumvent integration. The public schools "had no lockers, no cool water fountains despite the fact that the kids went to school in the hottest months," Randle said, adding that the library was not air-conditioned and had inadequate books.

Crime in the streets was a campaign issue, too, even when the streets were in small cotton-country towns. Mrs. Hamer and Randle asked repeatedly whether black people could safely walk the streets of their own hometowns in light of the slaying of Jo Etha Collier. In May 1971, just before the campaign began, Collier, who was 18, had been shot and killed as she stood in front of a grocery store while she was on her way home from graduation ceremonies at Drew High School. Three young white men, described as "very much under the influence of alcohol," were charged with the slaying. At the ceremonies Collier, named the most valuable member of the girls' track team, had received an award for her good conduct and attitude. The white principal of Drew High School commented: "She was a good girl. She was a black student but she was a good girl."[23]

Collier, who had been shot in the neck, was killed on a Tuesday night. The town was unsettled the next day, and Mayor W. O. Williford blamed demonstrations there on "outside agitators."[24] Meantime, Collier's mother had gone to Mrs. Hamer's house in Ruleville, where the two women talked to reporters. "It's a damned shame that kids were killed at Jackson State [in 1970] and nothing ever done, and now this," Mrs. Hamer said. "How much longer are things like this going to be allowed to happen?" Mrs. Hamer went to Drew to see what was going on, and she talked with the mayor. "I had felt that through her we might be able to reach some others," the mayor said, "but I can't see that we gained anything. She didn't promise anything except more demonstrations. With all due respect to Mrs. Hamer, I wish she would stay in Ruleville and tend to their business." In Ruleville, there was a demonstration on Thursday, during which thirty-one people were arrested. The charges were soon dropped after Mrs. Hamer met with Ruleville Mayor J. M. Robertson.

The following Sunday, hundreds of people gathered for the funeral at the same high school auditorium where the graduation ceremonies had been held. A handful of whites attended, including the mayor, the police chief, the Sunflower County sheriff, and the school superintendent—people who might never have attended such a funeral only a few years earlier. Mayor Williford, who had been in office twelve years, sat on the stage during the rites and said later that he was surprised himself at the turnout. "If that many Negroes had gathered in one place when I first took office, there surely would have been bloodshed. The only whites there came to go to the funeral, not to make trouble." Williford sent home the highway patrolmen put on duty in case of trouble.[25]

Mrs. Hamer was the first speaker. Three weeks earlier, she had been speaking in New York City about the black woman's plight; now she was living it again. She announced establishment of a fund to try to replace the dead girl's parents' rented home. "This family has suffered too much," she said. "In six months' time, we want them to have a home of their own," Mrs. Hamer said before she broke into tears.[26]

The Reverend Ralph David Abernathy, successor to Dr. Martin Luther King, Jr., as head of the Southern Christian Leadership Conference, delivered the eulogy, saying that the Mississippi Delta "has made its way on the map again. The forces of evil and destruction have robbed us of one of our brightest, most promising, talented young persons." Jo Etha Collier had not participated in civil rights activities, Abernathy said, "but she was black. We are all looked upon the same because we are black, so we all ought to get in the movement and make life better for ourselves and for our children."

Many local people felt that the shooting grew out of the tensions surrounding a voter-registration campaign for the 1971 statewide elections. NAACP officials pointed out that the previous Friday, a white grocer had killed a black man in northeast Mississippi and a white nightwatchman had killed a black man near Sumner that Sunday. Registration workers, some of them from out of state, had had their tires slashed and faced other abuse, NAACP state president Aaron Henry said. "Opposition to blacks registering to vote seems to have awakened the violent element of the white community," he added. Blacks outnumbered whites in the Delta then, and the Delta blacks felt that whenever they increased their political activity, white harassment increased as well.[27] "Jo Etha was smart and she was black," Mrs. Hamer said. "That was too much for the whites."

Despite the harassment, voter registration continued. John Lewis, the director of the Voter Education Project, and Julian Bond, a Georgia state senator and one of the South's leading black politicians, traveled to Mississippi and made thirty-nine stops in twenty-five counties over an eight-day period.[28] Mrs. Hamer, Lewis, and Bond would rotate their speaking order, and it fell Bond's turn to be speaking in Belzoni, scene of a major civil rights incident in the 1950s when Gus Courtts, an NAACP activist, had been shot on the courthouse steps. The voter-registration meeting was held in a church with forty or fifty people present. Bond was speaking when suddenly the doors swung open. A white man walked in and strode up the center aisle toward the pulpit. Bond froze. The man went into the pulpit, stuck out his hand, said he was the mayor, and welcomed them to Belzoni.[29]

Thus, the potential for violence—and the fear of it even when it no longer existed—was always present. Mrs. Hamer spoke of Jo Etha Collier during her campaign for the state Senate. The climate that had allowed the girl's death was the climate that she wanted to help change. She had a variety of objectives. One specifically was ousting James Eastland from office. Mrs. Hamer would tell people that after her state Senate race, Senator Eastland was her next target. She insisted that he was concerned about her challenge. Whether her words were simply to buoy her audience or whether she really believed that he was worried, one shall never know. On one trip north to raise money for Freedom Farm during her fall Senate campaign, Mrs. Hamer told students on the University of Wisconsin newspaper that owning land had given blacks an entering wedge into "the rich, white and racist" political machine that had always run Mississippi. "For the first time we are not beholden to the power structure," Mrs. Hamer said, adding that now "Big Jim" Eastland was calling her; he had never done that before.

"We call him Big Jim," she told the *Daily Cardinal* reporters. "You know, we think he's the biggest welfare recipient in the state. The government said they were gonna make it so nobody was gonna get more than $50,000 for not using the land [to grow crops], but Big Jim's real slick," she said, "and he's making good money."[30] In 1968 alone, Eastland had received $116,970 in federal farm payments, according to reports by one of the *Washington Post*'s top reporters, Spencer Rich.[31] That, to a man who refused to vote for programs to help poor blacks—or whites—in Mississippi through Head Start or job training or other aid.

History lost an opportunity to witness an epic political confrontation in 1972 because Mrs. Hamer was not healthy enough to follow through on her pledge to take on this powerful segregationist. Doubtless she would have lost, but the national press could not have avoided covering the race and would have had to focus on the truth of many of Mrs. Hamer's charges and on the basis for Eastland's power.

Despite her bravado outside the state, Mrs. Hamer knew the obstacles that she was up against. She had little money and could rarely buy air time to present her campaign issues to a broad audience. She was scared because violence still could occur at any time in Mississippi, especially because the national spotlight was, in the main, off civil rights activities in the state by 1971. The national press covered Evers's gubernatorial campaign spottily, and hers not at all. She called upon some of her new friends from the women's caucus to help her. In a letter to the NWPC Washington office, she urged the caucus to come to Mississippi for two weeks before November and then stay to watch the polls.

Betty Friedan rose to the challenge and traveled to the little town of Moorhead the Wednesday before the election. They were, on the surface, unlikely partners: this college-educated writer whose books and articles were debated on campuses and in feminist publications and the former Mississippi sharecropper. Friedan addressed a group, predominantly women, gathered at a small church. She said that she viewed the Mississippi election as her fight as well as theirs, that Mrs. Hamer's political work showed how strong the female bloc could be. The audience showed respect, but little animation, as Friedan talked about how few women there were in Congress and none on the Supreme Court. This was distant from their reality; Fannie Lou Hamer was expanding that reality by even trying to run for state office. "It's no joke now that a woman could be elected president in 1976," Friedan told the group. "Fannie Lou Hamer could be elected and would make a better President than the man in there now." That clicked; the audience, who, according to the *Delta Democrat-Times* reporter covering the event, "had been quiet for the better part of [Friedan's] brief, five-minute speech," responded with applause.

Talking to the reporter after her speech, Friedan said that her trip to Mississippi aimed at focusing national attention on the

Hamer campaign and perhaps strengthening it. "Electing women to offices in the state legislatures in 1971 is the first step toward bringing women into the mainstream of the American political system," she said. From the legislatures, the National Women's Political Caucus then hoped women could advance to Congress. "Replacing James Eastland with Fannie Lou Hamer would be a magnificent thing," she added. She had a particular score to settle against Eastland, she said, recalling her appearance a year earlier before the Senate Judiciary Committee hearing on President Nixon's nomination of G. Harrold Carswell for the Supreme Court. "Her usually quick Yankee voice turned to slow, Southern syrup when she recounted what Eastland told her," reporter Owen Taylor wrote. Friedan had opposed Carswell because she said he had a history of race and sex discrimination. " 'Sen. Eastland told me,' her voice going slow, 'I've never heard of anyone opposing a Supreme Court nomination simply on the basis of discrimination against women.' "[32]

Mrs. Hamer sent out other pleas for help. About three days before the election, she telephoned Liz Carpenter to ask her to come to Mississippi.

"Will it help?" Carpenter responded.

"Honey, anything will help," came the reply from Ruleville.

So off went Liz Carpenter. Xandra Kayden, a graduate student at Harvard, traveled with her. When the pair arrived in Mississippi, Mrs. Hamer was waiting, frying chicken for her guests. The campaigners borrowed a Winnebago camper and started tooling around the backroads. Mrs. Hamer wanted to visit the voters in person because she felt that calling them on the phone might be considered impersonal and would be resented. They rode for what seemed to Carpenter like six hours through cotton patches and around sleepy courthouse squares. The purpose was to visit as many radio and television stations in the district as possible. The candidate carried $2,000 wrapped in an old handkerchief to try to buy air time, and Carpenter was there to help her do it. As a former White House aide, Carpenter was one of the better interview catches to travel through that area for many a month. The stations would tape an interview with her, and she would talk about Mrs. Hamer's candidacy. She would also cite the federal law about selling air time on a nondiscriminatory basis, and so the stations would relent, realizing now that they might be reported if they failed to sell time to Mrs. Hamer.

Xandra Kayden recalled that Mrs. Hamer would point out trees that had been used for lynchings, plantations where particularly ugly violence had occurred. The two political women, the stocky Texan and the stockier Mississippian, sang at the top of their lungs as if to drive the fears away. They sang every hymn they knew, and they knew a lot, "Amazing Grace," and "His Eye Is on the Sparrow," and many more.

The campaigns of Charles Evers for governor and Fannie Lou Hamer for state Senate drew other veterans of the 1960s. Joe Rauh, with whom Mrs. Hamer had been so angry after the 1964 convention and during the 1965 congressional challenge, flew to the Delta for a rally and greeted his old friends with bear hugs. Jason Berry, working at the time for Evers, recalled the scene in his book *Amazing Grace:*

> Fannie Lou Hamer gave a thunderous speech, outshining everyone else. She was piping hot over the verdict handed down in the case of the killers of Jo Etha Collier. "Ah want to know how come they can gun down an innocent, holy li'l chile from Drew, Mississippi, a black girl who is an image of the Lawd, and they call that manslaughter—but when a white person gets killed, they call it murder!" Rauh turned to me after the speech and said wryly, "You know, two years ago they wouldn't even have gotten a guilty on any charge."

Rauh concluded his own speech to the rally by saying that he felt good knowing that "on November 3, Mr. Jim Eastland, who lives on a big plantation in Sunflower County, will be represented in the Mississippi Senate by none other than Mrs. Fannie Lou Hamer!"[33]

John Lewis also campaigned for Mrs. Hamer, appearing with her just before the election at a rally in a packed church in Rosedale in Bolivar County. "We are going to be mad as hell if they steal this one," Mrs. Hamer thundered to the enthusiastic crowd.[34]

Mrs. Hamer lost the election. The final result was Robert Crook, the incumbent seeking his third term, 11,770; Fannie Lou Hamer, 7,201. Charles McLaurin lost his bid to unseat incumbent state senator William B. Alexander, a Cleveland attorney and chairman of a powerful judiciary committee; Cleve McDowell and Carver Randle both lost their races. In Holmes County, Robert Clark narrowly retained his seat by 364 votes.

Thirteen candidates had run that fall as a slate called "the Concerned Citizens of Sunflower County to Elect Black Officials." None was elected. This, despite a voter-registration drive highlighted by an appearance in Indianola by Dr. Ralph Abernathy and by the participation of independent black candidates who drew out record numbers of voters. More people voted in the general election than in the primary in August, which was not usual. In addition, six thousand more people voted in the 1971 election than had voted in a 1963 gubernatorial election that had been hard fought—in a county that seemed to be losing population overall. The difference was that more blacks were registered to vote in 1971 than in 1963, and quite possibly more whites turned out to vote as a result. Still, as Richard Chesteen pointed out in his study of Indianola and Sunflower County politics, "despite the increase, no black came close to winning. Charles Evers received 617 more votes than the highest vote cast for any black seeking a county-wide office."

Why this dropoff? If blacks did not want to support local black candidates but were willing to vote for Evers, as Chesteen suspected, that explanation "does not speak well for black unity or success at the ballot box at the local level. Even the whites seemed to be surprised at the ease with which the local Democratic nominees defeated the independents since the slate included such prominent county Negro personalities as Fannie Lou Hamer, Carver Randle and Cleve McDowell." In Ruleville, Chesteen pointed out, Mrs. Hamer was defeated by 720 to 434 votes.[35]

Mrs. Hamer believed the election had been stolen. At a hearing that the NAACP held in Jackson a month after the voting, she told staff members from the national Democratic Party of harassment on election day. At one precinct in her two-county district, she said she had been met by someone calling himself a guard, who told her she could not go near the polling place. "People were intimidated worse than I have ever seen," Mrs. Hamer said.[36] Once again, Mississippi election officials around the state were charged with refusal to allow black candidates to have their own poll watchers, with changing the location of polling places, and with fraudulent assistance to illiterate voters. In *Amazing Grace,* Jason Berry told about events at the polling place in Shelby, a small town in Bolivar County, part of Mrs. Hamer's district. There was only one voting official black voters trusted but there were four voting machines. When the voting was over, three of the machines showed that white candidates had won handily over Mrs. Hamer and Charles McLaurin; the fourth machine showed the black candidates winning easily. A poll watcher from Princeton University complained that illiterate voters were "helped" by machine operators who entered false choices. Berry also reported that election supervisors in Indianola divided the ballot booths into eleven different rooms—"although there were only 1,200 voters"—so that black voters had no security in numbers as they were sent to separate rooms by the white officials.[37]

The results for black candidates statewide were almost as disastrous as in Sunflower County. There were 309 black candidates, and 259 lost. But 50 black candidates did win, meaning that Mississippi had more black elected officials than any other state in the South.[38] The victorious white candidate for governor, William Waller, courted black votes. This mixed picture set analysts wondering. The mobilization of black voters "misfired seriously," concluded Vanderbilt's Lester Salamon, because its main effect was "to mobilize white anxieties" instead of turning out support for black candidates. "All my land and everything I own is in this county," one white banker told Salamon, "and the same goes for my neighbors. If the blacks take control, we're finished. Now you don't expect us just to stand by and see that happen, do you?"[39] White voters turned out as never before, urged to the polls by Senators Eastland and John Stennis, who both stumped the state.

There was one more factor. "In a land where no one has great power," Jason Berry commented, "a person who suddenly obtains some of it, no matter how little, becomes the subject of envy," and people are reluctant to vote for those they envy.

> In a place like Sunflower County in the Delta, the situation was desperate. A brave woman, Mrs. Hamer was respected in enlightened circles across the land. In Mississippi, she was something of a legend. Even her influence could not settle the difficult problems of her community, however. Sunflower County was involved in a bitter dispute over Head Start funds, and a splinter group had broken off. The order of our campaign—both from [Evers] and Sunflower folks—was to stay clear of the situation. Let Sunflower County handle it. But it was doubtful that they could straighten things out by November 2.[40]

Her allies in Ruleville think to this day that her stand in the Head Start controversy cost her the election. That divisiveness hardly helped, but Mrs. Hamer's friend Unita Blackwell doubts that it was decisive. "The vote wasn't out there in the first place. We couldn't win it. But Mrs. Hamer ran because it was right to run, and it was a political showing that we needed as black people, that [they] could run for office, whether they win it or not."[41]

Some black voters also felt black candidates for office were not qualified. That perception came from years of dependence on whites, whether qualified or not. They were in charge, and that was all that mattered for survival. Harry Bowie, Mrs. Hamer's ally in many Delta fights, found that leadership in the civil rights movement was not considered sufficient qualification to hold office by many black voters, who held black candidates to a higher standard than they demanded of whites.[42] Political science surveys buttressed Bowie's conclusion. Reporting on black candidates who had run in the South between 1965 and 1970, Lester Salamon found that those who won "were generally not as active in the movement as the losers; they tended more to be later-comers who joined the movement after much of the personal danger had subsided but who quickly rose to the top thanks to their command of the traditional sources of prestige, and perhaps to the support they received from whites."[43]

Aaron Henry was one of the few major early-day civil rights leaders elected to office, and he was considered far more open to compromise than his friends like Fannie Lou Hamer; even so, he was not elected to the state legislature until 1979. "If I had to depend on the white community, I wouldn't have made it," Henry said of his election. Henry expressed the greatest affection for Congressman Mike Espy, elected from the Delta district in 1986 as Mississippi's first black U.S. representative since Reconstruction, but he added that Espy had not been as active in the movement as had Robert Clark, who tried twice to win the congressional seat. "People who have been on the cutting edge seldom, if ever, get involved in the leadership situation."[44]

Blacks' economic dependence on whites still led to political dependence in Mississippi. Fannie Lou Hamer was increasingly aware that she was dealing with an almost insoluble dilemma: How could blacks get decent educations and good jobs without some clout in the political process, but would they have the nerve to exercise their potential electoral strength without economic independence? How could you get either when it seemed you could get neither? Small wonder she was frustrated even as she kept trying to bridge the economic and political gaps. By the time Mississippi reduced its official resistance, Fannie Lou Hamer was gone. Her last years were not without accomplishment, but the 1971 election had marked her last major attempt to exert direct political influence.

CHAPTER 16

"And the Movement's Movin' On"

FANNIE LOU HAMER'S health ruled her life for her last five years. Some days she functioned with absolute clarity. Some days she forced herself to travel and to make speeches. And some days she sat alone in frustration and in pain. She thrived on helping people, on having people around her, and in the end she rarely had people with her. Her husband, who made little money himself driving a Head Start bus, sometimes could get people to stay with her only if he paid them.

Ill health was no stranger to the poor people of the Mississippi Delta, black or white. Poverty has its own diseases—malnutrition, dysentery, hypertension among them. When doctors from Tufts Medical School took the first steps toward establishing the Delta Health Center in Mound Bayou in 1965, they found that infant mortality had been dropping for whites in the region but increasing for blacks. Virtually all white women had their babies in hospitals, attended by doctors, while nearly half the black women did not. Children who survived had such poor diets—especially low in protein—during their early years that they suffered irreparable damage. And children lived in homes with no indoor plumbing—sometimes not even an outhouse in the backyard. Families got their water from pumps sunk only twenty feet or so deep; thus, the water was contaminated by sewage. Others collected their drinking water in oil drums stored in their backyards. Food couldn't be properly stored because refrigerators were too expensive for most people; many probably didn't have electricity anyway. Heaters also cost too much, so in the winter children huddled around a stove made out of an oil drum.

Mississippi had about half the national average of doctors, and of the state's nearly 1,500 physicians, only 59 were black. There were only 37 black dentists out of 465 and 376 black registered nurses out of 4,444. White doctors who would see black patients sometimes never touched them. As one person told a reporter from the *Boston Globe,* "Most often I sits on one side of the office and he sits on the other asking questions. There ain't no listening or thumping or looking in the mouth like white folks get."[1] Many hospitals demanded cash in advance, and if someone couldn't pay, he'd have to go to the charity hospital in Vicksburg, 100 miles away, or even farther to Memphis. Mrs. Hamer's daughter died after just such a futile drive to try to find medical treatment.

"Mrs. Hamer was born in an era when you weren't sick unless the boss man decided you were sick," said L. C. Dorsey, who today runs the Delta Health Center. "I'm not saying he decided as a medical person; he decided on the basis of economics. He decided whether you were sick because he had to spend for and pay for your health care and you were sick when you couldn't work. And you got health care when he decided or if he decided that you were valuable enough to invest the money to be taken care of. There have always been from slavery times until now people who were good or bad or indifferent toward the people that they cared for."[2] When Mrs. Hamer was growing up, preventive health care was not emphasized anywhere as much as it is today, and certainly not on Mississippi Delta plantations. "We didn't have access to information during that period that told us how to take care of ourselves or told us what to eat," Dorsey recalled. Had people known what to eat, they wouldn't have had the money to buy the most nutritious food. Furthermore, they grew up in cotton fields sharing the environment with pesticides and other chemicals.

As a child, Fannie Lou Hamer had a diet that was low in protein, high in starch, when there was food at all. As an adult, she was overweight and would explain that "just because people are fat, it doesn't mean they are well fed. The cheapest foods are the fattening ones, not the most nourishing."[3] But she and her neighbors wanted to learn about taking better care of themselves and eating better, and they especially wanted to take better care of their children. To try to help people learn about nutrition, Mrs. Hamer would invite Dr. Aaron Shirley, who had just become the first black specialist at the University of Mississippi Medical School, to share his knowledge with her community. He would drive from Jackson to Ruleville and back in the same day. Shirley gave them medical information, but "I think . . . I was there more for the inspiration— sort of, 'see, he can do it'—than for the nutrition information."[4]

   In early 1972, after her race for the state Senate, after the stress of unending speaking engagements, after the tensions surrounding the Head Start merger and the bomb attempt on her home, after the turmoil involved when Jo Etha Collier was killed in nearby Drew, Mrs. Hamer collapsed and had to be hospitalized. She had spent most of one January day on a picket line in front of a white-owned grocery store near her home. A boycott had been under way for nearly two weeks because the store owner had allegedly kicked a black teenage girl. That night Mrs. Hamer was hospitalized in Mound Bayou for what was described as near nervous exhaustion.[5] Later she was moved to a hospital in Nashville because so many people had come to see her in the hospital closer home.[6] She continued to try to accept speaking engagements around the country but at times had to cancel them because of ill health. She had thrived on the travel, which also helped her raise money for Freedom Farm and other causes; her body was starting to deny her that avenue of fulfillment, and she would be in and out of hospitals the remainder of her life. She frequently was depressed and frustrated.

   No wonder. She had been supported, emotionally more than financially, by the Student Non-Violent Coordinating Committee, which was dying. Her leadership had come under question during the Head Start controversy. She had money problems. She had been paid by the National Council of Negro Women until she ran for the state Senate; then, explained NCNW president Dorothy Height, the organization felt compelled to remove her from the payroll because of that partisan political activity. Whatever attention she had received through her national involvement had largely disappeared; she had also lost her state platforms because the Mississippi Freedom Democratic Party was virtually gone, the Child Development Group of Mississippi was gone. National leaders, the press, even state politicians stopped visiting.

   "On top of that," Voter Education Project director Ed Brown said,

   you see Johnny-come-latelies, people with no allegiance to the movement, having the upward mobility that you don't have, and you're still living with some deprivation. You have to come to terms with those realities. It's an understandable thing. You believe you've done [your work] for good and noble and unselfish reasons, and you haven't done anything to warrant the inattention you're now getting. And you don't understand national politics—that this happens. It happens to old Presidents who are no longer President; it happens to old Supreme Court justices who are no longer Supreme Court justices. It's a phenomenon in terms of people, in terms of leaders. But you miss the attention.[7]

Still not well by summer, Mrs. Hamer nevertheless insisted on attending the Loyalist Party meetings in Jackson. "She was beginning to decline," remembered Ed Cole, today the state Democratic Party chairman.[8] Almost immediately she became embroiled in a fight not of her own choosing over who would be the national committeewoman from Mississippi. Each state party selects two members of the Democratic National Committee, a man and a woman. To set themselves apart from the regular Democrats in their ongoing fight for party control within the state and nationally, the Loyalists' leaders wanted everything about their party to be scrupulously balanced between black and white. If one official was black, the other should be white. Aaron Henry, who had been the Loyalist leader since the middle 1960s, had been selected as national committeeman, replacing Charles Evers. Under the Loyalist scheme of things, the committeewoman should therefore be white. Patt Derian of Jackson, who later became assistant secretary of state in the Carter administration, had been serving in that post since the 1968 convention.

In Mississippi politics, as in Mississippi life, nothing is ever as it seems, and there are as many versions of the national committeewoman fight as there were people involved. Mrs. Hamer ran and lost. Whether she was a pawn or a willing participant is subject to argument. One side, the old allies, white and black, of the MFDP, didn't want Delta moderates to have control over the state's Democrats. They fought to maintain militancy. They asked Mrs. Hamer to run, and she agreed, despite ill health. "It was not pre-ordained that there couldn't be two black members sent from Mississippi," said Owen Brooks, one of those backers.[9] In 1972, Mrs. Hamer still symbolized the grass-roots flavor of what had been the MFDP, but she did not have the strength or possibly even the will to fight hard for the post, telling Patt Derian at one point that she had left her sickbed with a headache to come to the meeting.[10]

Ed King, one of Mrs. Hamer's backers, argued that she lost because her opponents unfairly undermined her candidacy. As King recalled it, Derian's supporters said that Mrs. Hamer couldn't afford to travel to Washington for the meetings and that the party could not afford to pay her way.[11] The other side—Derian, Hodding Carter, Aaron Henry, Charles Evers—felt that Mrs. Hamer was being used by those who did not see the importance of the absolute racial balance in the party at that time. Thus, as Carter said, Mrs. Hamer had to be beaten.[12] "There are some of us who seem to have a desire to be involved in a losing battle," said Aaron Henry, thinking about those times. "It gives us a martyr complex. If the party position was to make sure that we were biracial and represented both sexes, then it was not kosher to try to violate that."[13]

The national committeewoman election represented the biggest political fight ever between Mrs. Hamer and Charles Evers. "If we were saying we were against segregation, we had to be integrated," he recalled. "The SNCC folks wanted Fannie Lou to run. She didn't want to run at first, but they convinced her. I wasn't against Fannie Lou. How could you be against Fannie Lou? I said how about Hodding and Fannie Lou, and they wouldn't go along with that." So he backed Derian.[14]

Wes Watkins, a Loyalist delegate in 1968 and Carter ally, was far more outspoken. He felt Mrs. Hamer simply could not say no to people she cared about. "I personally felt like they used her in a very inhumane kind of way. She was their power. . . . She should have been in a hospital. They propped her up there and she was an icon. I felt very sorry for her and very angry."[15]

Mrs. Hamer was easily elected as a delegate to the 1972 national convention in Miami Beach. She delivered a passionate speech at the state meeting about how far black and white had come and about how much still needed to be done. She was honored to be selected, she said, even though she might not be able to attend. But attend she did, even though everyone who saw her knew that she shouldn't have done so, had health been the sole determinant. But her need to participate after struggling so hard for the right to do so carried her to Miami. "She would perspire all the time," Ed Cole recalled. "It was kind of scary to watch her. You didn't know whether she was fixing to have a heart attack or what. Obviously, her legs were in pain."[16]

Mississippi Democrats still were sparring over who would be recognized by the national party and who would control the state and local election machinery. The Loyalists had the national recognition, and the regulars still had most of the machinery. Aaron Henry, Hodding Carter, Patt Derian, Ed Cole, and others engaged in lengthy negotiations with the party regulars, now headed by Governor William Waller, who had been elected over independent candidate Charles Evers in a runoff election in 1971. The two factions found themselves unable to resolve their differences before the convention. In the kind of turnabout that only Mississippi could produce, the Waller contingent then challenged the Loyalist delegation, the group that had been seated at the 1968 convention. The Waller challengers lost. But they retained control of the party in the state until the two factions finally merged in 1976.

Only a handful of the original 1964 Freedom Democrats attended the Miami convention as delegates: Aaron Henry, Mrs. Hamer, and one or two others. Mrs. Hamer said she "felt disgusted because the people they had pulled in with the Loyal Democrats didn't know what suffering is and don't know what politics is about." Racially balanced as the 1972 delegation was, it was run by whites, she fervently believed. Black people "had nothing to say there at that convention, from Mississippi," she fumed to an interviewer not long afterward.[17] "Hodding Carter made one of these big flamboyant speeches. Well, I like Hodding," she added, conceding that it might not have been intentional that the whites seemed so visible. But she still grieved for the Freedom Democratic Party and adamantly insisted that the Loyalists were organized to break down MFDP because it was more militant against the Vietnam War and supported grass-roots economic programs.

Mrs. Hamer's feminist friends propelled her into the one role she played at the convention as part of its minidrama, the vice-presidential nomination. When Congresswoman Shirley Chisholm, who had been the first black woman to run for president, demurred about being a vice-presidential candidate, a group in the fledgling feminist political movement sought another woman to run. Plotting strategy in a women's rest room, they decided to back Frances "Sissy" Farenthold, a Texas state legislator who had made a strong second-place showing in that state's Democratic gubernatorial primary earlier that year.

The convention team assembled by Senator George McGovern of South Dakota, who by then had sewn up the nomination, had already steamrolled over the feminist contingent in two key fights. The women, led by Gloria Steinem and Bella Abzug, first challenged the seating of the South Carolina delegation, which had only eight women among thirty-two members. They lost. Then they brought up a strong reproductive rights platform and, after a bitter fight that divided even some couples among the liberal delegates, the feminists lost again, fifteen hundred to eleven hundred.[18] There was still the vice presidency. McGovern had already tapped Senator Tom Eagleton of Missouri as his choice, but the participatory democracy being preached, if not fully practiced, dictated that the delegates have a chance to put in nomination whatever other candidates they wanted.

After Senator Mike Gravel of Alaska, an opponent of the

Vietnam War and of secrecy in government, was nominated, convention chair Yvonne Braithwaite Burke recognized Steinem. Sissy Farenthold, said Steinem, "meets all the standards apparently being used in this 1972 vice presidential search: she is from Texas; she is an experienced and very successful campaigner; she is a Catholic and she is a fighter for the issues that have brought George McGovern to victory at this convention."[19] In Texas, she continued, Farenthold had put together a coalition of women, blacks, Chicanos, young people, and working people for her primary campaign for the governorship.

People representing various elements of that coalition rose to second the nomination. Mrs. Hamer was trying to make it to the platform but had to rest on the way. Texas delegate David Lopez went first, saying, "A great American wanted to precede me to this microphone tonight to second the nomination of Sissy Farenthold, but though her heart is strong, her body has temporarily given her a little trouble. I refer to that courageous Democrat from the State of Mississippi, Fannie Lou Hamer." Lopez read what Mrs. Hamer wanted to say: "This has been a good week for all Americans. This week the people, the people of our country, have been represented here by their own kind, other people just like them. Many of us have worked many years for this week. Now I ask you to make it all very real. Help to be born tonight a new America. It is struggling to be born. Help it. Vote for my fellow Southerner and a fine human being, Sissy Farenthold of Texas." Lopez described Farenthold's support for McGovern, her opposition to the war, and her campaign, which had "electrified Texas." He, too, urged the delegates to vote for Sissy Farenthold so "with all of us you can say Viva Sissy."

By then Mrs. Hamer was able, with help, to reach the podium. Her appearance was brief. "Madame Chairman, fellow Democrats and sister Democrats, I am not here to make a speech but just giving support and seconding the nomination of Sissy Farenthold for vice president. If she was good enough for Shirley Chisholm, then she is good enough for Fannie Lou Hamer. Thank you."[20] The delegates voted overwhelmingly for Eagleton.

The convention took its toll on her health, and Mrs. Hamer went home to rest. She continued to have her good days and her bad days. Sometimes she was frustrated, as when she talked to visiting journalists about Mississippi's requirement that people reregister. Sometimes she was not lucid, as Jeff Goldstein from Madison found out on one visit and June Johnson saw on various occasions. At times in 1973, Johnson said, Mrs. Hamer "did not

know who I was. She really didn't know. She was paranoid and that
was painful to me. . . . Her skin turned so dark, the texture of her
skin was not the same as I was used to seeing Mrs. Hamer. She was
a very glowing, sophisticated looking woman, and her eyes were like
they were bloodshot, just red, and she was just like a kid, no longer
in control, you know."[21]

It was during this period that Mrs. Hamer wrote to her friend
Jean Sweet in Madison that she had no energy. "I wasn't goin'
anyplace. I just stayed most of the time in the house in the bed. I
wasn't able to do my housework or anything."[22]

Some issues, such as conditions at the notorious Mississippi
State Penitentiary at Parchman, could still summon her passions.
Mississippi had jailed some of the early civil rights demonstrators at
this flat outpost only a short drive north from Ruleville. Parchman,
which the state considered a self-supporting cotton plantation,
farmed out inmates to work in the fields for neighboring landowners. Guards were harsh, conditions inhospitable. Mrs. Hamer
was involved with the inmates' lives and the conditions in which
they lived, frequently receiving calls seeking help for them. On one
occasion in 1971, for example, a young man was denied permission
to attend his father's funeral. Mrs. Hamer couldn't undo that problem, but she got a letter from a prison official explaining the mixup,
apologizing, and extending an offer to let the young man visit his
father's grave with his mother.[23]

In 1971, a group of inmates sued the state, charging that prison
authorities denied them certain constitutional rights. The court
agreed, outlining a litany of unequal and inferior treatment for black
prisoners.[24] In his 1972 decision, Judge William Keady ordered
sweeping reforms in the prison. That same year, Governor Waller,
new in office and seeking better ties with the black community,
named Cleve McDowell of Drew as the first black member of the
State Penitentiary Board. Slowly, the prison was opened to outside
scrutiny. In mid-January 1973, black leaders from around the state,
including Mrs. Hamer, visited the prison. It was the first time, she
said, that she had ever "crossed the tracks" to see inside the penitentiary even though she had lived and worked in the area for years.

"I was treated as a human being. We were allowed to go any
place we asked to go. I didn't really believe I was over there myself.
It was something that was long overdue but to see it happen now
means a lot not only for the black prisoners but a lot to all of us that
are out here in the free world." Mrs. Hamer's group, which included Amzie Moore, was guided through Parchman by its assistant superintendent, Clifford Jennings, the highest-ranking black

staff member. Mrs. Hamer and the others said they saw many changes, "but not enough. We know with people like Mr. McDowell and Mr. Jennings, it can mean a whole lot of change." In the past, Mrs. Hamer said, the inmates had been treated like slaves. Now, she had been told by some of the female prisoners, they felt better because of the recent changes of attitude.[25]

In 1974, Mrs. Hamer's nephew was sentenced to Parchman. A fourteen-year-old girl had been found strangled to death behind a doctor's office in Ruleville in November 1973, and a twenty-year-old nephew of Mrs. Hamer was charged with murder. Johnnie Walls was working in the Legal Services office in Greenwood, and Mrs. Hamer asked him to take the case. She was not sure about the circumstances of the case, Walls recalled, but she wanted her nephew to have the fairest trial possible. The case was a difficult one for the black community in Ruleville; many people had known the young girl who died. Mrs. Hamer helped Walls interview people who might have known of the young people's relationship. Her health was not good, but when the trial began in June 1974, she went to court each day. She could have thrown her weight around, could have claimed her nephew was being railroaded, Walls said, but she didn't; she was simply there to see that he received justice. The young man was convicted of manslaughter and sentenced to seventeen years in Parchman.[26]

With these strains, Mrs. Hamer's health did not improve. In 1974 she applied for disability income from the state and was turned down. But her application came to the attention of a physician with whom she had worked in the 1960s, Dr. Robert Smith. A graduate of Howard University Medical School, Smith had returned to his native Mississippi and had helped organize black doctors to obtain hospital privileges and to provide medical care for injured or jailed civil rights demonstrators. "Our paths crossed because we were basically trying to do the same things. . . . Many of the indignities that Mrs. Hamer went through, I went through also as a physician." By the time her disability income application was turned down, Smith had been named to the state disability review board because he had complained about the number of patients he felt had been unjustifiably rejected. "I was able to get her records and get her some disability."[27]

Despite her ailments, Mrs. Hamer continued to administer Voter Education Project (VEP) grants. In 1975, for example, she once again coordinated Sunflower County registration efforts. Indianola was a major target in that drive because it still had a large number of unregistered blacks. John Lewis was VEP director, and the campaign was highlighted by another fifteen-county mobilization tour as Lewis and Mrs. Hamer went from community to community to encourage people to sign up to vote.

In 1975, Mrs. Hamer also helped Henry Kirksey when he ran for governor. Kirksey, who had done much of the movement's printing during Freedom Summer, was later elected as one of Mississippi's first black state senators. In the gubernatorial race, Kirksey knew he had about as much chance of being elected as he had of emptying the Atlantic Ocean with a teaspoon. "But I was running to get known," he said. "I had gone to Washington to talk to some of the black members of Congress about school integration— or about how slow school integration was—and they asked if I had a letter of introduction from anyone." In short, he had no credibility, even though it was his name on one lawsuit that ultimately produced fairer legislative redistricting in Mississippi. Faced with this indifference to his opinion, Kirksey decided to run for office so he would be taken seriously.

> So I went to Fannie Lou and we talked about it. She was already in ill health and I knew she wouldn't campaign for me. I just wanted her endorsement. It was important to me to have on my campaign literature that she endorsed me. And she did. And it may have been just as well that she couldn't campaign for me. Because if she had, everyone would have been saying, "Did you hear what Fannie Lou Hamer said?" And no one would have heard of Henry Kirksey. I would have been completely overshadowed by her.
>
> Fannie Lou had the ability to get the people worked up, much more so than Martin Luther King. Martin Luther King was on more of an intellectual level than Fannie Lou Hamer. Fannie Lou Hamer was a very poorly educated intellectual. . . . If Fannie Lou Hamer had had the same opportunities that Martin Luther King had, then we would have had a female Martin Luther King.[28]

International visitors as well as state politicians made the trek to Ruleville to meet Mrs. Hamer and see the work that she had done. In early July 1975, twenty women from developing nations toured the Mississippi Delta after attending the first International Women's Year meeting in Mexico City. Traveling under the auspices of the National Council of Negro Women and led by its president, Dorothy Height, the women saw community centers and government-financed housing in Cleveland and then traveled north to Mound Bayou. Women in Ruleville had planned a reception for their guests, but, as inevitably happens with community tours, the group ran behind schedule. When it reached Ruleville, only Mrs. Hamer was still waiting.[29]

Endorsements, Mrs. Hamer could do; greeting foreign visitors, she still could do. But speeches became increasingly rare. In January 1976, she did travel to Madison, Wisconsin, to help observe the tenth anniversary of the founding of Measure for Measure, which had helped with fund-raising and management of Freedom Farm, by then virtually abandoned. She mixed appreciation for the help of the people of Madison with sharp words about President Nixon, who had left office in disgrace a little over a year earlier. "If the country ever was headed for dictatorship," she said, "it was under the Nixon Administration. But, you know, God always have a way. An innocent black man was curious about what tape was doing on a door and uncovered Watergate," she said, referring to the security guard who found the signs of the break-in at the Watergate building headquarters of the Democratic National Committee that led to Nixon's resignation. The 1976 presidential primary races had begun by the time Mrs. Hamer visited Madison, and she lamented the nature of the campaign. "The country has become so conservative that nobody among the presidential candidates is saying much. . . . What kind of choice do I have to vote for?" But times were changing, she added. "For the first time in the history of Mississippi, I was invited to Governor [Cliff] Finch's inauguration."

She gave her Madison audience another example of how Mississippi was changing, describing her plane ride two weeks earlier to Mississippi from Washington with Champ Terney. Mrs. Hamer said that she and Terney, who had been the opposing attorney in the school cases in which she was involved, always went "nose-to-nose because if he's for it, I always was against it even if I hadn't heard what it was. But just knowing who he was, I was against it," Mrs. Hamer told her amused Madison listeners. She was on her way back from Martin Luther King Day observances at HEW in Rockville, Maryland, January 15, 1976.

> We was in National Airport and who walks in but the son-in-law of Senator Eastland. His name is attorney Terney. When he walked in—now this is one thing that we have in the South that you don't have in the North that it's hard for me to get used to—nobody speak in the North. But you can be fixing to fight a person in the South, but before you hit him, you say, "Good morning." You got that kind of respect for each other.
>
> So when I saw him in the airport, I said, "Good evening, attorney Terney." He said, "Well, there's Mrs. Hamer." So he shook hands with me, and he had another old guy with him and he said . . . "This is Mrs. Fannie Lou Hamer from Mississippi." So the guy looked at me real funny. He said, "Howdy, Fannie Lou," and I said, "Howdy." So we didn't talk anymore.

In Memphis, Mrs. Hamer met Terney again. She was trying to convince the airline attendants to let her carry on the plane two pictures she had received in Rockville. When she boarded the plane, she saw Terney and she recalled that he said, "Hold, it, Mrs. Hamer. Now you done fought to ride in the front. You don't go back there in the back. You sit right down here with me. I sat right down and we talked, you know, from Memphis to Greenville. . . . He said to me when we got to the airport, if there's nobody there, I'll carry you on home. So that's come a long way because I've known the time that he'd have gotten off the plane rather than ride with me."[30]

Asked to speak at a conference on crime in Jackson that March, she couldn't say no, and she carried her plea for black men to become more active in their communities to that audience at New Hope Baptist Church. "God has been left out" of society, and so criminals come in, she said. One problem in Jackson was that "there are so many homes without a father." "Gentlemen," she added, "you're going to have to go into the neighborhoods and be a father to these kids. You have a responsibility, and don't say it can't be done because with God, anything is possible."[31]

That spring of 1976, Mrs. Hamer had breast cancer surgery. "I had it when you was down here," she wrote in a letter to me, "but I kept hoping it would go away." Her left breast was removed. She lacked the money for a prosthesis, and on one of her trips to New York City, her old friend Eleanor Holmes Norton learned of her situation. " 'You know what I got in here?' Mrs. Hamer said, gesturing toward her breast. " 'Some socks rolled up.'

"And I said, 'Oh, Mrs. Hamer, you should have a prosthesis,' " Norton recalled. "And I remember going and getting one for her and going with her. And it just seemed to me that here was a woman regarded as a heroine of the movement and something as basic as this she didn't have. . . . I remember asking her about the lump in her breast. I said, 'Mrs. Hamer, when did you first feel the lump?' " It had been a long time earlier.[32]

In the last year of Fannie Lou Hamer's life, her days were often empty. She was recovering from surgery and could travel only a little. She had no money to give away then, and fewer people came by the house. Vergie, the surviving girl she had helped raise, was no longer in Mississippi, leaving behind an ailing Mrs. Hamer and her husband and children, "so I could get myself together," she wrote to Mrs. Hamer from Memphis that year. "No matter how wrong I been," she said, "I never stop loving you all."[33]

For June Johnson, these days offered a sad contrast to the vital, hearty woman she had known. Every time she had visited in days past, she'd be greeted with a big hug and a helping of blackeyed peas or cornbread or whatever Mrs. Hamer had been cooking. "She always had something to put on the welcome table, not just to sit at the table but to be able to get something off of it," Johnson said. But now she was no longer able to greet guests with her old exuberance, as Johnson saw when she stopped by Mrs. Hamer's home one day on her way to visit some inmates at Parchman. Mrs. Hamer was sitting at the window.

> I went to ask her what was wrong with her. And she started crying. I had never seen Mrs. Hamer without her hair in its proper place because she was very particular about her hair. She was in her rocking chair at the window, and she broke down and started to cry. I said, "Why are you crying? What's the matter?" She said that it was a shame that she couldn't use her arms. She said, "I can't get people to come and do anything for me." And she wanted her hair combed. And I said, "Oh, Mrs. Hamer, don't cry about that."

She had sent for a woman to help her a few hours earlier, but the woman never came. "I said, 'Don't cry about that. I'm here now. I have time to comb your hair and brush it.' . . . I think it was not so much just combing her hair—she needed for somebody to be there and pamper and give her a little bit back. And I stood there and . . . I brushed her hair. And she was just as relaxed and just as calm. That just made her day."[34]

Pap Hamer complained bitterly about the way his wife was treated in her last years. "My wife loved people, but people didn't love her," he told L. C. Dorsey.

> I would come to this house and it would be so many people in here I couldn't hardly get in the door. They came to get clothes, food, money—everything. But when she fell sick and was in the hospital at Mound Bayou, the only way I could get people to stay with her was when I paid them. I tried to warn my wife. I told her, "You can't do everything." But still they called on her. . . . As soon as she got in [from a trip], they would call her again. They wore her down. She raised lots of money and she would come back and give it to people. And when she died, she didn't have a dime.[35]

Her movement friends knew that she had had breast cancer and that she had not been cured. They felt it was time for memorials while she could still hear the tributes. On September 25, 1976, the Congressional Black Caucus presented her with its annual George

W. Collins Memorial Award for Community Service at its gala dinner in Washington. The award had been established to give formal recognition to local people who exemplified the "quiet and efficient life and work styles" of the late Congressman George Collins of Chicago—although, as a *Delta Democrat-Times* reporter wrote soon afterward, " 'quiet' would hardly be an adjective that most people would use to describe Fannie Lou Hamer." Honored with Mrs. Hamer were comedian and activist Dick Gregory and Representative Gus Hawkins of Los Angeles. The party was an annual splashy affair, drawing Coretta Scott King, magazine publisher Earl Graves, presidential candidate Jimmy Carter's wife Rosalynn, vice-presidential candidate Walter Mondale, and Mrs. Hamer's old friend, Andrew Young, then a congressman from Georgia. Ella Fitzgerald entertained with a twenty-minute concert of works by black composers, and there was a dramatic presentation of poetry and speeches on black history called "The Advocates among Us," written by playwright Lonne Elder. Barbara Jordan was the dinner speaker.[36]

Mrs. Hamer received recognition back home in Ruleville, too: the town held another Fannie Lou Hamer Day in late October 1976. Charles Evers was the featured speaker, and he urged the audience to vote in the upcoming election. "We've got to take care of business for a woman who done so much and suffered for us," he said. "We don't have enough power in the Capitol to dot an 'i.' We've got to fight to make sure Fannie's work was not in vain." Evers pointed to members of the audience and admonished them by name to contribute to Mrs. Hamer's hospital bills. He led the way with a $500 bill and raised nearly $2,100 of the $2,500 he said was needed. The Alpha Phi fraternity used the occasion to present Mrs. Hamer with its Paul Robeson Award for humanitarian contributions, and a fraternity representative traveled from Ohio to speak at the celebration. A nearby PTA group presented her with a certificate of appreciation. Mrs. Hamer's longtime ally in the civil rights movement, Amzie Moore from Cleveland, reminded the audience that only 40 percent of blacks registered to vote did so. "We've got to stop begging and get something for ourselves," he added. Ruleville mayor Virginia Tolbert presented a proclamation declaring Fannie Lou Hamer Day and called Mrs. Hamer "one of Ruleville's most noted and famous citizens." Mrs. Hamer herself spoke briefly. "We've come a little way here in Ruleville and we've got a long way to go," she said. "I'll continue to fight to right these things as long as I can." She ended the ceremonies by singing a song expressing the love in her heart that day.[37]

"The place should have been packed but it wasn't," said Robert Clark, the state legislator who was one of the speakers. Fewer than one hundred people attended, and Clark said that if she had died and were stretched out in front, "there would be so many people that not only could you not get in, you couldn't get on the grounds. Then everybody would have her picture on the wall. I said, 'Fannie Lou, I want you to come down off the wall and give 'em hell.' " And when she died, I couldn't get in there were so many people."[38]

After the program in her honor, Mrs. Hamer invited everyone to her house. "We had a ball. We ate. We laughed. We talked," June Johnson recalled. "She was in bad health that day, but she was happy. . . . She was used to people being around her."[39]

Mrs. Hamer was visited by a reporter for the *Delta Democrat-Times* for the last time in October 1976. Lloyd Gray wrote, "Times have unquestionably changed in Ruleville and Sunflower County, as they have in all parts of Mississippi and the South in the last decade, and with those changes people like Fannie Lou Hamer have drifted from the spotlight. No longer are the circumstances so intense that they call forth simple, uneducated farm folk like Fannie Lou Hamer and turn them overnight into national—even international figures."

Although the glitter was gone, the fight for economic development and political participation went on, and Fannie Lou Hamer had been, as Gray noted, concentrating on those local issues all along. "There's such a thing as loyalty and love, loyalty to my people and love for my people. And I love Ruleville." She mused that day about the changes that she had seen some whites bring about in Ruleville, about the respect she felt some whites in Ruleville now gave her. She hadn't thought she'd see those changes in her lifetime. "I didn't believe that I would be the one that would sit with a white parent, you know, and could talk because we had kids in the school that were active, kids that needed from the beginning to know each other. And that's been the whole ripoff—you hadn't learned about me and my people." She had passed the leadership to younger people, she told Gray, but she still went to meetings that they called "because they're the leaders and I respect them."

Her faith in the South remained intact because she said she had always felt great hypocrisy in the North about racial matters. "Look at what's happening in Boston. Our little kids go to school together right around the corner from here every day. You go to a PTA meeting, and there's black and white together—and I would be shocked if somebody threw a rock." There would always be "some hellcats even the devil ain't gonna want," Mrs. Hamer added, but nonetheless she felt that the South could lead the country in creating respect for each human being. People simply have to realize, she added in an echo of her earliest speeches in the movement, "that whether he's white as a sheet or black as a skillet, out of one blood God made all nations."[40]

The interview might have made a reflective coda for a full life, but she was never one to stay out of the news when there was a call to answer. A few days after the interview appeared, Mrs. Hamer was off to Jackson for another protest, even though she had said she wasn't as strong as she used to be. The state's Medicaid Commission, operating under a directive from the legislature to control expenses, had decided that people receiving help under the program should pay 50 cents for each drug prescription and refill; previously, the government had paid the entire cost of prescriptions. The action took effect July 1 despite protests from Charles Evers, Dr. Aaron Shirley, and others that the poor would be hurt by even a 50-cent co-payment requirement. By fall, there had been no movement on the issue, so Evers led some three hundred demonstrators in a protest at the state capitol building in Jackson.

The capitol rotunda is a mix of architectural styles, a baronial place, graced, if that is the word, by a bronze statue of the archsegregationist U.S. senator Theodore Bilbo. Both a populist and a white supremacist, Bilbo had opposed bills that would have curbed lynching and eliminated the poll tax. His statue was thus a convenient backdrop for demonstrators seeking to embarrass state government by playing off a notorious figure from its history. The demonstrators gathered in the rotunda shortly before noon that October day. Fayette mayor Evers said the group wanted the governor and other state officials "to know they are wrong for imposing Medicaid pressure on not just blacks, but all poor people." Then the demonstrators met with Governor Cliff Finch, telling him they did not want to embarrass him but rather wanted to get his help in ending the 50-cent charge. Finch promised to look into the matter.

Mrs. Hamer led the group in singing "This Little Light of Mine." Standing in front of the Bilbo bronze, she shook her finger in its direction and said she was dedicating the singing of the civil rights anthem, "We Shall Overcome," to "this sick statue."[41] She had seen bigots like Bilbo come to power and lose power, and she was still there, protesting.

What was probably the last interview Mrs. Hamer gave was to the daughter of Tracy Sugarman, one of the Freedom Summer volunteers. Mrs. Hamer had often stayed with the Sugarmans on her fund-raising trips north, and on those trips the two Sugarman children talked with her about her experiences. Laurie Sugarman called Mrs. Hamer late in 1976 for help on a paper for a college class. The conversation was warm and loving and reveals Mrs. Hamer's mood only three months before she died. She was still concerned about random violence, about a young black man who had been murdered in nearby Cleveland. She was still annoyed that professional people who had jobs "have become complacent and very satisfied and really don't care what's going on with the people that's been doing the suffering." And she was disgusted at the fact that Mississippi still made people reregister to vote. The one bright spot she saw focused on the children. "They getting along good. We never had no trouble at the schoolhouse that I know of," Mrs. Hamer said.

"We have in Boston," Laurie said, referring to battles over court-ordered integration of the public schools there.

"We're ahead of Boston," Mrs. Hamer replied. "The parents and the kids—everybody go out to see their kids perform because we have the same thing in common." The performances occur in the auditorium, and "occasionally, you know, you find yourself talking to the person right by you because you sharing the same thing. You know, school was out today for Christmas and my youngest little girl, she got her little gift from her little white friend, you know." That would have been unheard of fifteen years ago, she added. "You wouldn't have believed it. But you know what I'm saying—we still haven't arrived. We got a long way to go. We just have to keep working at it."

Then Mrs. Hamer talked about the spirit of sacrifice of the young people who had gone to Mississippi in 1964. Believing in people was her weakness, she said, and she felt people could do anything.

> A living example was Andy Goodman, James Chaney and Michael Schwerner that come down here. And I remember talking to them the Sunday before they went to Oxford, Ohio, for the orientation where we had to drill or talk to them about what they might be faced with. Even when Christ hung on the cross, he said greater love has no man than the one who is willing to lay down his life for his friends. Even though they was aware they might die, they still came. These are the things we have to think about. These are the things we can't sweep under the rug. And these are the things that still give me hope.[42]

As she became more and more ill, she wanted to clear any remaining debts of Freedom Farm as well as her personal debts.

She did not want to leave life owing anybody anything, but she lamented that she could no longer travel to raise funds. She also made her last contacts with her friends. "Toward the end," said Unita Blackwell, "she called me one day and said, 'Girl, I'm real sick. I don't want to die, but I made my peace with God.' If anybody ever get to heaven, it was Mrs. Hamer. She was a powerful lady. God set her aside to do work. And her time was up."[43]

Early in 1977, Mrs. Hamer entered the Mound Bayou Community Hospital for treatment of cancer, diabetes, and heart disease. June Johnson saw her last on March 4. "She recognized us, but she was not in good spirits. She was sitting in a wheelchair, crying. She stated she was so tired, she wanted all of us to remember her and to keep up the work. She wanted us to understand that she had taken care of business. She felt her house was in place, and that everything was in order with God, because she was a very religious person."[44] On March 14, 1977, she died. In the very end, her heart failed, the only time it ever did.

CHAPTER 17

"Go Home
to My Lord and
Be Free"

THE TRAVELING, the speaking, and the singing had ended for
Fannie Lou Hamer. Now others would travel to Ruleville to speak
and sing in her honor. Hundreds of people gathered for her funeral
at the Williams Chapel Baptist Church. It was, by all accounts, a
day on which the movement reassembled and could have rekindled
its fires. But the activists of the 1960s were pulled in too many
different directions in the 1970s, so the moment passed, if indeed
it had existed at all. Some of those who had worked with Mrs.
Hamer had gone into government—national, state, or local. Others
had become lawyers out of state, or teachers, or social workers, all
with their own lives. Others had grown increasingly militant and
separatist. Even when they had worked in the state, they had agreed
on little beyond their overriding abhorrence of the white supremacist system, so why start agreeing now? Mrs. Hamer, representing
the grass-roots people, had been a keystone, a unifying force.
"None of the others could command so much respect," said her
farm co-op ally, Ron Thornton.[1]

On the day of the funeral, United Nations Ambassador An-
drew Young landed in a government plane at the Indianola airport.
Assistant Secretary of State Hodding Carter arrived. Michigan
Congressman Charles Diggs attended, as did Vernon Jordan of the
National Urban League, Dorothy Height of the National Council
of Negro Women, and activist Ella Baker. Stokely Carmichael, in
Memphis for a speech, showed up, as did H. Rap Brown, both
former Student Non-Violent Coordinating Committee leaders.
Austin Scott, who had covered the civil rights movement and who
reported on Mrs. Hamer's funeral for the *Washington Post*, mar-
veled in print that the small Delta town had never seen a funeral

quite like it. "People denounced only 15 years ago as 'outside agitators' and 'troublemakers' were here today as honored guests."[2]

Mississippi highway patrol officers directed traffic. Hundreds of local people—people who didn't have the big names of Young or Hodding Carter or Carmichael—couldn't get into the packed church for the services, and some of the activists felt that Mrs. Hamer's real friends were ignored. The overflow crowd was accommodated at a separate memorial service at Ruleville Central High School.

Mrs. Hamer loved wearing white, and she was buried in a white dress. She also loved flowers, so her open casket at the front of the tiny church was surrounded by bouquets. After an organ prelude and the invocation, the congregation sang what has become the black anthem, "Lift Every Voice and Sing." Solomon Gort, a friend from Greenwood and a Baptist minister, read scripture and the Jackson State University Community Choir sang.

Wearing an open-collared shirt and showing his old fire, Stokely Carmichael strode to the lectern to speak. "Why do we come to pick out Mrs. Hamer?" Some people who live do bad things and others are happy when they die; some live indifferent lives so no one knows when they die. But others give their blood and sweat, he said, and "these are the ones we come to honor." Mrs. Hamer, to Carmichael, represented "the very best of us." Any one of those present, he added, could become a Fannie Lou Hamer. "Her life shows that any sharecropper can rise to consciousness" and that "there is inevitable victory in our cause."

Dorothy Height spoke about the women from the Wednesdays in Mississippi group who had come together to support those who, like Mrs. Hamer, had participated in the history-making events of the summer of 1964. Ella Baker, who had been the behind-the-scenes intellectual to Mrs. Hamer's out-front galvanizer, talked about how Mrs. Hamer not only spoke about the movement's ideas and ideals but lived them. Vernon Jordan remembered the 1964 Mississippi Freedom Democratic Party convention in Jackson. It occurred the same summer that the three civil rights workers had disappeared in Neshoba County, and there was considerable fear in the air. Mrs. Hamer, he recalled, led the singing of "Ain't Gonna Let Nobody Turn Me Around." He, too, had been afraid, especially because he had to drive from Jackson to Memphis alone after that meeting. "After I heard Mrs. Hamer sing, I was not afraid."[3]

Among those who had the most fear had been white Mississippians. "I think history will say that among those who were freed more totally and earlier by her were white Mississippians who were finally freed, if they had the will to be free, from themselves, from their history, from their racism, from their past," said Hodding Carter as he looked out over Mrs. Hamer's casket at the mourners. Tears seemed to well in his eyes as he added: "And I know that there's no way for us who have been freed to adequately thank those who freed us except to try also to continue the work which Mrs. Hamer and so many of you began, are continuing and will continue in the future. I'm glad I had a chance to be here. I'm gladder yet that I can say that I am from here because of Mrs. Hamer and because of many of you."

After the Tougaloo College choir sang, Andrew Young, who had gone to Winona to free Mrs. Hamer and the others from jail in 1963, read from Isaiah and from Revelations in the Bible. He said that the first time he had heard of Mrs. Hamer was when Willie Peacock, Sam Block, and James Bevel would write about how they would get together and sing spirituals with the people in the Delta. They relied heavily on freedom songs because they didn't have the nerve to talk to people about "redishing" to vote. But Mrs. Hamer had the nerve, and she had to leave the Marlow plantation because of it. Bevel called Young, he remembered, to ask whether they could scrape up $50 to haul her furniture into town. Most of the black people in Ruleville then didn't want to have anything to do with her. Fifteen years later, Young said, people from the U.S. government had come to pay their respects to Mrs. Hamer. "She literally, along with many of you, shook the foundations of this nation, and everything I learned about preaching, politics, life and death, I learned in your midst. The many people who are now elected officials would not be where they are had we not stood up then. And there was not a one of those that was not influenced and inspired by the spirit of this one woman, Mrs. Hamer."

Young, who had been appointed to his UN job by fellow Georgian Jimmy Carter, recalled an evening waiting for the 1976 election results. By 3:00 A.M., they still hadn't heard from Hawaii or Mississippi. When he thought it might hinge on Mississippi, he thought, "Lord, help us." But "when they said that Mississippi went our way, I knew then that the hands that had been pickin' the cotton had finally picked the President. Yet the picking of the President is just one more step along the way. For picking a President and not having picked a single black elected official in Sunflower County can't be considered a victory. . . . Memorializing Fannie Lou Hamer abroad and not carrying on her work at home is to betray everything she lived and stood for." When Young finished speaking, he led a hand-clapping version of "This Little Light of Mine." The services were over.

Over the years since her death, the issues that Fannie Lou Hamer addressed throughout her life—racism, poverty, war, and political powerlessness—have remained the issues at the core of American political debate. Was Fannie Lou Hamer's history, was her struggle, in vain? Given the disparity in the lives of black and white that one can still see in Ruleville and in Mississippi, had it mattered that she lived there and worked there? Yes, of course.

On the practical level, Mrs. Hamer led the way for hundreds of thousands of black Mississippians to register to vote, to participate in the political life of their communities. "Her greatest victory," Ed Brown of the Voter Education Project told me, "was that ultimately she did in [Senator] Eastland. He decided not to run again because he would not win again. . . . He was the arch symbol of what we were against. And she had registered people and gotten things to the point that he could not win again."[4]

Nine years after the services at the Williams Chapel Church, there was a second funeral—at the Ruleville Methodist Church one mile away—that drew dignitaries from around the nation. James O. Eastland died February 19, 1986. Who will be better remembered?

There are those who will tell you that Jim Eastland was the most consummate politician Mississippi ever had. That may be. In the end, though, Fannie Lou Hamer did overcome James O. Eastland. She and Victoria Gray and Annie Devine and Unita Blackwell and the other civil rights workers campaigned for the vote and for jobs and food and housing for people who had had little before they began their efforts. Many still have little. But "people became aware, most for the first time, that they had a right to enjoy whatever the society, the country, has to offer," said Victoria Gray Adams years later in looking back on their work. Mississippi had truly been a closed society, for white as well as black, a society that killed the possibilities for everyone. To have altered that situation—and the movement did alter the situation—was a lasting accomplishment.[5]

Smaller-scale accomplishments occurred as well, things the ear could hear, the heart could sense. These were "the little intangibles—the races regarding each other as people, whites learning that blacks loved their families, wanted to work, wanted to educate their kids, cry when a baby dies," said Mrs. Hamer's Indianola ally, Carver Randle. Mrs. Hamer helped win daily courtesies, like being called *Mrs.* Hamer or *Mr.* Randle. "White people had a tendency to think of blacks as less than human. She did a lot to improve that."[6]

Sunflower County produced two giants of twentieth-century Mississippi history. Both Fannie Lou Hamer and James O. Eastland showed that one person can make a difference. Mrs. Hamer resisted being beaten down, literally and figuratively, by a political system that refused to give poor people like her, white or black, a voice in running their lives. Eastland simply resisted.

Through time, there has been a touch of organizational claim jumping over who "found" Fannie Lou Hamer. She had worked with all the groups that shared her aims—signing up people for the NAACP, working for SCLC and attending some of its citizenship education sessions, and working for SNCC, to which she gave the most credit for turning Mississippi around. After her death, Julian Bond addressed the question: "Some people thought they'd 'discovered' Fannie Lou Hamer, the way entertainers are discovered by talent scouts looking for something new. But she discovered herself, celebrated herself, lived for herself and her people, and died because she could not stop trying."[7]

Fannie Lou Hamer also inspired younger women like Dorie Ladner, who had been with her the day she first tried to register to vote; Euvester Simpson Morris and June Johnson, jailed with her in Winona; Marian Wright Edelman, a civil rights attorney who handled many cases in Mississippi and is now president of the Children's Defense Fund; and Mary Hightower, who still works as an organizer for the Freedom Democratic Party in its remaining outpost in Holmes County, a rural area near the center of the state. Whenever she would call on Mrs. Hamer in the troubled days of the 1960s, "she would always be there. She would always speak out; she wasn't afraid," Hightower told me. "Having people like Mrs. Hamer and Mrs. Devine and Mrs. Gray encouraged us and gave us more confidence. Knowing that they were doing it and sacrificing made us think it's all right, we can join in. The commitment overrode the fear."[8]

Hollis Watkins also worked closely with Mrs. Hamer as a young man. Graying now, he recalled that she challenged those around her to give their talents. She defined those talents as a light, he said, and "she challenged all of us to use those talents against injustice and evil wherever we were."[9]

Fannie Lou Hamer held her light over some of the dark places in the American soul. She recognized that a web of power had been woven to keep some people up and some people down. She worked to make people recognize that web, and she tried to sweep it away, to create a fairer balance in society so that people for whom and among whom she worked might someday be able to say that they were no longer "sick and tired of being sick and tired." That was her lament in life, and those are the words on her tombstone in a dusty, weedy field in Ruleville. They remind us of her history and her mission, the latter as yet unfulfilled. Someday, we must believe, commitment will again override fear.

Chronology

October 6, 1917—Fannie Lou Townsend was born, Montgomery County, Mississippi.

c. 1919—Parents, Jim and Ella Townsend, moved to Sunflower County, Mississippi.

c. 1923—First field work.

c. 1925—Joe Pullum lynching.

c. 1930—Left school to help support family.

1939—Father died.

1944—Married to Perry Hamer, settled on W. D. Marlow plantation outside Ruleville, Mississippi.

1953—Ella Townsend became an invalid, cared for by Hamers.

1950s—Raised as their daughters Dorothy Jean and Vergie.

1955—Emmett Till's mutilated body found in the Tallahatchie River.

1961—Fannie Lou Hamer sterilized without her knowledge or permission; mother died.

August 1962—Attended mass meeting after Student Non-Violent Coordinating Committee workers came to Ruleville; unsuccessfully attempted to register to vote August 31; evicted from Marlow plantation.

September 1962—Sought refuge with friends in Ruleville, then left for Tallahatchie County after outbreaks of violence.

November 1962—Returned to Sunflower County, committed to civil rights activity.

December 1962—Became a fieldworker for SNCC; moved to frame house on Lafayette Street in Ruleville near Williams Chapel Church; tried again to register.

January 1963—Learned that she had passed the voter registration test; signed voter rolls in Ruleville.

April 23, 1963—Took citizenship education course at Dorchester, Georgia.

June 1963—Arrested at Winona, Mississippi, bus station while returning from voter-registration training in Charleston, South Carolina. Beaten severely by two inmates on orders from law officers and learned of the death of Medgar Evers on release.

September 9, 1963—U.S. Justice Department filed criminal charges against Winona police chief, Montgomery County sheriff, Mississippi highway patrolman, and two others in Winona jailing and beating incident.

November 1963—Aaron Henry ran for governor and Ed King for lieutenant governor in the Freedom Vote; SNCC debated inviting white students to work in Mississippi; SNCC conducted Washington conference at which Mrs. Hamer spoke and sang.

December 1963—Testified at trial of law officers in federal court in Oxford, Mississippi; officers acquitted by all-white jury.

February 1964—Sovereignty Commission investigator visited Ruleville to check on Mrs. Hamer's activities distributing clothing.

April 26, 1964—Mississippi Freedom Democratic Party established at Jackson meeting as possible alternative to all-white Democratic Party.

June 1964—Lost bid for Congressional candidacy in Democratic primary.

June 1964—Spoke at Washington, D.C., hearing in preparation for Freedom Summer in Mississippi; predicted possible violence because of whites "riding with the guns."

June 1964—Helped orient summer volunteers at Oxford, Ohio.

June 25, 1964—Firebombing attempted at Williams Chapel Church.

August 6, 1964—Appeared at MFDP state convention in Jackson; selected as vice chairman of the delegation to challenge the regulars in Atlantic City.

August 22, 1964—Testified at the credentials committee hearing at the Democratic National Convention in Atlantic City about how she attempted to register to vote, lost her job, and later was jailed and beaten. If the MFDP challengers were not seated, she said, "I question America."

August 25, 1964—Democratic convention accepted the compromise that called for an end to discrimination at all future conventions, a compromise the MFDP had rejected.

September 1964—Traveled to Guinea with other SNCC workers and Harry Belafonte.

November 1964—Attempted to run for Congress in fall election; ran in Freedom Vote open to all.

December 4, 1964—With Victoria Gray and Annie Devine, launched challenge to the Mississippi congressional delegation.

December 20, 1964—Appeared twice with Malcolm X at rallies in Harlem.

January 4, 1965—House of Representatives voted to seat the five Mississippi congressmen, referred challenge to election committee.

April 23, 1965—Filed lawsuit, *Hamer v. Campbell,* to try to block elections in several Sunflower County communities on grounds that black voters had not had opportunity to register.

June 1965—Bolstered efforts by striking members of the Mississippi Farm Labor Union.

June 1965—More than one thousand people, including Annie Devine, arrested in Jackson in protests over new state laws aimed at curbing civil rights demonstrations.

June 19, 1965—Victoria Gray and eleven MFDP supporters jailed for sitting in at the office of the clerk of the House of Representatives in protest over his refusal to print challenge documents.

August 6, 1965—President Johnson signed the Voting Rights Act.

September 13, 1965—Testified before the closed hearing of House elections subcommittee; told members that if "Negroes were allowed to vote freely, I could be sitting up here with you right now as a Congresswoman."

September 17, 1965—Challenge dismissed by Congress.

March 1966—Federal appeals court overturned district court decision in *Hamer v. Campbell;* new elections ordered in two small Sunflower County towns.

June 1966—Walked with the Reverend Martin Luther King, Jr., in Meredith March.

October 8, 1966—Spoke at Jackson rally in support of the Child Development Group of Mississippi as part of efforts to save grass-roots Head Start programs.

January 1967—Attended conference in Oxford, Mississippi, co-chaired by Annie Devine, at which black women learned how to write grant proposals.

Early 1967—Raised money to support election activities in towns of Sunflower and Moorhead.

April 1967—Defeated in bid for election to board of Sunflower County anti-poverty agency.

May 2, 1967—Watched voting activity as black candidates lost in Sunflower and Moorhead.

Spring 1967—Shaken by death of daughter, Dorothy, who was not accepted at a nearby hospital and died before she could reach the hospital in Memphis; the Hamers formally adopted her daughters, Lenora and Jacqueline, in 1969.

May 29, 1967—Pap Hamer arrested in Drew; Hamers filed suit, charging harassment in voter registration activities.

June 27, 1967—Organized attendance by local women at Indianola conference with Sunflower County officials.

January 2, 1968—Robert Clark from Holmes County seated as the first black state legislator since Reconstruction after dispute over bonding in which he was helped by Mrs. Hamer.

May 5, 1968—Spoke to mule train as it prepared to leave for the Poor People's Campaign in Washington.

August 7, 1968—Selected to be a delegate to the 1968 convention in Loyalist Democratic party meeting at Winona.

August 1968—Led protest at the anti-poverty agency in Indianola as county attempted to eliminate grass-roots Head Start program.

August 20, 1968—Seated as a delegate at the Democratic convention in Chicago and spoke in behalf of a challenge to Alabama delegation.

1968—Created Pig Bank, with help of the National Council of Negro Women.

Early 1969—Bought first forty acres of Freedom Farm with help of funds from around the country, especially from Measure for Measure in Madison, Wisconsin.

February 1969—Aided students boycotting Mississippi Valley State College in Itta Bena.

March 3, 1969—U.S. Supreme Court ruled, in *Whitley v. Johnson,* that the Voting Rights Act's preclearance provisions applied to qualifications of candidates as well as voter registration laws, clearing the way for Mrs. Hamer, who was a named plaintiff, to run for state office in 1971.

December 1969—Attended White House Conference on Food, Nutrition and Health.

March 1970—Fannie Lou Hamer Day held at Ruleville Central High School.

May 17, 1970—Filed lawsuit, *Hamer v. Sunflower County,* charging that county schools were not desegregating properly.

January 28, 1971—Firebomb attempt at Hamer home; FBI investigation, no prosecution.

Early 1971—Traveled to Office of Economic Opportunity regional office in Atlanta for appeal hearing on merger of Head Start programs in Sunflower County.

May 1971—Honorary chairman of the International Walk for Development.

May 1971—Jo Etha Collier slain in Drew; Mrs. Hamer spoke at her funeral, helped organize aid for her family.

July 10, 1971—Participated in founding meeting of the National Women's Political Caucus.

Fall 1971—Ran unsuccessfully for Mississippi state senate; Betty Friedan and Liz Carpenter helped her campaign.

January 1972—Hospitalized for nervous exhaustion.

July 1972—Lost election to be Democratic national committee-woman; delegate to the national convention in Miami Beach, where she gave a seconding speech for vice-presidential candidacy of Frances Farenthold.

January 1973—Visited Mississippi State Penitentiary at Parchman as part of citizens committee.

March 1973—Testified in federal court in Greenville as an expert witness in the lawsuit of two Drew school employees fired for having illegitimate children.

January 1974—Hospitalized for nervous breakdown; Freedom Farm lost all but forty acres to creditors.

1974—Turned down for disability income but aided on appeal by a doctor friend from early movement days.

July 12, 1974—Hamers observed thirtieth wedding anniversary at a party in Greenville.

August 5, 1974—Joe Harris, Freedom Farm manager, died of a heart attack.

July 1975—Hosted visitors from developing nations after International Women's Year meeting.

Spring 1976—Had breast cancer surgery.

September 25, 1976—Received award from Congressional Black Caucus at its dinner in Washington, D.C.

October 1976—Led the singing at a protest about new Medicaid requirements in the state capitol at Jackson.

Late October 1976—Fannie Lou Hamer Day in Ruleville, Mississippi; Charles Evers led in efforts to raise money for her medical bills.

March 14, 1977—Died of heart failure brought on by cancer, diabetes, and hypertension.

March 20, 1977—Funeral and burial in Ruleville, Miss.

Cast

These identifications are based upon individuals' connections with Fannie Lou Hamer and do not include subsequent leadership positions.

Ella Baker—Staff member at the Southern Christian Leadership Conference at the time of the founding of the Student Non-Violent Coordinating Committee, whose independence and grass-roots organizing focus she supported; spoke at the 1964 Mississippi Freedom Democratic Party convention in Jackson, and at Fannie Lou Hamer's funeral.

Harry Belafonte—Singer who helped raise money for civil rights activities in Mississippi; arranged 1964 trip to Africa for Mrs. Hamer and others; longtime friend.

James Bevel—Organizer for the SCLC. Spoke at the meeting at which Mrs. Hamer decided to try to register to vote.

Unita Blackwell—MFDP delegate to the 1964 convention, member of the delegation seated in 1968. Worked on housing programs in the Delta for the National Council of Negro Women; later mayor of Mayersville, Mississippi.

Julian Bond—Director of communications for the Student Non-Violent Coordinating Committee office in Atlanta. Traveled to Africa in 1964 with Mrs. Hamer. Later elected to the Georgia Senate and organized a challenge to the Georgia delegation to the Democratic convention in 1968.

Harry Bowie—Episcopal priest who moved to Mississippi in the 1960s. Active in the Mississippi Freedom Democratic Party and in community organizing in both McComb and Green-ville areas.

John Brittain—Attorney with the North Mississippi Rural Legal Services office who represented Mrs. Hamer and others in their suit against the Sunflower County school system.

Owen Brooks—Massachusetts native who moved to Mississippi to work in civil rights after hearing Mrs. Hamer speak at a rally. Later worked in Greenville for Delta Ministry and for Representative Mike Espy.

Liz Carpenter—Former press secretary for Lady Bird Johnson; helped Mrs. Hamer campaign for state senate in 1971.

Hodding Carter III—Editor of the *Delta Democrat-Times,* succeeding his father, Hodding Carter, Jr., and a leader in the Loyalist Democrats at the 1968 and 1972 national conventions. Spoke at Mrs. Hamer's funeral.

Mae Bertha Carter—Former sharecropper, activist in Drew, Miss. Sued the Drew school system for failing to desegregate schools fully.

Shirley Chisholm—New York congresswoman allied with Mrs. Hamer in urging the new National Women's Political Caucus not to forget racism as it fought sexism.

Robert Clark—Holmes County teacher who, in 1967, became the first black person elected to the Mississippi legislature since Reconstruction.

Claude F. Clayton—Federal judge in Oxford, Mississippi, who presided at the trial of the Winona law officers; also heard the case of *Hamer v. Campbell* and was overruled by appeals court.

Dorothy Cotton—SCLC citizenship training teacher at Dorchester, Georgia, center; went to Winona to help get Mrs. Hamer and others out of jail.

Polly Cowan—Founder, with Dorothy Height, of Wednesdays in Mississippi, a group of women who visited Mississippi to try to build bridges with black and white women in the summers of 1964 and 1965; later worked with Mrs. Hamer on Indianola conference.

Patt Derian—Jackson activist, member of the 1968 and 1972 Loyalist delegations to the Democratic conventions; opposed by Mrs. Hamer for national committeewoman in 1972.

Annie Devine—Canton, Mississippi, activist. Member of the 1964 MFDP delegation and challenger with Mrs. Hamer and Victoria Gray of the Mississippi congressional delegation in 1965.

Charles Dorrough, Sr.—Mayor of Ruleville during Freedom Summer.

L. C. Dorsey—Former sharecropper who worked with the North Bolivar County Farm Cooperative and helped Mrs. Hamer with Freedom Farm before earning a doctorate in social work and directing the Delta Health Center.

James O. Eastland—U.S. senator from 1941 to 1978; chairman of the Senate Judiciary Committee; major landowner and power in Sunflower County.

Marian Wright Edelman—Civil rights attorney in Mississippi in early 1960s who then became active with the Child Development Group of Mississippi.

Len Edwards—Law student and 1964 summer volunteer, who lived with the Hamers.

Charles Evers—NAACP field secretary, leader in Loyalist Democratic delegations to 1968 and 1972 conventions; mayor of Fayette, Mississippi, and candidate for congressman and governor.

Medgar Evers—NAACP field secretary until his death at the hands a sniper in June 1963.

Cora Flemming—One of the founders of the Associated Communities of Sunflower County Head Start program; challenged Mrs. Hamer's position in that dispute.

James Forman—Student Non-Violent Coordinating Committee worker in Sunflower County; spoke the evening Mrs. Hamer decided to try to register and traveled to Africa with her in 1964; later wrote *The Making of Black Revolutionaries*.

Betty Friedan—Feminist writer and activist who helped found the National Organization for Women and the National Women's Political Caucus; campaigned for Mrs. Hamer for state senate in 1971.

Victoria Gray (Adams)—Palmers Crossing activist, member of 1964 MFDP delegation and later its national committeewoman; challenger against the congressional delegation in 1965.

Lawrence Guyot—SNCC worker in Greenwood in the early 1960s; jailed with Mrs. Hamer in Winona and beaten; later chairman of the MFDP.

Perry Hamer—Married Fannie Lou Townsend in 1944; tractor driver later employed by Head Start.

Jack Harper, Jr.—Chancery clerk of Sunflower County.

Dorothy Height—President of the National Council of Negro Women; helped organize Wednesdays in Mississippi and the 1967 Indianola conference.

Aaron Henry—Longtime NAACP activist in Clarksdale, Mississippi; headed the Council of Federated Organizations in the summer of 1964 and chaired the 1964 MFDP and 1968 Loyalist delegations to Democratic conventions.

Hubert Humphrey, Jr.—Senator from Minnesota who sought to become vice-presidential nominee in 1964; charged with working out a solution to MFDP challenge.

June Johnson—Greenwood activist who, as a teenager, was jailed with Mrs. Hamer in Winona, later worked for North Mississippi Rural Legal Services; helped arrange Mrs. Hamer's funeral.

Lyndon B. Johnson—President of the United States; sought nomination in his own right at 1964 convention and tried to prevent southerners from walking out over civil rights.

Wilhelm Joseph—President of Mississippi Valley State College student body during demonstrations there.

William F. Keady—Federal judge in Greenville; heard the school cases in which Mrs. Hamer testified; also ruled on other school desegregation cases and on Parchman.

The Reverend Martin Luther King, Jr.—Headed SCLC; counseled accepting the proposed compromise at the 1964 Democratic convention; backed 1965 Congressional challenge; joined by Mrs. Hamer during the 1966 Meredith March. Single most influential black leader of the era; in his approach to organizing he relied more on top-down direction rather than the grassroots approach of SNCC.

Arthur Kinoy—Attorney for the congressional challenge.

William Kunstler—Attorney for the congressional challenge.

Dorie Ladner—SNCC volunteer in Ruleville in 1962.

John Lewis—Freedom Rider who became a SNCC activist, later chairman, then headed the Voter Education Project.

Malcolm X—Black nationalist leader; when Mrs. Hamer appeared with him in December 1964, only months before he was assassinated, he introduced her as a brave "freedom fighter."

Joe and Rebecca McDonald—Early supporters of SNCC drive in Ruleville.

Charles McLaurin—SNCC worker with most ongoing responsibility in Ruleville; longtime ally of Mrs. Hamer.

Leslie McLemore—1964 MFDP delegate to Atlantic City; later wrote his dissertation on the Freedom Democrats.

Victor McTeer—Attorney who represented Katie Mae Andrews, in whose discrimination case Mrs. Hamer testified as an expert witness.

Walter Mondale—Attorney general for Minnesota; headed the credentials committee subcommittee charged with resolving the impasse over whom to seat at the 1964 convention; as U.S. senator, represented Hubert Humphrey's campaign at 1968 Loyalist convention.

Amzie Moore—Cleveland, Mississippi, employee of Post Office who was a longtime organizer for the NAACP and who put SNCC workers in contact with Mrs. Hamer.

Robert Moses—Harvard graduate who traveled to Mississippi to help organize registration drives; went to Indianola with Mrs. Hamer the day she tried to register; key figure in the 1964 convention challenge.

Eleanor Holmes Norton—Law student who tried to get Mrs. Hamer out of jail in Winona; later active with the MFDP and the National Committee for Free Elections in Sunflower.

Annell Ponder—SCLC field secretary in Greenwood who was jailed with Mrs. Hamer and beaten because she would not say "Sir."

Joseph F. Rauh, Jr.—Attorney for the 1964 MFDP challenge; opposed the 1965 congressional challenge. Campaigned for Mrs. Hamer in 1971.

Walter Reuther—President of the United Auto Workers; helped engineer the proposed compromise at the 1964 convention.

William Fitts Ryan—Manhattan congressman who introduced the challenger to the Mississippi delegation in 1965.

Pete Seeger—Folk singer who often appeared with Mrs. Hamer.

Euvester Simpson (Morris)—Teenager jailed with Mrs. Hamer in Winona in 1963.

Henry R. Smith—Ruleville Central High School principal whose job was saved through Mrs. Hamer's organizing school suit.

Martha Bucy Smith—Measure for Measure member and good friend.

Morton Stavis—Attorney for the 1965 congressional challenge.

Gloria Steinem—Feminist activist who helped organize seconding speeches—one of which Mrs. Hamer gave—for Frances Farenthold to be 1972 vice-presidential nominee.

Tracy Sugarman—Artist and later filmmaker who was a 1964 summer volunteer in Ruleville; Mrs. Hamer later stayed with him and his wife, June, when she went to Connecticut on fundraising trips; wrote *Stranger at the Gates*.

Jean and Charlie Sweet—Measure for Measure activists with whom Hamer stayed in Madison, Wisconsin.

Mike Thelwell—Head of the MFDP Washington office during the congressional challenge.

Pascol Townsend—City attorney in Drew who later represented Mrs. Hamer in Freedom Farm matters and in adoption of Lenora and Jacqueline Hamer.

Mary Tucker—Ruleville neighbor of Mrs. Hamer who invited her to her first mass meeting.

Johnnie Walls—Law student at University of Mississippi when Mrs. Hamer spoke there; represented her nephew in murder trial.

Hollis Watkins—Early SNCC worker in McComb and Mississippi Delta.

Wes Watkins—Lawyer for the 1968 Loyalist delegation.

Jamie Whitten—Senior member of Congress, one of the targets of 1965 congressional challenge.

Douglas Wynn—Member of the regular Democratic delegation in 1964, and the Loyalist delegation in 1968, for which he was also an attorney.

Andrew Young—Congregationalist minister, directed SCLC leadership program in Dorchester, Georgia; went to Winona to bail out Mrs. Hamer; key aide to the Reverend Martin Luther King, Jr., and later Georgia congressman and ambassador to the United Nations; delivered the eulogy at Mrs. Hamer's funeral.

Notes

CHAPTER 1

1. Interview with Rims Barber, Jackson, Miss., Aug. 21, 1989.

2. June Johnson told me that relatives of the Hamers believe Mrs. Hamer may have been born not in Montgomery County but in a neighboring county. Mrs. Hamer, however, always listed her birthplace as Montgomery County.

3. Martha Bucy Smith, "Fannie Lou Hamer," biographical sketch, Measure for Measure archives, State Historical Society of Wisconsin, Madison.

4. J. H. O'Dell, "Life in Mississippi: An Interview with Fannie Lou Hamer," *Freedomways*, Second Quarter 1965, pp. 231–232.

5. L. C. Dorsey, "Harder Times than These," *Mississippi Writers: Reflections of Childhood and Youth*, vol. 2, Nonfiction, ed. Dorothy Abbott (Jackson: University Press of Mississippi, 1986), pp. 167–168.

6. *The Independent Eye*, Cincinnati, Ohio, Dec. 23, 1968–Jan. 20, 1969.

7. Interview with Ben Sklar, Ruleville, Miss., Nov. 20, 1989.

8. Fannie Lou Hamer, "To Praise Our Bridges," *Mississippi Writers: Reflections of Childhood and Youth*, pp. 323–324.

9. Fannie Lou Hamer, "Songs My Mother Taught Me," tape produced by Bernice Johnson Reagon, financed by the We Shall Overcome Fund and the National Endowment for the Humanities, 1980. Songs taped by Worth and Long and quoted with his permission.

10. *The Independent Eye*, Cincinnati, Ohio, Dec. 23, 1968–Jan. 20, 1969.

11. Ibid.

12. Elton C. Fox, "Fannie Lou Hamer," *Contemporary Black Leaders* (New York: Dodd, Mead, 1970), p. 115.

13. Hamer, "To Praise Our Bridges," pp. 322–323.

14. Stephen J. Whitfield, *A Death in the Delta: The Story of Emmett Till* (New York: Free Press, 1988), pp. 48–49.

15. "Report of a Study of the Education for Negroes in Sunflower County, Miss.," Bureau of Educational Research, University of Mississippi, March 1950, quoted in Neil R. McMillen, *Dark Journey: Black Mississippians in the Age of Jim Crow* (Urbana: University of Illinois Press, 1989), p. 84.

16. June Jordan, *Fannie Lou Hamer* (New York: Thomas Y. Crowell Co., 1972), pp. 10, 12.

17. Smith, biographical sketch of Fannie Lou Hamer, Wisconsin Archives.

18. Fannie Lou Hamer, speech to the Systematic Training and Redevelopment Program, Jackson, Miss., Sept. 17, 1969. Tape in the Audiovisual Collection of the Mississippi Department of Archives and History, Jackson.

19. Ibid.

20. O'Dell, "Life in Mississippi," p. 232.

21. Ibid.

22. Phyl Garland, "Builders of a New South," *Ebony,* August 1966, p. 29.

23. Conversation with W. Dave Marlow IV, Ruleville, Miss., Mar. 14, 1991.

24. Interview with Mae Bertha Carter, Drew, Miss., Nov. 29, 1989.

25. Hamer, "Songs My Mother Taught Me."

26. Hamer, "To Praise Our Bridges," p. 324.

27. Interview with Andrew Young (telephone), Washington, D.C., Dec. 24, 1989.

28. Interview with Unita Blackwell, Mayersville, Miss., Nov. 28, 1989.

29. John Egerton, *A Mind to Stay Here: Profiles from the South* (New York: Macmillan, 1970), p. 104.

30. O'Dell, "Life in Mississippi," p. 239.

31. Edwin King, "Go Tell It on the Mountain: A Prophet from the Delta," *Sojourner,* December 1982, p. 18.

32. Interview with John Lewis, Washington, D.C., Jan. 23, 1990.

33. Ibid.

34. Interview with Cora Harvey, Ruleville, Miss., Nov. 25, 1989.

35. Sklar interview, Nov. 20, 1989.

36. Interview with Harry Belafonte, Los Angeles, Calif., Jan. 28, 1991.

37. Interview with Pete Seeger, Beacon, N.Y., Feb. 20, 1990.

38. Belafonte interview, Jan. 28, 1991.

39. Tape of interview with Dale Gronemeier, summer 1964, courtesy of Tracy Sugarman.

40. Jerry DeMuth, " 'Tired of Being Sick and Tired,' " *The Nation,* June 1, 1964, p. 549.

41. Perry Deane Young, "A Surfeit of Surgery," *Washington Post,* May 30, 1976, p. B1.

42. Interview with Bob Moses, Cambridge, Mass., Oct. 21, 1989.

CHAPTER 2

1. Interview with Mary Tucker by Tracy Sugarman, Ruleville, Miss., early 1980s.

2. Fannie Lou Hamer, oral history interview, Oral History Department, Moorland-Spingarn Research Center, Howard University.

3. Among the histories that explore pre-1960s resistance are Neil R. McMillen, *Dark Journey: Black Mississippians in the Age of Jim Crow* (Urbana: University of Illinois Press, 1989); Herbert Shapiro, *White Violence and Black Response: From Reconstruction to Montgomery* (Amherst: University of Massachusetts Press, 1988), which includes black organizing efforts against white violence; August Meier and Elliott Rudwick, *CORE: A Study in the Civil Rights Movement* (Urbana: University of Illinois Press, 1975), which details the early years of the Congress of Racial Equality as well as its evolution during the contemporary movement; and Aldon Morris, *The Origins of the Civil Rights Movement: Black Communities Organizing for Change* (New York: Free Press, 1984), which is particularly illuminating in discussing the movement's support groups. There is also work on regional resistance, such as Ray Gavins, "The NAACP in North Carolina during the Age of Segregation," in *New Directions in Civil Rights Studies,* ed. Armstead Robinson and Patricia Sullivan (Charlottesville: Carter G. Woodson Institute Series in Black Studies, University Press of Virginia, 1991); William H. Chafe, *Civilities and Civil Rights: Greensboro, North Carolina, and the Black Struggle for Freedom* (New York: Oxford University Press, 1980); and Robert J. Norrell, *Reaping the Whirlwind: The Civil Rights Movement in Tuskegee* (New York: Alfred A. Knopf, 1985).

Three books deal with women in the developing fight against discrimination: Paula Giddings, *When and Where I Enter: The Impact of Black Women on Race and Sex in America* (New York: William Morrow, 1984); *Women in the Civil Rights Movement,* ed. Vicki L. Crawford, Jacqueline Anne Rouse, and Barbara Woods (Brooklyn: Carlson Publishing, 1990); and *Ready from Within: Septima Clark and the Civil Rights Movement,* ed. Cynthia Stokes Brown (Navarro, Calif.: Wild Trees Press, 1986).

4. Juan Williams, *Eyes on the Prize: America's Civil Rights Years, 1954–1965* (New York: Viking Penguin, 1987), p. 208.

5. Interview with John Doar, New York, Feb. 22, 1990.

6. Anthony Lewis, "U.S. Sues to Widen Mississippi Voting," *New York Times*, Aug. 29, 1962.

7. Clayborne Carson, *In Struggle: SNCC and the Black Awakening of the 1960s* (Cambridge: Harvard University Press, 1981), p. 46, and Taylor Branch, *Parting the Waters: America in the King Years 1954–63* (New York: Simon and Schuster, 1988), pp. 330–331.

8. Statistics from *Hamer v. Campbell*, 358 F. 2d 215 (5th Cir. 1966), cert. den., 385 US, October 10, 1966.

9. John Doar interview, Feb. 22, 1990.

10. Interview with Marian Wright Edelman, Washington, D.C., Jan. 2, 1990.

11. *Greenwood Enterprise*, Feb. 12, 1904.

12. Ibid.

13. *Greenwood Commonwealth*, Feb. 13, 1904. Also *New York Daily Tribune*, Feb. 8, 1904.

14. Ibid.

15. *New York Daily Tribune*, Feb. 8, 1904.

16. Quoted in Benjamin Brawley, *A Social History of the American Negro* (New York: Macmillan, 1927), pp. 317–318.

17. *Greenwood Commonwealth*, Feb. 13, 1904.

18. *Memphis Press-Scimitar*, quoted in a letter to Friends of SNCC, May 7, 1965, by Margaret Lauren, Student Non-Violent Coordinating Committee files, 1959–1972, microfilm, NYT Microfilm Corp. of America.

19. Quoted in Erle Johnston, *Mississippi's Defiant Years, 1953–1973* (Forrest, Miss.: Lake Harbor Press, 1990), p. 44.

20. Ibid.

21. Robert Sherrill, "James Eastland: Child of Scorn," *The Nation*, Oct. 4, 1965, p. 183.

22. John A. Salmond, *The Conscience of a Lawyer: Clifford J. Durr and American Civil Liberties, 1899–1975* (Tuscaloosa: University of Alabama Press, 1990), p. 166. See also Virginia Durr, *Outside the Magic Circle: The Autobiography of Virginia Durr* (Tuscaloosa: University of Alabama Press, 1985), pp. 254–266.

23. United Press International, "Eastland Says He's Reactionary," *Delta Democrat-Times*, Greenville, Miss., June 9, 1966.

24. Letter from Bob Moses to John Doar, Aug. 19, 1962, Voter Education Project files, Southern Regional Council Papers, 1944–1968, microfilm, NYT Microfilming Corp. of America.

25. "A Chronology of Violence and Intimidation in Mississippi since 1961," compiled by Jack Minnis, *Congressional Record,* Apr. 4, 1963, and contained in the SNCC files.

26. Civil rights efforts in Ruleville are well documented, in part because Fannie Lou Hamer became such a central figure and shared her recollections with journalists and historians in later years and in part because of the detailed, on-the-scene reports filed by Charles McLaurin. By the summer of 1964, Ruleville was a center of movement activity because of Mrs. Hamer, the Tuckers, the McDonalds, and others. The college students who worked there that summer wrote down what they saw, as did a writer and artist, now filmmaker, Tracy Sugarman. Years later, Sugarman interviewed Ruleville residents and McLaurin for a documentary about Mrs. Hamer, *Never Turn Back.* He has generously shared his tapes, which help trace Mrs. Hamer's growing involvement in the movement and the role of others around her.

27. Report on Ruleville, "A Small Town in Sunflower County, Mississippi, from August 18, 1962, til August 31, 1962: As Seen through the Eyes of Charles McLaurin," Voter Education Project files.

28. Charles McLaurin, "To Overcome Fear," SNCC files.

29. Ibid.

30. McLaurin report on Ruleville, Aug. 18–31, 1962, VEP files.

31. McLaurin, "To Overcome Fear."

32. Fannie Lou Hamer, oral history interview with Neil R. McMillen for the Mississippi Oral History Program of the University of Southern Mississippi, Apr. 14, 1972.

33. Interview with Charles McLaurin by Tracy Sugarman.

34. Charles McLaurin, "Voice of Calm," *Sojourners,* December 1982, p. 12.

35. Fannie Lou Hamer, oral history interview, Oral History Department, Moorland-Spingarn Research Center, Howard University.

36. McLaurin interview by Sugarman.

37. Perry Hamer interview by Tracy Sugarman.

38. Tucker interview by Sugarman.

39. Interview with Dorie Ladner (telephone), Washington, D.C., Apr. 6, 1991.

40. Tucker interview by Sugarman.

41. "A Chronology of Violence and Intimidation in Mississippi since 1961," compiled by Jack Minnis, *Congressional Record,* Apr. 4, 1963, and contained in the SNCC files.

42. Interview with Charles Evers, Jackson, Miss., Apr. 26, 1990.

43. McLaurin interview by Sugarman.

44. Ibid.

45. McLaurin, "To Overcome Fear."

CHAPTER 3

1. The history of the Student Non-Violent Coordinating Committee— from founding to foundering—is told in Clayborne Carson's *In Struggle: SNCC and the Black Awakening of the 1960s* (Cambridge: Harvard University Press, 1981).

2. Charles McLaurin, "Memories of Fannie Lou Hamer," from the program of an Oct. 8, 1978, memorial service at Ruleville Central High School, State Historical Society of Wisconsin, Madison.

3. Interview with Victoria Gray Adams, Petersburg, Va., Apr. 4, 1990.

4. Unita Blackwell interview, Nov. 28, 1989.

5. Charles Evers interview, Apr. 26, 1990.

6. Charles Payne, "Men Led, but Women Organized: Movement Participation of Women in the Mississippi Delta," in *Women in the Civil Rights Movement: Trailblazers and Torchbearers,* ed. Vicki L. Crawford, Jacqueline Anne Rouse, and Barbara Woods (Brooklyn: Carlson Publishing, 1990), p. 4.

7. Charles McLaurin, "Report on Activity in Ruleville and Sunflower County from August 19th to December 28th," 1962, Voter Education Project files.

8. Ibid.

9. "Memo from Bob Moses and Charles Cobb, Re: Shooting Incident in Ruleville," interview with Herman and Hattie Sisson, Sept. 14, 1962, VEP files.

10. Moses and Cobb memo, Sisson interview, VEP files.

11. Moses and Cobb memo, interview with Edward and Lucy Sally, VEP files.

12. Moses and Cobb memo, accounting of shooting at the home of Joe McDonald, VEP files.

13. Moses and Cobb memo, report of Charles Cobb, VEP files.

14. McLaurin, Ruleville report, August–December 1962, VEP files.

15. Ibid.

16. Charles Cobb and Charles McLaurin, "Preliminary Survey on the Condition of the Negro Farmers in Ruleville, Miss., at the Close of the Cotton Season," Nov. 19, 1962, SNCC files.

17. Ibid.

18. McLaurin, Ruleville Report, August–December 1962, VEP files.

19. Cobb and McLaurin, "Preliminary Survey," SNCC files.

20. McLaurin, Ruleville Report, August–December 1962, VEP files.

21. Charles McLaurin, "Ruleville and Sunflower County Report," Jan. 4–12, 1963, VEP files.

22. Cobb and McLaurin, "Preliminary Survey," SNCC files.

23. McLaurin, Ruleville Report, August–December 1962, VEP files.

24. Charles McLaurin, "Report on Progress in Ruleville and Other Counties," Nov. 22–29, 1962, VEP files.

25. McLaurin, Ruleville Report, November 1962, VEP files.

26. McLaurin, Ruleville Report, August–December 1962, VEP files.

27. Fannie Lou Hamer, University of Southern Mississippi oral history, p. 9.

28. McLaurin, "Ruleville and Sunflower County Report," Jan. 4–12, 1963, VEP files.

29. James Jones and Charles R. McLaurin, Report on Voter Registration activity in Ruleville and Sunflower County, January 1963, VEP files.

30. John Egerton, *A Mind to Stay Here: Profiles from the South* (New York: Macmillan, 1970), p. 98.

31. Charles McLaurin, "Report on Voter Registration Activities in Sunflower County from February 10–21, 1963," VEP files.

32. Candidate biography of Fannie Lou Hamer, released by the Mississippi Freedom Democratic Party, 1964 Freedom Vote campaign, MFDP files.

33. There is good background on Highlander and its role in Aldon Morris, *The Origins of the Civil Rights Movement: Black Communities Organizing for Change* (New York: Free Press, 1984), pp. 141–157.

34. Dorothy Cotton interview (telephone), Ithaca, N.Y., Dec. 19, 1989.

35. Andrew Young interview, Dec. 24, 1989.

36. Dorothy Cotton interview, Dec. 19, 1989.

37. Interview with Leslie McLemore, Jackson, Miss., Nov. 10, 1989.

38. Andrew Young interview, Dec. 24, 1989.

39. Dorothy Cotton interview, Dec. 19, 1989.

40. Interview with June Johnson, Greenwood, Miss., Mar. 2, 1990.

41. Ibid.

42. Johnson interview with Sugarman.

43. Paule Marshall, "Hunger Has No Colour Line," *Vogue*, June 1970, p. 126.

44. Fannie Lou Hamer, "To Praise Our Bridges," *Mississippi Writers: Reflections on Childhood and Youth*, ed. Dorothy Abbott (Jackson: University Press of Mississippi, 1986), p. 328.

CHAPTER 4

1. Among the most compelling histories of this period are Taylor Branch's *Parting the Waters: America in the King Years 1954–63* (New York: Simon and Schuster, 1988), and Juan Williams's *Eyes on the Prize: America's Civil Rights Years, 1954–1965* (New York: Viking, 1987), the companion volume to the stunning Public Broadcasting System documentary of the same name. For Evers's role, see also Myrlie Evers, with William Peters, *For Us, the Living* (New York: Doubleday, 1967).

2. June Johnson, "Broken Barriers and Billy Sticks," *Sojourner*, December 1982, p. 16.

3. June Johnson interview, Mar. 2, 1990.

4. Annell Ponder described the events in Winona, Miss., to Jean Levine of the Voter Education Project, SNCC files. Her report and that of Mrs. Hamer are reprinted in Pat Watters and Reese Cleghorn, *Climbing Jacob's Ladder: The Arrival of Negroes in Southern Politics* (New York: Harcourt, Brace and World, 1967), pp. 363–375.

5. Testimony by Marjorie Staley in the trial of *U.S. v. Earle Wayne Patridge, Thomas J. Herrod, Jr., William Surrell, John L. Basinger and Charles Thomas Perkins*, U.S. District Court for the Northern District of Mississippi, Western Division, Dec. 2–6, 1963. Criminal action No. WCR 6343.

6. The civil rights workers' narratives come from SNCC files, oral histories, interviews, and testimony during the trial of *U.S. v. Patridge*. The law officers' accounts come from the trial transcripts as well as their affidavits filed in a Justice Department civil suit in the case of *U.S. v. City of Winona; Martin C. Billingsley, mayor of the City of Winona, Thomas Herrod, chief of police of the City of Winona, and Earle W. Patridge, sheriff of Montgomery County*, civil docket WC 6331.

7. Ponder describing events in Winona, SNCC files.

8. Transcript, *U.S. v. Patridge et al.*

9. Fannie Lou Hamer reports on her jailing to Jack Minnis, SNCC files.

10. FBI interview with Fannie Lou Hamer, Atlanta, Ga., June 14, 1963, about Winona jailing, p. 3, from the FBI file on Fannie Lou Hamer.

11. Hamer report to Minnis, SNCC files.

12. Interview with Euvester Simpson Morris (telephone), Columbus, Miss., Apr. 2, 1991.

13. June Johnson interview, Mar. 2, 1990.

14. Fannie Lou Hamer, oral history interview, Oral History Department, Moorland-Spingarn Research Center, Howard University.

15. Interview with Hollis Watkins, Jackson, Miss., Nov. 10, 1989.

16. Virgi Stewart, "JSU Panelists Recall Civil Rights Pioneer," *Jackson Clarion-Ledger,* Mar. 18, 1983.

17. Watters and Cleghorn, *Climbing Jacob's Ladder,* p. 138.

18. "Five Fined in Winona Protest," *Delta Democrat-Times,* June 13, 1963, p. 1. The *New York Times* stories: "Negro Voter Aides Held in Mississippi," June 11, 1963, and E. W. Kenworthy, "U.S. Acts to Block New Trial of Six Negroes in Mississippi," June 18, 1963.

19. Affidavits of Fannie Hamer and Annell Ponder, Washington, D.C., June 15, 1963.

20. Interview with Lawrence Guyot, Washington, D.C., Dec. 29, 1989.

21. Milton Hancock memo to Bob Moses, VEP files.

22. Lawrence Guyot interview, Dec. 29, 1989.

23. Fannie Lou Hamer report to Jack Minnis, SNCC files.

24. Eleanor Holmes Norton helped enforce fair employment laws as chairman of the U.S. Equal Employment Opportunities Commission in the Carter administration. She became a law professor at George Washington University and was elected the District of Columbia's nonvoting member of the U.S. House of Representatives in 1990.

25. Interview with Eleanor Holmes Norton, Washington, D.C., Dec. 28, 1989.

26. Report on Winona, Miss., by Ida Holland, June 10, 1963, to the Student Non-Violent Coordinating Committee, SNCC files.

27. Andrew Young interview, Dec. 24, 1989.

28. Ibid.

29. Hamer report to Minnis.

30. Joanne Grant, "Way of Life in Mississippi," *National Guardian,* Feb. 13, 1964, p. 12.

31. Dorothy Cotton interview, Dec. 19, 1989.

32. Lawrence Guyot interview, Dec. 29, 1989.

33. FBI file on Fannie Lou Hamer.

34. Hamer report to Minnis, SNCC files.

35. Elsewhere in Mrs. Hamer's FBI file, 42 pages have been deleted from what appears to be the Memphis office's final report on the case, dated June 22, 1963. The FBI said information on those pages either might invade someone's privacy or had been supplied by confidential sources. Of 1,145 pages of Mrs. Hamer's FBI file requested under a 1990 Freedom of Information Act, only 480 pages were released.

Mrs. Hamer's file, at least that part of it that has been released, is largely about the investigation into the Winona jailing. But it also contains notes from special agents about her appearances at anti–Vietnam War and civil rights demonstrations as well as reports on newspaper accounts of her speaking engagements and notice of magazine and radio interviews. There is also a letter from J. Edgar Hoover to John D. Ehrlichman of the White House staff dated Oct. 6, 1969, indicating that Ehrlichman, like the Johnson staff before him, had requested a name check on Mrs. Hamer, among others. The undeleted portion indicates that she was active in civil rights activities and anti-war demonstrations. There is also a list, including Mrs. Hamer, of those who signed the Black Manifesto demanding reparations from white churches and synagogues. James Forman was the leader of this effort in 1969.

The file also contains reports of an investigation into threats against Mrs. Hamer in December 1965 and the investigation into the firebombing attempt at her home in January 1971 during the controversy over the Sunflower County Head Start program.

36. Memo to C. A. Evans about attorney general's interest, June 11, 1963, FBI file.

37. FBI report, June 12, 1963, FBI file.

38. Grant, "Way of Life," p. 12.

39. FBI report on interview of June 18, 1964, after Mrs. Hamer had testified at a Washington hearing on civil rights, FBI file.

40. John Doar and Dorothy Landsberg, "The Performance of the FBI Investigating Violations of Federal Laws Protesting the Right to Vote— 1960–1967," prepared in 1971. No page numbers. Lent to the author by John Doar.

41. In 1963, Burke Marshall, who headed the Justice Department's Civil Rights Division, responded to a letter from the American Civil Liberties Union on why the department had refused to supply marshals or FBI agents to protect civil rights workers by saying that preserving law and order and protecting citizens against unlawful conduct by others "is the responsibility of local authorities." Quoted in Howard Zinn, *SNCC: The New Abolitionists* (Boston: Beacon Press, 1964), p. 197. Deputy Attorney General Nicholas Katzenbach reiterated the Justice Department position in July 1964, saying that the department lacked manpower to do the job and would displace local police who were crucial to "maintaining law and order in a community gripped by racial crisis." Quoted in Steven Lawson,

Black Ballots: Voting Rights in the South (New York: Columbia University Press, 1976), p. 302. Without the force of the federal government behind them, workers like Bob Moses and Fannie Lou Hamer were beaten for their efforts in Mississippi; others were killed.

42. Quoted in Taylor Branch, *Parting the Waters: America in the King Years, 1954–63* (New York: Simon and Schuster, 1988), p. 824.

43. Interview with H. M. Ray (telephone), Jackson, Miss., Aug. 29, 1990.

44. Department of Justice news release on civil complaint, June 17, 1963, FBI file. Plus E. W. Kenworthy, "U.S. Acts to Block New Trial of Six Negroes in Mississippi," *New York Times,* June 18, 1963.

45. *U.S. v. Earle Wayne Patridge, Thomas J. Herrod, Jr., William Surrell, John L. Basinger and Charles Thomas Perkins,* U.S. District Court for the Northern District of Mississippi, Western Division, Dec. 2–6, 1963. Criminal action No. WCR 6343.

46. *U.S. v. City of Winona; Martin C. Billingsley, mayor of the City of Winona, Thomas Herrod, chief of police of the City of Winona, and Earle W. Patridge, sheriff of Montgomery County,* civil docket WC 6331.

47. June Johnson interview, Mar. 2, 1990.

48. Leon Friedman, "The Federal Courts of the South: Judge Bryan Simpson and His Reluctant Brethren," *Southern Justice,* ed. Leon Friedman (Cleveland: Meridian, 1967), pp. 189, 191.

49. Ray interview, Aug. 29, 1990.

50. Conversation with John Doar, Jackson, Miss., Mar. 16, 1991.

51. June Johnson, "Broken Barriers and Billy Sticks," *Sojourner,* December 1982, p. 17.

52. Ray interview, Aug. 29, 1990.

53. Looking back years later, H. M. Ray told the author that he had always been sad about the verdict. He thought they should have gotten a conviction. The jury evidently didn't want to "believe things like that happened here. . . . It was a matter of not wanting to face, I believe, a very, very flagrant violation of civil rights, and I had hoped that jury would be able to lay aside any subconscious or conscious prejudice."

CHAPTER 5

1. Interview with Annie Devine, Canton, Miss., Mar. 2, 1990.

2. Jerry DeMuth, " 'Tired of Being Sick and Tired,' " *The Nation,* June 1, 1964, p. 549.

3. Pat Watters and Reese Cleghorn, *Climbing Jacob's Ladder: The Arrival of Negroes in Southern Politics* (New York: Harcourt, Brace and World, 1967), p. 213.

4. Fannie Lou Hamer, appeal for funds, cars, and clothing, Sept. 30, 1963, SNCC files.

5. Jane Stembridge, field report from Greenwood, Miss., Nov. 20, 1963.

6. "Freedom Ballot for Governor, Platform," MFDP files.

7. Ivanhoe Donaldson, field report from Greenville, Miss., week of Oct. 3 through Nov. 5, 1963.

8. Howard Zinn, *SNCC: The New Abolitionists* (Boston: Beacon Press, 1964), p. 188.

9. Hollis Watkins interview, Nov. 10, 1989.

10. Zinn, *SNCC,* p. 189.

11. "Over 300 Attend SNCC Conference," *Student Voice,* Dec. 9, 1963, p. 2.

12. Ibid.

13. Ibid.

14. Interview with Mike Thelwell (telephone), Amherst, Mass., May 16, 1990.

15. Eleanor Holmes Norton interview, Dec. 28, 1989.

16. Interview with Dorothy Zellner (telephone), New York City, Dec. 13, 1990.

17. Interview with Erle Johnston, Forrest, Miss., July 10, 1990.

18. Ibid.

19. A Sovereignty Commission memo of Mar. 26, 1964, signed by Erle Johnston, details alleged links between Tougaloo College and the Southern Conference Education Fund, "branded as a communist front organization by the House Unamerican Activities Committee." Another dated Apr. 17, 1964, discusses Tougaloo as "more of a school for agitation than a school for education." A commission memo of June 28, 1964, reflects some activities aimed at discrediting the Child Development Group of Mississippi. See also articles in the Jan. 28, 1990, *Jackson Clarion-Ledger* by Jerry Mitchell and Michael Rejebian on commission activities.

20. Johnston interview, July 10, 1990.

21. The extent of commission files on Mrs. Hamer—and scores of other Mississippians—is unknown because those files are sealed and the subject of several lawsuits. A few papers have been opened, those in the personal files of former Governor Paul Johnson and now housed at the University of Southern Mississippi. Judging from what has leaked to the press, the files still sealed may well be far rougher. The files also indicate that some rights workers, wittingly or unwittingly, gave information to the Sovereignty Commission.

    In a state and a movement in which people remember twenty-five years later who sided with whom, opening those papers could indeed rock Mississippi and its former movement workers. But leaving those papers sealed does graver harm to history. Americans need constantly to be reminded that government can and does spy on its citizens, and not always for its stated aims of state sovereignty or national security.

The report of the U.S. Senate Select Committee to Study Governmental Operations with Respect to Intelligence—also known as the Church Committee after its chairman, Senator Frank Church of Idaho—detailed the spying on black leaders such as Dr. Martin Luther King, Jr., as well as the Mississippi Freedom Democratic Party at the 1964 convention. See chapter seven.

22. Tom Scarbrough, Sovereignty Commission investigator, memo about Sunflower County, Feb. 21, 1964.

23. DeMuth, " 'Tired of Being Sick and Tired,' " p. 551.

24. Ibid.

25. Jerry DeMuth, "Celebrity Boycott," *The New Republic,* Apr. 25, 1964, pp. 8–9, and "The VIP's Regret," *The Nation,* May 18, 1964, p. 497.

26. Zinn, *SNCC,* p. 113.

27. Report on Fannie Lou Hamer's 1964 congressional primary campaign, SNCC files.

28. Letter of Mar. 16, 1963, from Charles McLaurin to John Hannah of the U.S. Commission on Civil Rights, VEP files.

29. "The Move to the Hustings," *Southern Patriot,* Mar. 1964.

30. Fannie Lou Hamer, " 'Sick and Tired of Being Sick and Tired,' " *Katallagete, The Journal of the Committee of Southern Churchmen,* Fall 1968, p. 26.

31. James C. Cobb, " 'Somebody Done Nailed Us on the Cross': Federal Farm and Welfare Policy and the Civil Rights Movement in the Mississippi Delta," *Journal of American History,* December 1990, p. 923.

32. Report on 1964 campaign, SNCC files.

33. Ibid.

34. Mendy Samstein, "Congressional Campaign Workers Harassed in Ruleville, Miss., March 20, 1964," SNCC files.

35. Lawrence Guyot interview, Dec. 29, 1989.

36. Press statement sent to *Delta Democrat-Times,* Apr. 15, 1964, SNCC files.

37. Bob Cohen, "Mississippi Caravan of Music," *Broadside Magazine,* October 1964, quoted in Bernice Johnson Reagon, "Songs of the Civil Rights Movement 1955–1965: A Study in Culture History" (Ph.D. dissertation, Howard University, 1975), p. 152.

38. DeMuth, " 'Tired of Being Sick and Tired,' " p. 549.

39. Sue Cronk, "They've Already Lost Election," *Washington Post,* Apr. 7, 1964.

40. A transcript of the hearing was inserted into the *Congressional Record,* June 16, 1964. Quotations in this chapter are from pp. 13996–14009.

41. "The Job Ahead," *Southern Patriot,* June 1964, p. 1.

42. Tracy Sugarman, *Stranger at the Gates* (New York: Hill and Wang, 1966), pp. 15–16.

43. James W. Silver, *Mississippi: The Closed Society* (New York: Harcourt, Brace and World, 1966), p. 341.

44. Sally Belfrage, *Freedom Summer* (Charlottesville: University Press of Virginia, 1990), p. 3 (originally published by Viking Press, 1965).

45. Silver, *Mississippi: The Closed Society,* pp. 341–342.

46. Belfrage, *Freedom Summer,* p. 8.

47. Seth Cagin and Philip Dray, *We Are Not Afraid: The Story of Goodman, Schwerner and Chaney and the Civil Rights Campaign for Mississippi* (New York: Macmillan, 1988).

48. "The Sunflower County Project," Mississippi Freedom Democratic Party files, State Historical Society of Wisconsin, Madison.

49. Interview with Len Edwards, Palo Alto, Calif., June 25, 1989.

50. Sugarman, *Stranger at the Gates,* pp. 116–117.

51. Interview with Tracy and June Sugarman, Westport, Conn., Feb. 21, 1990.

52. Edwards interview, June 25, 1989.

53. "Report of Leonard Edwards, Sunflower County," SNCC files.

54. Sugarman, *Stranger at the Gates,* p. 84.

55. Edwards interview, June 25, 1989.

56. Len Edwards report, SNCC files.

57. Sugarman interview, Feb. 21, 1990.

58. Edwards report, SNCC files.

59. James B. Wilson, "Municipal Ordinances, Mississippi Style," *Southern Justice,* ed. Leon Friedman (Cleveland and New York: Meridian Books, 1967), p. 41.

60. Sugarman, *Stranger at the Gates,* pp. 114–116.

61. James Atwater, "If We Can Crack Mississippi . . . ," *Saturday Evening Post,* July 25–Aug. 1, 1964, p. 18.

62. Edwards report, SNCC files.

63. Sugarman interview, Feb. 21, 1990.

CHAPTER 6

1. Bob Moses interview, Oct. 21, 1989.

2. Interview with Joseph Rauh by Anne Romaine, "The Mississippi Freedom Democratic Party through August, 1964" (M.A. thesis, University of Virginia, 1970), pp. 301–302.

3. "Brief submitted by the Mississippi Freedom Democratic Party," p. 11, from the Joseph L. Rauh, Jr., papers, Manuscript Division, Library of Congress.

4. Platforms of the Freedom candidates in the June 2, 1964, primary, *The Mississippi Freedom Democratic Party* pamphlet, p. 3, MFDP files.

5. Fannie Lou Hamer, University of Southern Mississippi oral history, and Fannie Lou Hamer interview, *Freedomways,* Second Quarter 1965, p. 236.

6. Hamer interview, *Freedomways,* p. 236.

7. MFDP brief, p. 13.

8. MFDP report, MFDP files.

9. "Reading Ourselves Out of the Party," *Delta Democrat-Times,* Greenville, Miss., July 14, 1964.

10. MFDP brief, p. 13.

11. Sally Belfrage, *Freedom Summer* (Charlottesville: University Press of Virginia, 1990), pp. 200–203.

12. Hanes Walton, Jr., *Black Republicans: The Politics of the Black and Tans* (Metuchen, N.J.: Scarecrow Press, 1975). Walton makes the point that Herbert Hoover weakened the Black and Tans when he bargained with them to get the 1928 presidential nomination, then turned his back on them. He worked with the lily-white segment of the party in campaigning against Al Smith, a Catholic, in the South.

13. Interview with Ed Cole, Jackson, Miss., Apr. 24, 1990.

14. Kelso Sturgeon, Associated Press, " 'Freedom Party' Makes Plans for Challenge at Convention," *Jackson Daily News,* Jackson, Miss., Aug. 7, 1964.

15. Guyot did not attend the convention in Atlantic City because he had been jailed in Hattiesburg for civil rights activity there.

16. "Biographical Sketches of Delegates to the National Convention of the Democratic Party," SNCC files.

17. Interview with Victoria Gray Adams, Apr. 4, 1990.

18. Victoria Gray interview, and interview with Sandy Leigh by Anne Romaine, "Mississippi Freedom Democratic Party," p. 110.

19. Claude Sitton, "Mississippi Freedom Party Bids for Democratic Convention Role," *New York Times,* July 21, 1964.

20. Annie Devine interview, Mar. 2, 1990.

21. "Convention Program for Women," *Washington Post,* Aug. 23, 1964.

22. Interview with Joseph L. Rauh, Jr., Washington, D.C., Jan. 6, 1990.

23. Kelso Sturgeon, Associated Press, "Freedom Party,' Makes Plans for Challenge at Convention," *Jackson Daily News,* Jackson, Miss., Aug. 7, 1964.

24. Joseph Rauh notes, Joseph L. Rauh, Jr., papers, Library of Congress.

25. FBI file on Fannie Lou Hamer. John Doar told the author years later that the request probably had come from the White House. "We didn't have any investigation going on in that delegation. These were some of the finest people I ever knew. Their standards were especially high. Johnson was the kind of guy who wanted to know everything about what was going on. He didn't want any disruption at his convention. It wouldn't surprise me at all if he asked Dick Goodwin or Joe Califano to 'call Doar and see what he knows about these people.' I can tell you the civil rights division on its own wouldn't be asking the bureau for information about these people because we knew more about these people than the FBI—we worked with them."

26. Kenneth O'Reilly, *"Racial Matters": The FBI's Secret File on Black America, 1960–1972* (New York: Free Press, 1989), p. 187.

27. O'Reilly, *"Racial Matters,"* p. 186.

28. *Intelligence Activities and the Rights of Americans,* book 2, *Final Report of the Select Committee to Study Governmental Operations with Respect to Intelligence* [the Church Committee report], Aug. 22, 1976 (Washington, D.C.: U.S. Government Printing Office, 1976), p. 119.

   The FBI activities in Atlantic City were hardly atypical—the bureau had been wiretapping King for almost a year already—and it kept files under the category "racial matters" on civil rights leaders as well as black nationalists who supposedly had a "propensity for violence and civil disorder." Some did threaten violence; many caught up in the web did not, leading the Church Committee to conclude on p. 5 of its report that "too many people have been spied upon by too many government agencies and too much information has been collected."

29. Joseph Rauh oral history, Lyndon Baines Johnson Library.

30. Lyndon Johnson, *The Vantage Point* (New York: Holt, Rinehart and Winston, 1971), p. 101.

31. Ella Baker interview in *Never Turn Back* documentary film by Tracy Sugarman.

32. Fannie Lou Hamer oral history, University of Southern Mississippi.

33. James Forman, *The Making of Black Revolutionaries* (New York: Macmillan, 1972), p. 385.

34. Aaron Henry oral history, Lyndon Baines Johnson Library.

35. Aaron Henry oral history interview with Neil McMillen and George Burson, Clarksdale, Miss., May 1, 1972, Mississippi Oral History Program of the University of Southern Mississippi, Hattiesburg.

36. Reagon went on to earn a doctorate in history in 1975 from Howard University with her dissertation "Songs of the Civil Rights Movement 1955–1965: A Study in Culture History." Later, she became a curator at the Smithsonian Institution and held a MacArthur Foundation grant to pursue her work. She produced a tape of Fannie Lou Hamer's singing, called "Songs My Mother Taught Me," and she founded the singing ensemble Sweet Honey in the Rock. Among the songs the group performed regularly were tributes to Ella Baker and Fannie Lou Hamer.

37. Interview with Bernice Johnson Reagon by Bill Moyers, public television, Feb. 6, 1991, on "Moyers: The Songs Are Free, with Bernice Johnson Reagon." Moyers had worked for President Johnson, including during the period of the 1964 convention.

38. Interview with Mendy Samstein by Anne Romaine, "Mississippi Freedom Democratic Party," pp. 164–165.

39. Joseph Rauh interview, Jan. 6, 1990.

40. Leslie McLemore, "The Mississippi Freedom Democratic Party—A Case Study of Grass-Roots Politics" (Ph.D. dissertation, University of Massachusetts, 1971), p. 140.

41. Unless otherwise indicated, all material concerning testimony and questioning comes from the transcript of the Democratic Party's convention credentials committee hearing of Aug. 22, 1964, contained in the Joseph Rauh papers, Library of Congress.

42. Memo from Lee C. White to President, Aug. 13, 1964, PL1/ST 24, Box 81, White House Central File, Lyndon Baines Johnson Library.

43. "Brief of the facts and the law (with supporting affidavits) filed with the committee on credentials of the Democratic National Committee on behalf of the delegates of the regular Democratic Party in the state of Mississippi," Democratic National Committee Credentials 1964—Mississippi, Box 102, Lyndon Baines Johnson Library.

44. Credentials committee transcript, Joseph Rauh papers, Library of Congress.

45. Rauh interview, Jan. 6, 1990.

46. Nan Robertson, "Mississippian Relates Struggle of Negro in Voter Registration," *New York Times,* Aug. 24, 1964.

47. Rauh interview, Romaine, "Mississippi Freedom Democratic Party," pp. 306–307.

48. "Mississippi Compromise Denounced," *Los Angeles Times,* Aug. 24, 1964.

49. Edith Green oral history interview, Oral History Department, Moorland-Spingarn Research Center, Howard University.

50. Charles Sherrod, report on Atlantic City, MFDP files.

51. "Atlantic City: The Dilemma," *National Guardian,* Aug. 29, 1964.

52. Fannie Lou Hamer interview, Romaine, "Mississippi Freedom Democratic Party," pp. 214–215.

53. Edwin King interview, Romaine, "Mississippi Freedom Democratic Party," p. 271.

54. Fannie Lou Hamer interview, *Freedomways,* Second Quarter 1965, p. 240.

55. Rauh interview, Jan. 6, 1990.

56. Ibid.

57. Robert Penn Warren, *Who Speaks for the Negro?* (New York: Random House, New York, 1965), p. 118.

58. Mendy Samstein interview, Romaine, "Mississippi Freedom Democratic Party," p. 175.

59. Finlay Lewis, *Mondale: Portrait of an American Politician* (New York: Harper and Row, 1980), pp. 134–135.

60. Rauh interview, Jan. 6, 1990, and Milton Berlinger, "Pleas Eased Tension," *Washington Daily News,* Aug. 27, 1964.

61. Rauh interview, Jan. 6, 1990.

62. Ibid.

63. Hamer oral history interview, Moorland-Spingarn Research Center.

64. Ibid. An associate of Roy Wilkins—who admittedly was not present at the time—contended that Wilkins was too much of a gentleman to have spoken that bluntly, especially to a woman. Nonetheless, it is a story that Mrs. Hamer and others among her MFDP allies who had witnessed the incident told for years thereafter. Whether these were the exact words Wilkins used is unclear, but Mrs. Hamer felt this was plainly his message.

65. Aaron Henry oral history interview, Oral History Department, Moorland-Spingarn Research Center, Howard University.

66. Hamer oral history interview, Moorland-Spingarn Research Center.

67. Andrew Young interview, Dec. 24, 1989.

68. David Harris, *Dreams Die Hard* (New York: St. Martin's, 1982), p. 73.

69. Edwin King interview, Romaine, "Mississippi Freedom Democratic Party," p. 279.

70. Hamer interview, Romaine, "Mississippi Freedom Democratic Party," pp. 219–220.

71. He would repeat his argument the following winter in a controversial magazine article that would further sour his relations with the MFDP. In that article, Rustin argued that the civil rights movement was turning from a protest movement into a political movement, and to be successful in politics, it needed allies from labor unions and liberal and religious groups. Arguing that black youths were realists who understood their lack of opportunity and who needed to know that jobs would be available if they indeed completed their education, Rustin called for a massive national commitment to combat ghetto poverty. Blacks were too isolated to win this commitment alone and would remain so if the civil rights movement maintained its purist no-compromise, no-win policies. He praised MFDP for its actions in Atlantic City but said it made a "tactical error" in spurning the compromise. He reminded his readers that MFDP launched its drive to displace Dixiecrat power "within a major political institution and as part of a coalitional effort."

Rustin's article appeared in the February 1965 issue of *Commentary*, pp. 25–31. It is reprinted in *The Great Society Reader: The Failure of American Liberalism,* ed. Marvin E. Gettleman and David Mermelstein (New York: Random House, 1967), pp. 261–277.

72. Unita Blackwell oral history interview, Oral History Department, Moorland-Spingarn Research Center, Howard University.

73. Interview with Bob Weil (telephone), New Paltz, N.Y., May 29, 1990.

74. Robert Miles, Fannie Lou Hamer Lecture Series, Jackson State University, Jackson, Miss., Nov. 8, 1989.

75. Cleveland Sellers with Robert Terrell, *The River of No Return* (New York: William Morrow, 1973), p. 109.

76. Henry Sias, oral history interview, Oral History Department, Moorland-Spingarn Research Center, Howard University.

77. Victoria Gray Adams interview, Apr. 4, 1990.

78. Hamer interview, Romaine, "Mississippi Freedom Democratic Party," p. 221.

79. Hamer oral history interview, Moorland-Spingarn Research Center.

80. Hodding Carter III, "3 Mississippi Loyalists Say Home Folks Favorable," *Delta Democrat-Times*, Greenville, Miss., Aug. 27, 1964.

81. Interview with Douglas Wynn, Greenville, Miss., Mar. 18, 1991.

82. *Amsterdam News*, Aug. 29, 1964.

83. Hamer interview, Romaine, "Mississippi Freedom Democratic Party," p. 230.

84. Letter from Walter Adams to Walter Jenkins, Sept. 1, 1964, PL1/ST24, Box 81, White House Central Files, Lyndon Baines Johnson Library.

85. Sally Belfrage, *Freedom Summer* (Charlottesville: University Press of Virginia, 1990), pp. 245–246.

86. Interview with Johnnie Walls, Greenville, Miss., Feb. 28, 1990.

CHAPTER 7

1. Belafonte interview, Jan. 28, 1991.

2. Fannie Lou Hamer oral history interview (part II) with Neil McMillen, Ruleville, Miss., Jan. 25, 1973, Mississippi Oral History Program, University of Southern Mississippi.

3. Fannie Lou Hamer interview, *Freedomways*, Second Quarter 1965, p. 234.

4. Hamer oral history (part II), University of Southern Mississippi.

5. Fannie Lou Hamer interview, *Freedomways*, p. 241.

6. Henry Hampton and Steve Fayer with Sarah Flynn, "Postscript: Taking a Group to Africa," *Voices of Freedom: An Oral History of the Civil Rights Movement from the 1950s through the 1980s* (New York: Bantam Books, 1990), p. 204.

7. John Lewis interview, Jan. 23, 1990.

8. Harry Belafonte oral history interview, *Voices of Freedom*, p. 205.

9. Belafonte interview, Jan. 28, 1991.

10. Belafonte oral history interview, *Voices of Freedom*, p. 205.

11. Hamer oral history (part II), University of Southern Mississippi.

12. Bob Moses interview, Oct. 21, 1989.

13. James Forman, *The Making of Black Revolutionaries* (New York: Macmillan, 1972), p. 409. Also John Lewis and Julian Bond interviews, Jan. 23, 1990, and July 3, 1990, respectively.

14. Interview with Julian Bond, Washington, D.C., July 3, 1990.

15. Hamer oral history (part II), University of Southern Mississippi.

16. Bond interview, July 3, 1990.

17. Lewis interview, Jan. 23, 1990.

18. John Neary, *Julian Bond: Black Rebel* (New York: William Morrow, 1971), p. 73.

19. Hamer oral history (part II), University of Southern Mississippi.

20. Neary, *Julian Bond,* p. 73.

21. Hamer oral history (part II), University of Southern Mississippi.

22. Hamer interview, *Freedomways*, pp. 234–235.

23. Hamer oral history (part II), University of Southern Mississippi.

24. Forman, *Making of Black Revolutionaries,* p. 427.

25. Tracy and June Sugarman interview, as well as accounts in James Forman's *The Making of Black Revolutionaries* and Clayborne Carson's *In Struggle: The SNCC and the Black Awakening of the 1960s* (Cambridge: Harvard University Press, 1981).

26. Interview with Charles Neblett (telephone), Russellville, Ky., June 15, 1990.

27. "With Fannie Lou Hamer," *Malcolm X Speaks,* ed. George Breitman (New York: Grove Press, 1966), p. 105.

28. Ibid., pp. 106–108.

29. Ibid., p. 108.

30. Ibid., pp. 108–110.

31. "At the Audubon," *Malcolm X Speaks,* p. 125.

32. Ibid., p. 132–133.

33. Ibid., p. 133, 135.

34. Neblett interview, June 15, 1990.

CHAPTER 8

1. William Kunstler, *Deep in My Heart* (New York: William Morrow, 1966), pp. 325–326, and "House Document No. 284, Mississippi Election Contest," the record of the hearing of the House Subcommittee on Elections, Sept. 13 and 14, 1965, hereafter referred to as Hearing Record, pp. 50–52.

2. Mike Thelwell report on meeting of Nov. 18, 1964, Washington, D.C., to discuss the congressional challenge, SNCC files.

3. Arthur Kinoy, *Rights on Trial* (Cambridge: Harvard University Press, 1983), p. 271.

4. Victoria Gray Adams interview, Apr. 4, 1990.

5. "Rough Minutes of a Meeting Called by the National Council of Churches to Discuss the Mississippi Project," Sept. 18, 1964, SNCC files.

6. Kinoy, *Rights on Trial,* p. 262.

7. Interview with Arthur Kinoy, Newark, N.J., Feb. 19, 1990.

8. This 1964 suit illustrated the division between MFDP lawyers. Joseph Rauh, preparing to represent MFDP in Atlantic City, wrote to Bob Moses that he felt the part of the suit concerning the Democratic Party was "an unwise tactic." Kinoy, Kunstler, and Morton Stavis came, in contrast, out of a radical tradition that constantly upped the ante in dealing with the establishment and thus were more than willing to file the suit. Rauh prevailed. "We are going to tell the Democratic National Convention that it has the sole power to make the decision on which delegation to seat and must make that decision in our favor precisely because there is no other

tribunal to which we can appeal," he told Moses. Rauh suggested amending the *Gray v. Mississippi* complaint, leaving out the question of convention delegations, and that was done.

9. Kinoy interview, Feb. 19, 1990.

10. Kinoy, *Rights on Trial,* pp. 266–268.

11. Ibid., p. 269.

12. Mike Thelwell interview, May 16, 1990.

13. Kunstler, *Deep in My Heart,* p. 331.

14. Hearing Record, pp. 101–187.

15. Thelwell interview, May 16, 1990.

16. Leon Shull memo to national officers, national board, chapter chairmen of the Americans for Democratic Action, on "Challenge to Mississippi Congressmen at opening of 89th Congress," Dec. 19, 1964, in the Joseph L. Rauh, Jr., files, Library of Congress.

17. Mississippi Freedom Democratic Party executive committee memo to Leon Shull, "MFDP challenges to the M.C. Delegation," MFDP files.

18. *Freedom Primer No. 3: The Right to Vote and the Congressional Challenge,* pp. 3–4, MFDP files.

19. Susanna McBee, "Goal Is Misunderstood, Say Miss. Challengers," *Washington Post,* Jan. 4, 1965.

20. Thelwell interview, May 16, 1990.

21. Kinoy, *Rights on Trial,* p. 272.

22. Robert E. Baker, "Mississippi Delegates Win Seat in House," *Washington Post,* Jan. 5, 1965, and UPI, "Mississippi Delegation Is Seated," *Delta Democrat-Times,* Jan. 4, 1965.

23. "600 Marchers Hold Washington Freedom Vigil," *New York Worker,* Jan. 10, 1965, cited in Leslie McLemore, "The Freedom Democratic Party and the Changing Political Status of the Negro in Mississippi" (M.A. thesis, Atlanta University, 1965), p. 81.

24. Ken Tolliver, "Indianola Picketing Is Calm; 300 Demonstrate without Incident," *Delta Democrat-Times,* Jan. 5, 1965.

25. Thelwell interview, May 16, 1990.

26. "The Challenge Has Just Begun," *Southern Patriot,* February 1965.

27. "Swearing in of Members," *Congressional Record, House of Representatives,* Jan. 4, 1965, pp. 18–19.

28. Thelwell interview, May 16, 1990.

29. Kinoy, *Rights on Trial,* p. 274.

30. Drew Pearson, "Liberals Force a Roll Call," *Washington Post,* Jan. 8, 1965.

31. Ibid.

32. *Congressional Record,* House of Representatives, Jan. 4, 1965, pp. 50–51.

33. Ibid., pp. 52–53.

34. "The Voting Record of the Challenged Congressmen from Mississippi," by the MFDP Washington office, MFDP files.

35. Kunstler, *Deep in My Heart,* pp. 334–335.

36. Victoria Gray Adams interview, Apr. 4, 1990.

37. Interview with Jan Goodman, New York, Feb. 23, 1990.

38. Fannie Lou Hamer testimony in *Katie Mae Andrews et al v. Drew Municipal Separate School District,* 371 F.Supp. 27 (DC Miss. 1973), affirmed 507 F.2d 611 (5th Cir. 1975), writ of cert. improvidently granted, 425 US 559 (1976). Testimony was given Mar. 21, 1973, before U.S. District Court Judge William Keady in Greenville, Miss.

39. Ellen Blunt, "She Found No Freedom," *Washington Post,* Jan. 27, 1965.

40. John Childs, "Farm Workers Strike at Tribbett Plantation, *Delta Democrat-Times,* May 31, 1965.

41. John Childs and Noel Workman, "More Choppers Join Farm Labor Strike," *Delta Democrat-Times,* June 4, 1965. Additional coverage of the tractor drivers' strike was given by Donald Janson in the *New York Times,* June 3 and 7, 1965.

42. Interview with Thelma Barnes, Greenville, Miss., Nov. 17, 1989.

43. Claude Ramsay, "A Report on the Delta Farm Strike," Aug. 16, 1965, SNCC files.

44. Linda Davis, "Ruleville Report—Sunflower County," early 1965, SNCC files.

45. Ibid.

46. Morton Stavis, now with the Center for Constitutional Rights in New York, which grew out of the lawyers' work that winter, coordinated the effort in Mississippi along with Claudia Shropshire Morcum, who headed the Jackson office of the National Lawyers Guild.

47. George Slaff, "Five Seats in Congress: 'The Mississippi Challenge,' " *The Nation,* May 17, 1965, p. 527.

48. Ibid., p. 528.

49. Fred Powledge, "Mississippi Aides at Voter Inquiry," *New York Times,* Jan. 30, 1965.

50. Kunstler, *Deep in My Heart,* p. 340.

51. W. F. Minor, "Challenge to Delegation Seen as Serious Matter," *New Orleans Times-Picayune,* Jan. 31, 1965.

52. Letter from Hayden Campbell to Governor Paul Johnson, Jan. 26, 1965, Paul Johnson papers, University of Southern Mississippi.

53. Drew Pearson, "Washington Merry-Go-Round," *New York Post*, Mar. 19, 1965.

54. Quoted in Juan Williams, *Eyes on the Prize: America's Civil Rights Years, 1954–1965* (New York: Viking Penguin, 1987), p. 262.

55. Ibid., p. 267.

56. Charles E. Fager, *Selma 1965: The March That Changed the South* (New York: Scribner's, 1974), provides a detailed look at these events.

57. William Strickland memo to members of the New York Ad Hoc Committee for the Support of the Mississippi Freedom Democratic Committee, reporting on the national conference Apr. 24, 1965, SNCC files.

58. "State-wide meeting of the Mississippi Freedom Democratic Party," Jackson, Miss., May 16, 1965, MFDP files.

59. "King, Farmer and Lewis Backing the Challenge," May 1965, MFDP files.

60. "Judge Balks on Ruling to Free Rights Group," *Los Angeles Times*, June 20, 1965, and John Perdew, "Mississippi Legislature: Old Wine in New Bottles," July 14, 1965, MFDP files.

61. Letter from John Doar, Justice Department, to Representative Donald Rumsfeld, July 20, 1965, MFDP files.

62. Annie Devine interview, Mar. 2, 1990.

63. Richard Rovere, "Letter from Washington," *The New Yorker*, Oct. 16, 1965, p. 242.

64. Russ Nixon, "House Clerk Reneges on MFDP depositions," *National Guardian*, June 26, 1965, and "12 Arrested at Capitol Sit-In Fail to See Clerk of the House," *Washington Post*, June 20, 1965.

65. Adams interview, Apr. 4, 1990.

66. Stephen C. Rogers, "Capitol Sit-In Case Is Dismissed after House Speaker Intervenes," *Washington Post*, July 15, 1965.

67. Hamer oral history interview, Moorland-Spingarn Research Center.

68. Victoria Gray, "Testimony on Voting Legislation," Mar. 25, 1965, MFDP files.

69. Robert S. Allen and Paul Scott, "Printing Cost Hits $60,000 to Unseat State Delegation," *Jackson Daily News*, Aug. 17, 1965.

70. MFDP news releases, "Labor, Civil Rights and Religious Leaders Call on Congress for Vote on Mississippi Challenges This Session," Sept. 3, 1965, and "Civil Rights Movement Mobilizes against Move to Dismiss Challenges; MFDP Protests Exclusion of Mississippi People from Subcommittee Hearings," Sept. 10, 1965; also Sept. 9, 1965, statement by Dr. Martin Luther King, Jr., all in MFDP files.

71. MFDP news release of Sept. 10, 1965, MFDP files.

72. Lee Bandy, "FDP Challenge Evoked Frustration, Trouble," *Jackson Daily News*, Sept. 23, 1965.

73. All the material on the subcommittee discussion is from Hearing Record, pp. 25–84.

74. Hamer oral history interview, Moorland-Spingarn Research Center.

75. The Reverend Allen Johnson, a resident of an area in which there had been no Freedom Vote, testified about his interest in running for office in Mississippi. Johnson, who had been an officer in the army, spoke of leading a businessmen's parade in Jackson and being beaten during that peaceful demonstration. "It was during this demonstration that this white man who struck me said, 'You cannot walk on our street.' We have heard them say, 'My State.' We want to say, 'Our State.' We have fought for it, we have bled for it, we are concerned, our children are in it, and we want to help it."

   Another witness, Augusta Wheadon, of Columbus, Miss., testified that she, too, felt it unsafe to run in her First Congressional District in the fall election. "You ask me why I did not attempt to run in the election of November 1964?" she said. "I ask you then, do I have to risk my life to be a candidate for Congress in the United States of America?"

76. MFDP report on events of the week of Sept. 13–18, 1965, MFDP files.

77. John Herbers, "Move to Unseat 5 in House Loss," *New York Times*, Sept. 16, 1965, and "House Unit Blocks Party's Unseat Bid," *Memphis Commercial Appeal*, Sept. 16, 1965.

78. Minority report quoted in MFDP report of Sept. 13–18, 1965, MFDP files. In addition to Hawkins, those who voted for public hearings were Congressmen Samuel Friedel of Maryland, Jonathan Bingham of New York, John Brademas of Indiana, and Lucian Nedzi of Michigan.

79. MFDP report of Sept. 13–18, 1965, MFDP files; also Larry A. Still, "Dr. King Here as Freedom Party Faces Defeat on House Challenge," *Washington Star*, Sept. 15, 1965.

80. I. F. Stone, "For the First Time since 1882, Miss. Negroes Reappear on House Floor," *I. F. Stone's Weekly*, Sept. 27, 1965, p. 3.

81. Sovereignty Commission records on MFDP executive committee meeting in Washington, Sept. 18, 1965, Paul Johnson files, University of Southern Mississippi.

82. Adams interview, Apr. 4, 1990.

83. Don Irwin, "House Blocks Move to Unseat Mississippians," *Los Angeles Times*, Sept. 18, 1965.

84. Annie Devine interview, Mar. 2, 1990.

85. All material on the House debate comes from "Dismissing the five Mississippi election contests and declaring the returned members are duly entitled to their seats in the House of Representatives," *Congressional Record—House,* Sept. 17, 1965, pp. 24263–24291.

86. "The FDP Challenge," *Delta Democrat-Times,* Sept. 19, 1965.

87. Interview with Morton Stavis, New York, Feb. 23, 1990.

88. Adams interview, Apr. 4, 1990.

89. MFDP report of Sept. 13–18, 1965, MFDP files.

90. Letter from Lawrence Guyot on congressional challenge, Sept. 28, 1965, MFDP files.

91. MFDP report of Sept. 13–18, 1965, MFDP files.

92. Kinoy, *Rights on Trial,* p. 295.

CHAPTER 9

1. MFDP summary of *U.S. v. Campbell,* MFDP files, and Letter to Friends of SNCC, May 7, 1965, SNCC files.

2. Richard D. Chesteen, "Change and Reaction in a Mississippi Delta Civil Community" (Ph.D. dissertation, University of Mississippi, 1976), p. 452.

3. "Indianola Vote Registration Drive Keeping up Pace: City Clerk Gives up Harassment Tactics," MFDP news release, Apr. 21, 1965, MFDP files.

4. *Mrs. Fannie Lou Hamer et al. v. Cecil C. Campbell, Circuit Clerk and Registrar of Sunflower County,* filed Apr. 23, 1965.

5. Fannie Lou Hamer, speech in Norwalk, Conn., 1967.

6. *Hamer v. Campbell,* 358 F.2d215 (5th Cir. 1966), cert. den., 385 U.S. Oct. 10, 1966. Federal Appeals Judge John R. Brown issued the decision Mar. 11, 1966, setting aside the election. The Supreme Court refused to hear Mississippi's appeal Oct. 10, 1966.

7. *Enterprise-Tocsin,* Indianola, Miss., Apr. 29, 1965, cited in MFDP files.

8. Chesteen, "Change and Reaction," p. 451.

9. "Sunflower County: A Southern Preview," Southern Reporting Service, May 24, 1965, MFDP files.

10. Morton Stavis interview, Feb. 23, 1990.

11. Frank Parker, *Black Votes Count: Political Empowerment in Mississippi after 1965* (Chapel Hill: University of North Carolina Press, 1990), pp. 104–116. After nine trips to the Supreme Court and seventeen years of help from both the Lawyers' Constitutional Defense Committee and the Lawyers' Committee for Civil Rights under Law, *Connor v. Johnson*

yielded fairer redistricting in Mississippi. By 1990, blacks represented twenty districts in the state House of Representatives and two state Senate districts. In 1986, Mike Espy, a Democrat from Yazoo City, was elected to the U.S. House of Representatives from the Delta district that Fannie Lou Hamer might have represented had she ever been successful in her electoral pursuits. Espy was the first black person elected to Congress from Mississippi since Reconstruction.

12. *Hamer v. Campbell.*

13. Relying on *Hamer v. Campbell*, the Freedom Democrats had also tried to block the statewide Democratic Party primary in Mississippi in June 1966. The district court threw out that suit and was affirmed by the federal appeals court, which said that the exceptional circumstances that existed in the *Hamer* case were not present. That is, for a year there had been no serious impediment to black registration or voting and so these elections should not be put off. "The tight grip of a long dead hand is hard to break," the appeals court acknowledged, adding that "more than one summer may pass before that grip is broken and the effect of its clasp on the present completely undone."

14. Robert Analavage, "Mississippi Hopes Center in Sunflower," *Southern Patriot,* March 1967.

15. William A. Price, "Mrs. Hamer 'Briefs' U.S. on Sunflower election," *National Guardian,* Mar. 18, 1967.

16. *Southern Patriot,* March 1967.

17. Drew Pearson, "Voting Pitch Fails," *Washington Post,* Apr. 17, 1966.

18. Ibid.

19. Charles Ellis, "Gunfire Echoes in Philadelphia as King Talks at Yazoo City," *Delta Democrat-Times,* June 22, 1966.

20. James Forman, *The Making of Black Revolutionaries* (New York: Macmillan, 1972), p. 476.

21. Tracy and June Sugarman interview, Feb. 21, 1990.

22. Hamer, Norwalk, Conn., speech.

23. "Progress Report, April 6, 1967," National Committee for Free Elections in Sunflower, MFDP files.

24. "Mississippi Leader Charges Justice Department with Bowing to Eastland Demands, Scores Congress in Powell Ouster," release of National Committee for Free Elections in Sunflower, MFDP files.

25. For example, in several counties in that Senate race, the MFDP candidate, the Reverend Clifton Whitely, had even outpolled Eastland, although he lost badly statewide. Nicholas Chriss, "Negro Voting Fairly Heavy in Mississippi," *Los Angeles Times,* June 8, 1966.

26. Marlene Nadle, "Making the Vote Count on Eastland's Plantation," *The Village Voice,* Mar. 16, 1967.

27. "Analysis and statement on behalf of the Negro citizens of Sunflower County, Miss., to Ramsey Clark, attorney general of the United States, given April 26, 1967, by a delegation led by Rep. William F. Ryan and Bayard Rustin," issued by the National Committee for Free Elections in Sunflower, MFDP papers.

28. *Los Angeles Times,* June 8, 1966.

29. National Committee for Free Elections in Sunflower, Apr. 26 analysis.

30. *Southern Patriot,* March 1967.

31. "Negro Is Hopeful on Mississippi Bid," *New York Times,* Apr. 30, 1967.

32. Foster Davis, "FDP Rally Urges Sunflower Voting," *Delta Democrat-Times,* Apr. 17, 1967.

33. Otis Brown, Jr., campaign statement, Apr. 7, 1967, MFDP files.

34. Robert Analavage, "Views, Hopes of Sunflower Candidates," *Southern Patriot,* April 1967.

35. *New York Times,* Apr. 30, 1967.

36. Percy E. Sutton, "Report of Visit to the Mississippi Delta," Apr. 19, 1967, MFDP files.

37. Walter Rugaber, "2 All-Negro Tickets Defeated in Mississippi Delta," *New York Times,* May 3, 1967.

38. Walter Rugaber, "Federal Observers Watch Election in Mississippi," *New York Times,* May 3, 1967.

39. Robert Analavage, "Negroes Not Represented," *Southern Patriot,* May 1967.

40. Ibid.

41. Rugaber, "2 All-Negro Tickets," and Associated Press, "Negroes Suing over Miss. Vote," *New York Post,* May 3, 1967. The *Post* quoted Mayor Patterson as saying he had campaigned to get the votes of the "good Negroes," while the *Times* quoted him as saying "good niggers."

42. Robert Analavage, "Bitter Defeat in Sunflower," *National Guardian,* May 13, 1967.

43. Pic Firmin, "Order for New Election is Filed in U.S. Court," *Delta Democrat-Times,* May 14, 1967, and UPI story, "Court Is Asked to Void Ballots," *Memphis Commercial Appeal,* May 14, 1967.

The case was by this point known as *Hamer v. Ely* because Sam J. Ely had succeeded Cecil Campbell as Sunflower County clerk. The Campbell of *Hamer v. Campbell,* Circuit Clerk Cecil C. Campbell had decided not to run for office again in 1965. At seventy-two, after serving twenty-eight years, he told a historian in 1971 that he felt that he had been encouraged in his practice by the Sunflower County Board of Supervisors and then singled out as a scapegoat when times changed. "Campbell had gradually come under increasing strain as he found his office exposed to a constant flow of United States Department of Justice lawyers, militant civil rights workers and increasing streams of Negro vote applicants," wrote Richard D. Chesteen, who was studying Sunflower County politics, in "Change and Reaction in a Mississippi Delta Civil Community" (Ph.D. dissertation, University of Mississippi, 1976), pp. 446–447.

44. *Fannie Lou Hamer et al. v. Sam J. Ely et al.*, U.S. Court of Appeals, Fifth Circuit, Apr. 10, 1969, 410 Federal Reporter, 2d Series, p. 154.

45. Letter from Sandra Nystrom, administrator of the National Committee for Free Elections in Sunflower, to Representative William F. Ryan, June 9, 1967, Fannie Lou Hamer papers, Amistad Research Center, Tulane University.

46. Associated Press, "Harassment Charged in Suit," *New Orleans Times-Picayune,* June 4, 1967.

47. Letter from Bayard Rustin, John Lewis, and Eleanor Holmes Norton to John Doar, June 14, 1967, Fannie Lou Hamer papers, Amistad Research Center, Tulane University.

48. Letter from Sandra Nystrom to John Doar, June 26, 1967, Fannie Lou Hamer papers, Amistad Research Center, Tulane University.

49. Robert Analavage, "First Round Ends in Mississippi Elections," *Southern Patriot,* October 1967.

50. Fannie Lou Hamer platform, 1967, Fannie Lou Hamer papers, Amistad Research Center, Tulane University.

51. Victor Ullman, "In Darkest America, *The Nation,* Sept. 4, 1967, p. 180.

52. Jack E. Harper, Jr., memo "To Our Sunflower County Negro Citizens," Nov. 1, 1967, Fannie Lou Hamer papers, Amistad Research Center, Tulane University.

53. Letter to legal colleagues, National Committee for Free Elections in Mississippi, Nov. 24, 1967. The team was assembled by Alvin Bronstein, Arthur Kinoy, Bill Kunstler, Morton Stavis, Eleanor Norton, Robert Lewis, and Ben Smith.

54. Robert Analavage, "Struggle Changes in Mississippi, *Southern Patriot,* December 1967.

55. Mike Higson, "Mississippi's Black Legislator," *Southern Patriot,* December 1967; Walter Rugaber, "Negro Elected to All-White Mississippi Legislature," *New York Times,* Nov. 9, 1967; "Mississippi House May Expel Negro," *New York Times,* Dec. 10, 1967; and "Mississippi Seats First Negro Legislator in 74 Years," *New York Times,* Jan. 3, 1968.

56. Interview with Robert Clark, Ebenezer, Miss., Nov. 26, 1989.

57. *Never Turn Back* documentary by Tracy Sugarman.

58. UPI, "Negro Legislator 'Warmly Received,' " *Delta Democrat-Times,* Jan. 3, 1968, and William Peart, "Legislators Exhibit Restraint with Clark," *Delta Democrat-Times,* Jan. 14, 1968.

59. By 1991, three of the five county supervisors in Holmes and Humphreys counties were black; two each in Copiah, Issaquena, Panola Quitman, Sharkey, and Yazoo counties; and one in Bolivar, Coahoma, Leflore, Sunflower, and Washington counties. None of the supervisors in Tallahatchie County was black. *Black Elected Officials Listing, State of Mississippi,* Secretary of State's Office, December 1990.

60. Edward H. Blackwell, "Taste of Hunger on Menu," *Milwaukee Journal,* Feb. 23, 1971.

CHAPTER 10

1. "Closing the Communication Gap: The Problem-Solving Approach," a report of a demonstration rural training workshop, June 27–28, 1967, Sunflower County, Miss., p. 12, from the collection of the National Archives for Black Women's History, Washington, D.C.

2. Mike Higson, "Casualty of the Great Society," *Southern Patriot,* January 1967.

3. Polly Cowan, oral history interview, Oral History Department, Moorland-Spingarn Research Center, Howard University; and a report on Wednesdays in Mississippi sent to the White House in November 1964, HU 2/ST 24, Box 39, WHCF, Lyndon Baines Johnson Library.

4. Wednesdays in Mississippi report, Lyndon Baines Johnson Library.

5. Interview with Susan Goodwillie, Washington, D.C., Feb. 26, 1990.

6. Cowan oral history interview, the Moorland-Spingarn Research Center.

7. "Society Women in Rights Project," *New York Times,* Aug. 30, 1964.

8. Goodwillie interview, Feb. 26, 1990.

9. Wednesdays in Mississippi report, Lyndon Baines Johnson Library.

10. Ibid.

11. Miriam Davis, report on Wednesdays in Mississippi at the National Archives for Black Women's History.

12. Frances Haight, notes of Aug. 26, 1964, National Archives for Black Women's History.

13. Wednesdays in Mississippi report, Lyndon Baines Johnson Library.

14. Interview with Flo Kennedy, New York, Feb. 22, 1990.

15. Wednesdays in Mississippi report, Lyndon Baines Johnson Library.

16. Cowan oral history interview, Moorland-Spingarn Research Center.

17. Interview with Patt Derian, Chapel Hill, N.C., May 9, 1990.

18. Workshops in Mississippi Newsletter, March 1967, National Archives for Black Women's History. Material in all subsequent notes for this chapter is from files at this archive in Washington, D.C., unless otherwise noted.

19. "Background of NCNW Training Workshop, Sunflower County."

20. Polly Cowan, notes on a telephone conversation with William Seaborn of the Department of Agriculture, Apr. 18, 1967.

21. Raw notes by Susie Waldman, June 26–30, 1967.

22. Polly Cowan, memo to Dorothy Height, July 6, 1967, and Polly Cowan, letter to Lorna Scheide.

23. Present were three influential whites: the Sunflower County chancery clerk, Jack Harper, Jr.; R. J. Allen, Jr., board chairman for the local antipoverty agency; and Colbert Crowe, head of the Community Action Agency. Also attending was Walter Gregory, a young black man who was the county Head Start director.

24. Raw notes by Polly Cowan on Indianola meeting.

25. Ibid.

26. Ibid.

27. Raw notes by Susie Waldman, June 26–30, 1967.

28. "Closing the Communication Gap," pp. 5–6.

29. Ibid., p. 3.

30. Raw notes by Polly Cowan on Indianola meeting.

31. "Closing the Communication Gap," p. 2.

32. Raw notes by Polly Cowan on Indianola meeting.

33. Ibid.

34. "Closing the Communication Gap," pp. 8–15.

35. Raw notes of Polly Cowan on Indianola meeting.

36. Interview with Dorothy Height, Washington, D.C., Mar. 7, 1990.

37. Raw notes by Polly Cowan on Indianola meeting.

38. Interview with Jack Harper, Jr., Indianola, Miss., Mar. 5, 1990.

39. Hollis Watkins talk, Southern Conference Organizing Committee meeting, Birmingham, Ala., Dec. 2, 1989.

CHAPTER 11

1. "Summary Statement of the Child Development Group of Mississippi," *Examination of the War on Poverty,* hearings before the U.S. Senate

Subcommittee on Employment, Manpower and Poverty, Jackson, Miss., Apr. 10, 1967, appendix II.

2. John C. Donovan, *The Politics of Poverty* (Washington, D.C.: University Press of America, 1980), p. 84.

3. Annie Mae King oral history interview, Oral History Department, Moorland-Spingarn Research Center, Howard University.

4. Mary Tucker interview with Tracy Sugarman.

5. L. C. Dorsey interview with Tracy Sugarman.

6. Richard D. Chesteen, "Change and Reaction in a Mississippi Delta Civil Community" (Ph.D. dissertation, University of Mississippi, 1976), p. 329.

7. Franklynn Peterson, "Pig Banks Pay Dividends," *Memphis Commercial Appeal Mid-South Magazine,* Jan. 7, 1973.

8. Annie Mae King oral history interview, Oral History Department, Moorland-Spingarn Research Center, Howard University.

9. Polly Greenberg, *The Devil Has Slippery Shoes* (London: Macmillan, 1969), p. 523.

10. King oral history interview, Moorland-Spingarn Research Center.

11. Marlene Nadle, "Making the Vote Count on Eastland's Plantation," *The Village Voice,* Mar. 16, 1967.

12. Jack Harper, Jr., interview, Mar. 5, 1990.

13. "Sunflower County: A Call to Action," MFDP files.

14. Greenberg, *The Devil Has Slippery Shoes,* pp. 524–527, and report of the Associated Communities of Sunflower County, July 10, 1966, Collection on Legal Change, Coleman Library, Tougaloo College.

15. Jan Robertson, "Outgoing Anti-Poverty Chief Feels His Group Has Been Fair," *Delta Democrat-Times,* Apr. 24, 1966.

16. Chesteen, "Change and Reaction," p. 357.

17. Jack Harper, Jr., interview, plus letter from Colbert Crowe to the U.S. Senate Subcommittee, *Examination of the War on Poverty* (Washington, D.C.: U.S. Government Printing Office, 1967), appendix I—Materials Submitted by Senator Eastland, p. 1040.

18. Greenberg, *Devil Has Slippery Shoes,* pp. 524–527.

19. Ibid., p. 605.

20. Ibid., pp. 608–609.

21. Aaron Henry oral history interview, University of Southern Mississippi.

22. Nicholas von Hoffman, "Manna from OEO Falls on Mississippi," *Washington Post,* Oct. 13, 1966.

23. Nicholas von Hoffman, "3000 Jackson Negroes Flay Head Start Cut-off," *Washington Post,* Oct. 9, 1966.

24. Mrs. Hamer did not rely strictly on government efforts against poverty. In 1966, she joined Amzie Moore and Unita Blackwell among the first members of the board of directors of the foundation-financed Mississippi Action for Community Education, which helped grass-roots groups form organizations to combat local problems. Mrs. Hamer insisted that the MACE program not become like so many others designed to help local people, that is, top-heavy with administrators and out of touch with the people they were supposed to organize.

25. Chesteen, "Change and Reaction," p. 358.

26. Fannie Lou Hamer testimony before the U.S. Senate Subcommittee hearings, *Examination of the War,* p. 581.

27. Ibid., pp. 581–582.

28. Ibid., p. 595.

29. Unita Blackwell testimony before the U.S. Senate Subcommittee hearings, *Examination of the War,* pp. 584–585.

30. Telegram from Walter Gregory and Colbert Crowe to the U.S. Senate Subcommittee, *Examination of the War,* p. 698, and letter from Colbert Crowe, ibid., pp. 1040–1041.

31. Quoted in "An Appeal to the Directors of the Office of Economic Opportunity and the Office of Child Development, from the Associated Communities of Sunflower County," July 1971.

32. Robert C. Maynard, "Poor Mass at Miss. Town to Start D.C. March Today," *Washington Post,* May 6, 1968.

33. Bob Boyd, "Sunflower Head Start Protest Is Persistent, Quiet," *Delta Democrat-Times,* Aug. 18, 1968.

34. Betsy Fancher, "Mississippi Replay," *South Today,* Leadership Project of the Southern Regional Council, 1970, Fannie Lou Hamer papers, p. 4, Amistad Research Center, Tulane University.

35. Chesteen, "Change and Reaction," pp. 322–323.

36. Interview with Walter Gregory, Indianola, Miss., Apr. 30, 1990.

37. Interview with Pascol Townsend, Drew, Miss., Mar. 12, 1991.

38. Sallie Anne Neblett, "Head Start Agency Seeks Federal Hearing," *Delta Democrat-Times,* Feb. 5, 1971.

39. Interview with Cora Flemming, Indianola, Miss., Nov. 30, 1989.

40. Gregory interview, Apr. 30, 1990.

41. Report from the Jackson, Miss., office of the FBI on the attempted firebombing of the residence of Mrs. Fannie Lou Hamer, Feb. 18, 1971.

42. Townsend interview, Mar. 12, 1991.

43. Harper, interview, Mar. 5, 1990.

44. Interview with David Rice, Washington, D.C., Feb. 12, 1990.

45. Unita Blackwell interview, Nov. 28, 1989.

46. Cora Flemming interview, Nov. 30, 1989.

47. Interview with Robert Buck, Greenville, Miss., Mar. 5, 1990.

CHAPTER 12

1. Elton C. Fax, *Contemporary Black Leaders* (New York: Dodd, Mead, 1970), p. 129.

2. Bill Sartor, "Wynn Says State Dems Are far from 'Dead,' *Delta Democrat-Times,* Sept. 2, 1964.

3. Interview with Douglas Wynn, Greenville, Miss., Mar. 18, 1991.

4. Memo of Douglas Wynn, to Jake Jacobsen at the White House, HU 2/ST 24, Box 40, White House Central Files, Lyndon Baines Johnson Library.

5. Aaron Henry oral history interview, Lyndon Baines Johnson Library.

6. Douglas Wynn memo, Sept. 9, 1966, PL/ST 24, Lyndon Baines Johnson Library.

7. The coverage of *Time* and *Newsweek,* as well as *U.S. News and World Report,* is analyzed in Richard Lentz, *Symbols, the News Magazines, and Martin Luther King* (Baton Rouge and London: Louisiana State University Press, 1991), pp. 134–135 and 171.

8. James Wechsler, "Showdown for the Democrats," *New York Post,* Feb. 23, 1967; "Democrats Reject Quota System," *Des Moines Tribune,* July 15, 1967; and Warren Weaver, Jr., "Democrats List Rights Pledges," *New York Times,* Oct. 11, 1967.

9. Hodding Carter III oral history interview, Oral History Department, Moorland-Spingarn Research Center, Howard University.

10. Brief Submitted by the Loyal Democrats of Mississippi to the 1968 Democratic National Convention, pp. 21–22, Joseph L. Rauh, Jr., papers, Library of Congress.

11. Richard D. Chesteen, "Change and Reaction in a Mississippi Delta Civil Community" (Ph.D. dissertation, University of Mississippi, 1976), p. 479.

12. Chesteen, "Change and Reaction," p. 482.

13. Interview with Wes Watkins, Washington, D.C., Dec. 26, 1989.

14. "First Integrated Dem Meet Slated," *Jackson Daily News,* June 30, 1968.

15. Charles Overby, "Seating Fight Seen for Dems," *Jackson Daily News,* July 3, 1968.

16. Chesteen, "Change and Reaction," p. 482. Included in that delegation were Carver Randle of the Indianola NAACP; Annie Mae King, who had run for town council in Sunflower the previous spring; and Joe Harris, a local MFDP leader. Two whites known for civil rights activities, Father Walter Smiegel and Margaret Kilbee, were also selected.

17. Interview with Hodding Carter III, Washington, D.C., Oct. 30, 1989.

18. Wynn interview, Mar. 18, 1991.

19. Harry Bowie oral history interview, Oral History Department, Moorland-Spingarn Research Center, Howard University.

20. Ibid.

21. Quoted in Steven F. Lawson, *In Pursuit of Power: Southern Blacks and Electoral Politics, 1965–1982* (New York: Columbia University Press, 1985), p. 98.

22. Lawrence Guyot interview, Dec. 29, 1989.

23. Owen Brooks, Fannie Lou Hamer Lecture Series, Jackson State University, Nov. 8, 1989.

24. Interview with Owen Brooks, Greenville, Miss., Nov. 16, 1989.

25. Wes Watkins interview, Dec. 26, 1989.

26. Walter Rugaber, "Humphrey Supports Mississippi Party Rebels," *New York Times,* Aug. 12, 1968.

27. Annie Devine oral history interview, Oral History Department, Moorland-Spingarn Research Center, Howard University.

28. Hollis Watkins interview, Nov. 10, 1989.

29. Fannie Lou Hamer oral history interview, Moorland-Spingarn Research Center.

30. Fannie Lou Hamer oral history interview, University of Southern Mississippi.

31. Unita Blackwell oral history interview, Moorland-Spingarn Research Center, Howard University.

32. Brief submitted by the Loyal Democrats of Mississippi to the 1968 Democratic National Convention, p. 12, Joseph L. Rauh, Jr., papers, Library of Congress.

33. Ibid., p. 22.

34. Marion Symington, "Challenge to Mississippi" (Honors thesis, Harvard University, 1969), p. 88, quoted in Jack Bass and Walter DeVries, *The Transformation of Southern Politics* (New York: Basic Books, 1976), p. 207.

35. Richard Cooper, "Credentials Panel Hears 5-Hour Challenge to Mississippi Slate," *Los Angeles Times,* Aug. 20, 1968, and W. F. Minor, "Miss. Bi-Racial Delegations Argue for Seats," *New Orleans Times-Picayune,* Aug. 20, 1968.

36. John Adam Moreau, "Credentials Unit Votes to Seat Challengers in Mississippi Dispute," *Chicago Sun Times,* Aug. 21, 1968.

37. Richard Cooper, "Democrats Vote Seat to Rebel Mississippians," *Los Angeles Times,* Aug. 21, 1968.

38. Wes Watkins interview, Dec. 26, 1989.

39. John Adam Moreau, "Credentials Unit Votes," *Chicago Sun Times,* Aug. 21, 1968.

40. Interview with Mildred Jeffreys (telephone), Detroit, Mich., Jan. 21, 1990.

41. Wes Watkins interview, Dec. 26, 1989.

42. Carter oral history interview, Moorland-Spingarn Research Center.

43. Unita Blackwell interview, Nov. 28, 1989.

44. UPI, "Georgia Challenge Backed by Henry," Aug. 27, 1968, MFDP files.

45. Lens News Service, Aug. 1, 1968, MFDP files.

46. Bessie Ford, UPI, "Persistence Paid Off for Fannie Lou," *Delta Democrat-Times,* Aug. 29, 1968.

47. "MFDP Platform Calls for Land Reform, Economic Rights and Peace in Vietnam," Aug. 24, 1968, news release, Fannie Lou Hamer papers, Amistad Research Center, Tulane University.

48. "Proposed Program of Mississippi Freedom Democratic Party," Fannie Lou Hamer papers, Amistad Research Center, Tulane University.

49. Letter from John Garner to friends, Dec. 30, 1968, Mississippi Department of Archives and History, Jackson.

50. Interview with Bob Kochtitzky, Jackson, Miss., Nov. 6, 1989.

51. Robert Clark interview, Nov. 26, 1989.

52. Hodding Carter interview, Oct. 30, 1989.

53. Lawrence Guyot interview, Dec. 29, 1989.

54. Fannie Lou Hamer speech, Madison, Wis., 1971.

55. Interview with Jeannette King, Jackson, Miss., Apr. 24, 1990.

56. Wes Watkins interview, Dec. 26, 1989.

57. Ibid.

58. Patt Derian, "Of Shadow and Substance," *New South,* Summer 1968, p. 55.

59. UPI, "FDP Shadowed by Doubts," *Delta Democrat-Times,* Jan. 6, 1969. Also Delta Ministry Reports, January 1969, Fannie Lou Hamer papers, Amistad Research Center, Tulane University.

CHAPTER 13

1. Roger Yockey, "King Co. 'Adopts' Sunflower Co., Miss.," *The Progressive,* Seattle, Wash., Mar. 7, 1969.

2. Fannie Lou Hamer, "Sick and Tired of Being Sick and Tired," *Katallagete, The Journal of the Committee of Southern Churchmen,* Fall 1968, p. 25.

3. Interview with Charlene Rogers, Greenville, Miss., Nov. 17, 1989.

4. Interview with Alvin Bronstein, Washington, D.C., May 28, 1990.

5. "Fannie Lou 'Tells It Like It Is,' " *Harvard Crimson,* Nov. 23, 1968.

6. "Mrs. Hamer Perks Up 'Sagging' Boycotters," *Delta Democrat-Times,* Jan. 9, 1969.

7. Interview with Wilhelm Joseph (telephone), New York City, June 5, 1990.

8. "Fannie Lou Hamer Backs Boycott," *Delta Democrat-Times,* Feb. 13, 1969.

9. Joseph interview, June 5, 1990.

10. Bob Boyd, "Student-Faculty Accord Ends Boycott at MVSC," *Delta Democrat-Times,* Feb. 14, 1969. Also Delta Ministry Reports, February 1969, Fannie Lou Hamer papers, Amistad Research Center, Tulane University.

11. Mae Bertha Carter interview, Nov. 29, 1989.

12. James W. Loewen and Charles Sallis, eds., *Mississippi: Conflict and Change* (New York: Pantheon, 1980), p. 282.

13. Bob Boyd, "Rights Leaders Announce Drive to Rebuild Burned Tchula School," *Delta Democrat-Times,* Jan. 5, 1970.

14. Bob Boyd, "Indy Plan Submitted," *Delta Democrat-Times,* May 17, 1970.

15. Marian McBride, "Nobody Knows the Trouble She's Seen," *Washington Post,* July 14, 1968.

16. *Fannie Lou Hamer et al. v. Sunflower County,* filed in U.S. District Court in Greenville, Miss., May 1970.

17. Ibid.

18. Ibid.

19. Sunflower County response, June 4, 1970.

20. William Keady, *All Rise: Memoirs of a Mississippi Federal Judge* (Boston: Recollections Bound, 1988), p. 104.

21. Ibid., pp. 86–87.

22. Interview with Allan Alexander (telephone), Oxford, Miss., Mar. 2, 1991.

23. Interview with John Brittain (telephone), Hartford, Conn., May 16, 1990.

24. *Hamer v. Sunflower County.* Keady's ruling was on June 15, and the U.S. Court of Appeals for the Fifth Circuit affirmed that ruling Aug. 13, 1970.

25. Brittain interview, May 16, 1990.

26. Fannie Lou Hamer, speech to Tougaloo students, Jan. 11, 1971, Mississippi Department of Archives and History, Special Collections, Audio-Visual Records, MP 80.01 Newsfilm Collection, Reel D-0321, Item 1103, Stennis/Hamer/Legislature/Police.

27. Interview with Henry R. Smith, Ruleville, Miss., Nov. 20, 1989.

28. Letter from C. M. Dorrough, Sr., to Fannie Lou Hamer, Mar. 26, 1970, Fannie Lou Hamer papers, Amistad Research Center, Tulane University.

29. Roger Yockey, "King Co. 'Adopts' Sunflower Co., Miss.," *The Progressive*, Seattle, Wash., Mar. 7, 1969.

On another occasion, speaking in Madison, Wis., Mrs. Hamer said that one reason she did not subscribe to separatism was that "a lot of my uncles and aunts are very white. I'd be separating myself from some of my own people." She didn't agree with the Black Panthers and Stokely Carmichael but added that "the shame is with the country that can make people like that." She called Carmichael one of the kindest people she had ever met, adding that she had watched him go to jail and could understand why he had changed. Gay Leslie, "Rights Matriarch Pleads for Action Now," *Wisconsin State Journal*, July 19, 1969.

30. Schedule of the program put on by the University of Mississippi Law Student Civil Rights Research Council, Apr. 18–21, 1969, Fannie Lou Hamer papers.

31. June Johnson interview with Tracy Sugarman.

32. *Katie Mae Andrews v. Drew Municipal Separate School District,* 371 F.Supp. 27 (DC Miss. 1973), affirmed 507 F.2d 611 (5th Cir. 1975), writ of cert. improvidently granted, 425 US 559 (1976). Brief of Respondents to the U.S. Supreme Court on writ of certiorari, October term 1975, p. 7. The remainder of the material about this case comes from the respondents' brief and the transcript of Mrs. Hamer's testimony on Mar. 21, 1973, before Judge Keady unless otherwise indicated.

33. Clark testified that he did not see "that unwed parenthood in itself interferes with either the technical academic competence of teachers or the ability of a teacher to communicate to students the genuine acceptance of the humanity of those students or qualities of kindness, sensitivity and love. I don't see how unwed parenthood in itself can do that any more than divorce can do it, or separation, or being unmarried."

34. Interview with Victor McTeer, Greenville, Miss., May 1, 1990.

CHAPTER 14

1. Andrew Young interview, Dec. 24, 1989.

2. Franklynn Peterson, "Fannie Lou Hamer: Mother of Black Women's Lib," *Sepia,* February 1970, and Franklynn Peterson, "Pig Banks Reap Dividends," *Dallas Morning News,* Jan. 31, 1973.

3. Measure for Measure news release, Ruleville, Miss., Apr. 1, 1968, Measure for Measure files, State Historical Society of Wisconsin.

4. Paule Marshall, "Hunger Has No Colour Line," *Vogue,* June 1970, p. 126.

5. Nan Robertson, "Severe Hunger Found in Mississippi," *New York Times,* June 17, 1967.

6. Nick Kotz, *Let Them Eat Promises* (New York: Doubleday Anchor, 1971), pp. 1–2.

7. Ibid., p. 88.

8. Whitten was first elected in 1941 at age 31.

9. James C. Cobb, " 'Somebody Done Nailed Us on the Cross.': Federal Farm and Welfare Policy and the Civil Rights Movement in the Mississippi Delta," *Journal of American History,* December 1990, p. 923.

10. *Hunger—American Style,* documentary filmed in Sunflower and Tallahatchie counties, Miss., Feb. 7–10, 1968, shown on public television Feb. 25, 1968. Nick Kotz was the reporter.

11. Charles Kern, "Miss. Leader Tells of Plans to Win Historic Poll," *UE News,* Mar. 20, 1967.

12. *Hunger—American Style.*

13. Memo from Concerned Mississippians for Hunger and Poverty, Mar. 7, 1969, Fannie Lou Hamer papers, Amistad Research Center, Tulane University.

14. Measure for Measure statement, Mar. 15, 1970, Measure for Measure files, State Historical Society of Wisconsin.

15. Measure for Measure news release, Dec. 31, 1968, Measure for Measure files.

16. James M. Fallows, "Miss. Farmers Fight for Co-op," *Harvard Crimson,* Jan. 27, 1969.

17. Harry Belafonte appeal, May 1969, Fannie Lou Hamer papers.

18. Harry Belafonte interview, Jan. 28, 1991.

19. Peterson, "Pig Banks."

20. Fannie Lou Hamer tape recording, National Archives for Black Women's History, Washington, D.C.

21. Report by consultant Robert A. Hall on visit to pig program, Jan. 17–25, 1969, National Archives for Black Women's History.

22. Pascol Townsend interview, Mar. 12, 1991.

23. Alvin Bronstein interview, May 28, 1990.

24. Years later, Townsend had the grace to say that William Keady had probably made a better federal judge than he would have.

25. Franklynn Peterson, "Pig Banks Pay Dividends," *Memphis Commercial Appeal Mid-South Magazine,* Jan. 7, 1973.

26. Jack Rosenthal, "President at Food Parley, Pledges Fight on Hunger," *New York Times,* Dec. 3, 1969.

27. Leroy F. Aarons, "Hunger Caucus Planned on Eve of Conference," *Washington Post,* Dec. 2, 1969.

28. Interview with John Kramer (telephone), New Orleans, Nov. 6, 1990.

29. Spencer Rich, "Moderates Battle Hunger," *Washington Post,* Dec. 7, 1969.

30. Spencer Rich, " 'Crisis' Hunger Program, *Washington Post,* Dec. 4, 1969.

31. Interview with L. C. Dorsey, Cleveland, Miss., Apr. 30, 1990.

32. Paule Marshall, "Hunger," p. 126.

33. Fannie Lou Hamer, "It's in Your Hands," in *Black Women in White America: A Documentary History,* ed. Gerda Lerner (New York: Vintage, 1973), p. 613.

34. Peterson, "Pig Banks."

35. Fannie Lou Hamer letter, Apr. 23, 1970, Measure for Measure files.

36. Peterson, "Pig Banks."

37. Ibid.

38. Peterson, "Fannie Lou Hamer."

39. "Domestic Project—Mississippi Freedom Farms Cooperatives," undated 1971 release, Measure for Measure files.

40. Fannie Lou Hamer speech, Madison, Wis., 1971, courtesy of Jean Sweet.

41. Fannie Lou Hamer letter, Apr. 23, 1970, Measure for Measure files.

42. Edward H. Blackwell, "Hike Workers Given Taste of Hunger," *Milwaukee Journal,* Feb. 22, 1971.

43. Fannie Lou Hamer speech, Madison, Wis., 1971, courtesy of Jean Sweet.

44. Interview with Jeff Goldstein (telephone), Madison, Wis., December 1990.

45. Freedom Farm report on 1972 operations, Fannie Lou Hamer papers, Amistad Research Center, Tulane University.

46. Jeff Goldstein interview, December 1990.

47. Freedom Farm report on 1972 operations, Fannie Lou Hamer papers, Amistad Research Center, Tulane University.

48. Martha Smith's report after visit to Mississippi, Dec. 5–11, 1972, Measure for Measure files.

49. Letter from Joe Harris to Mrs. Eugene Wilkening, Jan. 23, 1973, Fannie Lou Hamer papers, Amistad Research Center, Tulane University.

50. Fund-raising appeal from Harry Belafonte, June 1973, Measure for Measure files.

51. Fund-raising appeal from Bunny Wilkening (undated), Measure for Measure files.

52. Letter from Ron Thornton to Kay Mills, July 1990. Author's files.

53. L. C. Dorsey interview with Tracy Sugarman.

54. Letters from Fannie Lou Hamer and Joe Harris to Charles Bannerman, Mar. 12, 1973, and in reply from Bannerman, Mar. 20, 1973, in Fannie Lou Hamer papers, Amistad Research Center, Tulane University.

55. Letter from Bunny Wilkening to Joe Harris, Aug. 29, 1973, Fannie Lou Hamer papers, Amistad Research Center, Tulane University.

56. Letter from Joe Harris to Mrs. Helena Wilkening, Oct. 4, 1973, Fannie Lou Hamer papers, Amistad Research Center, Tulane University.

57. Measure for Measure general meeting minutes of Jan. 20 and Feb. 17, 1974, Measure for Measure files.

58. Measure for Measure board meeting minutes of June 23, 1974, Measure for Measure files.

59. Letter from Charlene T. Rodgers to Mr. and Mrs. Jim Taylor, June 26, 1974, Measure for Measure files.

60. Measure for Measure meeting minutes, July 22, 1974, Measure for Measure files.

61. Ibid.

62. Letter from Fannie Lou Hamer to Mrs. Nancy Taylor, Nov. 29, 1974, Measure for Measure files.

63. Thornton letter, July 1990.

64. L. C. Dorsey interview, Mound Bayou, Miss., Nov. 30, 1989.

CHAPTER 15

1. Fannie Lou Hamer, "It's in Your Hands," pp. 609–612.

2. Fannie Lou Hamer speech, "Is It Too Late?" 1971, Fannie Lou Hamer files, Coleman Library, Tougaloo College, Jackson, Miss.

3. Ibid.

4. Jean Otto, "Milwaukee, Mississippi the Same: Rights Leader," *Milwaukee Journal,* Feb. 16, 1970.

5. Fannie Lou Hamer speech, Madison, Wis., 1971, courtesy of Jean Sweet.

6. "Women's Political Power," *Congressional Record—House,* July 13, 1971, p. 24787.

7. *Congressional Record—House,* July 13, 1971, p. 24788.

8. Marcia Cohen, *The Sisterhood* (New York: Simon and Schuster, 1988), p. 315.

9. Eileen Shanahan, "Women Organize for Political Power," *New York Times,* July 11, 1971.

10. Tim O'Brien, "Women Organize for More Power," *Washington Post,* July 11, 1971.

11. Transcript of Fannie Lou Hamer's speech at the first session of the National Women's Political Caucus organizing conference, author's files, courtesy of Joanne Edgar.

12. Interview with Shirley Chisholm (telephone), Williamsville, N.Y., Jan. 19, 1990.

13. Interview with Liz Carpenter, Washington, D.C., mid-1970s.

14. Tim O'Brien, "Women's Caucus Seeks Ban on Sex Bias," *Washington Post,* July 13, 1971.

15. Eileen Shanahan, "Women Organize."

16. Fannie Lou Hamer speech at NWPC organizing conference, author's files.

17. W. F. Minor, "Suit Attacks Election Law," *New Orleans Times-Picayune,* Oct. 21, 1966.

18. *Whitley v. Johnson,* 260 F.Supp. 630 (S.D. Miss. 1966) (three-judge court), 296 F.Supp. 630 (S.D. Miss. 1967) (three-judge court), rev'd sub nom. *Allen v. State Board of Elections,* 393 U.S. 544 (1969). The quotation is from the appellants' brief submitted to the U.S. Supreme Court in its fall term 1968, p. 19.

19. "Statement of the Mississippi Freedom Democratic Party," Mar. 5, 1969, Fannie Lou Hamer papers, Amistad Research Center, Tulane University.

20. Frank Parker, *Black Votes Count: Political Empowerment in Mississippi after 1965* (Chapel Hill: University of North Carolina Press, 1990), p. 99.

21. Lester Salamon, "Mississippi Post-Mortem: The 1971 Elections," *New South,* Winter 1972, p. 43.

22. Interview with Carver Randle, Indianola, Miss., Nov. 21, 1989.

23. Bill Rose, "Drew Black Girl Slain," *Delta Democrat-Times,* May 26, 1971.

24. George La Maistre, Jr., "Calm in Drew, Arrests in Ruleville," *Delta Democrat-Times,* May 27, 1971.

25. Jules Loh and Roland Draughon, Associated Press, "Reaction in Drew: A Change in South," *Washington Post,* June 20, 1971.

26. Philip D. Carter, "Both Races Mourn Death of Miss. Girl," *Washington Post,* May 31, 1971, and George La Maistre, Jr., "Abernathy: Love, not Hate," *Delta Democrat-Times,* May 31, 1971.

27. Loh and Draughon, "Reaction in Drew."

28. 1971 Annual Report of the Voter Education Project, Fannie Lou Hamer papers, Amistad Research Center, Tulane University; and *Jackson Clarion-Ledger,* June 15, 1971.

29. Julian Bond interview, July 3, 1990.

30. Megan Landauer and Jonathan Wolman, "Fannie Lou Hamer '. . . Forcing a New Political Reality,'" *The Daily Cardinal,* Madison, Wis., Oct. 8, 1971.

31. Spencer Rich, "Big Jim Ain't So Big Agin' Them California Boys," *Washington Post,* May 22, 1969.

32. Owen Taylor, "Women's Rights Activist Backs Mrs. Hamer," *Delta Democrat-Times,* Oct. 28, 1971.

33. Jason Berry, *Amazing Grace: With Charles Evers in Mississippi* (Washington, D.C.: Three Continents, 1978), p. 292.

34. Report on 1971 by Jeff Goldstein, Measure for Measure files.

35. Richard D. Chesteen, "Change and Reaction in a Mississippi Delta Civil Community" (Ph.D. dissertation, University of Mississippi, 1976), p. 520.

36. UPI dispatch, *Delta Democrat-Times,* Dec. 5, 1971.

37. Berry, *Amazing Grace,* p. 299.

38. Salamon, "Mississippi Post-Mortem," p. 45.

39. Ibid.

40. Berry, *Amazing Grace,* p. 268.

41. Unita Blackwell interview, Nov. 28, 1989.

42. Harry Bowie, Fannie Lou Hamer Lecture Series, Jackson State University, Jackson, Miss., Nov. 8, 1989.

43. Lester M. Salamon, "Leadership and Modernization: The Emerging Black Political Elite in the American South," *The Journal of Politics,* August 1973, p. 644.

44. Interview with Aaron Henry, Clarksdale, Miss., Nov. 22, 1989.

CHAPTER 16

1. Carl M. Cobb, "Mississippi Medicine," *Boston Globe,* July 17, 1967.

2. L. C. Dorsey interview, Nov. 30, 1989.

3. Charles Kerns, "Miss. Leader Tells of Plans to Win Historic Poll," *UE News,* Mar. 20, 1967.

4. Interview with Aaron Shirley, Jackson, Miss., Apr. 23, 1990.

5. "Fannie Lou Hamer Hospitalized," *The Drummer,* Mississippi Black Community Newspaper, Feb. 7, 1972.

6. "Mrs. Hamer Ill," *The Tennessean,* Nashville, Mar. 23, 1972.

7. Interview with Ed Brown, Washington, D.C., June 28, 1990.

8. Ed Cole interview, Apr. 24, 1990.

9. Interview with Owen Brooks, Greenville, Miss., Feb. 28, 1990.

10. Patt Derian interview, May 9, 1990.

11. Interview with Edwin King, Jackson, Miss., Nov. 9, 1989.

12. Hodding Carter interview, Oct. 30, 1989.

13. Aaron Henry interview, Nov. 22, 1989.

14. Charles Evers interview, Apr. 26, 1990.

15. Wes Watkins interview, Dec. 26, 1989.

16. Cole interview, Apr. 24, 1990.

17. Fannie Lou Hamer oral history interview, University of Southern Mississippi.

18. Susan and Marty Tolchin, *Clout: Womanpower and Politics* (New York: Coward, McCann & Geoghegan, 1974), pp. 40–52.

19. "The Official Proceedings of the Democratic National Convention, 1972," July 13, 1972, p. 435.

20. Ibid., p. 437.

21. June Johnson interview, Mar. 2, 1990.

22. Letter to Jean Sweet, Jan. 29, 1976, Fannie Lou Hamer papers, Amistad Research Center, Tulane University.

23. Letter from Jack Byars, assistant superintendent at Parchman, to Pascol Townsend, Jan. 7, 1971, Pascol Townsend's office files.

24. David M. Lipman, "Mississippi's Prison Experience," *Mississippi Law Journal,* June 1974, pp. 685–755.

25. Ron Harrist, Associated Press, "State Black Leaders Pay Parchman Visit," *Jackson Daily News,* Jan. 16, 1973.

26. "Ruleville Man Is Held for Murder," *Enterprise-Tocsin,* Indianola, Miss., Nov. 22, 1973; "Testimony Heard in Trial Here," *Enterprise-Tocsin,* June 20, 1974; and Johnnie Walls interview, Feb. 28, 1990.

27. Interview with Robert Smith, Jackson, Miss., Apr. 26, 1990.

28. Interview with Henry Kirksey, Jackson, Miss., Apr. 29, 1990.

29. Kim I. Eisler, "IWY Delegates Tour Delta," *Delta Democrat-Times,* July 7, 1975.

30. Fannie Lou Hamer speech in Madison, Jan. 29, 1976, Wisconsin State Historical Society, Madison.

31. Bill Sierichs, " 'Sin-Sickness' Probed at Crime Meet," *Jackson Daily News,* Mar. 24, 1976.

32. Eleanor Holmes Norton interview, Dec. 28, 1989.

33. Letter from Vergie to Fannie Lou Hamer, Dec. 6, 1976, Fannie Lou Hamer papers, Amistad Research Center, Tulane University.

34. June Johnson interview, Mar. 2, 1990.

35. L. C. Dorsey, "Epilogue," Fannie Lou Hamer files, State Historical Society of Wisconsin, Madison.

36. Jacqueline Trescott, " 'The Black Caucus Comes of Age,' " *Washington Post,* Sept. 27, 1976, and Erma Lee Laws, "Congressional Black Caucus Dinner Is Soulful," *Tri-State Defender,* Memphis, Tenn., Oct. 2, 1976.

37. Barbara Wright, "Fannie L. Hamer Day Celebrated," *Bolivar Commercial,* Bolivar County, Miss., Nov. 1, 1976.

38. Robert Clark interview, Nov. 26, 1989.

39. Johnson interview, Mar. 2, 1990.

40. Lloyd Gray, "The Glitter Is Gone, but the Fight Goes On," *Delta Democrat-Times,* Oct. 3, 1976.

41. Otis L. Sanford, "Group Protests New Medicaid Fee," *Jackson Clarion-Ledger,* Oct. 8, 1976; Andrew Reese, UPI story on Medicaid protest, Oct. 10, 1976; and WLBT film from Oct. 7, 1976, Mississippi Department of Archives and History, Jackson.

42. Fannie Lou Hamer interview with Laurie Sugarman (telephone), Ruleville, Miss., December 1976, courtesy of Tracy and June Sugarman.

43. Unita Blackwell interview, Nov. 28, 1989.

44. Austin Scott, "Fannie Hamer, Civil Rights Leader Dies," *Washington Post,* Mar. 17, 1977.

CHAPTER 17

1. Ron Thornton letter to author, July 1990.

2. Austin Scott, "A Tribute in a Delta Town," *Washington Post,* Mar. 21, 1977.

3. Tape of Fannie Lou Hamer funeral by Jane Petty and Patti Carr Black, Trans Video, Ltd., Mississippi Department of Archives and History, Jackson.

4. Ed Brown interview, June 28, 1990.

5. Victoria Gray Adams interview, Apr. 4, 1990.

6. Carver Randle interview, Nov. 21, 1989.

7. Julian Bond tribute to Fannie Lou Hamer, in *Seven Days,* Apr. 25, 1977, p. 37, Fannie Lou Hamer collection, Tougaloo College, Jackson, Miss.

8. Interview with Mary Hightower (telephone), Lexington, Miss., Apr. 9, 1991.

9. Hollis Watkins remarks, Southern Conference Organizing Committee meeting, Birmingham, Ala., Dec. 2, 1989.

Acknowledgments

Fannie Lou Hamer touched the lives of so many people who have in turn touched my life as I gathered material for this book. Their recollections enrich these pages; without them, the book could not have been written. I have listed their names at the end of these acknowledgments, but they shaped the beginning, middle, and end of this work.

Lawrence Guyot suggested that I write this book in 1973 after my first trip to Mississippi. He calls it "our book" and, beyond his own detailed recollections, he provided me with many contacts. Years later, when I began the project with some certainty that it might actually be completed, Marian Wright Edelman took what I am sure were rare breaks in her schedule to show me how important the women of Mississippi had been to her life. She also sent me to Mae Bertha Carter in Drew, without whose "get-on-back-out-there" admonitions when the work was dragging me down I might not always have kept going. June Johnson became a staunch ally in my efforts, taking me with her to revisit the Winona jail where she and Mrs. Hamer had both been beaten, opening the doors of the Delta to me and providing countless other invaluable contacts. Bob Moses is a man of few words, but those few were always the right ones in the right places. Rims Barber remains very much on the scene in Jackson, and always helpful. And, of course, Victoria Gray Adams, Annie Devine, and Unita Blackwell are key players in the story. Their insights inform; their courage inspires.

Tracy and June Sugarman lent me tapes of their own interviews about Mrs. Hamer, an act of genuine generosity. I appreciate, too, permission to quote from a conversation that their daughter, Laurie, had with Mrs. Hamer in the last months of her life. Sight unseen, Jean and Charlie Sweet in Madison, Wisconsin, and Noel and Liz Workman in Greenville, Mississippi, housed and fed me on research trips and took a bit of the loneliness out of a life on the road. Winifred Green in Jackson and L. C. Dorsey in the Delta were always supportive and helped set the context for the book. Time and again, Jim and Cynthia Abbott at the *Enterprise-Tocsin* in Indianola provided a crucial local link.

The bulk of the research for this book was done with the help of a Rockefeller Foundation humanities fellowship at the Carter G. Woodson Institute for Afro-American and African Studies at the University of Virginia, for which I thank both the foundation and the Woodson Institute. At the institute I particularly appreciated the help of Armstead L. Robinson, Patricia Sullivan, William E. Jackson, Gail Shirley, and Mary Rose. My fellow Civil Rights Fellow, Ray Gavins of Duke University, and Pat Sullivan both helped steer me to the historical sources for my work. Janette Greenwood and Julia McDonogh shared the grind in the Woodson Annex. The support of Clayborne Carson and Estelle Freedman of Stanford University and Dean Mills of the University of Missouri aided immeasurably in obtaining the Rockefeller grant.

I also received research help through a Moody Grant from the Lyndon Baines Johnson Foundation in Austin, Texas, for travel to the Johnson Library. I appreciate the help of library staff members Bob Tissing and Linda Hanson.

Without the work of archivists and oral historians, the documentation for this book would have been impossible. I appreciate the help of Avril Madison, oral history librarian at the Moorland-Spingarn Research Center at Howard University in Washington, D.C.; Professor Neil McMillen of the University of Southern Mississippi, who directed me to its oral history collection and who shared his ideas with me; Virgia Brocks-Shedd at the the Coleman Library of Tougaloo College in Jackson and Jo Ann Bowmar, archivist for its civil rights collection; Dan Den Bleyker, curator of audiovisual records at the Mississippi Department of Archives and History in Jackson; Marya McQuirter of the National Archives for Black Women's History, which houses the collection of the National Council of Negro Women, in Washington, D.C.; Kenneth Coleman at Amistad Research Center of Tulane University in New Orleans; Karen M. Lamoree of the Wisconsin State Historical Society in Madison; Clinton Bagley of the Greenville, Mississippi, Public Library; and Anice Powell of the Sunflower County Public Library in Indianola, Mississippi. I especially thank Janet Lundblad of the *Los Angeles Times* library, who helped with countless magazine articles, reference questions, and microfilm location—plus encouragement—and Cecily Surace, for allowing her to help me. I also had research help from Sherry Hunter of the clerk's office at the U.S. District Court in Oxford, Mississippi, Joyce Almond in the clerk's office at the U.S. District Court in Greenville, and Rick Boylan at the Democratic National Committee in Washington, D.C. Sheriff Robert H. Tompkins and his deputy, Bill Thornburg, provided access to the Montgomery County Jail in Winona, Mississippi. In the serendipity department, Victor McTeer of Greenville lent me the transcript of Mrs. Hamer's testimony in the Andrews case, and Joanne Edgar unearthed her speech at the first National Women's Political Caucus meeting.

I need also to thank all the fine photographers whose work is used because it adds a dimension to the story that words could never give. In the early 1960s especially, they were there, often at some peril.

Once again, I thank my agent, Diane Cleaver, who had faith in another of my pet projects, and Alexia Dorszynski and Deborah Brody, my editors at NAL/Dutton, who shared my excitement about putting Fannie Lou Hamer on paper. The suggestions of John Paine at Dutton consistently helped me focus on the main story, not the tangents. The book has benefited from reading by Eileen Shanahan, Ann R. Lane, Leola Johnson, Julian Bond, Dean and Sue Mills, Susan Henry, and my mother, Mary S. Mills.

Either for bed and breakfast, or response to telephoned pleas for research help, or encouragement whenever, I would also like to thank Connie Koenenn, Wendy Lazarus, Mary Bryant, Gayle Pollard Terry, Solveig Torvik, Karen West, Pam Pettee, Christine Sauceda, Jordan Mo, Suzanne Rosentswieg, Margie and Bill Freivogel, Glenda Holste, Jane and Ned Cabot, Saralee Tiede and Dan Van Cleve, Jean Campbell, Marj Paxson, Kathy Haq and Marc Sani, Bernice Buresh, Sharon Rosenhause, Pamela Moreland, Richard Foster, Connie Curry, Charles and Carol Horwitz, Debbie Bell, William Ferris, Betsey Wright, Julie and Tom Ashbrook, Ellen and Gary Dolan, Enid Slack, Melinda Voss, Jack and Jeanette Partridge, Richard Schweid, Pat Hanscom, and, most of all, my mother.

The following people provided recollections that helped me write this book:

Victoria Gray Adams, Allan Alexander, Rims Barber, Thelma Barnes, Harry Belafonte, Unita Blackwell, Julian Bond, Ted Borodofsky, Harry Bowie, Bob Boyd, John Brittain, Alvin Bronstein, Owen Brooks, Ed Brown, Robert Buck, Liz Carpenter, Hodding

Carter III, Mae Bertha Carter, Shirley Chisholm, Robert Clark, Ed Cole, Peggy Jean Connor, Dorothy Cotton, Ken Dean, Armand Derfner, Patt Derian, Annie Devine, John Doar, L. C. Dorsey, Marian Wright Edelman, Len Edwards, Ruby Edwards, Shirley Edwards, Charles Evers.

Martha Fager, Frances "Sissy" Farenthold, Rose Fishman, Cora Flemming, Jeff Goldstein, Susan Goodwillie, Jan Goodman, Walter Gregory, Lawrence Guyot, Perry Hamer, Jack Harper, Jr., Cora Harvey, Juanita Harvey, Dorothy Height, Aaron Henry, Mary Hightower, Charles and Carol Horwitz, Winson Hudson, Millie Jeffrey, June Johnson, Erle Johnston, Wilhelm Joseph, Xandra Kayden, Flo Kennedy, Edwin King, Jeanette King, Arthur Kinoy, Henry Kirksey, Bob Kochtitzky, Nick Kotz, John Kramer, Dorie Ladner, Joyce Ladner, Ken Lawrence, Mel Leventhal, John Lewis.

W. D. Marlow IV, Cleve McDowell, Leslie McLemore, Victor McTeer, Euvester Simpson Morris, Robert Moses, Charles Neblett, Eleanor Holmes Norton, Frank R. Parker, Carver Randle, Joseph R. Rauh, Jr., H. M. Ray, David Rice, Bernice Robinson, Charlene Rogers, Ed Scott, Pete Seeger, Aaron Shirley, Ben Sklar, Henry R. Smith, Robert Smith, Morton Stavis, Gloria Steinem, Tracy and June Sugarman, Jean and Charlie Sweet, Mike Thelwell, Ron Thornton, Pascol Townsend, Johnnie Walls, Hollis Watkins, Wes Watkins, Pearlie Winford, Bob Weil, Douglas Wynn, Andrew Young, Bob Zellner, and Dorothy Zellner.

Index